Education and War

EDUCATION AND WAR

Edited by

ELIZABETH E. BLAIR

REBECCA B. MILLER

MARA CASEY TIEKEN

HARVARD EDUCATIONAL REVIEW

REPRINT SERIES NO. 45

Library of Congress Control Number 2008942557

ISBN 978-0-916690-49-6

Published by Harvard Educational Review,
an imprint of the Harvard Education Publishing Group

Harvard Educational Review
8 Story Street
Cambridge, MA 02138

Cover Design: Perry Lubin

The typefaces used in this book are New Baskerville for text and Franklin Gothic Condensed for display.

Education is the most powerful weapon which you can use to change the world.

—Nelson Mandela

Contents

Editors' Introduction 1

PART ONE: REFORMS OF EDUCATION AMIDST CONFLICT 7

Introduction 9

Jesuit Education for Justice: The Colegio in El Salvador, 1968–1984 11
Charles J. Beirne, S.J.

Resistances to Knowing in the Nuclear Age 33
John E. Mack, M.D.

The Contradictions of Bantu Education 45
Mokubung O. Nkomo

Identifying Alternatives to Political Violence: An Educational Imperative 61
Christopher Kruegler and Patricia Parkman

Developing Cultural Fluency: Arab and Jewish Students Engaging in One Another's Company 71
Jocelyn Anne Glazier

Black Dean: Race, Reconciliation, and the Emotions of Deanship 95
Jonathan David Jansen

"I Was Born Here, but My Home, It's Not Here": Educating for Democratic Citizenship in an Era of Transnational Migration and Global Conflict 117
Thea Renda Abu El-Haj

PART TWO: NEW FORMS OF EDUCATION AMIDST CONFLICT 149

Introduction 151

The Flying University in Poland, 1978–1980 153
Hanna Buczynska-Garewicz

"Not Bread Alone": Clandestine Schooling and Resistance in the Warsaw Ghetto during the Holocaust 169
Susan M. Kardos

An Interview with Khalil Mahshi 203

Forming the National Character: Paradox in the Educational Thought of the Revolutionary Generation 219
David Tyack

Women and Education in Eritrea: A Historical and Contemporary Analysis 231
Asgedet Stefanos

Nicaragua 1980: The Battle of the ABCs 263
Fernando Cardenal, S.J. and Valerie Miller

About the Contributors 291

About the Editors 295

Editors' Introduction

For most Americans, the phrase "education and war" evokes disturbing images in which the familiar iconography of schooling is corrupted by haunting features. Some imagine children sitting attentively at their desks, their orderly rows and smiling faces surrounded by battle-scarred walls and gun-wielding patrolmen. Others picture similar groups of earnest students, obediently crouching underneath their desks in a duck-and-cover position, anticipating a bomb attack. Though these images are striking and upsetting—juxtaposing standard-issue desks, lively children, and attentive teachers with the brutal symbols of organized violence—they obscure the complexity of the relationship between education and war. Throughout history and across the globe, war-torn people and states have pursued educational change in their efforts to satisfy both their wartime goals and their postwar aspirations. Schooling has not simply been a casualty of conflict, but rather has been implicated in the conduct, resistance, and aftermath of wars in complicated ways.

This volume—an examination of the interconnections between education and war—comes at a time when intense political conflict is raging in nearly every region of the world, and when the importance of educational opportunity and quality is both widely acknowledged and scrutinized. To enrich our understanding of the roles that education plays in conflict-ridden contexts, we look to lessons from the past. We searched the archives of the *Harvard Educational Review* to uncover stories and studies of teaching and learning amidst violent political turmoil, to replace the standard, simplistic conception of wartime schooling with a more multifaceted and challenging set of ideas about the forms and purposes of education during and after war.

At first, the lessons of prior conflicts appear to have little relevance today, in part because warfare itself seems to have evolved. Where previous wars were typically waged by powerful governments or regional factions, today's militias seem more diffuse or informal. Where armies in the past relied mostly on bullets and bombs, today's arsenals also include sophisticated microscopic, economic, and technological tools. Where the political and economic ramifications of war were once relatively contained, today the effects reverberate worldwide. Despite these developments in form, the root causes of war—struggles for power or resources, ethnic or religious domination, and political or social ideology—remain unchanged. Moreover, the social and political divisions that drive war continue to be entangled with educational institutions and programs, regardless of when and where wars happen or sophistication of the war being waged. This collection reveals how people embroiled in conflict consistently reconsider and reshape education to reflect or resist the commitments, ideals, structures, and effects of wartime. Constituents use educational institutions to disseminate and reproduce dominant ideologies or to empower and inspire those marginalized; or to simultaneously promote both oppression and liberation. The articles and essays in this volume indicate that the uses and consequences of education in times of conflict are neither incidental nor insignificant.

The fact that education plays a pivotal role in wartime is unsurprising. Educational sociologists, from Emile Durkheim to Prudence Carter, have explored the dynamic relationship between schools and societies and the co-occurrence of educational and social change. It stands to reason that these interconnections would be maintained, or even amplified, in times of violent unrest, yet there are surprisingly few published examinations of these connective threads, particularly across geographic and political contexts. While political violence itself receives abundant attention in the media and among scholars, few journalists or academics consider the role of education in these conflicts. The most prominent recent works to explore these themes focus on education as it addresses childhood trauma or promotes democratic ideals—leaving underexamined the ways schools have been used to advance or obstruct the social and political agendas underlying conflict.

In this collection, we explore the purposes and forms of educational change in wartime and postwar contexts to understand why communities and political groups consistently seek to reform or create educational opportunities in the midst or aftermath of violent turmoil. What do the various approaches to education in these contexts reveal about the roles of educational institutions for those engaged in conflict or post-conflict action? How is education implicated—intentionally or not—in the social and political aims of individuals, organizations, communities, and governments engaged in war or postwar recovery?

The Relationship between Education and War

To understand the many ways in which education is implicated in the conduct of war, we selected articles that examine both formal and informal educational settings—any spaces where teachers and students meet and join in the work of teaching and learning. Because conflict at any scale can affect the lives of students, families, and teachers, we considered manuscripts that focus on any context in which nations or factions use violence to advance their sociopolitical agendas, whether in brief skirmishes or decades-long combat. The pieces included here illuminate the multiplicity of approaches adopted by conflict-torn communities and governments attempting to reshape education in order to promote their social and political goals, and highlight both the intended and unintended effects of these efforts.

The manuscripts in the *Harvard Educational Review* archives tend to emphasize the hope and promise that education offers. While we cannot dispute the powerful potential for education to oppress and colonize, we find that the articles in this volume primarily demonstrate education's potential to liberate, resist, reinvent, empower, and transform, sometimes in unexpected ways.

We have deliberately chosen not to prioritize "neutral" perspectives. The authors represented in this volume have diverse backgrounds and roles: they are teachers, organizers, historians, activists, observers, and scholars. They take implicit and explicit political positions with respect to their subjects, reflecting the partisan reality of both conflict and educational politics. We ask readers not to look *past* these authors' stances, but rather to look *inside* their portrayals of conflict to see how education is used by and for people with particular political commitments.

Reading through the authors' positions and across wide-ranging contexts, we found recurring themes that reveal the ways in which schooling is employed as a tool of warfare and defense. First, we find evidence of the ways in which educational institutions are instrumental in the development of political, ethnic, or religious identities. Within the Nazi-run Warsaw ghetto, for example, secret schools sustained the practices, history, and customs of Jews targeted for genocide and cultural obliteration. Elsewhere, schools have been spaces in which identities are forged anew: in post-Revolutionary America political leaders called on schools to carry out republican indoctrination to inculcate the principles underlying the new nation's political structures. In other educational spaces, identities are contested: today's Palestinian American high school students struggle to maintain ties to the Palestinian people while both adopting and challenging the American norms and values propagated in their schools.

Education is also revealed as a force in the negotiation of power relations, serving as a tool for political resistance, social mobility, and/or economic development. We find that in both an El Salvadoran school and a Nicaraguan literacy campaign, enterprising twentieth-century curriculum reformers sought to remediate their countries' socioeconomic inequity by cultivating students' critical consciousness and social awareness. In the other hemisphere, Eritreans expanded educational access for women in an attempt to end gender inequality and build the human capital of their newly independent nation. Schools can also simultaneously reproduce and disrupt the social order. For instance, though the Bantu people were provided a separate curriculum meant to reinforce their subordinate status in apartheid South Africa, these educational programs also helped them develop cultural solidarity and a collective will to resist the political system of their oppressors.

Finally, the articles in this volume show that in times of conflict schools can cultivate communal dispositions toward either hope or fear. Schools promote hope through the transformative power of small acts—for instance, in an elementary school that educates Arab and Jewish students together, or in an underground university that defied the communist Polish government's restrictions on intellectual freedom. Yet this collection also reveals that schools can shelter anxieties by failing to challenge collective fears, assumptions, and biases, by implicitly sanctioning violence, or by neglecting to teach the possibilities of peace.

Together these articles and essays suggest that no aspect of education is untouched by war; school structures, curriculum, pedagogy, access, outcomes, and personal and emotional ties to schools and colleagues are reconsidered in the wake of violence and political upheaval. Moreover, they uncover—across different contexts and conditions and through various approaches—a shared set of concerns about belonging, power, sustenance, and agency that come to the fore during times of violence and political turbulence. The numerous forms of educational change in the midst of war and recovery confirm not only that educational institutions are deeply situated in their surrounding communities and states, but also that education is often used instrumentally and intentionally to advance the wartime political and social goals of peoples and governments—often with unforeseen consequences. Across this volume, we confront both the immense potential of education to promote justice and transform societies, and the limits and disappointments of that potential.

Approaches to Educational Change During War: Reforms and New Forms

We have organized this volume around the familiar question of how educational changes happen—as reform or revolution, from the inside-out or the outside-in. We acknowledge that this dichotomy may be overly simplistic, yet this simplicity also reveals a deeper truth—that the purposes and consequences of educational change are often analogous regardless of where the change originates.

The first section of the book, *Reforms of Education Amidst Conflict,* explores wartime educational changes that originated from within existing educational systems, and how social and political change are reflected in, or leveraged by, these changes. The second section of the volume, *New Forms of Education Amidst Conflict,* investigates how education during conflict has been reconfigured from outside the institutionalized systems. These articles consider the purposes and impacts of new educational programs and structures, emerging in response to conflict, to abandon or oppose established approaches.

The pieces in each section reflect these two divergent approaches to educational change, yet we anticipate that readers will find more similarities than differences across these sections. The accounts in this collection show that wartime and postwar educational initiatives, whether originating within or outside existing systems, produce expected as well as unanticipated social and political ramifications, and may succeed and fail as agents of change.

Education and Conflict Today

We offer this book at a time when America is engaged in military battles half a world away, and Americans grapple with a diffuse "war on terror" that is both everywhere and nowhere. Even though the country is embroiled in conflict, many Americans have largely been shielded from its impact, and are rarely forced to consider how education is affected by and involved in these battles. While there are no armed soldiers or duck-and-cover drills in today's American classrooms, our schools are no less implicated in contemporary conflicts than are those examined in this collection. Educators today, like those in past wars, are struggling with how to teach their students about political and global conflicts and about their country's involvement and influence around the world. Educational institutions continue to shape students' developing and shifting identities, contributing to the perpetuation or contradiction of forms of racial, ethnic, and religious oppression that incite violent conflicts around the world. Classrooms in America, like those in other war-torn nations, harbor collective hope for social change and improvement, as well as people's fears of the distant and unfamiliar.

This book offers lessons for educators around the world to consider how conflict affects and engages all teachers, learners, schools, and societies. In particular, we challenge the educational community in America to abandon the simplistic images that come to mind when we think about education and war. We invite readers to reflect on the ways our own teaching practices, interactions with students, and research agendas take certain approaches and political ideas for granted. We ask educators to contemplate the ways in which violent political conflict shapes and pervades our lives and work, despite the distance of geography and years that may separate us from war. Most important, we call on each reader to consider how to uncover and disrupt the ideological agendas and persistent fear that keep us from using education as a means to envision and enact a more peaceful and just world.

Elizabeth E. Blair
Rebecca B. Miller
Mara Casey Tieken
Editors

PART ONE

Reforms of Education Amidst Conflict

PART ONE

Introduction

Moments of conflict and social unrest are often seen as opportunities for political and social transformation. Across the articles in this volume, authors describe educators, community members, and students responding to war and violent circumstances by pursuing particular social agendas through schooling. These stakeholders often adopt different approaches to producing educational and social change.

This section, *Reforms of Education Amidst Conflict*, explores the ways in which students, educators, and communities utilize existing educational systems to enact politically motivated change. Authors in this section explore the complicated terrain of identity, fear, oppression, and resistance when teaching or learning in a conflict-ridden system. From the murder of Jesuit priests promoting educational access to discrimination against Palestinian students in the United States after September 11, these articles describe the great costs presented by subverting or challenging established educational systems. This section also reveals the potential opportunities arising from these transformations—opportunities for developing collective student resistance, for changing minds and habits through innovative curricula, and for providing educational access to those historically underserved.

This section begins with Charles Beirne's compelling account of the 1968–1984 egalitarian transformation of an El Salvadoran Jesuit school and the violent opposition to this reform. Amidst broader political conflict in the country, the Colegio expanded access to those outside the wealthy elite class and introduced a curriculum that confronted El Salvador's social and economic inequities. In examining the violent consequences of a seemingly straightforward educational reform, Beirne reveals how educational access and curricula can challenge systems of power in a society, and the high price some reformers pay for their convictions. Next, John Mack helps us understand the motivations for such violent opposition to educational change. He draws upon American parents' and educators' fears of teaching young people about the threat of nuclear war in 1984 to show how individual psychology and popular assumptions can obstruct efforts to educate about and in the midst of conflict.

Mokubung Nkomo's examination of segregated Bantu higher education in apartheid South Africa complicates Mack's assertion that educators must confront the fears and commitments that sustain conflict in order to challenge it. Nkomo shows how educational institutions in conflicted regions are not just spaces in which immediate (and potentially oppressive) political aims are enacted, but may also be sites where the conditions for change build slowly, over generations, and through the accumulation of small acts. Amid apartheid violence, the South African government sought to codify the subordinate role of the Bantu people by providing them with a distinctive curriculum rooted in their culture. Nkomo shows how, contrary to the government's goal, the state-supported higher educational system actually inspired Bantu solidarity, black empowerment, and resistance to discrimination and oppression.

Next, we shift from considering curriculum as a tool of oppression or resistance in wartime to considering the potential of curriculum to challenge war itself. In their 1985 article on alternatives to political violence, Christopher Kruegler and Patricia Parkman discuss the value of nonviolent responses to conflict and call for continued research and new forms of teaching that advance nonviolent strategies for confronting and ending war. They highlight how a new curricular focus can advance well established but often overlooked nonviolent ideals and actions amid more commonplace violent responses.

The final three articles in this section look inside wartime and post-conflict educational institutions, exposing the complexity of working towards the peaceful ideal that Kruegler and Parkman introduce. In her 2003 article about a bilingual school for Arabs and Jews in Israel, Jocelyn Anne Glazier shows how the existing school structure can be modified in ways that promote peace and cooperation. By welcoming a mixed student population and adopting programs to promote cultural fluency, Glazier explores how traditional schools can address the ongoing conflict in the region. Yet her work also reveals the limitations of schools' responses to conflict in a culture of entrenched hatred and violence.

David Jonathan Jansen focuses on complex intergroup relationships in a conflict-torn region. In his 2005 article, Jansen documents his experience as the first black dean in a traditional Afrikaner university in post-apartheid South Africa. He vividly describes the compromises he made, the way he coped with his often-conflicting emotions, and the policies he instituted to promote transformation of the university culture. Jansen's account highlights the challenges involved in establishing respectful and constructive interpersonal relationships between once-opposed groups in a post-conflict school, as well as the difficulty in establishing institutional and cultural changes in this context.

Finally, Thea Renda Abu El-Haj examines Palestinian students' complicated negotiations of identity and experiences of violence and discrimination in a post-9/11 American high school. This 2007 article explores how students' identification with the Palestinian people was implicated in their everyday clashes with peers and teachers. These students confronted and negotiated notions of citizenship, belonging, and conflict in school spaces, calling attention to the tangible ramifications for students and schools of conflicts half a world away. Like other articles in this section, this study raises questions about how oppression and conflict are negotiated and resisted within the school walls, highlighting the inability of those walls to contain or obstruct the impacts of war.

Jesuit Education for Justice: The Colegio in El Salvador, 1968–1984

CHARLES J. BEIRNE, S.J.

On September 30, 1980, Oscar Romano Calderón and Rafael Santos Chávez strolled down to the front gate after they had taught their classes at Externado de San José, the Jesuit colegio in San Salvador.[1] Minutes later shots rang out; the two teachers slumped to the ground dead. The previous March, gunmen had murdered José Trinidad Canales, another teacher at the school. That same year, thirteen of their colleagues fled El Salvador after receiving repeated death threats.

Why did some elements in Salvadoran society find a school so threatening that they killed teachers, machine-gunned the school building, and paid for newspaper advertisements accusing the faculty of subversion?

The Catholic church experienced and initiated many changes after Pope John XXIII called the bishops to the Second Vatican Council in 1963. The church became more involved in the world and began to believe it was important to take an active part in the creation of a more just society. Jesuit education, an international system, attempted to make radical changes in curriculum and ideology in response to the recommendations of the Second Vatican Council.

The case of the Externado de San José in El Salvador from 1968 to 1984 illustrates those radical changes. The Externado was a changing school in the middle of a changing church and changing society. The events that occurred have implications for educational policy and practice in all developing nations.[2]

Jesuits in El Salvador

The Jesuit order was founded by Ignatius Loyola in 1540 as the Society of Jesus and established its first New World colegio twenty-eight years later in Lima, Peru.[3] Most of the students were the sons of *peninsulares* (Spanish-born people) and *criollos* (the descendants of *peninsulares*), and in spite of the efforts of the Jesuits to identify benefactors who could endow the schools so that attendance would not depend on ability to pay tuition, the school re-

Harvard Educational Review Vol. 55 No. 1 February 1985, 1–19

mained a place for a small number of scions from the native *cacique* (politically powerful) families.[4]

As early as 1694 colonial officials hoped that the Jesuits would establish a colegio in El Salvador, but they had to content themselves with sporadic missions throughout the nation. Ever since its "discovery" early in the sixteenth century, El Salvador has endured colonial socioeconomic structures and their latter-day equivalents—a monocrop-dominated economy and a stratified society headed by a few oligarchical families and policed by their trusty allies in the military.[5] In the nineteenth century, elites from both the Liberal and Conservative parties exchanged the presidency, their rule punctuated by occasional military takeovers to "insure peace." Power shifted from the Conservatives (dye producers) to the Liberal elite (coffee producers), the latter distinguished by a strong desire for free trade and control over Catholic church influence.

As in most of Latin America, the efforts of the church hierarchy to bring Jesuits back to Central America after the suppression of the order "were frustrated by the intrigues of the Liberals."[6] A government spokesman lamented in 1858 that "the number of Salvadoran students in the Guatemala colegio is large and growing every day. Within a short time, the State will have its youth totally educated with this limitation."[7] Until that time, only upper-class students were educated in the Guatemalan colegio.

When five Jesuit priests and two brothers, who were expelled from Mexico in 1914, landed in El Salvador and began teaching in the local seminary,[8] many upper-class Salvadoran parents urged the provincial superior to open a colegio, but he had no staff available. In 1921, in response to the parental requests, the Jesuits began to allow lay students to take classes with the seminarians. At the end of the school year, the seminary rector announced that the Externado de San José, a Jesuit colegio, and the seminary would begin to share the seminary building. Jorge Meléndez Mazzini was the first student to register in 1921.[9] His father and uncle had both served as president of El Salvador, and his grandmother had donated two of the school buildings. Until the mid-1960s, the sons of the "fourteen families" and others who aspired to elite social positions attended the Externado. They received a classical education: Spanish grammar and literature, theology, philosophy, history, and some math and science.

A 1930 account of religious practice at the Externado describes a rigorous program. The day began with morning prayers and mass. Later in the day, brief visits to the chapel were encouraged. Two special sermons a week and sung litanies on Saturdays prepared the students for more solemn liturgies on Sundays and feast days. Spiritual guidance, retreats, special devotions, and religious organizations were also included in the program.[10]

In 1932 the massacre of more than fifteen-thousand *campesinos* (rural peasants) consolidated the power of the dictatorship of General Maximiliano Hernández Martínez, who ruled El Salvador from 1931 until 1944 and strengthened the hold of the fourteen families.[11] A series of military officers controlled the country without strong opposition until the late 1960s.

In 1955 the new rector at the Externado, Ignacio Amezola, S.J., announced the foundation of Academia Loyola, "a night school for workers who wanted secondary education." With regular faculty members, supplemented by Externado alumni, the Academia opened its doors in 1956 "to elevate the needy classes of society."[12] In 1959 twenty-seven of the original seventy students received diplomas. The addition of a night school left the structure of the colegio intact, especially its well-to-do clientele and traditional curriculum.

During the next decade the Externado continued to thrive. In 1956 it announced that the eleven best students in academics and discipline would receive full scholarships "which would stimulate student efforts in a marvelous way each day as they strove to be the best in the class and thus gain the scholarship that would bring them a prominent place within the student body."[13] National championships put the name of the school in headlines on the sports pages of the national newspapers. The campus was completed in 1963 with the construction of a chapel that seated more than one thousand adults.[14]

Meeting of the Jesuit Provincial Superiors in Rio, 1968

Aware that the Latin American bishops would be meeting in Medellín, Colombia, in September 1968, the Jesuit provincial superiors of the region gathered in Rio in May to determine guidelines for change of the educational institutions. The superiors identified "personal conversion from selfishness" and "admission of past failures" as prerequisites to evaluation and renewal of specific institutions. Whenever possible, Jesuits should share the lifestyle of the poor to give credibility to their "clear position in favor of social justice on behalf of those who lack the fundamental means of education without which development is impossible." The superiors continued, "Our high schools and universities should accept their role as active agents of social justice in Latin America. Conditions in Latin America require a radical change: to develop in our students first of all an attitude of service to the society in whose transformation they should collaborate, and an effective concern for marginal people for whose development they should labor." They called for "some authentic social service on behalf of the community" as a "part of the curriculum," and equal access for all persons, allowing "no privileges of class or money."[15]

Although the superiors cautioned against the use of "political criteria," they added that Jesuits should insist on helping people to overcome "the religious separation between their private and professional lives. Neither violence inspired by hatred nor passivity induced by fear of the consequences of commitment should characterize involvement." To further specify the forms this social justice commitment might take, the superiors called for pilot projects, adult education, mass communication, and transformation of the curriculum in the traditional institutions of the order. Jesuits should not rely on images or roles of power but should work in close cooperation with other groups in the church that seek to create a society permeated by gospel values.

The Jesuit superiors left the development of concrete strategies and programs to all members of the community. They committed themselves by assigning members of the order to graduate studies to prepare for their roles as developers of programs. They encouraged creative thinking but warned of the reactions that would "bellow forth" from the upper class, the traditional clientele of the order's institutions. "Our apostolate, inspired by this truly universal and evangelical spirit, will stimulate unavoidable reactions; we will not provoke them [the upper class] by partisan attitudes but we will continue to preach the gospel of the poor whatever the reaction." We will work for a society that is "more just, more free and more peaceful."[16]

Meeting of the Latin American Bishops in Medellín, Colombia, 1968

Four months after the Rio meeting of the Jesuit provincial superiors, the Latin American bishops gathered in Medellín, Colombia, to formulate renewal guidelines for the Catholic church.[17] Although less specific and radical than the Rio statement, Medellín committed the church to "liberate people from all servitude and to help them ascend from less than human conditions." With remarkable faith in its potential they celebrated education as "the best guarantee of personal development and social progress . . . a means toward full integration into society with full social, economic, cultural, political and religious participation."[18]

The bishops' pointed criticism, however, tempered this optimistic portrait. They characterized current educational practices as "too abstract and formalistic," and "more concerned with maintenance of existing social and economic structures than with their transformation." The bishops objected to current pedagogy as uniform, passive, and "geared toward having more rather than being more." Democratization of educational opportunities required, they said, "that all social sectors, without discrimination, have access to the Catholic schools and acquire in them an authentic social conscience which informs their lives."[19]

Unlike the Rio document of the Jesuit superiors, the bishops' Medellín statement makes no mention of the risks and difficulties implicit in such a transformation, nor of doubts that the goals could be accomplished. Both the Rio and Medellín documents, however, express a similar faith in education as the most effective agent of social change and the creation of a society permeated by the values espoused in the gospel.[20]

Developments in El Salvador

With the Rio and Medellín documents in hand, the Jesuits of Central America, under the leadership of their thirty-six-year-old Salvadoran superior. Miguel

F. Estrada, S.J., surveyed the order's educational institutions.[21] As leader of the Jesuits of Central America, Estrada was responsible for overseeing the educational institutions operated by the Jesuits in El Salvador. A local Jesuit assembly expressed satisfaction with the high academic standards of the Externado de San José in 1969 but criticized the elite socioeconomic status of the school's students. "If the current type of student is not the most appropriate to bring about the necessary social transformation to which the provincials committed the Society in Rio, then it is obvious that we have to get a different clientele."[22]

In 1970 and 1971 the Externado staff explored the possibility of transferring ownerships of the school to the Salvadoran Ministry of Education or to *Fe y Alegría,* a church-sponsored educational group, in order to receive a financial subsidy that would eliminate the need to collect tuition, thus opening the school to all qualified students regardless of ability to pay. The Ministry and *Fe y Alegría* turned down the offer.[23] Then the Externado staff settled on the Turno Vespertino, a school within a school that would provide education in the afternoon for economically needy but academically qualified students in seventh to ninth grade. Turno Vespertino students would be charged tuition according to their ability to pay, and the resulting financial shortage would be augmented by surplus funds from the regular Externado sessions. The Turno Vespertino replaced the 1956 project, Academia Loyola.[24]

Students who finished ninth grade in the Turno Vespertino were later integrated into the tenth- to twelfth-grade programs of the morning division. The staff believed that the differences in academic preparation and social and cultural backgrounds of the two student populations made it necessary to integrate the new students gradually. Interviews with some of the teachers revealed that an initial high dropout rate of the new Turno Vespertino students diminished during the first few years, and most of the students made a smooth transition into the tenth- to twelfth-grade program. Some of the upper- and upper-middle-class families resented this structural change and cited it for years as "proof" that the Externado had lowered its standards.[25]

By 1971 the Externado had no outstanding debt, so that all surplus income could subsidize the combined schools. The staff recruited students who could benefit from this program by going personally to the public schools in economically disadvantaged areas of San Salvador to explain the Turno Vespertino to school officials.

Although some of the older Jesuits helped design and implement the project, differences in approach to the Turno Vespertino and other programs led to the creation of a separate Jesuit community late in 1971. The older group of Jesuits had received very different religious training than the younger ones, much more rigorous and focused on such traditional subjects as classical languages and scholastic philosophy and theology. The younger group had been sent to graduate studies in Europe and the United States and, therefore, had a wider horizon from which to look at the country's problems. The older group tended to work on more strictly religious questions and did not feel that they had to get involved in reforming the socioeconomic conditions of the country. This is not to imply that the older Jesuits were insensitive to the needs of the poor but only that they worked to alleviate the more oppressive aspects of the lives of the poor rather than to change the social structure. While these changes were occurring, the Jesuits at the *Universidad Centro Americana, José Simeón Cañas* (UCA), especially the younger community, began a collaboration with the innovators on the Externado staff that later became crucial to the Externado's success.

The Turno Vespertino inaugurated classes in 1972. That same year, Rutilio Grande, S.J., assumed charge of the Aguilares parish, a center for experimental pastoral programs to aid the poor in El Salvador. That year also marked the torture and exile of José Napoleón Duarte after the military refused to allow him to take office as president of the Republic.

In the midst of these events, the Externado began to phase in the *bachillerato,* the official reformed tenth- to twelfth-grade curriculum. The Salvadoran Ministry of Education had recently rearranged the early years of schooling into a six-three-three system, with diversified diplomas and additions to the curriculum such as sociology and seminars, that would bring the students into closer contact with the socioeconomic reality of the country. Some criticized this governmental initiative as "reformist," a substitute for real transformation, but others saw it as a wedge that could lead to structural change.[26] The Jesuits decided to adopt the new structure because, with a military government in power, more drastic changes in the elite educational system seemed unlikely.

Externado staff members assigned students to survey socioeconomic conditions in the community and accompanied them on other projects such as coffee-picking, teaching in public schools, and reforestation. In the next few years, approximately 30 percent of the Externado students participated in the community service programs, and almost all became involved in the survey projects connected with the sociology classes. School officials explained the programs to parents, who generally supported these changes.

Although the math and science professors still taught their subjects in the traditional lecture style with some laboratory experiments, the sociology, religious studies, literature, and psychology teachers shifted toward research projects, field studies, and discussions. Such themes as institutional violence, poverty, political repression, and injustice appeared on the course syllabuses and in class discussions.

During the middle of the 1972 school year, Javier Colino, S.J., the rector, left for his final period of Jesuit training in Spain with the intention of returning to El Salvador for the beginning of the 1973 school year in February. He left the administration of the school to Robert Zarruk, S.J., the prefect of studies, who wrote to Externado parents that "an era of the Externado de San José was ending." He cited two sections of the Salvadoran educational reform that called for "the development of creative capabilities of a speculative and practical sort" and "social consciousness that would help the students understand the problems and needs of the community, and which would stimulate efforts of service." Zarruk said the Externado would implement these ministry directives by "forming highly qualified Christians, familiar with the national reality of El Salvador" and, consistent with this, the teachers would abandon techniques that rendered the students passive. "We have opted clearly for deschooling our learning, and we will send our students out into the field to do first-hand research."[27] He used "de-schooling" in a much more restricted sense than those who wanted nonformal education to substitute for schooling. He also invited parents to meetings of each grade level where they could ask questions about the changes.

1973: The Explosive Year

In January 1973 Zarruk hired several faculty members to teach the second-year sociology classes. Early in February, Colino returned from Spain, and on the nineteenth of that month he canceled their contracts. A strong protest from the staff forced a reversal of his decision, but the incident revealed his serious reservations about the new direction of the Externado. Polarization sharpened between the two Jesuit communities in the school.

Early in the school year, the Externado had begun an extensive study of the sociology program. In March, without the permission of Colino, a teacher mimeographed copies of a liturgical ceremony, the *Via Crucis* (Stations of the Cross) composed by Fabián Amaya, a priest of the San Salvador archdiocese. Bishop Arturo Rivera y Damas of San Salvador had previously refused permission for its publication because he considered its denunciation of injustice too inflammatory.[28]

At about the same time, Salvador Samayoa, a lay staff member, used *Conozcámonos* (Let's Get to Know Each Other), the regular publication of the Parents Association, to publish without their permission an explanation of the school's new direction. Illustrating the text with cartoon characters and writing in a whimsical style to downplay the extent of the changes, Samayoa quoted the Medellín documents and described those Externado programs which were designed to bring the students into greater contact with the social reality of El Salvador.

On April 6 the assistant to Pedro Arrupe, S.J., the Jesuit father general in Rome, wrote to Estrada, who was ultimately responsible for the school, to express Arrupe's concern about reports of disunity within the Jesuit community of the Externado. He indicated that an avalanche of complaints had inundated Rome.[29]

The dam finally broke when officers of the Parents Association wrote a letter to Colino, the school's rector, strongly attacking the new orientation of the Externado.[30] The parents condemned "the excessive attention given to socioeconomic themes to the neglect of other academic subjects and the religious formation of the students." They cited what they called "the tendentious approach" the teachers were taking to sociology because, they wrote, "when our sons come back from their field work in marginal zones with their teachers, who should be orienting them with a Christian spirit instead of class conflict, they begin to accuse their families of living like bourgeoisie, as if trying to work hard to improve one's economic position were a crime." All this "is causing real division in the families."[31]

They also decried the elimination of obligatory attendance at mass and charged that the teachers were unqualified. They termed Samayoa's special edition of *Conozcámonos,* their own publication, as a distortion of the bishops' Medellín document. "The Association demands that you remove these unqualified teachers immediately, along with the prefect of discipline, Joaquín Samayoa," whom they confused with his brother, the author of *Conozcámonos.* They maintained that even though they agreed with the post-Vatican Council orientation of the church, they were "worried that the Externado was going to take an extremist direction such as that of the so-called 'Christians for Socialism'." They closed their letter with protestations of loyalty to the Jesuit order.

Both the interviews cited in this paper and the correspondence in the provincial archives indicate that Colino explicitly encouraged this letter from the Parents Association so that he might gain support against the younger faculty members who championed the reforms. In a letter to Estrada dated two days after the parents' letter, Colino clearly indicated his opposition to the new orientation of the Externado.[32] On May 14 he responded in writing to the Parents Association's officers to thank them for their letter, assuring them that the Externado would study their complaints. He wrote that the administration of the school was seriously determined to take whatever steps were necessary to correct the faults and answer the complaints that the parents had noted in their letter.[33] Shortly afterwards, Colino left for Rome to complain about Estrada's approach, which he believed was encouraging radical reforms.

Estrada, who received a copy of the parent's letter, also responded. He thanked the parents for their letter and assured them that their complaints would be studied. But unlike Colino, Estrada reminded the parents of "the importance of social formation . . . the key role of lay staff members in a Jesuit school," and the need for "a well-rounded education."[34] That same day Estrada called together his consultors to discuss the problem, and on May 16 he named Juan Moreno, S.J., the master of novices, as his delegate to investigate the charges.

During the same month, the faculty committee which had been appointed at the beginning of the school year to study the sociology department turned in its report.[35] They suggested some revision of curriculum material and some toning down of overly zealous classroom presentations by one of the Jesuit teachers, but they found the program basically sound and in conformity with Ministry of Education guidelines.

As part of its research, the faculty committee surveyed the students, 90 percent of whom responded. Responses to two of the questions are of particular interest:

Do you feel that the sociology class has tried to impose certain ideas on the students without allowing criticism and dialogue?

		Percentage	
	Yes	*No*	*Not Sure*
1st bacchillerato—Grade 10	20.0	74.0	6.0
2nd bacchillerato—Grade 11	7.5	86.2	6.3

Do you have the impression that the teachers wanted you to identify fully with Marxist ideology?

		Percentage	
	Yes	*No*	*Not Sure*
1st bacchillerato—Grade 10	25.0	75.0	—
2nd bacchillerato—Grade 11	3.7	91.2	5.0

The faculty committee concluded that "the emphasis in the course is on field work which is meant to give students an opportunity to confirm or disprove the hypotheses formulated in the classrooms. If the hypothesis states, for example, that there is destitution in San Salvador, the student is not obliged to believe it, but is sent to investigate whether it exists." Although the evaluation found the teachers more sympathetic to Marxist categories of analysis than to the more traditional ones, they felt that the teachers "took a serious approach to the subject." They suggested that perhaps some of the students were not sufficiently mature to handle the subject, and they recommended better communication and orientation with both students and parents.

Nine days after his letter to the parents and the meeting with his consultors, Estrada wrote a long letter to Arrupe in Rome. He pointed out that the younger staff members "had demonstrated to him their discontent because they feel the school is moving too slowly in its reform." He admitted that the publication of the *Via Crucis* and *Conozcámonos* had left the school vulnerable to attack and that a strong figure was needed to lead the sociology department. There was no such person on the Externado staff, so he had to rely on academically qualified but inexperienced teachers.

"The real problem," Estrada wrote, "was the presence of some parents who disagree with the approach the Jesuit order had decided to take in all its schools, and the presence of some Jesuits who also disagree with the approach. Before anything else we have to define ourselves, indicate what is our educational thrust. Basing myself on the documents of the father general himself, Oaxtepec, etc., I wrote my response to the Parents Association." He assured Arrupe that the Externado would not make an issue of defending the publications but would stick to its educational objectives. "These difficulties were foreseen and are even logical; possibly they will not be the last ones we will have to face."[36]

Estrada had kept Archbishop Luis Chávez y González and Bishop Arturo Rivera y Damas informed of the change process in the Externado and received their encouragement.[37] But Bishop Oscar Romero, the editor of *Orientación,* the Catholic weekly newspaper, published an attack on May 21 "against schools that taught demagoguery and Marxism." "We bring up this problem," he said, because "pamphlets and literature of known Red origin are being used in a certain colegio. . . . Such teachers," he maintained, "should not even call themselves Christian."[38]

Estrada strongly criticized Romero in a letter for interfering in the Moreno study, for not contacting the Externado before his public attack, for not hearing the teachers before judging them, and for false accusations of Marxism.[39] As for Romero's statement that the teachers should not consider themselves Christian, Estrada termed the charge intolerable and demanded formal rectification. "If it does not occur," he threatened, "then I will be forced to take more serious steps." He closed by saying: "These points constitute an attack so unjust, serious and without foundation, that it requires a public retraction."

Romero responded that he had sent both the *Orientación* editorial and Estrada's letter to the Vatican ambassador in El Salvador "to whose criteria and judgment I commit the matter."[40] On June 7, Estrada once again demanded a public apology.[41] By this time, the issue had become front page headlines in the national newspapers. The following month the exchange ended. Estrada wrote to one of the other bishops: "I was asked, for the good of the church, to maintain silence [over the Romero attack], and I did so, despite the fact that this editorial served as the basis of subsequent attacks against the Externado."[42]

The *Diario Latino* announced on June 6 that the Ministry of the Interior was launching an investigation of the Externado program which is taught, it said, "by a group of foreign priests. If found guilty of socialist-communist propaganda, they would have to leave the country in 48 hours." On June 12 Minister of Education Rogelio Sánchez presented complaints against the Externado to the attorney general of El Salvador.

This quotation typifies the sort of attack that appeared daily in all the newspapers which were controlled by the members of the Right who were obsessed with a fear of Marxism or any other force that might threaten their economic and political power.

> To their unapostolic love of power and money, for which the Jesuits are notorious, is now added the sordid business of corrupting the young minds of wealthy students who have been put in their charge by families who still believe that the Society of Jesus is of the Church of Christ.
>
> The Jesuit counter-church is the vanguard of the Red Revolution in the Catholic world, especially in Latin America. And this is nothing new. The Jesuits

> paved the way for the betrayal of Chile to communism. Jesuits in Argentina prepared the Cordoba outbreak in 1969. Mexican Jesuits headed the 1968 disturbances. How much blood has been spilled because of the Jesuits!

Meanwhile, letters continued to go to Rome from parents, from other critics, and even from Jesuits within the community who still lived in the Externado building but agreed with the charges. On the very day of the first newspaper attacks, June 5, Arrupe wrote to Estrada: "I do not doubt your zeal in trying to transform education at the Externado along the lines of Medellín, Rio, etc., but I ask once again whether the means chosen will lead to that end."[43] Estrada replied on June 22: "I see as very difficult any process of renovation or adaptation in the institutions or in the communities without conflict. It is not that we are looking for it, but reality itself and the persons involved make confrontation inevitable."[44]

On June 11 Moreno, who had become the Externado's acting rector, in a memorandum to the secondary school administrators, observed that "the uproar that has been produced, obviously out of proportion . . . has served undoubtedly to commit the school to continue along the lines of change implemented already, changes I consider irreversible." He counseled them to forget the storm raging outside and concentrate on the evaluation and adjustment of the project and on staff development.[45]

That same day, witnesses began testifying before the attorney general about the "Marxist indoctrination" perpetrated at the Externado. The president of the Parents Association, Nicolas Estéban Nasser, was the first witness, and other parents also testified against the school.[46] The *Diario Latino* headline for June 16 proclaimed: "Marxism in Externado Says Parent, Gerardo Ramos!" Zarruk, the prefect of the school, and Moreno also appeared at the hearing, and the newspapers criticized their testimony as incomplete and ambiguous.[47] Others attacked the Externado program and the Jesuits. One witness expressed indignation that Externado students had gone to a hacienda owned by his wife to check on the living conditions of the *campesinos*.[48] Another witness and his son claimed that the youngster had been expelled from the Externado because he opposed Marxism. The parent argued that "getting rid of the Marxist Jesuit teachers would not be enough. It was necessary to rip out this evil at the roots since it comes in orders from Father General Arrupe."[49]

At the crescendo of attacks rose higher, the younger Jesuits of the Externado and the Samayoa brothers were meeting with the younger Jesuit community at UCA to write a concise statement of ideology. This document, *El Externado Piensa Así* (This Is What the Externado Thinks), began to appear in paid national newspaper installments on June 15 because the authors feared that, if left to editorial discretion, the newspapers would distort the presentation as they had in similar situations. In this document the authors explained how the Externado carried out, at the local level, the more general concepts of Rio, Medellín, and Oaxtepec.[50]

The first section of the document countered the charges of Marxist indoctrination, partisan politics, and the undermining of family ties. It then traced changes in the Latin American church and the Jesuit order and spelled out the theological and pedagogical rationale for the changes made in the Externado curriculum. The statement also included an extensive description of the Salvadoran educational reform implemented at the Externado.

El Externado Piensa Así stated: "Parents are free to send their children wherever they please. But if they choose the Externado they should realize that their children will be educated for justice."[51] To accomplish these goals, the statement continues, the Externado offers "an active pedagogy that deepens the students' appreciation of various aspects of human understanding, not that they may just content themselves with the discovery of truth but rather put it at the service of the community."[52]

Four days after the first statement appeared in the newspapers, and while witnesses were still attacking the school before the attorney general, the official organization of the San Salvadoran priests appointed a committee to investigate the charges. They visited the school, interviewed the teachers and students, and submitted their report a week later. They found the sociology teachers "well qualified," using Paulo Freire's pedagogy rather than that of Karl Marx, "worthy of admiration and respect," and "taking seriously the directives of the Ministry of Education."[53]

On the same day the priest's report was issued, Bishop Rivera y Damas declared that "no one can conclude in justice from the evidence that the Colegio Externado de San José had a Marxist orientation. . . . On the contrary . . . it is based on the Christian faith. Any defects in pedagogy are already being corrected, and they were exaggerated out of proportion, a disfigurement of reality." He termed the accusations "unjust and subjective," and said he deplored "the attitude of those who with criteria conditioned by ignorance, bad faith or a lack of Christian spirit have placed obstacles in the way of an education committed to the national reality."[54] The Salvadoran Conference of Major Religious Superiors also published on the same day a statement supporting the Externado.[55]

The UCA faculty and students also published an affirmation of their confidence in the Externado faculty and programs that week.[56] The press continued to focus attention on the school by reporting that the prefect of studies and two of the Jesuit teachers of sociology were Nicaraguans, thus implying a foreign conspiracy.[57] On June 29 the Turno Vespertino parents took out a newspaper advertisement to voice their support of the Externado.[58] The national teachers' union and the student council of the University of El Salvador also expressed support for the Externado.[59]

Some of the public uproar abated during July, but the Externado still awaited the verdict of the attorney general. Moreno wrote on the 6th: "The fight has been hard because there really is a small group of powerful families bent on blocking anything that even smells like serious social change." He recognized the crucial nature of the current controversy. "At this present time in the colegio's history, we Jesuits have decided openly for a liberating education. If it does not achieve its goal sufficiently and show that it is indeed possible to stimulate social change through a colegio, such a failure will have repercussions in the whole vice province."[60]

Moreno called for a referendum of the parents who had heard both the complaints and the school's response to them, especially through *El Externado Piensa Así*. On July 12 he wrote to the president of El Salvador, Arturo Molina, that "support of the parents is massive, which confirms that the discontented ones are a reduced minority."[61] Two days later he wrote: "After the investigation made by the Externado itself and the Archdiocesan Priests Senate, we find ourselves in a position to assure Your Excellency categorically that the Externado students have not been subjected to any Marxist indoctrination."[62] Most of the participants in the controversy, however, believed that the number of parents opposed to the new orientation of the school was much larger than Moreno judged.

Moreno also reported to Arrupe: "All this controversy has served to raise the consciousness of thousands of persons because the Externado has been at the center of national life for some time; its publications have been read with great interest. The public image of the Externado has changed from a colegio of the elites to one which has decided to do something for the people."[63]

President Molina called a meeting for July 31 in the presidential palace, to which he invited Archbishop Chávez y González; Luis Acherándio, S.J., rector of UCA; Ignacio Ellacuría, S.J., of the UCA staff; Dr. Román Mayorga, vice-rector of UCA; and Estrada and Moreno. Also in attendance were the vice-president of the republic, the vice-minister of the presidency, and the sub-minister of the interior. President Molina announced that "the attorney general had concluded that three Nicaraguan Jesuits had violated the Constitution of the Republic of El Salvador." Archbishop Chávez y González asked what sections of the Constitution the Jesuits had violated. They taught "anarchist and anti-democratic doctrine," replied Molina. He added that the minister of education agreed with this conclusion, and that there were two alternatives: to apply the immigration law and expel the Jesuits, or to fail to apply it and allow them to stay. In his letter to Arrupe reporting on the meeting, Estrada said that "the president suggested that I remove them from the country as if this were a normal organizational decision of the Jesuit order."[64]

Estrada requested time to reflect on the matter and suggested a private meeting with the president at a later date. President Molina agreed, and Estrada met with the president, Ellacuría, and Mayorga at Mayorga's home. The president brought along all the documents accumulated by the attorney general. Ellacuría reported that the president said he would not leave the meeting until they had convinced him that the Jesuits were innocent of the charges.[65]

The meeting lasted from 7:00 P.M. until midnight. Estrada told the president, "we do not accept the conclusions of the attorney general" because they are based on "spurious or incomplete information taken out of context." Estrada argued that he could not transfer the three Jesuits "because it would be unjust," and he asked the president to trust him to take care of the matter.

Estrada reported that after many hours of painstaking review of the evidence and argument, "the president decided that we were right and he gave me a free hand." He even expressed interest in meeting the three Jesuits so that "he could tell them that he had nothing against them. Finally he told me that he would put the attorney general's documents at my disposal and that I could do anything I wanted with them, even burn them." The president actually took the documents home with him, but that meeting ended the crisis.[66]

The polarization of the two Externado Jesuit communities increased after the controversy died down. The older Jesuits objected to "lax discipline," schedule changes, and, later, to the appointment of Joaquín Samayoa as prefect of studies.[67]

1974–1980: Years of Consolidation

The internal battle among the Jesuits smouldered in the background, but the change in social awareness and pedagogy took root. An experienced Jesuit from the UCA, Segundo Montes, S.J., took over the direction of the sociology department and the rectorship of the school. Only about 7 to 8 percent of the students decided not to return for the new school year, and even the major protesters, who came from the upper-middle class rather than from the most affluent, left their sons in the Externado until graduation.

During this period the community activities of the school increased dramatically. In 1974 the Externado provided shelter for one hundred families who were victims of a hurricane. The following year, the school established *Socorro Jurídico,* a legal aid service for the poor in the San Salvador area. At first the staff handled bureaucratic and relatively minor legal problems of the poor, but with the closing of the University of El Salvador's legal aid office and tightened political repression, the demand for services increased and Externado students supplemented the legal aid staff as part of their studies. In 1977 the Archdiocese of San Salvador incorporated *Socorro Jurídico* as an official agency of the Church, but the office remained in the Externado building, maintained by the continued funding and involvement of the school.[68]

The Externado's religious-pastoral program was also changed to match the school's new purpose. The traditional classroom approach with testing and marks was abandoned early, but the students did not take seriously the new program that stressed religious experience over theology. Later, the school shifted the religious experience program to the afternoon. That did not work very well either. Finally, in the late 1970s, under the direction of Manuel Santiago, S.J., the program was divided into two sections: classes of Catholic theology for all students and personal religious experiences, such as retreats, for those who showed interest. The school still sponsored large-group celebrations of mass but also offered small group liturgies tailored to individual needs.[69]

Field work in sociology classes continued, and about a third of the students became involved in the more extensive projects. The increased political repression and human rights violations in the country, however, began to radicalize the students politically. In about equal proportions, students from both the original morning school and the Turno Vespertino sessions moved toward organizations in opposition to the military regime of President Molina, and later of General Romero.[70] Since many of these graduates have been killed or exiled, it has not been possible to study this part of the school's history in detail.

In 1975 the Jesuit order convened the Thirty-Second General Congregation, the highest authority in the Society of Jesus. The meeting produced a decree entitled "Our Mission Today: The Service of Faith and the Promotion of Justice." It was an affirmation of the integral relationship between faith experience and the creation of a just society. In 1976 Arrupe raised Central America to the status of a full province, just as the internal problems of the Jesuits there were most serious. To clear the air, the new provincial, César Jeréz, S.J., challenged both the older and younger Jesuit groups at the Externado to design plans that described their approach to change in the school. Although he was perceived as favoring the younger group, Jeréz promised to review both plans with his consultors, turn over the administration of the school to one group, and reassign the other group to different works.

The older Jesuits' plan for the Externado maintained that they could better accomplish the goals expressed in *El Externado Piensa Así,* but their proposals were primarily criticisms of the younger group who were the principal authors of that document.[71] The younger group prepared a lengthy document that summarized much of the data from *El Externado Piensa Así* but also spelled out in detail how they would continue to develop this vision. Unlike the document of the older group, their plan included the admission of female students.[72]

The consultors felt that the older Jesuits lacked vision and the younger group lacked experience, but they recommended that Jeréz decide in favor of the younger group, which he did on October 4, 1976.[73] A group of parents claimed to have gathered six-hundred signatures on a petition asking that Jeréz delay implementation of his decision because, they said, they had been generally unaware of the tensions in the community and were afraid they would lose some of the Jesuit teachers. But the provincial moved ahead and appointed Luis M. Ormaechea, S.J., as the new rector. Arrupe reluctantly accepted Jeréz's decision, but he expressed deep concern about the disunity that had provoked it.[74]

In 1977 electoral fraud gave the Salvadoran presidency to General Carlos Humberto Romero. A new archbishop, Oscar A. Romero (no relation to the general), author of the *Orientación* attack against the Externado, succeeded the aging Archbishop Chávez y González. On March 12 Rutilio Grande, S.J., at whose Aguilares parish some Externado students had been working, was shot to death as he drove to church to say mass. The death of Grande and similar instances of persecution of the church had a remarkable effect on Archbishop Romero. Within a relatively short time, he changed from an ally of the oligarchy into an eloquent spokesman for the poor.

A group calling itself the White Warriors promised the Jesuits a fate similar to Grande's if they did not leave El Salvador within thirty days. Jeréz defied this threat by keeping all the Jesuit institutions open, but dispersed the Jesuits to private houses and other religious communities each night. The Central American Jesuits also contacted their American counterparts, who influenced President Jimmy Carter of the United States to communicate to the president of El Salvador his concern for the safety of the Jesuits. Arrupe also cabled President Romero and wrote to Jeréz that he "was filled with joy to see the manner in which the various communities were putting up with the trials to which they were subjected."[75] Although the threats forced a cutback in Externado field work projects, the pedagogical changes gained a more lasting place in the school.

Chaos in the streets and government of El Salvador increased. On October 15, 1979, a military coup forced President Romero into exile, and its leaders appointed the rector of the UCA, Mayorga, to head the government. Mayorga had been the host of the dramatic meeting of Estrada and President Molina in 1973, but he had little power. After four months Mayorga and his civilian colleagues resigned and fled into exile. A member of a military death squad assassinated Archbishop Romero while he said mass on March 24, 1980. As noted at the beginning of this paper, three Externado teachers met their deaths that year and thirteen escaped into exile. In November, Ellacuría, by then the UCA rector, also left El Salvador after he was warned that he was a target of military plots.

Security forces raided the Externado campus on July 7, ransacked the files of *Socorro Jurídico,* and removed photos and transcripts of testimony that implicated security forces in extensive killing. The newspapers alleged that a cache of arms had been found in the school.[76] Security forces surrounded the Externado on November 27 and kidnapped several opposition leaders who were meeting there. Their tortured, dead bodies were found along a roadside several hours later. On December 2, four U.S. churchwomen were killed by the National Guard.

The school continued to operate and develop during the turmoil. Arrupe commended the excellent service provided by the Externado staff, noting that they offered their lives, their works, and especially what he referred to as their "pilot project" under the sad and difficult circumstances through which the country was passing.[77]

1981–1984: Conclusion and Implications

Although many professionals, *campesinos,* and labor leaders still lose their lives in El Salvador, no priests or members of religious orders have been attacked since the murder of the four U.S. churchwomen. These murders provoked such public outrage and so endangered U.S. congressional support that the government security forces and their death-squad allies found safer targets. As a precautionary move, however, Jeréz relocated the Jesuit communities of the Externado and UCA to an old novitiate outside San Salvador. By 1983 both communities had returned to their original residences, and Ellacuría had returned to the UCA presidency. The Jesuit residences have been searched by security forces since their return, and a bomb destroyed the front gate of the UCA Jesuit community in October 1983.

In the last few years, the Externado curriculum changes have become institutionalized, but the community service programs have been judged too dangerous to continue. The Turno Vespertino has prospered, and the integration of its students into the three final years of the morning session runs more smoothly as fewer social differences separate the two groups. Many of the elite now attend the British School or one of the other foreign schools in San Salvador, or they study in the United States.

The current staff is generally satisfied with the religious-pastoral program. Most of the seventy-five faculty members hold full-time positions, and eight recently graduated alumni teach classes while pursuing their own studies at the UCA. Extensive in-service programs in pedagogy, socioeconomic problems, religious and ethical questions, and the school's mission have shored up the staff development program. Although the continuing economic deterioration of El Salvador raises serious questions about the school's financial condition, the tuition has not been raised in five years nor has the size and quality of the Turno Vespertino been cut. The faculty has also gone five years without a raise in salary.

Several factors stand out as crucial in this change process at the Externado de San José: the decisive leadership and qualifications of the major actors and their skill in resisting opposition; the clarity of vision or ideology and its reformulation to meet changing circumstances; the development of strong coalitions of support groups, locally, nationally, and internationally; and the 1968 educational reform in El Salvador which provided a structure within which the ideology could be made real.

Estrada launched the change process, implemented many recommendations, and stood firm despite criticism from Rome, some local Jesuits, and the school's clientele. Jeréz consolidated these changes and skillfully managed the 1977 and 1980 crises. In time, Arrupe strongly supported the new orientation of the Externado, although his major contribution was his own heroic transformation, over eighteen years, of the whole Jesuit order.

Clear formulation of the religious and educational ideology at the international, national, and local levels, and wide participation of the personnel in its formulation, provided basic criteria to evaluate existing institutions and to develop new policies and strategies. The Externado staff and their UCA colleagues made frequent use of the Rio, Medellín, and Oaxtepec documents. Local documents such as *El Externado Piensa Así* and *Los Jesuitas Ante El Pueblo Salvadoreño* (Jesuits before the Salvadoran People) not only helped formulate policy and plans but also served to encourage all the participants. Such clearly formulated statements, and the process that produced them, proved essential in the face of strong, opposing ideologies. Several coalitions strengthened the process at crucial moments: the collaboration with the UCA; personal contact with the president of the Republic, local and international church officials, local educational groups, and the new clientele of the school.

The national educational reform program, despite its limitations and its gradual abandonment by the Ministry of Education, made it easier to implement the Externado ideology. The staff used the state reform as a vehicle to legitimize its new orientation and cited it in self-defense before President Molina and the outraged parents.

It would seem that all four factors have to be present in some significant way if any large-scale process of educational change is to succeed. Dramatic steps, followed by periods of consolidation, also proved decisive at the Externado. Under other circumstances a more incremental approach might be prudent and effective, but such a gradual process might give opposing forces time to water down the changes or neutralize them altogether.

Reformers have to be willing to pay the price of their convictions. They must suffer opposition from inside and outside the structure without becoming so defensive that they freeze the process at any point. The Externado's relatively successful efforts to distinguish the main project from the means to achieve it allowed them to minimize the discussion of ideology and substitute policies and plans when circumstances required. The Jesuits who directed the Externado knew when to stand and fight, and when to regroup their forces. All along they stressed staff development and wide participation in the design and implementation of the project. Staff motivation was strengthened by religious convictions that inspired them to work for justice.

Notes

1. A colegio is the equivalent of a high school but often includes an elementary school section and a college-level course.
2. Scholars have recently stressed the value of looking at the individual school as the locus of change. See, for example, John I. Goodland, *A Place Called School: Prospects for the Future* (New York: McGraw-Hill, 1983) and Sara L. Lightfoot, *The Good High School: Portraits of Culture and Character* (New York: Basic Books, 1983).
3. Luis Martin, S.J., *The Intellectual Conquest of Peru: The College of San Pablo, 1568–1767* (New York: Fordham University Press, 1968), p. 12.

4. John W. Donohue, S.J., *Jesuit Education: An Essay on the Foundation of Its Idea* (New York: Fordham University Press, 1963), p. 7. For a study of similar problems, see John W. Padberg, S.J., *Colleges in Controversy: The Jesuit Schools in France from the Revival to the Suppression, 1818–1880* (Cambridge: Harvard University Press, 1969), p. 126; Carmelo Sáenz de Santa María, S.J., *Historia de la Educación Jesuítica en Guatemala,* Parte I (Madrid: Universidad de Duesto, Bilbao, 1978), p. 55; see also William V. Bangert, S.J., *A History of the Society of Jesus* (St. Louis: Institute of Jesuit Sources, 1972).
5. The best general histories of El Salvador that set the stage for the period covered in this article are Alastar White, *El Salvador* (Boulder: Westview Press, 1973); and Ralph Lee Woodward, Jr., *Central America: A Nation Divided* (New York: Oxford University Press, 1976). For the colonial period, see Mudro J. MacLeod, *Spanish Central America: A Socioeconomic History, 1520–1720* (Berkeley: University of California Press, 1973); and Miles L. Wortman, *Government and Society in Central America, 1680–1840* (New York: Columbia University Press, 1982). For the recent era, see Enrique A. Baloyra, *El Salvador in Transition* (Chapel Hill: University of North Carolina Press, 1982).
6. Santiago Malaina, S.J., "La Compañía de Jesús en El Salvador, C.A., Desde 1864 a 1872," *Revista Del Departamento De Historia y Hereroteca Nacional Del Ministerio de Instrucción Publica,* 3 (1940), 5.
7. Malaina, "La Compañía de Jesús en El Salvador," p. 25.
8. Malaina, "La Compañía de Jesús en El Salvador," *Estudios Centroamericanos,* 6 (1951), 483.
9. "Externado de San José: Publicación Especial del Cincuentenario," a newspaper-like publication on the 50th anniversary, 25 March 1971; a copy can be found in the archives of the Central American Province of the Society of Jesus (Jesuits), San Salvador. This source is hereafter cited as ASJCA. A more detailed socioeconomic study of early Externado classes had been contemplated but not implemented due to unanimity of sources on this point.
10. ASJCA, "Informe Sobre La Religión Religiosa en El Externado de San José."
11. Thomas P. Anderson, *La Matanza* (Lincoln: University of Nebraska Press, 1971).
12. ASJCA, House Diary, Externado de San José, 30 Oct. 1955.
13. *La Prensa Gráfica,* 14 May 1956.
14. *Estudios Centroamericanos,* 17 (1963), 367.
15. *Estudios Centroamericanos,* 22 (1968), 260–63
16. *Estudios Centroamericanos,* 22 (1968), 260–63.
17. Conferencia General Del Episcopado Latinoamericano (CELAM), "Educación," in *Segunda Conferencia General Del Episcopado Latinoamericano, Medellín, 1968, Documentos Finales* (Lima: Arquidiocesano de Pastoral, 1968). For a discussion of the Limitations on Church leverage to effect social change, see Brian H. Smith, "Religion and Social Change: Classical Theories and New Formulations in the Context of Recent Developments in Latin America," *Latin American Research Review,* 10 (1975), 18; and Ivan Vallier, *Catholicism: Social Control and Modernization in Latin America* (Englewood Cliffs: Prentice-Hall, 1970), p. 8.
18. CELAM, "Educación," in *Segunda Conferencia General Del Episcopado Latinoamericano.*
19. CELAM, "Educación," in *Segunda Conferencia General Del Episcopado Latinoamericano.*
20. These criteria received confirmation when the Catholic bishops gathered at the synod in Rome and wrote *Justice in the World* (Boston: Daughters of St. Paul, 1971).
21. La Comisión Central Del Survey S.I. de C.A., *Análisis de las Obras Apostólicas S.I., Vice Provincia de Centro América,* Vol. VIII of *Apostolado de los Colegios,* (San Salvador: ASJCA, 1970), p. 42.
22. La Comisión Central, *Análisis de las Obras Apostólicas S.I.,* p. 65.
23. Xavier Ibánez, S.J. (Externado staff member), unpublished interview, May 1984.
24. José Santamaría, S.J. (currently rector of the Externado), unpublished interview, May 1984.

25. Luis M. Ormaechea, S.J. (past rector and current administrator at the Externado), unpublished interview, May 1984.
26. *Estudios Centroamericanos* dedicated the whole of its August 1978 issue to an analysis of the Salvadoran educational reform ten years after its inception.
27. ASJCA, 16 Oct. 1972.
28. ASJCA, Miguel F. Estrada, S.J., to Pedro Arrupe, S.J., 18 May 1973.
29. ASJCA, Vincent O'Keefe, S.J., to Miguel F. Estrada, S.J., 6 April 1973.
30. ASJCA, Asociación De Padres De Familias Del Externado de San José to Javier Colino, S.J., 28 April 1973.
31. ASJCA, Asociación De Padres De Familias Del Externado de San José to Javier Colino, S.J., 28 April 1973.
32. ASJCA, Javier Colino, S.J., to Miguel F. Estrada, S.J., 30 April 1973.
33. ASJCA, Javier Colino, S.J., to Asociación De Padres De Familias Del Externado de San José, 14 May 1973.
34. ASJCA, Miguel F. Estrada, S.J., to Asociación De Padres De Familias Del Externado de San José, 9 May 1973.
35. ASJCA, Jose Santamaría, Luis M. Ormaechea, and Salvador Samayoa, "Evaluación De Las Clases De Sociologiá Estudios Sociales De Bachillerato En el Colegio 'Externado de San José'," May 1973.
36. ASJCA, Miguel F. Estrada, S.J., to Pedro Arrupe, S.J., 18 May 1973.
37. Miguel F. Estrada, S.J., unpublished interview, May 1984.
38. Oscar A. Romero, Editorial, *Orientación,* 21 May 1973.
39. ASJCA, Miguel F. Estrada, S.J., to Oscar A. Romero, 28 May 1973.
40. ASJCA, Oscar A. Romero to Miguel F. Estrada, S.J., 31 May 1973.
41. ASJCA, Miguel F. Estrada, S.J., to Oscar A. Romero, 7 June 1973.
42. ASJCA, Miguel F. Estrada, S.J., to Benjamín Barrera y Reyes, 26 July 1973.
43. ASJCA, Pedro Arrupe, S.J., to Miguel F. Estrada, S.J., 5 June 1973.
44. ASJCA, Miguel F. Estrada, S.J., to Pedro Arrupe, S.J., 22 June 1973.
45. ASJCA, Juan Moreno, 11 June 1973.
46. *La Prensa Gráfica,* 12 June 1973.
47. *El Diario De Hoy,* 16 June 1973.
48. *El Diario De Hoy,* 16 June 1973.
49. *El Diario De Hoy,* 20 June 1973.
50. *El Externado Piensa Así* (San Salvador: Talleres Gráfico, UCA, 1973); also published in *Estudios Centroamericanos,* 28 (1973), 399–422.
51. *El Externado Piensa Así,* p. 16.
52 *El Externado Piensa Así,* p. 17.
53. ASJCA, "Informe, Senado Presbíteral de San Salvador, Presentado por la Comisión Especial por Mandato General," 25 June 1973.
54. ASJCA, Arturo Rivera y Damas, 25 June 1973.
55. *La Prensa Gráfica,* 26 June 1973.
56. ASJCA, mimeographed pages for distribution.
57. *El Diario De Hoy,* 28 June 1973.
58. *La Prensa Gráfica,* 29 June 1973.
59. *La Prensa Gráfica,* 29 June 1973.
60. ASJCA, Juan Moreno, S.J., to Benigno Achaerandio, S.J., 6 July 1973.
61. ASJCA, Juan Moreno, S.J., to Coronel Arturo Molina, 12 July 1973.
62. ASJCA, Juan Moreno, S.J., to Coronel Arturo Molina, 12 July 1973.
63. ASJCA, Juan Moreno, S.J., to Pedro Arrupe, S.J., 7 July 1973.
64. ASJCA, Miguel F. Estrada, S.J., to Pedro Arrupe, S.J., 21 Aug. 1973.
65. Ignacio Ellacuría, S.J., unpublished interview, May 1984.
66. Miguel F. Estrada, S.J., unpublished interview, May 1984.

67. ASJCA, Vincent O'Keefe, S.J., to Miguel F. Estrada, S.J., 21 Sept. 1973.
68. Former Rectors Luis M. Ormaechea, S.J., and Segundo Montes, S.J., unpublished interview, May 1984.
69. Manuel Santiago, S.J., unpublished interview, May 1984.
70. José Santamaría, S.J., unpublished interview, May 1984.
71. ASJCA, "Plan De El Externado para 1977, Presentado Por Comunidad De Externado I," July 1976.
72. ASJCA, "Plan Sexenal Del Externado (1977–1982), Elaborado por la Comunidad Externado Il y los Srs. Joaquín y Salvador Samayo," 28 August 1976.
73. ASJCA, César Jeréz, S.J., to Padres de Estudiantes del Externado de San José, 4 Oct. 1976.
74. ASJCA, Pedro Arrupe, S.J., to César Jeréz, S.J., 12 Oct. 1976.
75. ASJCA, Pedro Arrupe, S.J., to César Jeréz, S.J., 10 June 1977.
76. *La Prensa Gráfica,* 8 July 1980.
77. ASJCA, Pedro Arrupe, S.J., to César Jeréz, 28 April 1980.

This study was made possible by a grant from the New York Province of the Society of Jesus, an appointment as Associate in Education at Harvard University Graduate School of Education, and the cooperation of the Central American Jesuits. The author is particularly grateful to Noel F. McGinn of the Harvard faculty for his invaluable assistance in structuring this study, especially his conceptual framework on the interrelationships among ideology, actors, strategies, and coalitions to effect change.

Resistances to Knowing in the Nuclear Age

JOHN E. MACK, M.D.

The publication in 1983 of several guides that provide instructional materials for teachers on the subject of nuclear weapons and nuclear war stirred a national controversy about the inclusion of such materials in school curricula. The controversy has focused upon whether the materials provide "a balanced treatment" (Maeroff, 1983) and involve teaching in a "normally accepted" sense (*Washington Post,* 1983) or are intended instead as "propaganda" to advocate a particular political position. *Choices: A Unit on Conflict and the Nuclear War,* a teaching unit developed by the Union of Concerned Scientists (UCS) and the National Education Association (NEA) (1983), brought forth the polar extremes of the controversy. In attacking the lesson plan, Albert Shanker, president of the American Federation of Teachers, called it "lopsided propaganda" and objected that it contained "no discussion of the Soviet takeover of other countries, no treatment of Soviet aid to Communists around the world to help overthrow other governments, no facts on the Soviet political system . . . , the Gulags, the psychiatric tortures, etc. What the NEA lesson plan sees as irrational fears, many of us feel justified in viewing as not only rational but prudent" (Shanker, 1983, p. E7). In a letter supporting *Choices,* Henry W. Kendall of UCS and Terry Herndon, director of NEA, wrote that the curriculum was designed "to respond to widespread fear and anxiety among young people on the issue of nuclear war" and to present options, choices, and contrasting views. Its purpose, they said, was not to advocate views or any political position, but "to present controversial subjects in an objective manner" (Kendall & Herndon, 1983). President Reagan himself entered the fray in a speech before Shanker's union in June 1983 when he attacked "curriculum guides that seem to be more aimed at frightening and brainwashing American school children than at fostering learning and stimulating balanced, intelligent debate" (Shribman, 1983, p. A12).

As a psychiatrist and psychoanalyst who has been studying the impact of the nuclear weapons competition on young people, I hold the view that the argument about balance and fairness, though important at one level, obscures a more profound educational and national dilemma. The development by

Harvard Educational Review Vol. 54 No. 3 August 1984, 33–66

educators of teaching materials about nuclear weapons and the nuclear arms race has occurred in response to a felt need in the society, especially on the part of children, adolescents, and their parents and educators. In several clinical studies and surveys and in countless less formal communications, many young people have expressed their fears—a sense of powerlessness and of things being out of control—and uncertainties about the future in the face of the threat of nuclear annihilation (Bachman, 1983; Beardslee & Mack, 1982, 1983; Goldenring & Doctor, 1983; Goodman, Mack, Beardslee, & Snow, 1983; Mack, 1983, 1984). Many young people feel that the situation is now hopeless and that nuclear war will occur before they have a chance to complete their lives. Some adolescents say the nuclear danger dominates their lives and is their greatest concern.

It would appear to be an appropriate response on the part of parents and educators to address, through reliable, carefully prepared educational materials, the sense of helplessness and hopelessness which adolescents feel about the nuclear threat. Obtaining knowledge and information and debating possible alternative policy positions are initial steps to securing a sense of power and control. Indeed, when one considers the centrality of the nuclear issue for the lives of U.S. young people and the hunger among adolescents for education on this subject, it is remarkable how little attention has been given to it in our schools. Some adolescents even attribute their anxiety and sense of powerlessness directly to their ignorance of basic facts about nuclear weapons and the arms race. Teachers and other adults feel equally powerless in relation to the enormity of the nuclear threat. Teachers' sense of helplessness is in itself a kind of first barrier to approaching the problem of what and how to teach about nuclear weapons and the arms race. One curriculum for high school students, developed recently by Snow and her colleagues (1983), states explicitly that "perhaps the most striking reason for including nuclear education programs in our schools is that adolescents are asking for help in understanding a world that seems out of control, uncertain, and without choices. The evidence that adolescents are deeply affected by the fear of nuclear annihilation demands a concerned response from us, as adults and teachers" (p. 2).

On the surface these arguments seem reasonable enough. In a democratic society, we expect young people to be thinking for themselves—developing choices—in matters that powerfully affect their lives. From a civic point of view, it has long been believed that a well-informed citizenry can, on the whole, make better decisions on important public questions than can an ignorant population. Yet, in the case of the nuclear problem, do we really want this? Let us consider the minimum agreed-upon facts about nuclear weapons and nuclear war that a balanced curriculum, free of political bias, would include. It would describe the properties of the weapons and the extent of their physical, climatic, and biological destructive effects. It would include the numbers and kinds of weapons in the possession of the nuclear powers. A historical account of the nuclear predicament would have to be provided so students might understand the current situation in which the United States and the Soviet Union possess about 50,000 nuclear devices, many thousands of which are deployed in battlefield, theatre, or "strategic" situations and are ready to be used under several potential military circumstances; the resulting risk is that human life on earth might be ended, perhaps forever. There would be some discussion of U.S. and Soviet policy with respect to nuclear weapons, including the regrettable knowledge that the United States and the Soviet Union are prepared, however reluctantly, to accept the sacrifice of hundreds of millions of innocent people, perhaps the entire human population and much of the rest of the planet's life, in defense of their respective political systems and values. In addition, this discussion would consider possible ways a nuclear war might start—through escalation of a regional conflict involving U.S. and Soviet interests, direct superpower confrontation, human error, or technical failure—and some assessment of the likelihood of each of these possibilities.

Deeper Issues

It is here, I believe, that the deeper problem of nuclear education resides. For it may be the case that no balanced teaching, nor any information about the Soviet system, can distract teenagers from our failure to secure for them a reliable and minimally safe future. Even the threat of Soviet militarism may fail to justify the proliferation of nuclear weapons. We may not be able to hide from young people the fact that these weapons have not provided them with a sense of security or freedom from the Soviet threat. We now know that it is likely, judging from the scientific report of Turco and his colleagues, that our own weapons, if used for only a moderate-sized first strike, will result in the death of our own entire population, even if the other side never fires a single missile (Turco, Toon, Ackerman, Pollack, & Sagan, 1983). Confronted with a minimum amount of factual information about the nuclear reality, young people are likely to ask difficult questions of their teachers, parents, and government leaders. They have already begun to ask why we have not done a better job of ordering the world and providing for their futures. They ask ethical questions about the propriety of threatening to kill such vast numbers of people as an acceptable solution to conflict between nations. These questions make us uncomfortable, and we have no good way to answer them. There is probably no balanced curriculum, no politically neutral position for teaching about the nuclear issue that can fail to confront young people with the fact that all of our lives have been placed in imminent jeopardy by nuclear weapons. I believe it is this realization, which we all share at some level, that lies behind the controversy over nuclear education in American schools. We are not prepared for the hard questions that children and adolescents will surely ask of us if we provide them with solid information and open the classroom to a discussion of the nuclear problem.

I maintain that the controversy surrounding nuclear education is illustrative of the conflicts which beset the society *as a whole* with regard to nuclear weapons and nuclear arms policy; it reflects the resistances to confronting the nuclear problem that operate throughout the adult community. As a result of these resistances, decisions concerning nuclear weapons have been left to a small group composed largely of men thought to be qualified on the basis of their possession of technical knowledge and a limited number of government and military officials whom they hold in their thrall.

Recognition is dawning in our society that policymaking with regard to nuclear weapons is more than a military matter of national security in the traditional historical sense. This is true for a rather simple reason involving the nature of the weapons themselves. Nuclear devices are, from a military point of view, essentially unusable except to inspire fear by the threat of their use or as instruments of global murder/suicide; their targets are not just the cities or military installations of a designated enemy but the minds of the enemy's political and military leaders and the people themselves. However, the actual impact of the nuclear threat upon the intentions and behavior of another nation's leadership and people is virtually unknown. Because this is largely a human or psychological matter, having to do with the emotions and behavior of individuals and groups under stress, the question may be raised whether military leaders and experts with technical knowledge are any better qualified to make judgments in this area than the rest of the nation's citizens.

The responsibility, I suggest, for recognizing and coming to grips with the nuclear problem lies far more in the hands of the citizenry as a whole than has been the case in the past with matters of military policy and national security. Along the same lines, we may discover that solutions to the nuclear dilemma, and to achieving real security in the nuclear age, lie far less in the realm of military policy and action than we have heretofore realized.

Resistances to Knowing

In light of the above discussion, I will now examine some of the forces or, as I prefer to call them, the *resistances* which have stood in the way of our recognizing and dealing with the nuclear peril.

Individual Resistance

When we consider resistance from a psychological point of view, we are most familiar with those avoidances of reality and emotion that operate at a personal and individual level. In relation to the horror and despair which confront us when we consider the possibility of a nuclear holocaust, we pull away, wanting urgently to consider less painful matters. Our minds and hearts cannot grasp the meaning of a million Hiroshimas or the possible deaths of hundreds of millions, if not billions, of human beings, so we turn away in a kind of benumbed horror and address ourselves to problems of a more manageable scale. This kind of personal, individual resistance can be overcome, at least to a degree that permits involvement, by psychological work that reduces the margin between intellectual and emotional knowing. Films like *The Day After* (1983) and documentaries which depict the actual effects of nuclear explosions can be useful in breaking through the barriers to awareness of the threat. They reach us at a human level and make the danger more real. Community affinity groups[1] and other supportive organizations provide settings in which feelings can be shared and constructive education and action—perhaps the only real therapy for the fear of nuclear annihilation—can be planned in collaboration with one's neighbors, colleagues, relatives, and friends.

Collective Resistance

But there are additional resistances to knowing the truth about nuclear weapons and the arms race which act at another level, often quite subtly. These might be called collective resistances, as they operate in relation to the group: at the level of society or the nation as a whole and its organizations and institutions. Collective resistances have the explicit or tacit support of the community. They are a product of the way a nation and its institutions organize their basic assumptions about the world. These assumptions are held in conformity with what the society regards as its essential political and economic purposes, values, and ideologies.

Historically, we know that an accurate view of the physical nature of the universe can be sacrificed, and factual certainties rejected, if new empirical data challenge, at least by implication, the shared assumptions of the community. The threats of Darwin's discoveries to religious theories of humankind's place at the pinnacle of creation and of psychoanalysis to our collective conceit of self-mastery and awareness are well-known examples. In the present age, we struggle against the notion that human life after a nuclear war will not exist. We reject data such as the findings of Turco, Toon, Ackerman, Pollack, and Sagan (1983) which reveal the likely climatic and biological effects of a nuclear war, and we continue to plan civil defense programs, knowing that shelters cannot help us. As a recent editorial in *Science* notes, "The completely new strategic implications of the nuclear winter scenarios have not yet received any great public attention or discussion" (1984, p. 775). To know in the fullest sense the nature of the destructive monster we have created delivers a kind of double blow to our experience of reality and ourselves. On the one hand, it confronts us with the failure of our political and military system to order its affairs in a way that provides security for its people in relation to other nations. At the same time, such knowledge brings us face to face with the fact that our policy of a "credible" nuclear deterrent requires the willingness to annihilate most, if not all, of human life in the service of national goals—a piece of societal self-knowledge that is potentially devastating to our collective self-regard.

Our society as a whole, especially as represented by its government and corporate leaders, resists knowledge or public discourse about nuclear weapons and the threat of nuclear war. But collective resistances also operate within individual citizens, although we may be quite unaware of their presence. We become identified with a kind of collective mind, allying, often quite unconsciously, our individual selves with the values, purposes, and prejudices of the larger group, which functions as a parent to whom we surrender authority and our powers of discrimination. Despite the fact that we might know better, we find comfort in reassurances by the president that our expanding nuclear arsenal has made the world a safer place. Or we may resist a deeper knowing of the nuclear danger out of fear that we may be criticized for raising questions, especially if we become "active." Our self-image in relation to the larger group may not include "activist," whatever that word may imply. We take comfort in identification with the organization or group—the nation, the company, or the school—and go along with it, wherever it may take us. To raise questions, to challenge and confront, creates anxiety and revives ancient fears of being cast out of the group or family. The advanced nature of nuclear technology may serve to augment all forms of emotional distancing that relate to the nuclear threat. The sense that the problems are too technical or remote, require special knowledge to understand, or will be solved by new technological advances, can be used to remove us from responsibility for what is essentially a human problem.

At the level of the nation, our collective resistance is most prominently manifested in relation to the representation of an enemy. To maintain the attitude of belligerence necessary to sustain a giant war effort—in the nuclear age, a war preparedness—a society must have both a worthy enemy and a willingness to kill on a mass scale. As Warnke (1983) pointed out recently, the accommodation with China (no longer "Red" China) has required that the full burden of our national enmity fall on the Soviet Union. When we question the prudence of unquestioning hostility toward Russia or speak of the dangers of policies which rely solely upon threat and intimidation, we feel slightly unpatriotic, perhaps even a little seditious. This feeling is but the tip of an iceberg of fear and inhibition (not in relation to the Soviet Union itself, which is another kind of fear) that grows out of challenging deeply held articles of national faith, which our foreign policy directly reflects. The very nature of thermonuclear devices and their international and intercontinental delivery systems, which indiscriminately spew radioactive fallout around the globe and cross national borders with ease, has brought into question the assumption that "national" security in the nuclear age can be achieved by *any* nation acting on its own. But the recognition of the interdependence of the United States and its adversaries, the realization that security can only be achieved mutually, brings into question deeply held beliefs about the functions of the nation-state and about the meaning of national sovereignty. Traditionally, one of the most fundamental responsibilities of a national government has been to protect its people through military power. To doubt the capacity of the nation to defend its borders militarily evokes fears which are, to use Shanker's words, "justified," "rational," and "prudent." But the nature of nuclear devices challenges something deeper. It undercuts our mental representation of the nation as a powerful, autonomous, protective institution which can secure survival by military means. The anxiety this evokes will be resisted by leader and follower alike. As Tolstoy observed in 1898, the most intelligent persons will "seldom discern even the simplest and most obvious truth if it be such as obliges them to admit the falsity of conclusions they have formed . . . of which they are proud, which they have taught to others, and on which they have built their lives" (quoted in Dyson, 1984).

Resistances to knowing and to changes of thinking forced upon us by the development of nuclear technology occur also in subnational collectives, at what might be called the corporate level. Subnational collectives include military and other national and local governmental entities connected with the national security system, organizations and industries involved in weapons research and production, and labor unions and other social institutions which have a vested interest in resisting the revolution in thinking that nuclear technological developments require. By vested interest I mean something more than direct economic or political gain which results from participation in one or another corporate aspect of the nuclear weapons production system. I include also the psychological attachment and personal emotional security afforded by the alignment with the organization and its associated mission and ideology. To challenge the corporate consensus, much less to break away in protest, appears to evoke very deep anxiety. Ellsberg (1984) has said that, for many of his colleagues in the government, his act of defiance in breaking with the government and releasing the Pentagon papers was terrifying. To them, it was as if he had sent himself "spinning into a black void." A primal force seems to operate here, the fear of a kind of tribal ostracism that goes beyond the actual danger of criticism or censure. This fear prevents most members of the group from breaking with its assumptions and acting independently. It accounts for the rarity with which people resign from government or corporate positions, even when they know they are participating in policies they consider dangerous or are involved in producing weapons systems whose mass-murderous effects they find morally repugnant.

Implications for Nuclear Education

Secondary schools are themselves corporate structures. Public schools administered by local municipal committee structures, private nondenominational schools governed by citizen boards often dominated by corporate leaders, and religious schools administered by clergy are all deeply embedded in the collective structure of the larger society and participate in its purposes and prevailing ideology. In our secondary schools young people, whether by conscious intent or happenstance, undergo the political socialization which will adapt them to the larger society. Schools, and especially school systems, may resist educational materials that stimulate questions about the basic assumptions of the society as a whole, even though teenagers and their parents may express the wish for such programs. This sort of resistance may be quite unconscious. Extraneous reasons—for example, that the information is too upsetting to children—may be offered as the basis for rejecting this material in the curriculum. It is true, of course, that the facts about nuclear weapons and the arms race *are* upsetting to children and adolescents. But preliminary research shows that many young people are troubled about the nuclear threat in any event and that education offers them at least some opportunity for mastery. I believe that the deeper and truer reason for the avoidance of this topic in school curricula is fear of change and the challenge that education about nuclear issues is likely to pose to prevailing assumptions embedded in the social system.

Looked at from this point of view, the controversy around nuclear education in the schools has some features in common with the furor around sex education two decades ago. The argument is not fundamentally about balance of presentation or about offering all sides of the issue. The debate is fueled by the topic itself and its disturbing nature. I am not saying that there are not courageous teachers, union leaders, school administrators, and even school governing boards willing to take on the challenges of offering educational materials in this disturbing area. But they do so in the face of a structural reluctance in the school systems and in the nation as a whole. A first step is to confront in ourselves the fear that is the very sign of our struggle to become free of the benumbing effect of our inevitable identification with the larger collectivity and its prevailing assumptions and ideologies.

Let us consider, for example, teaching high school students about the Soviet Union in relation to the nuclear arms race. To be "balanced," such instruction might include, together with available facts about the Soviet political system, some account of how the Soviet leadership and people see the nuclear danger, *their* view of security, and *their* fears of U.S. and Chinese military power. No amount of emphasis upon unacceptable behavior of the Soviet regime, including the Gulags and "the psychiatric tortures," can prevent American young people from discovering that there *is* a Soviet point of view, that the Russians *do* fear nuclear war, and, most important, that our prevailing nationalistic ideology tends to stereotype negatively the Soviet Union. It is precisely a "balanced treatment" which those who resist nuclear education in our schools fear. U.S. adolescents, with their characteristic sense of fair play, are reluctant to stereotype the Soviet Union to begin with, as one pilot study has already suggested (Goodman, Mack, Beardslee, & Snow, 1983). They may resist even further being conscripted into an attitude of enmity should they receive an even-handed exposure to the complexities of Soviet society and the United States-Soviet relationship and come to see Soviet children and adults as real people with human feelings. I do not argue here whether a reluctance to stereotype is good or bad for national security. I simply suggest that this fear—that adolescents may question and challenge the dichotomizing and dehumanizing view of the Soviet Union which predominates in our collective mentality—may be a powerful conscious and unconscious obstacle to our providing objective teaching about the Russians.

Or consider the effect on adolescents of learning about the history of the arms race, the opportunities missed on both sides to halt and reverse it, and the decisions made in most instances by U.S. and Soviet leaders to engage in technological escalation rather than to pursue initiatives for weapons reductions and peace. Are they not likely to ask troubling factual and moral questions, indict our generation for the failure to protect their futures, and become disillusioned and distrustful of their government and society, as many young people already have? The worry that nuclear curricula will "win the young for the cause of nuclear disarmament" (Maeroff, 1983) may in one sense be well founded. Many teenagers, even after they have learned the rationale for the arms race, recoil in horror from the absurdity of the nuclear predicament and see in disarmament the only hope for the planet. Some begin to work actively toward this end.

We may worry that some teenagers will go further than this. Hyde (1983) has written, "Adolescence is marked by that restless, erotic, disturbing inquisition: Is this person, this nation, this work, worthy of the life I have to give?" (p. 97). When exposed to the realities of the nuclear threat and encouraged by teachers to question openly and deeply the mental attitudes and choices which give rise to it, their inquisition may become disturbing indeed. Their questioning may reach beyond the arms race, extending to the political system which gave rise to it and even to the school system and the school itself, if these are seen as accomplices in the evil they discern.

Literature and art inside and outside the classroom can be powerful forces for revealing a nation's betrayal of its own values. In Hyde's words, "Art does not organize parties, nor is it the servant or colleague of power. Rather, the work of art becomes a political force simply through the faithful representation of the spirit. It is a political act to create an image of the self or of the collective. . . . So long as the artist speaks the truth, he will, whenever the government is lying, or has betrayed the people, become a political force whether he intends it or not" (p. 198). In the mid-nineteenth century, Walt Whitman, with his characteristic emotional bluntness, put the matter directly: "Under and behind the bosh of the regular politicians, there burns . . . the divine fire which . . . during all ages, has only wanted a chance to leap forth and confound the calculations of tyrants, hunkers, and all of their tribe" (quoted in Hyde, p. 198). Exposing our teenagers to "divine fire" may be precisely what we most assiduously resist, lest they discover that not all the "tyrants" and the "hunkers" reside among the ranks of the designated enemy. The embarrassing insistence of adolescents that a nation live up to its proclaimed ideals in its dealings with other nations may be considered by "the regular politicians" and much of our "tribe" as the very essence of a lack of patriotism, to be avoided at all costs.

Conclusion

In our democracy we value highly citizen participation and responsibility in relation to the important issues facing society. Yet, in the choices surrounding nuclear weapons policies, citizens have been excluded—or have excluded themselves—to an extraordinary degree, especially when one considers that our lives and our futures depend on these decisions. On the surface it appears to be the arcane technical/military complexities of nuclear devices that have restricted the debate, at least until recently, to a relatively small number of officials and specialists with technical expertise. Yet, as I have argued in this essay, nuclear weapons policies are based on human decisions about the imagined impact of the threat of one or another weapon system on an imagined adversary's mind. The problem is essentially a human one that affects all of our lives and for which we each must assume responsibility.

For most citizens the principal road to responsible involvement leads through our schools and the educational system. A great deal of information is available on nearly every aspect of the history, science, technology, geography, and politics of nuclear weapons and the nuclear arms competition. Nevertheless, efforts to bring teaching materials of high quality into our schools have run into powerful obstacles. Some nuclear educational programs have been opposed on the grounds that they do not offer a "balanced treatment." I have suggested that the deeper source of the obstacle to nuclear education in our schools is a resistance to knowing that is both personal and collective. I have argued that if we fail to recognize the desire not to know which operates in ourselves as individuals and as members of a nation or its associated institutions and organizations, advocacy for nuclear education in our schools—no matter how well-intended or impassioned—will not succeed.

The sense of helplessness or powerlessness which so many people feel in relation to the nuclear threat is in part the result of the enormity of the problem and the scope of the forces arrayed to support the perpetuation of the arms race. But our helplessness, too, can be the expression—and I suspect this is the more important element—of our experience of individual and collective resistance and our fear of involvement. After all, we each know many people whose individual efforts have made an extraordinary difference in opening up and extending the debate about nuclear weapons policy that is now taking place in the United States. The nuclear age has many large and small heroes in the quest for peace and global security.

In a recent article, Powers (1984) wrote that the "bad news" about nuclear weapons can arrive in many ways. By bad news Powers meant "a belief, an inner conviction, an awareness deep in the primitive center of the brain, that these weapons are really out there, they work, and that they will be used if we go on as we are" (p. 35). I have discussed another kind of bad news that concerns our relationship to nuclear weapons and nuclear weapons policies. This second sort of bad news is psychological or psychosocial, analogous perhaps to the message brought by Freud and psychoanalysis which forced us to confront the irrational, aggressive, and erotic dimensions of our individual selves.

This second kind of bad news about the nuclear threat is that we created it ourselves, that it is the outgrowth of our own individual and collective fear and hostility, amplified by a technological, genocidal exuberance that is peculiar to the last four decades of the present century. It is not at all clear that we wish to uncover the historical and inner psychological forces that have led us to the present frightful impasse. Resistance to nuclear education is an expression of a conscious and unconscious desire not to know. The most powerful resistance grows out of our identification with the prevailing purposes and ideology of the nation and its associated corporate or institutional structures, including the mass media, which tend to locate the problem largely elsewhere—in the present context in the Soviet Union. Through this identification, we surrender individual responsibility and allow ourselves to be mollified by reassuring words communicated by national leaders through television, radio, and newspapers. But to question, to separate ourselves from the national consensus, evokes a fear that is like being cast out into the unknown. There is also a kind of good news, a corollary to the fact that the nuclear deadlock is a human creation. For, by this same token, the present course can be reversed if we make the commitment to find alternatives to war in the settlement of conflicts between nations. If we do not have this courage, if in the nuclear age we do not assume the risks of knowing, we face the disaster that will come about inevitably as a result of our inability to distinguish the threat which emanates from outside ourselves and the danger which is our own continuing creation.

Notes

1. Community affinity groups refer to support groups which meet around common social concerns.

References

Bachman, J. (1983). How American high school seniors view the military. *Armed Forces and Society, 10,* 86–104.

Beardslee, W. R., & Mack, J. E. (1982). The impact on children and adolescents of nuclear developments. In *Psychosocial Aspects of Nuclear Developments* (Task Force Report No. 20). Washington, DC: American Psychiatric Association.

Beardslee, W. R., & Mack, J. E. (1983). Adolescents and the threat of nuclear war: The evolution of a perspective. *Yale Journal of Biology and Medicine, 56,* 79–91.

Dyson, F. (1984, February 27). Reflections: Weapons and hope [Pt. 4]. *New Yorker,* p. 54.
Ellsberg, D. (1984, January). Lecture at Cambridge Hospital, Department of Psychiatry, Cambridge, MA.
Goldenring, J. M., & Doctor, R. M. (1983, September 20). *Adolescents' concerns about the threat of nuclear war.* Prepared statement before the Select Committee on Children, Youth, and Families, U.S. 98th Cong., 1st Sess., H. Rept. (Washington, DC: GPO, 1984), pp. 61–66.
Goodman, L., Mack, J. E., Beardslee, W. R., & Snow, R. M. (1983). The threat of nuclear war and the nuclear arms race: Adolescent experience and perception. *Political Psychology, 4,* 501–530.
Hyde, L. (1983). *The gift: Imagination and the erotic life of poetry.* New York: Vintage Books.
Kendall, H. W., & Herndon, T. (1983, April 15). Letter to the editor. *Washington Post.*
Mack, J. E. (1983, September 20). *The psychological impact of the nuclear arms competition on children and adolescents.* Testimony to Select Committee on Children, Youth and Families, U.S. 98th Cong., 1st Sess., H. Rept. (Washington, DC: GPO, 1984), pp. 47–91.
Mack, J. E. (1984). Research on the impact of the nuclear arms race on children in the U.S.A. *Report, 2,* (IPPNW) 7–9. Published by International Physicians for the Prevention of Nuclear War.
Maeroff, G. I. (1983, March 29). Curriculum addresses fear of atomic war. *New York Times.*
Papazian, R. (Producer), & Meyer, N. (Director). (1983). *The Day After* [Film]. New York: American Broadcasting Company.
Powers, T. (1984, January). What is it about? *Atlantic Monthly,* pp. 35–55.
Science (1984, February 24). Editorial, p. 775.
Shanker, A. (1983, April 17). Where we stand [Advertisement]. *New York Times,* p. E7.
Shribman, D. (1983, July 6). Reagan accuses NEA of brainwashing efforts. *New York Times,* p. A12.
Snow, R., Austill, C., Bowditch, B., Burt L., Landenburg, T., Lewis, E., Phillips, C., Schotz, M., and Stoskopf, A. (1983). *Decision making in a nuclear age.* Weston, MA.: Halcyon House.
Turco, R. P., Toon, O. B., Ackerman, T. P., Pollack, J. B., & Sagan, C. (1983). Nuclear winter: Global consequences of multiple nuclear explosions. *Science, 222,* 1283–1292.
Union of Concerned Scientists and the National Education Association (1983). *Choices: A unit on conflict and nuclear war.* Washington, DC: National Education Association.
Warnke, P. (1983, October 30). Discussion of presentations by R. Fisher, J. Mack, and C. Pinderhughes. In *Aggression and its alternatives in the conduct of international relations.* Symposium at the meeting of the Psychoanalytic Society and Institute, Boston.
Washington Post (1983, April 5). Editorial, P. A14.

The author wishes to thank Dorothy Austin, Lisa Goodman, and Roberta Snow for their helpful suggestions in the preparation of this article.

The Contradictions of Bantu Education

MOKUBUNG O. NKOMO

A chronic turbulence has characterized South Africa's African universities over the last decade. Much of the protest arises from opposition to the policy of separate development in general and Bantu education in particular.[1] Ironically, the protesters are the very people who were supposed to be docile workers in the urban industrial areas of South Africa and complacent citizens of the homelands.[2]

The underlying proposition of this article is that African student behavior did not follow the intent of government policymakers because the Africans' reactions to Bantu education were never taken into consideration. Specifically, two explanations for the contradictory outcomes of Bantu education and the subsequent uprisings of recent years are suggested.[3] The first is that Bantu education has developed a culture of its own which is at odds with official intentions. The second is that forces external to in-class instruction have exerted as great an influence as the official curriculum—perhaps greater.

Historically, Africans in South Africa have not been involved in the formulation of government policies that affect them. Disenfranchisement has been a cardinal principle of white Afrikaner domination, although recently the right to participate in electoral politics has been allowed in the homelands. Exclusion from policymaking has engendered protest and resistance, which extends to the education system. Opposition to discrimination in education was first expressed in 1923, when African conferences, attended by government officials and African leaders and held in the cities of Bloemfontein and Pretoria, demanded that the Union government take full control of African education policy (Troup, 1976; Walshe, 1971). The demand was not met. Vociferous protests greeted the Bantu Education Act when it was introduced in 1953 (Kuper, 1971; Tabata, 1960; Troup, 1976). Its expressed aim was to educate Africans according to their ethnic identities and to provide basic literacy and numeracy skills needed by a burgeoning economy. Critics saw the act as an effort by the dominant white group to control the development of Africans, and thereby to steer that development in a direction that would ensure perpetual peonage.

Harvard Educational Review Vol. 51 No. 1 February 1981, 126–138

Such fears were intensified by the statements of leading Afrikaners, in particular those of Hendrik Verwoerd, once minister of native affairs and later prime minister, who stated: "Education must train and teach people in accordance with their opportunities in life, according to the sphere in which they live" (Welsh, 1971, p. 225). Their "opportunities in life" and the "sphere in which they live" were to be defined not by Africans but by whites, who believed they were invested with this right to rule by "divine" authority. Furthermore,

> the Bantu must be guided to serve his own community in all respects. There is no place for him in the European community above the level of *certain forms of labor*. . . . For that reason, it is of no avail for him to receive training which has as its aim absorption in the European community while he cannot and will not be absorbed there. Up till now, he has been subjected to a school system which drew him away from his own community and partially misled him by showing him the green pastures of the European but still did not allow him to graze there. (Welsh, p. 225, emphasis added)

So, while the purpose of Bantu education was ostensibly to school Africans within their own cultural groups and patterns, its actual goal was to produce a semiliterate industrial force to meet the needs of an expanding economy. In a racially defined society such as South Africa, the stratification of labor along racial lines is institutionalized. Whites get stable jobs with high wages and a future, while blacks get high-turnover, dead-end, low-wage jobs (Magubane, 1979). Bantu education, critics charged, was designed to ensure the subordinate position of Africans in the South African social and political hierarchy.

In the last ten years, opposition to Bantu education, led by African students, has been widespread. While grievances against specific policies, such as insistence on Afrikaans as the primary language of instruction, have generated confrontations, participants have consistently related their protests to the general socioeconomic conditions to which Africans are subjected. This has been a common thread in reports to the Van Wyk Commission appointed to investigate disturbances at the University of Western Cape, the Snyman Commission (Note 1) that investigated disturbances at the University of the North; the Jackson Commission (Note 2) that investigated the status of Africanization at the University of the North; and the Cillie Commission that investigated the 1976 Soweto protests.

Although the policy of separate development provides outlets for political expression by creating homelands where Africans can have a sense of participation, this psychological valve has neither abated frustration nor eliminated opposition in the urban areas, where the majority of black South Africans live. This denial of a political voice in the larger society has led to feelings of ambivalence toward apartheid institutions. On the one hand, there is opposition to the policy of separate development, on the other, separate institutions have been used by African students to organize against government apartheid policies. For example, the general demands at the various black universities have been for control of these institutions, for effective involvement in decision making, and for greater Africanization of the teaching faculty and administrative staff.[4] These demands can be justified as fitting within the official framework of separate development. However limited in scope they may be, the institutions set up to maintain separate development seem to provide opportunities for African students to launch opposition against the overall apartheid structure.

When the Nationalist party came to power in 1948, it transformed the former practice of laissez-faire racial segregation into a systematic racial ideology. Education was to be a principal instrument to achieve the goal of separate development: "For education to serve the purposes of domination, the institutions must, of necessity, follow the model of the larger society. In this sense, the university is nothing more than a microscopic representation of Nationalist [party] aspirations, ideals, and values. Accordingly, there is a hierarchical arrangement of teaching staff, mirroring societal designations. The quality of education, especially methods of instruction, reflects as well as cements the surrounding racial structure" (K. Adam, 1971, p. 201).

The Bantu Education Act of 1953 was extended to the university level in 1959. As a result of this legislation, five university colleges were established: The University College at Westville, for Indians; the University of Western Cape at Bellville, for Coloreds; the University College of Fort Hare, for Xhosa-speaking Africans; the University College of Zululand at Ngoye, for Zulu- and Swazi-speaking Africans; and the University of the North at Turfloop, for the north and south Sotho, Tsonga, Tswana, and Venda ethnic groups. Since racial discrimination existed in the English-speaking universities before the 1959 act, the new institutions were not established primarily to ensure segregation but to encourage the fragmentation of the Africans into their separate ethnic groups, and, consequently to consolidate the power of the state (K. Adam, 1971). The expansion of the universities was also consistent with the government's goal of producing an African administrative corps to manage ethnic institutions in the homelands and, increasingly, to fill token middle-management positions that have little impact.

For many students, however, Bantu education seems to have promoted the notion of an undivided South Africa, rather than fragmentation among its various ethnic groups.[5] Power relations between whites and blacks became the defining variable. For many students, Bantu education instilled collective pride instead of ethnic rivalry and subservience. Socialized throughout their formal educational experience to identify with their own ethnic group, students have reacted by forming a culture of their own, one having an autonomous will, logic, and momentum quite contrary to official intentions.

The official curriculum contains elements that might serve either to reinforce apartheid or motivate resistance to it. Murphy's (1973) study points out how the preuniversity curriculum reinforces the idea that Africans are of inferior status. The geography syllabi, for example, stress the uniqueness of the various homelands within an interdependent economy, and portray the role of the Africans as junior rather than equal partners. The history syllabi, in focusing on the building of a modern republic, emphasize white development and denigrate African values, customs, institutions, and historical events.

Religion classes, or Bible studies, a mandatory subject for Africans in the lower grades, emphasize "love, joy, peace, long suffering, kindness, goodness, faithfulness, gentleness, justness, truth, inner compassion, humbleness and thankfulness, and above all these things . . . charity (love) which is the bond for perfectness" (Murphy, 1973, pp. 195–196). The official South African theology claims that the dominant-subordinate relationship between whites and blacks is divinely ordained. Since the separation of nations and races is God's desire, any attempt to alter the arrangement is to defy God and his will—a powerful idea to instill in youngsters.

Courses in citizenship and good conduct emphasize submissiveness to employers, territorial authorities, central government institutions, and appreciation and respect for the Influx Control System and the value of the Reference Book.[6] Despite the government's policy of separate development, Murphy found no syllabi that promoted attitudes such as independence, self-reliance, or skepticism about the social order.

The specific factors of the Bantu curriculum that motivate resistance are not so easily described. Murphy attributes the development of Bantu education's unintended culture to Western concepts of science and technology built into the curriculum. Interestingly, these concepts were included not to advance the students' analytic capacities, but to demonstrate the superiority of Western civilization. Inclusion of Western values, Murphy notes, fosters logical analysis, democracy, and, by inference, ideas of progressive development and power. Closely related is the notion that, for certain individuals, education, however inferior, promotes an analytic ability that leads to questioning the social order.

Whatever the exact causes of resistance, it does not seem accidental that the Black Consciousness movement gained popularity in the late 1960s, a period that roughly coincides with the emergence of the first Bantu-educated graduates. In one sense, Bantu education had achieved its goal of ethnic pride and had not misled its students into believing that "the green pastures of the European" were meant for their grazing. As Helen Suzman, member of the Progressive Federal party in Parliament, said at a March 1973 House of Assembly debate, "the government had spawned an indestructible black nationalism which was, after all, only a by-product of white nationalism" (South African Institute of Race Relations [SAIRR], 1973, p. 344).

Because of apartheid, very few blacks were members of the National Union of South African Students (NUSAS) in the 1960s. As one African student observed, "It does not help us to see several quiet black faces in the multiracial gathering which ultimately concentrates on what the white students believe are the needs of black students" (SAIRR, 1970, p. 245). Tensions within the organization had been developing and were heightened when African delegates to a 1967 NUSAS conference were housed in separate facilities. To the black delegates this discrimination symbolized the inability of a white liberal organization to bring meaningful change to South Africa. The time had come to form a black students' organization, and in July 1969 the South African Student Organization (SASO) was officially established. The SASO stated:

1. Black Consciousness is an attitude of mind, a way of life.
2. The basic tenet of Black Consciousness is that the Black man must reject all value systems that seek to make him a foreigner in the country of his birth and reduce his basic human dignity.
3. The Black man must build his own value systems, see himself as self-defined and not defined by others.
4. The concept of Black Consciousness implies the awareness by the Black people of the power they wield as a group, both economically and politically and hence group cohesion and solidarity are important facts of Black Consciousness.
5. Black Consciousness will always be enhanced by the totality of involvement of the oppressed people, hence the message of Black Consciousness has to be spread to reach all sections of the Black Community. (Snyman, Note 1, p. 206)

Rather than molding docile workers and complacent citizens of the homelands, Bantu education had produced critical and self-assured individuals concerned not only with their own ethnic group, but also with achieving a collective interest. Initially, the government regarded SASO as a healthy development and gave it the same recognition as its ethnically defined counterparts (NUSAS) for English-speaking students and Studentebond for the Afrikaans-speaking students. The Snyman Commission (Note 1) observed:

> SASO has some positive features. The idea that the Black man should help himself, that students should go out and serve their own people, that the Black man should build his future by his own efforts, is surely not wrong and is *compatible with the approach of the whites.* The Black man has after all *been encouraged to be himself,* to be proud of what is his own and not be a Black White. If he now in fact develops some pride, there is no need for alarm. (p. 136, emphasis added)

Any objectives beyond or contrary to the official policy of separate development, however, were regarded as subversive.

On the other hand, the Commission report also refers to SASO's "hatred for whites." SASO's policy manifesto, by contrast, specifically states that the exclusion of whites "from the struggle towards realizing our aspirations" is not to "be interpreted by Blacks to imply 'anti-Whiteism' but merely a more positive way of attaining a normal situation in South Africa." Separateness was not a belief, but an instrument of expediency. "South Africa," the manifesto states, "is a country in which both Black and White live and shall continue to live together" (Snyman, Note 1, p. 205). Ironically, black students, the recipients of an extremely race-conscious education, were depicted by the Commission as the ones responsible for racial hatred. Hence, the report changes its tone: "What is alarming, however, is the manner in which this organization implements its policy in its activities. The evidence before the Commission indicates that SASO advocates violent revolution and promotes racial hatred in South Africa" (Snyman, Note 1, pp. 137–138). When SASO addressed broader issues, it "exceeded the allowable boundaries" and joined the legions of organizations banned by the South African government.

One of the ongoing issues "legitimized" by the policy of separate development is Africanization—the process by which all institutions are ultimately to be run and controlled by the respective ethnic groups. In fact, it has become a contentious issue at the University of the North, where the Black Academic Staff Association (BASA) has noted: "It is suggested that the control of the University by Blacks follows logically from the policy of the State with regard to the homelands. It has never been suggested that the university constitutes an exception to the field of activities which Blacks are legitimately entitled to control" (Nkondo, 1976, p. 71).

The Jackson Commission, set up to investigate the problems at the University of the North, agreed that the call for Africanization, which had been attributed to SASO, had its basis in government promises. The Snyman Commission, for its part, acknowledged that in a "true interpretation of the policy of separate universities for Blacks, the ultimate goal must be to transfer each university to its own population group to be administered on its own account," but ultimately concludes that Africanization is "virtually an unattainable ideal" (Snyman, Note 1, p. 140).[7] As Wolfson noted in his 1976 report: "No one said how much control would be transferred to blacks but it was obviously intended that white academics would be slowly replaced by blacks, even if the process might never be completed" (p. 84).

The figures on the Africanization process are dismal (see Table 1). In 1969 there were 241 teachers in the three African universities at Fort Hare, Turfloop, and Zululand; of these, 39 (16 percent) were African and 202 (84 percent) were white (SAIRR, 1969). By 1976 the staff had increased to 413, with 96 (23 percent) African and 317 (77 percent) white. While the aggregate figures give a sense of some progress, they are misleading. The African faculty remains at the bottom rung of the academic ladder. BASA, in its response to Commissioner Snyman's questionnaire on events at the University of the North, lists African faculty who were bypassed in favor of whites for appointments and promotions despite their comparable or even superior academic standing (Nkondo, 1976). Table 2 shows the racial imbalance among the staffs of all the South African universities, that white universities have virtually all-white faculties, and those few Africans who teach at these are mainly in the African language departments.[8]

TABLE 1
Staff at African University—1976

University	Professors		Senior Lecturers		Lecturers	
	Africans	*Whites*	*Africans*	*Whites*	*Africans*	*Whites*
Fort Hare	1 (2)[a]	44 (98)	5 (9)	52 (91)	20 (39)	31 (61)
Turfloop	6 (18)	28 (82)	5 (13)	33 (87)	36 (51)	34 (49)
Zululand	2 (8)	24 (92)	4 (8)	47 (92)	17 (41)	24 (59)

Source: SAIRR, 1976, p. 367.
[a]Numbers in parentheses are percentages within each category.

TABLE 2
Numbers of Lecturers at South African Universities—1977, 1978

Universities for	*White*	*Indian*	*Colored*	*African*	*Totals*
1977					
Whites	5,453	64	6	20	5,543
Indians	177	78	n.a.	n.a.	255
Colored	n.a.	n.a.	n.a.	n.a.	n.a.
Africans	301	n.a.	n.a.	133	434
UNISA[a]	668	n.a.	n.a.	10	678
1978					
Whites	6,080	38	9	27	6,154
Indians	193	96	n.a.	n.a.	289
Colored	253	6	53	1	313
Africans	n.a.	n.a.	n.a.	n.a.	n.a.
UNISA	731	n.a.	n.a.	11	742

Source: SAIRR, 1978, p. 450.
n.a. = not available.
[a]The University of South Africa, located in Pretoria, is the only multiracial correspondence institution in South Africa

Africanization at the administrative level lags even further behind. This provoked the Student Representative Council of the University of the North to make these demands in March 1974: "that a capable black man should be appointed as Registrar so that he can learn on the job; immediate appointment of a black Chief Liaison Officer; a black chairman of Council and a black Chancellor and for all the Senate and Council joint committees to have about 50 percent black representation" (Wolfson, 1976, p. 82).

We now turn to our second explanation, that outside influences are partially responsible—perhaps even more decisively than the curriculum—for the contradictory outcomes of Bantu education. It is easy to see that, in a racially organized society such as South Africa, formal classroom instruction can be offset by the observation of discrepancies among lifestyles of specific groups, as well as the knowledge that alternative sociopolitical systems exist elsewhere. Some educational theorists argue that a significant portion of the knowledge held by any student is acquired through nonschool sources, including family, political organizations, observation of existing conditions, and so forth (Illich, 1971; Itzkoff, 1976). This section will first examine internal influences related to school or university conditions and the general sociopolitical situation within South Africa; and, second, external influences that originate outside South Africa but have an impact on the students' consciousness.

In many of the confrontations that have occurred at the University of the North, student and BASA demands centered on the disparity in salaries of black and white staff; unequal per pupil expenditures in white and black universities; and discrimination in black institutions (Nkondo, 1976).[9] While these grievances deal with issues outside the formal curriculum and appear to be university centered, they are in fact related to broader sociopolitical issues. This relationship was recognized by students, staff, and the investigating commissions. The Snyman Commission, in a moment of rare insight, observes that "on closer examination, neither the University authorities, nor the Black or white staff, nor the students, can be held solely responsible for the conditions that led to unrest at the University of the North. The university has in fact become ensnared in a much wider and deeper problem than a mere university situation" (Snyman, Note 1, p. 138). The Jackson Commission report also points out that the turbulence at the university is related to broader political goals beyond the scope of the university (Jackson, Note 2).

The June 16, 1976 student unrest in Soweto was, for example, ostensibly in opposition to Afrikaans as the mandatory language of instruction, but the Cillie Commission found the underlying grievance to be a rejection of the entire apartheid system. Similarly, among the grievances of students of three Colored high schools in Bonteheurel in August 1976 were "the system of apartheid and Colored education" and the "general behavior of police during the unrest in Black areas" (SAIRR, 1976, p. 73).

For the past twenty years, both black and English-speaking universities have been the arena for political debate. In 1972 Mr. Tiro, president of the Student Representative Council, was expelled from the University of the North for criticizing the system of segregated education in South Africa, an event that eroded the idea of the university as a place for the free expression of ideas. Confirming that such beliefs are not permitted at an African university, the Snyman Commission referred to them as the "students' distorted idea of 'academic freedom'" (Snyman, Note 1, p. 136). BASA noted, for example, that "there are significant differences between the autonomy of the University at Turfloop and the autonomy of the White universities, and that in the case of the University of the North, the State retains significantly larger measures of control" (Nkondo, 1976, p. 64). Such episodes bring to the surface the contradictions between official rhetoric and practice.

During the 1970s, the decolonization process was a major external development that influenced African students. The attainment of independence by Mozambique and Angola in 1975, and the national liberation struggle in Namibia, for example, have had a tremendous impact on black South Africans. When the Mozambique Liberation Front (Frelimo) assumed power, SASO called for demonstrations throughout South Africa. As the Jackson Commission noted, the internal contradictions and tensions were only heightened by these external developments:

> If Black students and staff can show that at a university-level of education, apartheid does not work, then, they would argue, the Government, in order to preserve a respectable international image might change or modify the system. *They may have been encouraged by the apparent success of terrorist tactics in political operations elsewhere in Africa*; they may think that in the long term, if their demands are insistent enough, and no compromises are sought or accepted, they will achieve a political victory. (Jackson Commission, Note 2, p. 9, emphasis added)

Another important external influence on the students seems to have been the civil rights movement in the United States and black power in particular, although SASO disclaims any associations with it.[10] Literature from abroad is severely censored, but the government exhibited a qualified tolerance for some black power literature, especially its separatist strand, because it fit into the scheme of homelands and separate development. Black power writings and the visits to South Africa by politically moderate U.S. black leaders had a modicum of influence on the students and played at least a supplementary role in the black movement in South Africa.

In the late sixties, student demonstrations in Japan, France, Germany, the United States, Brazil, Ghana, and elsewhere made headlines by challenging either universities or governments (Lipset, 1966; Seabury, 1966; Todara, 1977; Worms, 1966). Accounts of these events spread throughout the world and influenced others; South African students were no exception.

Toward the end of the 1970s, African high school and university students demanded the abolition of Bantu education and the implementation of equal education. Having described Bantu education as being "irrelevant to the pressing needs of the Black community," SASO set up an "education commission to study the ways of making education of Blacks relevant to the community" (Wolfson, 1976, p. 61). As a result, community education, literacy, and health projects were launched (SAIRR, 1972, p. 386). Members of SASO also opposed attempts to create a black middle class that would act as a buffer between the white power structure and the vast majority of black people

(SAIRR, 1976; Snyman, Note 1).[11] They viewed with suspicion the short-lived Polaroid experiment and the Urban Foundation's efforts to provide bursaries.[12] The Snyman Commission had actually called for differential treatment of educated blacks by recommending a "reappraisal of the conduct of Whites in general towards Blacks and more especially sophisticated Blacks. . . . With a little more courtesy and consideration in everyday contact with Blacks, the White public could do more than the university itself" (Snyman, Note 1, p. 147).

The interaction of these internal and external factors seems to have exerted a strong influence on the students. In the absence of a democratic process, the resulting confrontations and conflicts have brought about a gradual reformulation of Bantu education policy, although the needed fundamental change does not appear to be under way.[13] The Bantu Universities Amendment Act No. 57 of 1977 is essentially a cosmetic disguise of the old arrangement. Advisory Councils, composed mainly of Africans and virtually powerless, were abolished, except at the University of Fort Hare. Predominantly white University Councils, the real source of decision-making power, were retained, though with some minor variations in racial representation.

The behavior of the first African rector and vice chancellor of the University of the North, W. N. Kgware, seems to confirm Adam's observation that the intent of self-administration is not "total autonomy in decision-making for blacks in their own institutions but that self-administration can be an instrument for domination as well as legitimation" (K. Adam, 1971, pp. 206–207). The University of the North, where Kgware was rector, expelled Moako Ramatlhodi, a third-year law student for allegedly contravening the conditions of his admission to the university by participating in the organizational meeting of a March 21 Sharpeville commemoration. Ramatlhodi filed suit, and the Pretoria Supreme Court ruled in favor of his reinstatement. Ironically, the state legal machinery was legitimized while the highly placed black administrator, appearing insensitive to such a politically delicate matter as Sharpeville, became the culprit (SAIRR, 1979). Similar instances are common in African institutions where African administrators have been appointed.

The Jackson Commission's recommendations envisioned a gradual admission of white students to African universities at the graduate level and suggested that institutions with specialized academic areas admit students from all racial groups (Jackson, Note 2). The evidence indicates that a growing number of students do attend universities designated for other groups (SAIRR, 1978; SAIRR, 1979). Although these changes appear to reverse previous policy and practice, government officials view them not as a substantive change but as part of the effort to eliminate petty apartheid and achieve the ultimate goal of utopian apartheid.[14] The *Johannesburg Star,* on March 31, 1978, thought this to be a good development that would bring "a realization that contact does not mean integration or the loss of group identity." The practice is another example of the effort to modernize racial domination—an effort that stems from tensions and conflicts brought about by the Africans and not from change in Afrikaner social philosophy.

An Education and Training Bill was introduced and passed by the House in 1978. This bill was intended to replace the Bantu Education Act of 1953 and the Bantu Special Education Act of 1964, and would be based on the following principles:

1. That education in government-controlled schools shall have a Christian character but that religious persuasion will be respected in regard to religious instruction and ceremony.
2. That the universally approved principle of the use of the mother tongue as medium of instruction be observed. That wishes of the parents should be taken into account in application of principle after standard 4 and also in the choice of one of the official languages as medium of instruction.
3. To introduce compulsory education in all areas with the cooperation of parents.
4. Provision of education will take into account ability, aptitude and interest of the pupil as well as needs of country and appropriate guidance to be furnished.
5. Coordination with other departments regarding syllabuses, courses and examination standards.
6. Active involvement of parents and the communities in the educational system through parent teacher associations.
7. School health services be introduced in conjunction with Department of Health. (SAIRR, 1978, p. 403)

Reactions to the proposed bill were mixed. The African Teachers' Association of South Africa (ATASA) welcomed the Department's assumption of responsibility for preschool education and health services, and the removal of the power of school boards to appoint and dismiss teachers. But ATASA registered strong reservations about the bill, focusing on its "failure to bring the education for Africans under the Department of National Education" (confirming the government's commitment to separate development) and emphasizing "free and compulsory education whereas the draft bill merely stated that it was to be compulsory" (SAIRR, 1979, pp. 490–491).

The architects of apartheid, and of Bantu education in particular, developed their system employing the assumptions of a "functionalist" paradigm. According to this model, education merely responds to the demands of the society's technological-occupational structure. Education's specific function, therefore, is to provide the labor required by the occupational structure. That education can become its own force for change is not recognized by this model. Thus, questions of conflicting values, social class hierarchies, cultural systems, and the nature and effects of oppressive systems are not seriously considered—a fundamental flaw of functionalist models and studies, which seriously erodes their predictive value.

Bantu education was intended to produce subservient individuals with the skills needed to minister to the needs of the white economy rather than to develop critical thinkers. Its aim was, and is, to maintain—if not actually to create—a state of intellectual underdevelopment and dependency.

It has produced, instead, at least for a good portion of the student body, a distinct culture whose thrust and direction are contrary to the expectations of the system. Actually, the extension of higher education to Africans, given the nature of the South African polity, is itself, as Adam observed, "contradictory" (K. Adam, 1971, p. 197). Education appears to have become one of the principal disintegrative agents of the South African system. External factors that are not part of the official curriculum seem to have added powerful ingredients in producing the unintended consequences.

For the past eight years the South African government has embarked on an accelerated program of adjustment in response to the pressures by students and the larger black community. These concessions, however, are largely consistent with the program of separate development and have the effect of promoting the legitimacy of the regime. Whether the state will be able to maintain control of the culture that has been set into motion remains to be seen. A preliminary assessment seems to indicate that unless higher education for blacks is abolished, an action that is impossible to conceive of at this juncture, then greater contradictions, with their attendant structural dysfunctions, will emerge.

Notes

1. In South Africa, the term "Bantu," considered offensive by Africans, has been used to characterize the people who speak Bantu languages. In this paper, however, the term is strictly intended to reflect the usage of a writer being quoted or official references to Bantu education. Otherwise, the term "African" is used to refer to African people. In 1978, in response to Africans' intense resentment for the designation "Bantu," the government changed the Bantu Education Department to the Department of Education and Training.
2. The "homelands," commonly called Bantustans, are government-designated areas for African settlement. They represent approximately 13 percent of the land area to which more than 70 percent of the South African population is assigned on the basis of ethnic affiliation. It is in these overcrowded, economically depressed, and fragmented areas that Africans are to exercise their political rights. Of the nine homelands, three—the Transkei, Bophuthatswana, and Venda—have been granted "independence." Less than half the African population, 46.6 percent according to the 1970 census, lives in the homelands. The majority of Africans who live outside the homelands are opposed to the homelands (Rogers, 1976), which is the backbone of apartheid or separate development policies. The latter is a more "elegant" reformulation of apartheid, and purports to encourage equal and parallel social, economic, and political development with white South Africa based on the unique cultural heritage of the races.
3. African university closings, student suspensions, and expulsions have been increasing over the last decade. Major student protest took place at the University of the North in 1972, 1974, 1976, and 1980. Other universities were similarly beleagured in the past few years. The 1976 Soweto uprisings symbolized a generalized protest against Bantu

Education. In 1980 seventy-seven schools were closed by government decree because of protracted boycotts by students.

4. In black consciousness political parlance, the designation "black" refers to Africans, Coloreds, and Indians. This interpretation will be retained throughout as its usage has become widespread, especially among the youth of the three groups.
5. Murphy (1973) noted references to "our country" (meaning both black and white) in the official Bantu education syllabi, but which were contradicted by specific content in the curriculum that reinforces separation. Clearly, then, the students' demand for a unitary South Africa as stated in the South African Student Organization's constitution is partially based on the official curriculum.
6. The Influx Control System is composed of regulations and legislation designed to restrict the number of Africans entering, residing, or working in so-called white areas. Labor agencies, the police, magistrates' courts, and the Bantu Affairs Department are involved in its enforcement. The Reference Book, commonly known as the pass, insures the operation of the Influx Control System. All African adults sixteen years of age and above must carry the Reference Book at all times and produce it on demand.
7. This lends credence to the charge that independence or control of institutions in the homelands is not viewed by the Nationalist government in absolute terms, but only in relative terms. Ultimate control remains with the central government. A statement attributed to M. C. Botha, the minister responsible for the Bantustans (homelands), makes this very clear: "In the economic framework of the country, the economy of the homelands is interwoven with that of the Republic of South Africa and it stands to reason that the development of the homelands cannot be carried out at a pace which would have a detrimental effect on the economy of the country" (Sibeko, p. 15).
8. As of 1978 the exceptions were H. M. Njokweni, who was employed in the Industrial Sociology Department of the University of Cape Town, and Professor E. Mphahlele, who recently became the Director of the African Studies Institute at the University of Witwatersrand.
9. According to BASA calculations, the average per pupil expenditure in 1973 at the University of the North was approximately R180, or $205 based on the 1975 exchange rate of R1 = $1.14, (exclusive of capital expenditure). This figure constitutes, on the average, approximately 26 percent of the per pupil expenditures at the following universities: Pretoria, Witwatersrand, Cape Town, Stellenbosch, Potchefstroom, Orange Free State, and Rhodes. For an elaborated breakdown, see Nkondo (1976, pp. 47–48).
10. It is theoretically possible that common sociopolitical philosophies can emerge in separate geographical areas if similar conditions exist in both. Black power in the United States and South Africa may thus have had independent origins as an expression of negative reaction and alienation of peoples to conditions that have historically denied them their humanity and self-determination. This reaction tends to manifest itself in forms of cultural renaissance in an attempt to recapture a sense of identity that has not been allowed to flourish.
11. For a succinct, but perceptive, discussion of this question, see H. Adam (1979, p. 291).
12. In 1971 the Polaroid Corporation established the American-South African Study and Educational Trust administered by the South African Institute of Race Relations, which provided bursaries to African students. The Urban Foundation was founded in 1976 by leaders of industry and commerce whose proclaimed task was to assist in improving in South Africa the social problems of the underprivileged.
13. A closer examination of the concessions or the general reformulation of Bantu education shows it to be simply an effort at modernizing racial domination. While this strategy enhances the legitimizing mechanisms of separate development, the decision-making hierarchy remains intact.

14. The various forms of apartheid are defined by H. Adam (1971, p. 68):

    Micro-apartheid as the special relationships of contact or distance, that have evolved historically, between the race groups that were legalized by laws of petty apartheid.

    Meso-apartheid aims at the geographical separation of residential zones in the urban areas.

    Macro (or ideal) apartheid is directed toward the future coexistence of ethnically homogeneous nations. A recently coined phrase is the so-called "interdependent constellation of states."

    Utopian-apartheid is an attempt to overcome the expressive features of traditional apartheid. This endeavor aims at rendering petty apartheid obsolete.

Reference Notes

1. Snyman, J. H. *Report of the commission of inquiry into certain matters relating to the University of the North.* Sovenga, South Africa, 1975.
2. Jackson, S. *Report to the council on Africanization of the university.* Sovenga, South Africa, 1975.

References

Adam, H. *Modernizing racial domination: The dynamics of South African politics.* Berkeley: University of California Press, 1971.

Adam, H. Political alternatives. In H. Adam & H. Gilliomee (Eds.), *Ethnic power mobilized: Can South Africa change?* New Haven: Yale University Press, 1979.

Adam, K. Dialectic of higher education for the colonized: The case of non-white universities in South Africa. In H. Adam (Ed.), *South Africa: Sociological perspectives.* London: Oxford University Press, 1971.

Altbach, P. G., & Lipset, S. M. Student politics and higher education in the U.S. *Comparative Education Review,* 1966, *10,* 320–349.

Bunting, B. *The rise of the South African reich.* Baltimore: Penguin Books, 1969.

Kuper, L. African nationalism in South Africa, 1910–1964. In M. Wilson & L. Thompson (Eds.), *The Oxford history of South Africa* (Vol. 2). London: Oxford University Press, 1971.

Leroy-Beaulieu, A. *The institutions.* Part II. *The empire of the csars and the Russians.* New York: G. P. Putnam's Sons, 1894.

Levitan, S. A., Mangum, G. L., & Marshall, R. *Human resources and labor markets.* New York: Harper & Row, 1972.

Mafeje, A. Soweto and its aftermath. *Review of African Political Economy,* 1978, January–April 1978 (No. 11), 17–30.

Magubane, B. M. *The Political economy of race and class in South Africa.* New York: Monthly Review Press, 1979.

Malherbe, E. G. *Education in South Africa: 1923–1975* (Vol. 2). Johannesburg: Juta, 1977.

Murphy, E. J. *Bantu education: Its compatibility with the objectives of African self-development or white domination.* Unpublished doctoral dissertation, University of Connecticut, Storrs, 1973.

Nkondo, G. M. (Ed.). *The dilemma of a black university in South Africa.* Johannesburg: Ravan Press, 1976.

Piore, M. J. Notes for a theory of labor market stratification (Working Paper 95). Cambridge, Mass.: Massachusetts Institute of Technology, 1972.

Rogers, B. *Divide and rule: South Africa's Bantustans.* London: International Defense and Aid Fund, 1976.

Rhoodie, N. J., & Venter, H. J. *Apartheid.* Pretoria: HAUM, 1960.

Seabury, P. Student freedom and the republic of scholars: Berlin and Berkeley. *Comparative Education Review,* 1966, *10,* 350–358.

Sibeko, D. The sham of independence. *African Report,* 1976, *23*(3), 14–17; 56.

South African Institute of Race Relations. *Annual surveys of race relations in South Africa.* Johannesburg: Author, 1960–1980.

Tabata, I. B. *Education for barbarism.* London: Pall Mall Press, 1960.

Tiro, O. R. Bantu education. In G. M. Nkondo (Ed.), *The dilemma of a black university in South Africa.* Johannesburg: Ravan Press, 1976.

Todaro, M. P. *Economic development in the Third World.* New York: Longman, 1977.

Troup, F. *Forbidden pastures: Education under apartheid.* London: International Defense and Aid Fund, 1976.

Villa-Vicencio, C. The theology of apartheid. *Christianity and crisis,* 1978, *38*(3), 45–59.

Walshe, P. *The rise of African nationalism in South Africa.* Los Angeles: University of California Press, 1971.

Welsh, D. The growth of towns. In M. Wilson & L. Thompson (Eds.), *The Oxford history of South Africa* (Vol. 2). London: Oxford University Press, 1971.

Wolfson, J. G. E. (Ed.). *Turmoil at Turfloop.* Johannesburg: South African Institute of Race Relations, 1976.

Worms, J. P. The French student movement. *Comparative Education Review,* 1966, *10,* 359–366.

Identifying Alternatives to Political Violence: An Educational Imperative

CHRISTOPHER KRUEGLER
PATRICIA PARKMAN

Few would disagree that organized political violence has had disastrous consequences for human life and civilization in this century. War, dictatorship, terrorism, genocide, and systems of social oppression have conspired to take millions of lives, divert precious economic resources from other human enterprises, and place the continued existence of humanity in question.[1]

Yet, while we conclude rationally that we may not survive our collective dependence on violence, both nation-states and insurgent movements cling to its use. In the absence of the international rule of law or a just world order, organized violence appears to be the ultimate recourse against intolerable conditions and grave threats to our lives, interests, and values. It persists, on the one hand, because of a widespread but largely unexamined belief that it "works" and, on the other, because there are no generally recognized alternative means of resolving those critical conflicts in which one or both parties perceive the stakes as too high to permit compromise.[2]

In this article, we argue that the efficacy of organized violence is overrated and, more important, that nonviolent sanctions offer a greatly underrated and underdeveloped source of political power which could replace armed force and free humanity from its heavy costs and incalculable dangers. We see a major role for educators in breaking down the cultural conditioning that perpetuates reliance on violence and in making nonviolent sanctions more effective, and therefore, more relevant to the critical conflicts of our time.

To say that the efficacy of organized violence is overrated is not to say that it *never* works, but merely that its recent history is not one of unqualified success. On a tactical level, superior armed force can control many, if not all, situations. Any act of resistance that is limited in time and place can be negated by sufficiently ruthless opponents. On the strategic and political levels, however, the probable effects of violence become less easy to calculate. Most armed struggles involve at least one clear loser. Moreover, victory is often

Harvard Educational Review Vol. 55 No. 1 February 1985, 109–117

achieved at terribly high or unanticipated costs. Finally, stalemate must be considered as a possible outcome. These less desirable outcomes for one or both protagonists waging violent struggle have been frequent enough to warrant a serious investigation of nonviolent alternatives.

Political scientist John Stoessinger has observed that "no nation that *began* a major war in this century emerged a winner."[3] Aside from possible disagreement over which wars should be classified as "major," it is correct that those powers which have struck first in the larger wars of this century have met military defeat, despite the range of possible outcomes described above. Stoessinger analyzes the moments of decision when statesmen chose either war or escalation and finds that these moments were almost always characterized by mutual misperception of each other's intentions and capabilities and the potential risks of armed conflict. Thus, he suggests, war functions as a sort of reality therapy in which expectations are most often adjusted in a context of defeat or stalemate.[4]

The complete failure of military power to secure policy objectives is perhaps best typified by the U.S. experience in Vietnam, and the same fate may well await the Soviet Union in Afghanistan. These are examples of asymmetrical conflicts: the vast preponderance of power, conventionally understood, appears to be on one side. In such conflicts, the ostensibly weaker parties are sometimes able to control the political aspects of the conflict and turn even military defeats to their own advantage. Thus the Tet offensive of 1968, technically a military victory for the United States, became a watershed for American antiwar sentiment simply because the opponent was still able to mount a major offensive at that point in the struggle. The My Lai massacre stands as another tactical "victory," whose counterproductive political effects far outweighed its military value.

If the Vietnam War demonstrates the limits of military methods for a superpower like the United States, does it not conversely support a case for successful use of unconventional warfare by Vietnam? Here, the question of costs becomes relevant. Although Vietnam can claim that it won, as many as two million of its people died. Its countryside is poisoned with chemical toxins and defaced by some twenty million bomb craters.[5] Independence of a sort was achieved, but for the foreseeable future Vietnam will probably be a military, economic, and political dependent of the Soviet Union. Vietnam's authoritarian regime, a product of thirty years of warfare, has alienated many of its citizens. Continuing regional conflict is another legacy of this war.

Hidden costs may also accrue to the winners of less significant conflicts. Both the British victory in the Falklands/Malvinas crisis and the recent invasion of Grenada by the United States were hailed by their architects as unequivocal triumphs. The former victory, however, obliged the Thatcher government to commit itself to an indefinite and expensive military presence in another hemisphere, while the latter reaped for the United States the dubious political prestige that results from defeating such a small opponent.

Stalemate is an outcome that appears to be occurring with increasing frequency. The Korean War is probably the clearest example of a large-scale, painful struggle that ended in the frustration of both sides' objectives. The interminable wars of the Middle East, in which the local participants draw encouragement and support from their big-power sponsors, have also been inconclusive. Fifteen years of paramilitary struggle in Northern Ireland have not significantly changed the balance of power in favor of the separatist forces in that country, while military occupation, special police powers, and other repressive measures on the part of the British government have failed either to restore the status quo ante or to remove the threat of terror.

Despite this record, news media, history books, and popular culture consistently focus on the results achieved by violence. Moreover, they give more attention to violent struggles that fail to achieve their objectives than to nonviolent struggles that succeed. Hence, few people are aware of the alternative ways to wage serious conflict that have been widely used for centuries.

The Hidden History of Nonviolent Sanctions

Nonviolent sanctions are those punishments and pressures which do not kill or threaten physical harm but which, nonetheless, thwart opponents' objectives and cause them to alter their behavior.[6] The power of nonviolent sanctions is essentially that of denying opponents the support or cooperation which they need to attain their objectives. Many people associate nonviolent action exclusively with the work of Mohandas Gandhi and Martin Luther King, Jr. While the contributions of these men and their followers are extremely important, they do not encompass or exhaust the potential of this form of power. Its use does not require a commitment to nonviolence as an ethical principle, although its most effective deployment does require an understanding of the special dynamics of nonviolent struggle.

There is, in fact, a vast hidden history of nonviolent sanctions.[7] Much of this history has simply been overlooked because of the selective perception noted above. Nonviolent sanctions have also gone unrecognized because they were not consciously chosen and identified as such. In many cases they have been used side by side with violent sanctions. Lacking a conceptual framework from which to do so, historians have often failed to ask questions or collect data that would enable us to assess the significance of the nonviolent facets of a conflict.

Of the hundreds of conflicts in which nonviolent action has played a significant role, only a few have been sufficiently researched to assess the strategic effect of nonviolent sanctions. The three cases that follow are among those which have received such study. They challenge common stereotypes about the conditions under which nonviolent sanctions can be effective. In none of the three were the nonviolent protagonists committed to nonviolence as an ethical principle, nor were their opponents liberal democratic governments.

On the contrary, the opponent in each case was a dictatorship with a record of ruthlessness, and in two cases the opponent responded to the nonviolent action with violent repression.

Maximiliano Hernández Martínez was El Salvador's most notorious dictator, best known for the massacre of 1932 which followed a brief, easily suppressed peasant uprising. Estimates of the number of people executed in cold blood range from eight thousand to thirty thousand in a country that, at the time, had a total population of about one million. The Martínez regime then suppressed the fledgling labor movement and all political parties except its own.

Twelve years of one-man rule gradually alienated many people who initially supported Martínez, including the majority of the big landowners, businessmen, professionals, and junior military officers. On April 2, 1944, the small Salvadoran air force and two army regiments took up arms against the government. The revolt quickly became a tragicomedy of overconfidence, bungling, and division among the insurgent leaders. Troops loyal to the president crushed the revolt within forty-eight hours.

Two weeks later, with the surviving opposition leaders imprisoned, in exile, or in hiding, university students, women, and collaborators in various occupational groups began to organize a completely nonviolent general strike that escalated rapidly from May 5–8. At the height of the action, buses and taxis disappeared from the streets of the capital city. Market stalls, shops, banks, and professional offices were closed. Government employees abandoned their work. The nation's railroads stopped running, and the strike began to spread to other cities.

Taken by surprise, divided, and demoralized, the government took no effective action to counter the strike. When a frightened or trigger-happy policeman shot and killed a boy on May 7, angry, though peaceful, crowds filled the streets. Martínez' cabinet panicked and resigned. After hours of negotiations on May 8, Martínez announced his decision to give up the presidency. The next morning the National Assembly received the president's resignation and named his successor.[8]

How has the memory of these events been preserved in El Salvador? April 2—not May 9—was declared a national holiday. As late as 1976, ceremonies still commemorated a botched military coup. Salvadoran periodical literature abounds with memoirs by participants of the April 2 uprising and gives detailed reconstructions of the fighting, while the civilian movement which actually dislodged Martínez is rarely mentioned. The only book on the revolution of 1944 devotes thirty-five pages to the events of April 2–4, another twenty-two to the trials and executions of a number of the participants, and eight to a woefully inaccurate and incomplete account of the general strike.[9]

The first Russian Revolution of 1905 is not commonly understood as nonviolent. Indeed, it was accompanied by a great deal of politically motivated violence, mostly in the form of assassinations and peasant riots. On October 17, 1905, however, it was not violence that forced Tsar Nicholas II of Russia to take an unprecedented and, for him, repugnant step.[10] When Nicholas created Russia's first representative assembly, or Duma, he did so in response to a massive general strike, which has been described as one of the most complete in history, and a campaign of public defiance of civil laws that mobilized nearly the entire urban population of Russia.[11]

In addition to strikes, the nonviolent methods employed in this movement included the holding of political banquets during which petitions were drafted; mass demonstrations, processions, and demonstration funerals; the withholding of taxes; the usurpation of governmental prerogatives by illegal bodies; defiance of censorship laws; refusal of conscription; and the refusal of troops to carry out orders. Most of these methods were used in an improvised fashion. In the course of the struggle, new organizations such as unions, soviets, or workers' councils, and illegal political parties with a variety of orientations were formed. These gained invaluable experience during the revolution, and many of them persisted after it had run its course. Labor unions, for example, won the right to exist legally as a result of the struggle and continued to function openly for several years.

The Duma, which Nicholas called for in his manifesto of October 17, represented the first legal limitation on the autocratic power of the tsar. Its creation did not by any means constitute a complete victory over the tsarist system, but it was certainly a major step toward the disintegration of that system.[12]

The Danish response to occupation by Nazi Germany from 1940 to 1945 employed various forms of social, political, and economic noncooperation to preserve the integrity of Danish life and institutions in the face of a concerted attempt to integrate them into Hitler's New Order. Open resistance was not initially condoned by the Danish government, which remained nominally in power until August 28, 1943. Instead, the civil service and government officials who retained their positions worked to mitigate the effects of the occupation on the Danish people.

In this period, resistance mainly took the form of *schweikism,* or obstructionism disguised as apparent cooperation.[13] Government officials, for example, concealed increases in food production from the German authorities, leaked information about repressive actions to the intended victims, and generally slowed down orders which might have hampered other resistance activities.[14] German concerts were boycotted in favor of community songfests featuring traditional Danish music. German soldiers and their collaborators were ostracized. Danish national symbols and pro-Allied symbols became widely used as a means of expressing opposition at comparatively little risk.[15] Subtle forms of noncooperation prevented Nazi penetration of Danish governmental institutions for three years, during which time a psychological climate conducive to open resistance, by both violent and nonviolent means, was developed.

In August of 1943, an industrial strike movement, accompanied by widespread sabotage, provoked a crisis. Government officials resigned rather than implement the severe repressive measures demanded by German authorities.

The Danish government dissolved, leaving no legitimate authority in its place and removing the legal barrier to open resistance. Among the most notable achievements of the nonviolent branch of the resistance was the rescue of approximately seven thousand Danish Jews from Nazi persecution by means of clandestine evacuation routes to Sweden, thus frustrating the implementation of Hitler's "final solution."[16] Later, early in the summer of 1944, the German occupation authorities gave in to demands to revoke a series of repressive measures when they found that they could not control a general people's strike in Copenhagen, although they had killed over one hundred Danes in the attempt to do so.[17]

It is important to note the catalytic role played by violent sabotage in eliciting the repression which stimulated the governmental crisis of August 1943. This illustrates the sometimes complex relationship between violent and nonviolent sanctions when they are used in the same conflict by the same protagonists.[18] The degree to which the two types of sanctions are, or are not, compatible under specific circumstances is a matter which has yet to receive serious and systematic study.[19]

In these three cases, nonviolent sanctions achieved a great deal. These examples do not, however, lead to the conclusion that nonviolent sanctions offer a ready-made panacea to those looking for a means of waging conflict. Indeed, examination of the outcomes brings to light the limitations of these and many similar movements.

While the Danish resistance made Germany's military and economic exploitation of Denmark less efficient than it would otherwise have been, neither the nonviolent sanctions nor the combination of violent and nonviolent sanctions stopped that exploitation. The opposition to Martínez failed in its attempt to establish democratic government in El Salvador, which soon succumbed to a new military dictatorship. Similarly, analysts of the 1905 general strike in Russia have pointed out that the coalition of forces which frightened the tsar into issuing the manifesto of October 17 did not act effectively to consolidate its new position. Instead, it became embroiled in its own internal struggles for power and ideological leadership. It was unable to respond with a unified program when the autocracy began to renege on promised reforms, to limit the powers of the Duma, and to invoke harsh repressive measures in the months that followed.[20]

When violent sanctions fall short of achieving their objectives we do not usually conclude that violence has been tried and found wanting. We ask what conditions favored the winner and what did the loser do wrong. Nonviolent struggle should be judged by the same standards. Given the nature of the forces involved in the examples above, there is no reason to think that the nonviolent protagonists would have achieved more with violent sanctions. We can, on the other hand, see their weaknesses. In each case nonviolent sanctions were improvised under harsh conditions with little or no advance preparation on the part of those using them. The Salvadoran opponents of Martínez had no strategy for pursuing longer-range goals beyond his resignation, and the opposition to the tsar suffered from lack of agreed-upon leadership and mechanisms for decision making.

Analysis of these and other cases of nonviolent struggle ought to suggest ways in which nonviolent sanctions could be made more effective, just as military strategists learn from the study of past victories and defeats. Over the past three decades a small group of researchers has begun a systematic study of nonviolent sanctions which should lead to a much better understanding of both their limits and their potential.[21]

Potential of Nonviolent Sanctions

Nonviolent sanctions are already used with great regularity and proficiency in certain types of conflicts. Both sides in most labor disputes, for example, are skilled in the use of a variety of coercive yet nonviolent methods for attaining their ends. Domestic protest movements and civil rights movements in many countries rely heavily on nonviolent sanctions to advance their causes. The question before us now is whether, on the basis of historical experience and creative new thinking, it is possible to extend deliberately the range of issues and problems for which they are relevant and to which they can be applied with confidence.

It has been suggested that nonviolent sanctions might provide the basis of an alternative means of national defense.[22] This possibility was recently explored in a three-year study conducted by Britain's Alternative Defence Commission. The Commission's report, *Defence Without the Bomb,* argues that British national security would be enhanced by a reduced role in NATO, unilateral nuclear disarmament, and the adoption of a two-tiered defense system, combining elements of both conventional military defense and prepared nonviolent resistance by civilians. The sixteen-member commission felt that conventional coastal and anti-aircraft defenses could extract a high entry price from a hypothetical invader, and that this might have some dissuasive power. Should an invasion be accomplished, however, the best defense might be achieved by withholding any form of cooperation from the opponent and waging a protracted resistance against the invaders by exclusively nonviolent means.[23]

For many small countries, any degree of armed resistance against their prospective opponents might be futile, if not suicidal. For these countries, a purely "civilian-based defense" may well offer the best alternative to surrender, on the one hand, and devastating armed conflict against much larger powers, on the other.[24] Such a defense policy would entail, in times of national crisis, the transformation of all of society's ordinary institutions and organizations into resistance organizations, thus denying the opponents effective political control and ultimately forcing them to withdraw. Naturally, the adoption of a civilian-based defense policy would imply considerable knowledge of, and confidence in, the nonviolent sanctions that would be its principal weapons.

Nonviolent sanctions are also being looked at with renewed interest by people who find themselves faced with various forms of social, political, and economic oppression. The assertion that armed struggle is the only effective method of changing or removing oppressive regimes is open to question. As the cases described above demonstrate, even the most repressive governments are dependent to some degree on the cooperation and acquiescence of the people they rule. When this cooperation is withdrawn in a systematic way, the power base of the oppressive authorities may erode very quickly. A struggle of this type inevitably involves violent repression against those wielding the nonviolent sanctions. Thus, participants must organize themselves at the outset to endure hardships and to continue the resistance despite repression, as they would have to do in a violent struggle. Nonviolent struggles are currently being waged in a number of repressive states, including Poland, Chile, and the Philippines. Nonviolent sanctions might also play a meaningful role in many other societies if their dynamics were better understood.

An Agenda for Educators

Developing the potential of nonviolent sanctions requires much more empirical research on their successes and failures, as well as theoretical work on questions of strategy and tactics. This is a task for institutions of higher learning. At the present time, Harvard University's Program on Nonviolent Sanctions in Conflict and Defense is the only program in the world, of which the authors are aware, that is specifically dedicated to research in this field, and it has only two full-time researchers. A handful of students have produced useful case studies as theses and dissertations, but many more are needed.

One reason for the paucity of research is lack of attention to nonviolent sanctions in the instructional programs of colleges and universities. While the World Policy Institute's curriculum guide, *Peace and World Order Studies,* does not necessarily give a complete picture of what is offered, it is probably representative. Of the thirty-one undergraduate peace studies programs surveyed, only eight appear to offer one or more courses on nonviolent action.[25]

The need is not simply to increase course offerings, however. As educators at all levels have become sensitive to the presence of race and gender stereotypes in what is taught—often implicitly rather than explicitly—we should ask how the existing curriculum perpetuates the assumption that violence "works" and how it treats the role of nonviolent sanctions in human life. A critical examination of curriculum guides, textbooks, and audiovisual materials from this point of view would show us where the deficiencies are and what is needed in the way of new materials. To our knowledge no such study has been proposed or undertaken. This is new subject matter for most teachers, which again argues for course offerings on nonviolent sanctions in colleges and universities, as well as in in-service training programs.

Education is not only what goes on in schools. A total of perhaps two-dozen informal study groups have used either a draft study guide on civilian-based defense or *U.S. Defense Policy: Mainstream Views and Nonviolent Alternatives,* which gives substantial attention to civilian-based defense.[26] The fall 1984 catalogue of the Pittsburgh Peace Institute offers an imaginative workshop on "The Nonviolent Defense of Pittsburgh." Interest in such adult education offerings is clearly growing and presents a challenge for the development of more and better materials.

To meet this interest, library holdings on nonviolent sanctions must be expanded. There is an urgent need for the translation of the best literature into languages other than the original, and for publication of new literature as it is developed.

The entertainment industry also has a role to play. Nonviolent struggle is drama. Its history abounds in stories of courage, suspense, and victory against formidable odds. Yet for every *Gandhi,* how many fantasies like *Red Dawn* unrealistically glorify violence? Why should films and television not bring us the excitement of, say, the rescue of the Danish Jews from Nazi persecution? And why should fiction not explore the as yet untried possibilities of the eminently human power of nonviolence?

We began by citing the threat to human survival posed by the technology of organized violence. That threat poses a challenge to educators, and central to the challenge is the need to help people envision credible alternatives to armed conflict. The development of nonviolent sanctions points the way to one such alternative.

Notes

1. This assessment of the problem, and much of the analysis which follows, draws heavily on Gene Sharp's *Social Power and Political Freedom* (Boston: Porter Sargent, 1980), ch. 9 and 11 in particular.
2. This point was first made by Walter Lippmann in "The Political Equivalent of War," *Atlantic Monthly,* Aug. 1928, p. 181.
3. Stoessinger, *Why Nations Go to War* (New York: St. Martin's Press, 1978), p. 123. Emphasis added.
4. Stoessinger, *Why Nations Go to War,* pp. 227–231.
5. Stoessinger, *Why Nations Go to War,* p. 136.
6. Sharp, *Social Power and Political Freedom,* p. 289.
7. For a list of eighty-five major cases, see Sharp, *Exploring Nonviolent Alternatives* (Boston: Porter Sargent, 1971), pp. 115–123.
8. For a detailed reconstruction and analysis of this case, see Patricia Parkman, "Insurrection Without Arms: The General Strike in El Salvador, 1944" Diss. Temple University, 1980.
9. Francisco Morán, *Las jornados cívicas de abril y mayo de 1944.* (San Salvador: Editorial Universitaria, Universidad de El Salvador, 1979), pp. 61–96, 105–127, 127–136.

10. By the Julian calendar, used in Russia until 1918, thirteen days behind the Gregorian calendar used in the West.
11. Alan Moorhead, *The Russian Revolution* (New York: Harper, 1958), p. 58.
12. Only Peter Ackerman's "Strategic Aspects of Nonviolent Resistance Movements," Diss. Tufts University, 1976, and Sharp's, *The Politics of Nonviolent Action* (Boston: Porter Sargent, 1973), pp. 78–79, treat the specifically nonviolent character of this revolution.
13. This technique takes its name from the bungling soldier in Jaroslav Hasek's *The Good Soldier Schweik* (Harmondsworth: Penguin, 1951). This is a reprint of the posthumously published work, which Hasek had not completely finished at the time of his death in 1923.
14. Paul Wehr, "Aggressive Nonviolence," in *Response to Aggression,* ed. Arnold P. Goldstein, Edward G. Carr, William S. Davidson II, and Paul Wehr (New York: Pergamon Press, 1981), p. 485.
15. Jeremy Bennett, "The Resistance Against the German Occupation of Denmark 1940–1945," in *Civilian Resistance as a National Defence,* ed. Adam Roberts (Baltimore: Penguin Books, 1969), pp. 187–189.
16. Wehr, "Aggressive Nonviolence," p. 488. It is estimated that only 450 of Denmark's 8,000 Jews were actually apprehended.
17. Wehr, "Aggressive Nonviolence," pp. 489–490.
18. There is a lively discussion in the literature as to whether sabotage is by definition violent, and whether it is ever compatible with nonviolent struggle. See esp. Sharp, *The Politics of Nonviolent Action,* pp. 608–611; and Bennett, "The Resistance Against the German Occupation of Denmark 1940–1945," pp. 190–197. In this context, we refer primarily to bombings at industrial and military sites.
19. In addition to the sources cited above, further material on nonviolent resistance in Denmark can be found in Jorgen Haestrup's *European Resistance Movements, 1934–45: A Complete History* (Westport: Meckler, 1981).
20. Ackerman, "Strategic Aspects of Nonviolent Resistance Movements," pp. 371–376.
21. See esp. the work of Sharp, Adam Roberts, Theodor Ebert, Johan Galtung, Anders Boserup, and Andrew Mack on this subject. Boserup and Mack's *War without Weapons* (New York: Schocken, 1975) provides a useful bibliography of the major works.
22. The National Conference of Catholic Bishops, to cite one example, called for the development of nonviolent means of national defense in its 1983 pastoral letter, *The Challenge of Peace: God's Promise and Our Response* (Washington: United States Catholic Conference, 1983).
23. The Alternative Defence Commission, *Defence Without the Bomb* (London, Taylor & Francis, 1983), pp. 11, 204–205, 243.
24. Sharp, *Social Power and Political Freedom,* p. 232 ff., offers a definition and thorough discussion of this policy.
25. Barbara J. Wein, ed., *Peace and World Order Studies* (New York: World Policy Institute, 1984), pp. 629–667. Sample syllabuses can be found on pp. 70–126, although these are not all clearly focused on nonviolent sanctions as an alternative form of power.
26. Bob Irwin, *U.S. Defense Policy: Mainstream Views and Nonviolent Alternatives (A Macro-Analysis Seminar Manual)* (Waltham, MA: International Seminars on Teaching for Nonviolent Action, 1982).

Developing Cultural Fluency: Arab and Jewish Students Engaging in One Another's Company

JOCELYN ANNE GLAZIER

Stepping In

I am standing on the stairs that run above the playground at the Gal Bilingual/Bicultural School, the second school of its kind in Israel that brings together Arab and Jewish elementary students full time.[1] The fifteen Jewish and sixteen Arab first graders are engaged in various recess activities, as usual. I'm watching a group of boys who stand near me. Samair, Abdalla, Amir, Nibeala, and Salech, five Arab boys, prepare to play hide-and-go-seek. Eli and Tal, two Jewish boys, are eager to join. As the first five begin to set up the game, counting off in Arabic, Eli and Tal say in Hebrew, "Us too." They are ignored. When they repeat the request, Amir says "*La,*" Arabic for no. Eli responds, "*Cane,*" Hebrew for yes. Amir, joined by Samair this time, repeats "La." Eli and Tal repeat "*Cane,*" at which time Samair says, "*La — rak araveem*" ("No — only Arabs"), in mixed Arabic and Hebrew. At this point, Eli and Tal put their arms around each other in a statement of camaraderie, and Tal says with emphasis and standing-up-straight pride, "We're Jews." They remain at the periphery. Minutes later, the five Arab boys are just about ready to begin their game. They just need to decide who will count, the dreaded job in this game of hide-and-go-seek. Eli leaves Tal's side and stands closer to these five. He just won't give up; he wants to play. He's silent for a moment, watching, and then when the five boys are still trying to decide who will count, Eli volunteers. He's persistent — he repeats himself. Amir finally acknowledges him, and the Arab boys agree that Eli will serve this role. Eli puts his head down on the stone wall, shielding his eyes, and begins the job of counting: "*Echad, shtaim, shalosh*" ("One, two, three"), he begins in Hebrew in a loud voice. Then he pauses and begins again, this time in Arabic, "*Waahid, ithinin, thalatha.*"

In Israel, Arabs and Jews frequently live near but not next to one another. Although their households are often close, there is a great divide between them. Further, across Israel, Jews and Arabs historically have attended segre-

Harvard Educational Review Vol. 73 No. 2 Summer 2003, 141–163

gated schools. Contact between Jews and Arabs in the region I studied generally happens on two levels: via economic transactions and extracurricular school exchanges, the latter often referred to as co-existence opportunities.

In September 1998, through the efforts of the nonprofit Center for Bilingual Education in Israel, a new bilingual/bicultural school opened its doors to Jews and Arabs alike. The founders of the center and the school sought to create a network of bilingual/bicultural schools across the country. Their mission was to "create a new model of education in which children, their families and the surrounding community can experience and grow together among values of democracy, mutual respect, and tolerance, and ultimately this will make a valuable contribution toward greater coexistence between Arabs and Jews in our country" (Mission Statement, 1998). The school is public, funded by both government funds and private donations. As a "blooming school," where a new grade is added each year, the only children at the school the year of my study were thirty-one first graders, fifteen Jewish and sixteen Arab, along with one Jewish and two Arab teachers. During that year, all Arab students were Moslem. Since then, the school has enrolled Arab Moslems and Arab Christians. Parents apply to send their children to the school, and decisions about enrollment are based on a variety of criteria, such as commitment to the school's mission and whether a potential student has a sibling at the school. In 2002, the school's fifth year, it included grades one through five. As a participant-observer at the school, I investigated interactions among Jewish and Arab students to determine how curriculum and pedagogy influenced those interactions, aware that the goals of the school included both self-identity development and the strengthening of cross-cultural understanding.[2]

The Gal School, where students study in both Hebrew and Arabic, offers a formal opportunity for contact between Arabs and Jews within an educational setting throughout the school year. In an effort to do more than provide the casual and infrequent contact that often defines coexistence work, the founders of the school are making an effort to bring Arabs and Jews into intimate contact.

According to the school's principal, brief encounters sometimes only solidify stereotypes. The principal commented on an experience that happened a few years earlier:

> Some organization wanted [the Jewish elementary school] to have contact with the Arab children in [a local village]. We liked the idea. The children met a few times throughout the year. The last time they met was terrible. . . . The Jewish children here started the project [with] very good perceptions about Arabs and by the end of the year it changed and they didn't want to meet the Arabs anymore. So what did we gain? Nothing. (personal communication, July 1999)

One of the major differences between the Gal School and other coexistence efforts is that, as one of the two Arab teachers explained, "here the kids live together" rather than "visit" with one another. The contact between the students occurs five days a week, six hours a day. The principal remarked, "The children come to school every day, every single day, day after day, year after year. It's not that they meet once every two months for two hours. They really get to know each other. They grow up together" (personal communication, July 1999).

Theoretical Perspectives

Individuals who have pursued the challenge of deconstructing borders through peace education have sought to bring people on separate sides of a border together by providing opportunities for contact. Building on the contact hypothesis (Allport, 1954), many peace educators believe that bringing people into positive physical contact with one another will reduce prejudice. This idea, that "prejudice and hostility between members of segregated groups can be reduced by promoting . . . intergroup contact" (Miller & Brewer, 1984, p. xv), is the foundation of such programs in Israel and elsewhere.

Social scientists build on Allport's (1954) seminal work, *The Nature of Prejudice,* to suggest that certain conditions need to be applied to the intergroup contact situation to eradicate stereotypes and prejudice. Intergroup relations can be improved if the contact 1) allows for equal status among participants, 2) provides opportunity for intimate relations among individuals, 3) includes institutional support, and 4) involves cooperative rather than competitive interactions (Allport, 1954; Coates-Shrider & Stephan, 1997; Miller & Brewer, 1984). However, while some experiences of intergroup contact lead to a diminished sense of prejudice among participants, others lead to more prejudice and some lead to no change at all (Cairns, 1996; Connolly, 2000). These inconsistent results are not surprising, given the unattainable challenge of meeting all four of these conditions within an instance of contact. In particular, while an institution can provide the necessary support for contact to happen, "the manipulation of equal status within a contact situation may . . . be very difficult to achieve" (Ruddle & O'Connor, 1992, p. 24). Currently, there are few situations — either inside or outside of schools — in which individuals are completely equal. Furthermore, even if equal status were attainable within a school, personal experience and personal history reveal that the two sides may be quite unequal in the real world, a reality that is hard to forget or leave behind.

There are additional reasons why intergroup contact experiences may not be as successful as hoped. First, they often focus on participants' similarities "to the virtual exclusion of [their] differences" (Pettigrew, 1986, p. 179). Second, outcomes of this work are often anchored "largely on isolated, noncumulative" (p. 179) experiences, despite the fact that learning and transformation, particularly related to issues of diversity, occur over time (see, e.g., Glazier et al., 2000). Third, the experiences tend to focus on the destruction of something (prejudice) rather than on the construction of something (cultural fluency). Fourth, the goals of contact experiences are often ambiguous and unspecified. Fifth, this work is primarily an investigation of otherness: gazing at the other remains central, while exploration of the self is secondary and/or nonexistent. The final limitation of intergroup contact theories is their lack of focus on curriculum and pedagogy, apart from suggesting that participants engage in cooperative work (Johnson, Johnson, & Maruyama, 1984).

I suggest in this article that border-crossing requires moving toward a well-articulated and constructive goal — specifically, cultural fluency — via sustained experiences of "company." Cultural fluency is the ability to step back and forth between two cultures, to embrace your own culture while understanding its relationship to others.[3] It is about being able to communicate with and for the other, and being able to express another's perspective, another's cultural beliefs, alongside your own. It is about ease of interaction with the "other." It is about exploring and becoming aware of cultural differences, as well as, ultimately, understanding what impact those differences have on one's status and one's opportunities in the larger context. Prejudice reduction is one small part of cultural fluency, which is a lifelong process that can be enhanced by education. It cannot be developed in a single moment, but happens through the cumulative effects of individuals from different cultures engaging *in one another's company.*

Intergroup contact does not, in and of itself, allow individuals to move toward cultural fluency. I suggest that it is through being *in the company of others* that opportunities to develop cultural fluency are cultivated and nurtured. Contact leaves us still at the border — a safe place to remain. Contact is defined as "the mutual relation of two bodies whose *external surfaces* touch each other" or "a light pressure *upon the skin* or the sensation of this"(Simpson & Weiner, 1989, p. 805, emphasis added). To come in contact with is defined in part as "to meet, come across, be brought into practical connexion with" (p. 805). What these definitions share is the notion of contact as something very much on the surface. Company, on the other hand, moves beneath the surface, beyond simple contact. Company means "companionship, fellowship, society"(p. 589), all of which imply a certain commitment to others. It is an "assemblage, a collection . . . a gathering of people for social intercourse . . . a body of persons combined or incorporated for some common object, or for the joint execution or performance of anything" (p. 589). Thus, company-keeping involves individuals sharing participation in a task.

Cross-cultural interactions frequently remain at the level of contact, bringing individuals together physically but not necessarily socially or emotionally. It is no wonder that, despite being desegregated in name, schools, for example in the United States, remain segregated (see, e.g., Kozol, 1991). "Merely including youth or teachers of different races and ethnicities in the same school clearly does not produce an integrated school" (Fine, Weis, & Powell, 1997, p. 253). In contrast, company-keeping moves contact beyond the surface, allowing individuals to move across psychological, language, and physical borders, and requires a sustained commitment to each other and the task at hand. It is this commitment over an extended period of time that allows for learning and transformation, and in the educational context it is the curriculum that plays a critical role in the experience of company-building. Consequently, this article examines what being in contact with and in the company of another meant for students at the Gal School, how these children engaged in one another's company, and what they began to learn as they were keeping company.

Methods

My entrance into the Gal School happened by chance. I traveled to Israel in search of critical multiculturalism: specifically, educational experiences where people support meaningful cross-cultural understandings between Jews and Arabs. I learned about the opening of the Gal School before arriving and arranged to conduct research there. When I arrived in September I realized I had a rare opportunity to document the struggle of the Gal School community to define meaningful cross-cultural work. Thus, I spent the 1998–1999 school year examining how curriculum and pedagogy influenced the understandings that Gal students developed about themselves and one another. I wondered in particular what would happen in this context where Jews and Arabs met, as the school principal remarked, "every single day, day after day, year after year" (personal communication, July 1999).

I began the year by spending three days a week at the school. This soon stretched to five, and included evening meetings with parents, teachers, and others. Students and teachers got used to my presence and often involved me in classroom activities. As a participant-observer I used two methods to collect data: videotaping and field notes. Structured and unstructured interviews with the three teachers, parents, school founders, and administrators were another primary source of data. I also gathered school documents: teacher handouts, copies of notices to parents, photographs, samples of student work, teachers' lesson plans, minutes of committee meetings, and even birthday party invitations. In addition, I collected newspaper articles to mark events in Israel.

Toward the end of the school year, I conducted formal conversations with various members of the Gal School community. For example, in closing interviews and viewing sessions with the teachers, I asked them to look closely at videotapes of their teaching that I found provocative. I also interviewed the founders of the school, the principal, and the parents of six students, three Arab and three Jewish, who consistently participated in school activities.

As a researcher I constantly weighed the reality of the research context against my assumptions — as conditioned by my experiences as a woman, graduate student, teacher, teacher educator, Jewish American, and advocate of critical multicultural education. I recorded my assumptions in the margins of my field notes and, at times, in a personal journal. I collected data in Arabic, Hebrew, and English, but am only fluent in English. I developed enough proficiency in Hebrew to follow conversations about the school. In some ways, my own language learning mimicked that of the first graders who were also struggling to learn a second language. I relied on the teachers to translate for me at various times throughout the year. My lack of language proficiency prompted me to pay attention in my data collection to nonverbal behavior as much as to verbal interactions, both necessary in allowing me to better catalog — and ultimately understand — the experiences of the students at the school.

Observations from the Gal School

Cross-cultural contact in the school happened within two primary contexts: the classroom and the hallway/playground.[4] Contact was initiated by teachers, children, parents, and school officials. Across all contexts, physical contact occurred between Jews and Arabs.[5] However, contact moved into the area of company as 1) the teachers structured experiences that fostered joint participation in a task to which the students could potentially be committed, and 2) the students created these experiences for themselves. I will explore several examples of teacher-structured experiences and students' responses to them. I will then examine examples of student-structured experiences, identifying the ways these mimicked or diverged from those the teachers structured.

Teacher-Structured Experiences

Within the school context, teachers initiated regular contact between Arabs and Jews through seating arrangements; placing children in Arab/Jewish pairs for field trips; designing and implementing activities where children had to work in small, heterogeneous groups; and creating a number of pair activities, again assigning students to Arab/Jewish dyads. The teachers also facilitated group activities that included all students or a large number of them.

Teachers' main objectives for students as they worked in heterogeneous groups were that they learn to cooperate and share with one another, strengthen their second-language skills, and understand other aspects of Arab and/or Jewish culture. As one Arab teacher explained, "Besides learning to write, read and do math . . . they're getting to know each others' culture and [are gaining] a sense that there isn't one way, any right way of living" (field notes, January 1998). The teachers understood that learning occurs through relationships and wanted students to develop a "sense of togetherness" (Arab teacher, field notes, January 1998). Therefore, they assigned students to work on activities that allowed them to feel "it [was] in their own interest to become one," to develop "a tight group" (Arab teacher, field notes, January 1999).

In addition, teachers consistently tried to provide students with an engaging curriculum, an engaging "It" (Hawkins, 1974) around which learning could unfold. As Hawkins explains, "Without an It there is no content for the context, no figure and no heat, but only an affair of mirrors confronting each other" (p. 52). Dissatisfied with packaged curriculum models, the teachers created their own curriculum to engage students as active learners. As one of the Arab teachers explained, "We're teaching them to be human beings who have responsibility and the right things to search for answers. . . . Our target is to have not pupils or students but to have researchers" (personal communication, March 1999).

As will be seen in the following vignettes, classroom experiences offered opportunities for cross-cultural interaction and learning. Some opportunities left students at the edge of contact while others moved them into company. The overlap of the experiences is what was perhaps most transformative, contributing to the development of cultural fluency.

Teacher-Structured Experiences: At the Level of Contact

It is the beginning of January. The teachers have explained to the children that they will be working in pairs this morning to create stories on the computer in Arabic for the first time. The teachers commented that the Arab students will have to take the lead, since they are fluent in Arabic. The students are still struggling to learn one another's languages. The teachers hope that this activity will prompt students to practice one another's languages and strengthen their ability to work collaboratively.

Ari, an energetic Jewish boy who is a frequent participant in class discussions of all sorts, sits with Zaina, a shy Arab girl who participates infrequently. Zaina sits facing the computer and busily types. Ari, uncommonly quiet today, sits with his body facing Zaina, his head twisted to see the screen. Ari attempts to enter the activity initially by pointing to a letter, intent on pushing it, but Zaina shakes her head no and instead enters a few letters on her own. Soon she points to specific letters on the keyboard, "inviting" Ari to push the correct key. Ari participates in this way. There is no verbal conversation between these two students as they work. Ari's physicality is telling. During the course of their interaction (less than 10 minutes long), Ari turns away from the screen a number of times, while Zaina is fully focused on the screen and the keyboard, looking away only once. This is Zaina's text.

A second pair — two of the brightest students in the class — work together later in the morning. Yael, a Jewish girl, and Khaled, an Arab boy, sit head to head at the computer. They begin by searching the keyboard together. Khaled begins to type a couple of letters. Yael's hand is poised above the keyboard, waiting, but Khaled does not invite her to join. She looks intently at Khaled for nearly a minute, hoping perhaps that this will prompt him to invite her to participate. Essentially, Khaled creates the story on his own; Yael never touches the keyboard and no words pass between them. As time passes,

Yael repositions herself, moves away from Khaled, sits back in her seat, and eventually settles back from the computer. Later, Yael dips in close again, only to retreat shortly thereafter. This is Khaled's text.

The teachers initiate pair work in this case in the hope that students will be able to learn from one another and, more specifically, that the Jewish students may improve their Arabic while the Arab students experience the role of expert. The teachers are concerned that the Jewish students are learning Arabic at a much slower pace than the Arab students are learning Hebrew. Reasons for this are many. First, "despite the legal status of Arabic as the second language, Israel is not in fact a bilingual society. Hebrew is the dominant language" (Bar-Yosef, 1993, p. 121). The Hebrew language is found everywhere — less so in Arab villages, but still very evident. Everyday survival in Israel is much easier if one speaks and reads Hebrew. Furthermore, it is required that students in schools — both Arab and Jewish — study Hebrew through high school. Therefore, the parents of all of the students at the school — Arab and Jewish — are fluent in Hebrew. In short, to succeed in many arenas in Israel, knowing Hebrew is mandatory; Hebrew is the language of the culture of power (Delpit, 1988).

The case of Arabic is different than that of Hebrew. Arabic is the dominant language in Arab villages. Here you can find Arabic phone books, store signs, and billboards. In mixed cities, like Haifa, Arabic can be found in certain enclaves but is not nearly as common as Hebrew. "In Jewish schools, Arabic is an elective course" (Bar-Yosef, 1993, p. 121), and thus is not required through high school. The great majority of Jewish parents of children at the school are not fluent in Arabic and cannot support their children's learning of the language. The Jewish teacher explains, "The problem is that the Jewish parents, only some of them know reading and writing in Arabic. . . . And it's a problem because you can't help your child so how will you support him? . . . It won't be easy." Whereas the Arab children have multiple opportunities to practice their Hebrew even within their own villages, the Jewish children have many fewer opportunities in their communities to practice their developing Arabic. It is in part this language gap among the students in this school that prevents the possibility of equal status, a preferred condition for successful intergroup contact. Though the teachers struggle to promote equity in language within the school, the world outside seeps through the school walls.

Another example of a teacher-structured experience occurred in the spring, when Jews remember ancestors who perished in the Holocaust. The students at the Gal School learned about the Holocaust in two ways. First, the Jewish teacher read them a story of a child who hid in the forest during the Holocaust. Second, she asked the Jewish children to ask their parents about the Holocaust and come to class the next day prepared to share what they had learned.

On April 13, the students sat together in the classroom, in physical contact with one another. At Gal School, like in many early elementary classrooms, the children have assigned seats. The configuration of the room changed more than a few times during the course of the year, but one thing remained constant: Jewish and Arab children sat in alternating seats. Tal, a Jewish student, began the day by sharing the story of a relative who survived the Holocaust. Later, Leah assumed Tal's spot at the front of the room, sharing the story of her relatives who had left their country to escape the war. Next came Yael, sharing the story of a relative who hid from the Nazis and, as a result, survived the war.

At the end of the storytelling, the Jewish teacher rose to set up a series of six memorial candles, explaining that there was one candle for each million Jews killed during the Holocaust. Manhal, an Arab student, asked incredulously, "Six million were killed?" covering his mouth in astonishment. The teacher invited each of the six Jewish students who had shared their stories to come and light a candle. Whereas the Jewish students were at the periphery in the computer exercise, in this case the Arab students were unable to participate fully. As the activity was constructed, the Arab students could do no more than listen.

These activities contained all three of the conditions necessary for contact to be potentially transformative: they occurred within an institution that supports contact between Arabs and Jews, they provided opportunities for intimacy, and they were noncompetitive and intended to be cooperative. A close look at how the activities unfolded, however, reveals that the third condition was met only at a surface level.

There are many reasons why the computer exercise was not as collaborative as the teachers had hoped. First, the task was one that asked students who were not yet proficient writers in a first language, and certainly not in a second language, to create a collaborative story. The students, emergent readers and writers, were focused initially on finding the correct letters on the keyboard. Second, not only were they new to reading and writing, they were also becoming familiar with a keyboard that has the color-coded letters for Hebrew, Arabic, and English on each key. Third, this was a new task for students. They had written stories individually in their first language, sometimes on the computers, but this was the first time that they had written collaborative stories, and they needed a model for how to do it. The teachers described the assignment and circled the room to answer students' questions, but did not explicitly teach the students how to do this work. Finally, the students were not committed to the project or to one another, two critical factors that must be present if contact is to become company. For instance, Khaled made no effort to invite Yael to contribute to the text. His commitment seemed to be to the text only — to getting the story written — and he seemed to perceive Yael as irrelevant to that effort.[6]

Like the computer exercise, the Holocaust narrative activity remained at the level of contact for some. There were certainly differences between these two activities, but neither provided an opportunity for engagement with, or commitment to, the other. Though students had the opportunity to learn about self and, to an extent, about others, neither activity allowed the students to truly be in one another's company.

Teacher-Structured Experiences:
Approaching Company-Keeping through Drawing

Another example of cross-cultural activities that occurred nearly once a week for the first half of the school year was when students shared a single piece of paper to create a drawing together. For this activity teachers generally assigned students to Arab/Jewish pairs to encourage cooperation and to give them an opportunity to practice speaking their second language. The degree of company-keeping achieved varied over the year, depending on the activity and on the students involved.

Ramadan presented an opportunity to teach about Islam and aspects of Arab Moslem culture. From late December to January, the teachers engaged students in a number of activities related to the holiday: they created a "midnight" feast for the students complete with specific foods and prayers, had students work on puzzles that showed scenes from Ramadan, and showed a film about the holiday. Students also worked in pairs to create a drawing of what they had learned about the holiday. The teachers explained the activity in both languages, as was generally the case, and asked students to speak in Arabic as they worked together.

Abdalla, a sometimes serious, sometimes playful Arab boy, works today with Gil, a Jewish boy who wavers between being shy and being somewhat mischievous. Right away the two boys begin by negotiating, making decisions about what they will draw on this single 8-by-11-inch sheet of white paper. Abdalla points to something on the display of Ramadan symbols behind them. Created by the teachers, the display includes street lanterns, Moslem prayer beads, Arabic phrases from the Koran, and pictures of foods eaten in the evening. Gil asks Abdalla in Hebrew, "Necklace?" Abdalla repeats the word in Hebrew, nodding, then gets up to point out what he means. He taps Gil on the shoulder, signaling his move from the table. "This," he says to Gil in Hebrew, pointing to a plate that hangs beneath the prayer beads — or necklace, as Gil calls them. Gil nods — he understands now — and gets up to join Abdalla, pointing out what he plans to draw. The two return to their seats, smile at one another, and then begin to work. Moments later, Gil makes a joke, using hand gestures only, and the two boys giggle to one another, stifling their laughter a bit as they see the video camera on them. As they work together, the boys point to different parts of the drawing they are creating and also to the display behind them. They question one another, using hand signals and Hebrew, about crayon color and the like, and watch each other draw. At one point, Gil takes the crayon Abdalla is using and peels back some of the paper so that Abdalla will have an easier time drawing. The final drawing reveals a mosque at the center of the paper, with symbols surrounding it. The boys write their names, one right after the other, in the same corner of the paper.

Certainly other pairs worked differently than those described above. One example of this process unfolding differently occurred in February. When King Hussein of Jordan died, the teachers designed an activity for students to work in pairs to prepare cards to send to Hussein's family. Once again, the teachers hoped to support students' second-language learning and cooperative skills. Some students worked like the pair described above, while others worked independently. Though the teachers emphasized that the students were to create a single drawing together on the shared sheet, Leah and Maja began by drawing a line down the center of the paper. Leah worked on one side, drawing freehand and writing in Hebrew. Maja worked on the other side of the sheet in Arabic, using cutouts from the newspapers supplied by the teachers for the assignment. The most notable communication between the two girls occurred when Maja moved to cross the line to add something to Leah's work. Leah screamed and was asked by one of the teachers to leave the room until she calmed down. Later, the two finished the drawing without speaking to each another. In this example, drawing in pairs was a contact experience rather than a more intimate experience of company.

Besides drawing in pairs, students drew in larger groups. The teachers often defined the task and students worked together in teacher-designed groups. At such times, the teachers circulated around the room as students worked. During one such activity that occurred in late November, groups of four or five students looked at Arabic books, especially the illustrations, given that students were still struggling readers at this point. Once students "read" the books, they drew their impression of the story. Each student was to participate in the drawing to create a single page for each group.

Yael, a pensive Jewish girl, Amira, an Arab girl sporting two long braids, Samair, an energetic Arab boy, Fozi, a quiet Arab boy, and Ruti, a Jewish girl who never tired of waving to the video camera throughout the year, were assigned to work together on this particular project. After students flipped through their copies of the text, they figured out what to draw. Amira began drawing a house, modeled on the illustrations from the text, in the middle of the paper. Meanwhile, Samair casually took the black marker from Ruti, who sat to his left, and wrote a word in the small sun in the upper-left-hand corner of the paper. When he finished, Ruti used the same marker and wrote in Hebrew directly underneath Samair's words. Though the page was small, these five students figured out how to negotiate that space. At times, all five worked together on different parts of the paper, their heads practically touching. On the paper, they drew a single house with windows and a door, trees and flowers beside the house, a cloud-covered sky, and the sun above the house. They engulfed the paper, their hands and arms at work on the drawing, their bodies flat against the tabletop. At other times, one or two of the students rested their chin on their hand and watched as the others drew. On two occasions,

Amira got up from her spot and moved to Samair's right to work on that part of the drawing. The students shared the page, shared the table, shared one another's markers.

In two examples of drawing activities, students had the chance to engage in one another's company, producing a shared text. They attempted to communicate, borrowed markers and ideas, negotiated roles, and played around with the tasks. These actions indicated a moving beneath the surface of contact into a more intimate relation between individuals. A commitment to the tasks and to one another was revealed, for example, in Gil's small but critical move of peeling back the paper on Abdalla's crayon, allowing him to be a full participant.

There are various ways to analyze Leah and Maja's experience. Their reluctance to cooperate could be a reasonable aspect of life in first grade (or any grade). Children, and adults for that matter, do not always share work equally, something teachers must be conscious of when making assumptions about the potential strength of cooperative learning experiences. Another way to look at an interaction like this is from the standpoint of the specific students involved. How do different individuals, with different personalities, influence whether or not an experience becomes one of company? Over the year, these drawing experiences offered students the opportunity to work with various students on a variety of projects. I discerned that the more opportunities students had to draw together, the more chances they had to be in the company of one another.

Collaboration on these drawings was more probable than on the computer assignment, given the abilities of the students when observed. Unlike the computer work, all participants in this case knew how to draw and had the knowledge needed to complete the task together. They came to drawing prepared. In addition, drawing enabled the students to overcome some of the language barriers they still encountered. They used other signs and symbols (e.g., hand gestures, drawings), critical tools in a bilingual classroom, to communicate.

The level of student engagement varied depending on whether or not the activity was teacher-facilitated. When students worked without a teacher, there often was not significant conversation across cultural lines. Instead, Arabs spoke with Arabs in Arabic, Jews with other Jews in Hebrew. In contrast, when a teacher facilitated the work, students moved closer to an experience of company. Teachers asked students to converse with one another and prompted them to enter into one another's space. The teachers' role in moving a teacher-structured experience of contact into one of company is critical.

When the teachers did not act as facilitators in these teacher-structured experiences, students still sometimes exhibited characteristics of company-keeping. As described, the students moved across borders by, for example, sharing resources (e.g., Ruti and Samair using the same marker). At the beginning of the school year, Jewish students shared with other Jews, Arab students with other Arabs, to the point that some students would take a long trip around the room in search of a marker or eraser rather than borrow from their neighbor of another culture. This pattern eased during the year as students began to share resources across cultural lines. Ultimately, asking for permission to borrow became extraneous. Once initial permission was granted, the resources were considered common, readily borrowed by Jews and Arabs alike. I interpreted this sharing across boundaries as a marker of students moving toward company-keeping, particularly since these elementary school students took pride in and ownership of their resources. In a class conversation about friendship, students indicated that sharing reflected friendship. More than one student commented that, among other things, friends are those with whom you "share your markers." I do not argue that being in the company of someone else necessarily implies friendship. However, I do believe this sharing practice is an indication of students' willingness to move across borders, to conceive of friendships beyond cultural boundaries.

Teacher-Structured Experiences:
Building Company through Difficult Conversations

The teachers at the Gal School often spoke about not wanting conversations and classroom activities to get "political," according to one of the Arab teachers, "not 'cause we're afraid, but because they're [only] in first grade" (personal communication, January 1999). Researchers have suggested that the most effective coexistence work between Arabs and Jews happens when politics are left by the wayside (Ben-Ari & Amir, 1986). However, Israel is a country fraught with political and racial tension, where history is not easily agreed upon or forgotten. Thus, talk of politics is unavoidable and frequently enters the conversation at the school, in response to events such as elections, holidays, and the death of Jordan's King Hussein.

During the school year, I had the opportunity to listen to and participate in a number of conversations that felt difficult to me. These conversations occurred among parents, teachers, and students. They were marked by changes in tone from mild to loud, by changes in tempo from rapid to sudden halting, by changes in body posture from casual leaning to crossed arms and legs. I believe that these difficult conversations, often avoided in classrooms, are opportunities to develop cultural fluency.

One such conversation took place in late March, around Land Day. Land Day commemorates a day in 1976 when Israel's Labor government made land in northern Israel, previously settled by Arabs, available to Jews. On March 30, 1976, there was an Arab general strike throughout Israel in protest of this land resettlement. A number of Arab demonstrators in Galilee, including residents from a village where some of the Gal School students live, were killed by members of the Israeli army. Every year, on March 30, demonstrations in commemoration of Land Day are held all over Israel.

Land Day is not a topic regularly discussed in either Jewish or Arab schools. The Gal School teachers, however, realized the need to bring this topic into the classroom, knowing that the students would no doubt bring it there themselves. I wrote in my field notes:

> Usually, when kids file into the room to sit on the rug for an activity, they sit where they want. Today, though, as they come in a few at a time . . . [the teachers] tell them where they should sit. Ari points out as he sits down "*Aravee, yehoodee, aravee, yehoodee*" [Arab, Jew, Arab, Jew] and continues till he points to everyone sitting on the carpet. He's right. [The teachers] are sitting the kids in that order, to the extent that that's possible on the rug. (March 1999)

Students were generally aware of the two distinct cultures within the classroom, as well as the moves the teachers made to integrate them. In this setting, differences often avoided in contact situations could not be avoided on this day or any other.

On the morning of Land Day, a teacher begins the conversation by saying she will talk about a subject that is difficult, even sad. She says she realizes that some students will want to talk; others might want to just listen. She then asks who knows something about Land Day. Tal, a Jewish boy and a voracious reader, speaks first, stating in Hebrew that land was taken from the Arabs and given to the Jews to build houses. Fozi, a quiet, introspective Arab student, speaks next, in Arabic. All students speak their native language during this discussion, a practice that is fairly common in class discussions. At this point in the year, however, students are more able to understand one another's languages. Fozi explains that a long time ago, Jews took land from the Arabs and five people were killed. He points out that some of the victims came from the village of some of their Arab classmates. Nibeela, in his native Arabic, corrects Fozi and says that six people were killed. Sara, a Jewish student, mistakes Land Day with Yom Siveeva, Environment Day. The teachers correct her. Ruti, another Jewish student, has the final comment. She begins, "Jews — " and then backtracks to explain more vaguely that certain people took other people's land. It is as if through this switch, Ruti works to maintain the fellowship of the classroom. I believe Ruti's word choice here, like Eli's pointing out "Jew, Arab, Jew, Arab," indicates her awareness of a tension that exists between Jews and Arabs and her understanding that both populations exist in this classroom.

The teachers explain the story of Land Day in both Hebrew and Arabic. One of the things that the teachers make clear is the fact that the initial event occurred a "long time ago." When I ask the teachers about their repetition of this phrase, they suggest that they did this consciously, not wanting the children to be fearful of one another as Arabs and Jews. The teachers venture into controversial waters, but avoid discussion that might divide the students, who are beginning to feel comfortable with one another.

The students seem to continue being in one another's company even after the discussion, something that has not occurred frequently before. As they work on individual projects with clay, creating scenes that come to mind when thinking about the topic of land, the students look to one another's structures. Samair and Yitzchak, an Arab boy and a Jewish boy sitting across from each another, construct bridges — perhaps an appropriate metaphor for what consistent company can create. Through acknowledging the past, the present, and the Arab/Jewish dichotomy, the school seeks to interrupt history and acknowledge the students as Arab and Jewish children caught in this shared tension of old and new.

Teacher-Structured Experiences: Building Company through a Common Project

Sunflowers seem to grow everywhere in Israel from May through July. Driving down roads, it is not unusual to see row after row of tall, yellow flowers, faces turned toward the sun. The teachers introduce the theme of sunflowers toward the end of the school year. The students planted sunflowers in plastic bottles, drew pictures of them, and read about them in Arabic and Hebrew. At the end of the year they put on a production about sunflowers. The teachers developed a bilingual script that incorporated ideas and characters from two of the stories the students had read during the last month of the school year, one about clouds and another about sunflowers.

The students spent days drawing pictures of sunflowers that would cover the stage. They spent hours rehearsing their lines and learning the dances the teachers choreographed for the play. When students rehearsed, they tapped each other or shouted across the room to remind one another when it was time to speak. They sometimes mouthed the lines as their peers spoke them. Sometimes they corrected one another. Students spoke their lines in both Arabic and Hebrew, crossing language boundaries. The teachers and students were tireless in their preparation.

When the curtain opened, the performance was flawless, as far as first-grade plays go. The teachers were off stage, so the students were not able to rely on them for cues or hints. Thus, the students had to look to one another for help — in essence, they had to be in each other's company. From the stage, students waved their peers in from backstage. They tapped each other to remind a peer to speak. When they stood to dance, they helped one another line up. They passed props. They whispered to one another about when to sing. They negotiated the space on the stage, making room for one another. They looked to their peers as they moved in time to the music. They relied on one another as actors in a theater company might, committed to the production and to each other's participation.

In the final number, the children waved their hand-held streamers, practically entwining them. Arab, Jew, Arab, Jew, girl, boy, girl, boy, child next to child: borders had been crossed for the moment. Their experiences of being first in simple contact with one another — sitting side by side at their desks, for example, or even at the computer — and next, in one another's company — learning one another's languages, drawing together, being in the same space, sharing resources and stories — enabled them to communicate onstage across cultural boundaries. By the end of the school year, the students had begun to learn to move from contact into company.

Student-Initiated Company-Keeping

Students were well aware of what the teachers expected when they assigned joint work. As one student remarked to a teacher, "When you put us in groups, we work together" (field notes, April 1999). What would happen if students chose with whom to work? How would students work with one another when the teachers were not present? Having learned to work together through teacher-initiated contact, would the students do the same outside of the teachers' sight?

It was common for students to segregate themselves on the playground and play in homogeneous groups, a practice not uncommon in integrated schools (Rogers, Hennigen, Bowman, & Miller, 1984). As the school principal remarked,

> What always interests me is to see if and how the children play or learn together, Arab and Jewish children, in official time and unofficial time. Official time is when the teachers give them assignments . . . and they work together very nicely. However, when they are off — recess, on their way to the bus — they don't always mix. (personal communication, July 1999)

I was interested to notice when students did choose to "cross over," in either academic or non-academic instances, unprompted by teachers or parents. I found that when the Gal School students initiated company, they borrowed from "official" classroom experiences. They brought a variety of tools with them to their unchaperoned company-keeping, which happened most often in the latter part of the school year. They could be intimately engaged with one another because they had practiced doing so through a number of different activities over a long period of time. I describe here moments when students chose to keep one another company, rather than remain at the level of contact.

It's 11:30 in the morning, six days before the end of the school year. The children are involved in one of their final individual writing activities, writing about what they have learned this year. Yitzchak, a Jewish boy, sits next to Manhal, an Arab boy. They have often played soccer together on the school playground, sometimes amicably, other times not.[7] Today they sit at their assigned seats, side by side. They have shared this table for months. Yitzchak looks up from the sheet on which he is writing in Arabic. Now more proficient in both languages, students could choose in which language they wrote. Yitzchak looks over to Manhal and asks him how to spell *la,* the Arabic word for no. Manhal uses his pencil and writes the word on the table. Yitzchak leans closer to Manhal to get a better view, his head nearly touching Manhal's shoulder. Manhal looks from his writing to Yitzchak and back as if to be sure Yitzchak is watching. As he writes, Manhal repeats "*la, la,*" emphasizing the letters for Yitzchak's benefit. Yitzchak points to what Manhal has written and says aloud "*low,*" Hebrew for no, playfully mispronouncing the word. He then turns to Manhal and smiles, revealing the gaps where his two front teeth will soon grow. Gripping an eraser, Yitzchak turns his attention back to his paper. Manhal follows Yitzchak's gaze and says "*Llllaaaa,*" further emphasizing the letters. Yitzchak erases and Manhal watches as Yitzchak works. Manhal repeats "*la*" twice as Yitzchak writes. Yitzchak's gaze, meanwhile, moves from his paper to the table where Manhal has written the word, and back again. He reaches over Manhal to borrow an eraser. As Yitzchak relaxes back into his seat, Manhal reinforces his teaching by repeating "*llaa,*" retracing the word he has written for Yitzchak on the table. Seconds later, as Yitzchak completes the task, Manhal rubs the word out, leaving little trace of what occurred between the two.

Across the same table stands Khalil, paper in hand. Dressed in a black-and-white T-shirt, he holds his paper in one hand and points to a word on it with his forefinger. Ruti, in a sleeveless pale blue T-shirt, her hair held back in a ponytail, is his audience. Khalil has asked Ruti how to write a word in Hebrew. Arabic is Khalil's first language, but he has chosen to do this exercise in Hebrew. Ruti, sitting, writes the word on the table in pencil. Khalil stands over Ruti as she writes. She points to a word on her own paper and then writes on the desk. As Ruti writes, Khalil moves his eyes from his own paper to the desk and back. He then points to a letter on his own paper and asks in Hebrew, "*Mah zeh?*" ("What is this?"). Ruti continues writing on the desk and Khalil begins to cross-check his paper against what Ruti has written. At this point, Yitzchak walks over and writes the word Khalil needs on the desk. Khalil looks over Yitzchak's shoulders in a way that mirrors what Yitzchak was doing moments before with Manhal.

This example resembles a number of similar episodes that occurred during the year when students, working on independent projects, sought help from one another, particularly when working in their second language. In this way students supported one another's learning. The resources around the room, organized and provided by the teachers, enabled the students to do this. Students often escorted one another to the various letter boards around the room to point out a letter, and they also used the chalkboard to write a word for a friend. Rarely did they violate a peer's text by writing directly on it. It was as if the paper itself was the private domain. They did, however, seek alternative resources to help one another, writing on the desks, for example. The desk appeared to be the public domain or the common, shared space.

Students also initiated company on the playground. I watched the scenario presented in my introduction, the hide-and-seek game, with some awe, recording the following in the margins of my field notes:

> After I watch part one — and the rejection of Eli and Tal by Samair — I hurt for them. I feel this pain deep in the pit of my stomach. I want to . . . do something more meaningful — to intervene somehow and yet I watch, amazed though

> sadly not surprised. . . . This short interchange forces me to question everything, to wonder what difference this school experience is making for these kids. . . . Mesmerized by the event, I keep watching. I watch as Eli mills at the side of this group, wanting to play, refusing to take no for an answer. . . . And then he gets to play and he begins to count . . . in Hebrew and then, as if he knows the rules, . . . code switching, . . . he begins to count again in Arabic. I feel ready now to burst into tears. I can hardly contain myself, my emotions. Is this a triumph? What does Eli's move say? It's what gives me hope, essentially. It's in the individual moves, perhaps, that peace — not the word I want, though — comes. (December 1997)

The teachers perceived the event as I did, as an example of crossing cultural divides, and asked me to share what I saw with the principal. The principal remarked that she was troubled by the boys' comment, "No Jews can play — only Arabs." Understandably, she read this as an example of division rather than inclusion. Another, perhaps more critical, reading of this episode would be its resemblance to the status quo: here is a Jewish boy "hunting" Arabs. However, in this case the Jewish boy is playing by the Arabs' rules — he is not the master of the game, so to speak. Eli's persistence and the boys' eventual willingness to let him play is the part of the story that differs from the societal norm. The boys ultimately engage with one another. What Eli does in this experience is cross a cultural divide through, in essence, code switching, or fluidly using two languages interchangeably (Gumperz & Hernandez-Chavez, 1972). He seeks "earnest crossing, with the intent of full participation" (Thorne, 1993, p. 121), using language as the mediating tool (Cole, 1996; Vygotsky, 1978). Therein lies the story of inclusion.

Concluding Thoughts: The Additive Potential of Company to Develop Cultural Fluency

Earlier in this article, I discussed the four conditions considered necessary for intergroup contact to be successful: equal status, acquaintance potential, a collaborative atmosphere, and institutional support. I argued that, though equal status was not feasible, the other three conditions seemed both possible and important when asking people to begin to cross borders. However, I questioned whether prejudice reduction was enough of an endpoint, and whether it was too undefined. I suggested that we need to strive instead for the development of cultural fluency. I wondered further if intergroup contact as commonly construed continued to leave participants interacting at a surface level, leaving borders between individuals intact. Contact alone will not allow us to arrive at cultural fluency, will not move us across the borders. Individuals must engage in ongoing, meaningful, and shared tasks in order to develop cultural fluency.

Much of the learning facilitated in this classroom was the result of the curriculum and pedagogy, two critical components often left out of the intergroup contact equation. The teachers encouraged students to be in one another's company, and to learn about themselves and others. A number of activities were designed by teachers to encourage students to be in one another's company, to learn about themselves and others, and to begin to develop cultural fluency. The curricula most influential in allowing students to engage with one another in meaningful ways was connected to the students' own lives. Creating such a curriculum is complicated in this setting, due to the sometimes radical differences between the lives of the children as Arabs and Jews, that is, as members of a minority and of a majority.

I argue that this classroom is not so different from others across the globe. In diverse classrooms teachers too often reach for an uncomplicated and uncontroversial curriculum that fails to address students' own lives and experiences. A common topic of conversation around which students at this school were engaged was that of holidays. I, like others (e.g., McLaren, 1995; Singer, 1992; Sleeter, 1995), have been critical of multicultural approaches that remain at the surface, such as food fairs and holiday celebrations. At the Gal School, holidays were often addressed in a way that flew in the face of the safe multiculturalism teachers often practice. In Israel, and in this classroom, holidays such as Land Day are controversial. In contrast to teachers in many other schools, Gal School teachers did not ignore the tensions that naturally entered the classroom context on such occasions.

In addition to connecting to students' lives, the curriculum — as the teachers came to realize — must reach students in a shared zone of proximal development (Vygotsky, 1978). For example, the computer activity failed to challenge all the students at an appropriate level. Other activities were more successful because they more appropriately allowed students to participate. As I watched students draw together in November, I wondered whether this practice became pedestrian over time. Teachers frequently asked the children to work in pairs to draw pictures for guests. This often involved writing "welcome" in both Hebrew and Arabic. I eventually realized that perhaps the pedestrian nature of this task actually enabled other things to happen within these groups, as the students no longer had to focus entirely on the task at hand. They no longer had to figure out how to negotiate space and how to share markers. The routine performance potentially enabled the students to "play" across borders, to test boundaries. Students could support one another's completion of the task by doing anything from the simple (e.g., helping a student open a bottle of glue) to the more challenging (e.g., helping a student with a language task). Thus the task was no longer joint in name only, but also in action. Familiarity, bred of practice, allowed students to move beyond the task into one another's lives, even if only momentarily.

As students moved beyond contact and engaged with one another, they had opportunities to learn first about themselves and their distinct cultures — a critical piece of the cultural fluency puzzle. In heterogeneous settings, individuals are "constantly called upon to explain [their] differences to each other" (Paley, 1995, p. 56). While they were being questioned by their peers, students became experts on their own languages and cultures (Sidorkin, 1999). As the school principal commented,

> You strengthen your identity much more if you know the other people, not just if you're with your own all the time. It's really . . . absurd but it is [true]. [If] you live in your community all the time, you don't even ask questions because there's no reason. Once you meet other people, you start asking questions: "Who am I? What do I stand for? What's my heritage?" and so on and that makes you stronger. (personal communication, July 1999)

In addition to helping students learn about themselves, having consistent and varied opportunities to engage in one another's company gave students the chance to learn about each other. This learning occurred through work on projects, like the Ramadan drawing exercise, during dialogic activities, such as the Land Day discussion, and when they worked side by side and sought each other's help, as in the experiences of Ruti and Khalil, and Yitzchak and Manhal.

Too often, experiences of intergroup contact look, feel, sound, taste, and ultimately are the same. It is perceived that there is one route to a certain end, and while some individuals may benefit from experiences such as a discussion group between Arab and Jewish youngsters or an event to bring together Blacks and Whites, these experiences will not touch everyone similarly. Simply put, each learner experiences the world differently and through different means of learning. Ultimately, it is the overlap of experiences of being in one another's company — thus creating a company zone — that allows students to begin to develop cultural fluency.

As stated earlier, I define cultural fluency as the ability to move back and forth between two cultures, to embrace one's own culture while understanding its relationship to the cultures of others. It is about being able to examine who you are, to examine your own cultural identity, which, perhaps ironically, cannot happen without being in the company of another (Bakhtin, 1984). Cultural fluency involves becoming multilingual, not simply in terms of verbal discourse, but also in terms of nonverbal communicative styles, as revealed in the drawing exercises. It is about ease of interaction, ease of movement, a code-switching that happens without giving up who you are, as in the case of the game of hide-and-seek. It is about being able to communicate both with and for the other, and being able to express another's perspective alongside your own. It is exploring and becoming aware of cultural histories and differences. Finally, cultural fluency is evident in activities or experiences in which speech patterns, ideas, and physical actions emerge and converge to occupy the same, equal terrain.

Students' cultural fluency begins to develop in large part because of and through their engaging consistently in one another's company. I remind the reader, however, that this is simply a beginning. Fluency continues to develop throughout one's lifetime. The Gal School students face many challenges as they develop cultural fluency, both inside and outside of the school. In particular, the world outside does its best to strengthen the walls between Jews and Arabs, rather than trying to tear them down. Segregation makes it difficult for Arab and Jewish children and adults to experience being in one another's company, thus limiting their opportunities to develop cultural fluency. In this classroom, the dividing walls were at least beginning to crumble.

Epilogue

The first graders whose experiences appear in this article are now taller, smarter, and trilingual, speaking Hebrew, Arabic, and English. They are fifth graders, the oldest of the five classes now at the school. The fifth-grade class is smaller than the original class of thirty-one. A few students have left over the years for various reasons, including fear. The political situation in Israel, particularly during the fall of 2000, has made this coexistence work at the school, and in the country, increasingly difficult. But the teachers, now five Arabs and five Jews, persist. And parents continue to enroll their children, although Arab parents, seeking educational opportunities for their children, are often the first to register their children.

Despite the tensions, there has been a growth in the bilingual/bicultural school movement across Israel, including the growth of the Gal School. In fact, the success of the Gal School has prompted the construction of a permanent school building, and the children and teachers will move there before the end of the 2002–2003 school year. The organization responsible for founding and promoting this school, the Center for Bilingual Education in Israel, has launched similar blooming schools. More than two hundred students are currently enrolled in these new schools, and a new generation is beginning to grow up under an educational model that may ultimately enable cultural fluency to flourish across the country.[8]

Notes

1. Gal is a pseudonym for the school, and all student names included in the text are pseudonyms.
2. Although I realize the heterogeneous nature of these broad cultural categories, I discuss the Jew/Arab dichotomy because it is the one stressed in Israel.
3. The term *cultural fluency* comes from the business field and describes how individuals work to understand and engage productively in another culture. Cultural fluency as described here stems from a close analysis of what occurred in this particular educational setting as Arab and Jewish students and teachers engaged in one another's company.
4. Contact also occurred beyond the school. These experiences included joint birthday parties, play dates, parents' meetings, family outings (e.g., a family beach trip organized by school officials), and field trips. This out-of-school context will not be discussed here.

5. One of the goals of the school is to have a ripple effect, its influence resonating beyond the school.
6. Another possible explanation for this work remaining at the level of contact may have to do with the fact that a number of pairs of students were not simply cross-cultural but cross-gender as well. However, examples cited later in this text suggest that this may not be the central issue.
7. The children often played soccer during recess. Cross-cultural participation during these games was inconsistent throughout the year. Sometimes the Jewish and Arab boys — the girls never participated — played together on mixed teams. At other times only the Arab boys played; the Jewish boys appeared less interested in playing. Further discussion of homogeneous groupings at the school can be found in Glazier (2000).
8. I am indebted to the teachers, students, parents, administrators, and founders of the Gal School for their willingness to allow me to spend a year learning with and from them. In addition, I want to thank the reviewers of this work, Melissa King and Jen de Forest, for their attention to detail, their helpful suggestions, and their guidance through the editorial process.

References

Allport, G. (1954). *The nature of prejudice.* Cambridge, MA: Addison-Wesley.

Bakhtin, M. (1984). *Problems of Dostoevsky's poetics.* Minneapolis: University of Minnesota Press.

Bar-Yosef, R. (1993). Melting-pot, multiculturalism and pluralism: The Israeli case. In K. Yaron & F. Poggler (Eds.), *Meeting of cultures and clash of cultures* (pp. 111–129). Jerusalem: Magnes Press.

Ben-Ari, R., & Amir, Y. (1986). Contact between Arab and Jewish youth in Israel: Reality and potential. In M. Hewstone & R. Brown (Eds.), *Contact and conflict in intergroup encounters* (pp. 45–58). Oxford, Eng.: Basil Blackwell.

Cairns, E. (1996). *Children and political violence.* Oxford, Eng.: Blackwell.

Coates-Shrider, L. N., & Stephan, W. G. (1997). The role of affect in cooperative intergroup contact. In R. Ben-Ari & Y. Rich (Eds.), *Enhancing education in heterogeneous settings: Theory and application* (pp. 47-67). Ramat-Gan, Israel: Bar Ilan University Press.

Cole, M. (1996). *Cultural psychology: A once and future discipline.* Cambridge, MA: Belknap Press.

Connolly, P. (2000). What now for the contact hypothesis? Toward a new research agenda. *Race, Ethnicity and Education, 3,* 169–193.

Delpit, L. D. (1988). The silenced dialogue: Power and pedagogy in educating other people's children. *Harvard Educational Review, 58,* 280–298.

Fine, M., Weis, L., & Powell, L. C. (1997). Communities of difference: A critical look at desegregated spaces created for and by youth. *Harvard Educational Review, 67,* 247–284.

Glazier, J., McVee, M., Wallace, S., Shellhorn, B., Florio-Ruane, S., & Raphael, T. (2000). Teacher learning in response to autobiographical literature. In N. Karolides (Ed.), *Reader response in secondary and college classrooms* (2nd ed., pp. 287–310). Mahwah, NJ: Erlbaum.

Glazier, J. (2000). *Balancing at the borders: Building cultural fluency in the company of others.* Unpublished doctoral dissertation, Michigan State University.

Gumperz, J., & Hernandez-Chavez, E. (1972). Bilingualism, bidialectalism, and classroom interaction. In C. Cazden, V. John, & D. Hymes (Eds.), *Functions of language in the classroom* (pp. 84–108). New York: Teachers College Press.

Hawkins, D. (1974). I, thou, and it. In D. Hawkins (Ed.), *The informed vision: Essays on learning and human nature* (pp. 48–62). New York: Agathon.

Johnson, D., Johnson, R., & Maruyama, G. (1984). Goal interdependence and interpersonal attraction in heterogeneous classrooms: A metanalysis. In N. Miller & M. Brewer (Eds.), *Groups in contact: The psychology of desegregation* (pp. 187–212). Orlando, FL: Academic Press.

Kozol, J. (1991). *Savage inequalities: Children in America's schools.* New York: Crown.

McLaren, P. (1995). *Critical pedagogy and predatory culture: Oppositional politics in a postmodern era.* London: Routledge.

Miller, N., & Brewer, M. (1984). Beyond the contact hypothesis: Theoretical perspectives on desegregation. In N. Miller & M. Brewer (Eds.), *Groups in contact: The psychology of desegregation* (pp. 281–302). Orlando, FL: Academic Press.

Paley, V. (1995). *Kwanzaa and me: A teacher's story.* Cambridge, MA: Harvard University Press.

Pettigrew, T. (1986). The intergroup contact hypothesis reconsidered. In M. Hewstone & R. Brown (Eds.), *Contact and conflict in intergroup encounters* (pp. 169–195). Oxford, Eng.: Basil Blackwell.

Rogers, M., Hennigen, K., Bowman, C., & Miller, N. (1984). Intergroup acceptance in classroom and playground settings. In N. Miller & M. Brewer (Eds.), *Groups in contact: The psychology of desegregation* (pp. 213–227). Orlando, FL: Academic Press.

Ruddle, H., & O'Connor, J. (1992). *A model of managed co-operation: An evaluation of Co-operation North's school and youth links scheme.* Limerick, Ireland: Irish Peace Institute.

Sidorkin, A. (1999). *Beyond discourse: Education, the self and dialogue.* Albany: State University of New York Press.

Simpson, J. A., & Weiner, E. S. C. (Eds.). (1989). *Oxford English dictionary* (2nd ed., vol. 3). Oxford, Eng.: Oxford University Press.

Singer, A. (1992). *Multiculturalism and identity. Democracy and Education, 6*(3), 24–28.

Sleeter, C. (1995). White preservice studies and multicultural education coursework. In J. Larkin & C. Sleeter (Eds.), *Developing multicultural teacher education curricula* (pp. 17–29). Albany: State University of New York Press.

Thorne, B. (1993). *Gender play: Girls and boys in school.* New Brunswick, NJ: Rutgers University Press.

Vygotsky, L. S. (1978). *Mind in society: The development of higher psychological processes.* Cambridge, MA: Harvard University Press.

Black Dean: Race, Reconciliation, and the Emotions of Deanship

JONATHAN DAVID JANSEN

As I drove through the gates of the University of Pretoria, I was already tense. Years of living under apartheid had involuntarily stressed the muscles and sharpened the mind to attack even the slightest hint of racial aggression when entering unfamiliar, White territory. It did not help that the entrance was guarded, as if by design, by one of the tallest buildings on the South African campus — a cold, white, rectangular edifice that dwarfed any soul entering the gates. The two security guards at the "boomgate" approached the car. I felt some relief, as both were Black: "Brothers," I thought. I announced that I was the new dean of education and that I would therefore appreciate entrance through the gates. One of the guards laughed uncontrollably: "Nice one, comrade, I've heard that one before." I burst out laughing, imagining myself in his shoes. I would certainly share the same incredulity if a Black man, coming through the gates of this former bastion of apartheid, suddenly declared himself dean. I went through the motions of filling out the visitor's form, having learned a long time ago that you do not argue with the person at the tail end of an authoritarian system — whether it be a university or a shop or a church. As I moved through the gates, I said to myself, "If I struggle with you, comrade, how on earth am I going to make it with my White colleagues?"

First Impressions: Symbols, Images, Uncertainty

I introduced myself to the vice principal of the university.[1] A wonderful person, I thought, who spoke English (rather than Afrikaans) and appeared quite genuine in his manner. This relaxed me. Together we walked over to the faculty of education, where I would take up the position of dean — the first Black dean in more than 100 years in this faculty.

The walk through the main entrance of the faculty building was riveting, and my tension returned. On the walls hung the imposing frames of four seri-

Harvard Educational Review Vol. 75 No. 3 Fall 2005, 306–326

ous-looking White men, all Afrikaners, all former deans. I tried to stare back, wondering how any student, Black or White, could possibly feel welcome and at home under the glare of these serious patriarchs. I had to take down these portraits, I thought. All along the corridor — a long bureaucratic hall with little doors, one alongside the next — ran a string of old black-and-white photographs dating back to the early part of the century, including one of the first graduating education classes of the University of Pretoria. In every photograph there were somber-looking individuals, grey and uniformed. Each photograph told a story. One was of the De Lange Commission: A few Black faces betrayed the identities of those regarded in much of the Black community as "sell-outs" and "collaborators" with the apartheid government of the 1980s as it sought, under pressure, to bring minimalist reforms to a crumbling, racist education system. Coming to this White university, was I simply another collaborator?

I had been invited to serve as dean at the University of Pretoria by its new and charismatic vice chancellor, who was determined to transform this former White Afrikaans university into an African institution that was, as he put it, locally relevant and internationally competitive. His vision and commitment created the space and the opportunity for bold leadership in the deanship. In order to make my decision to accept, I had consulted many friends, most of them radicals, then and now. Many of them felt that this was a chance to assist in creating a genuinely South African university rather than let this formidable institution continue as a White remnant of apartheid. Others reminded me, correctly, that I had always insisted I would never work in a White South African university. But surely things had changed, I rationalized. This was a South African university that needed to be transformed to serve all South Africans.

The Role of Emotions

I write about the deanship in terms of the emotional experiences of leadership by a Black person within what was once (and to some still is) regarded as one of the bastions of White Afrikaner power. To me "emotions" signal not a discussion about weakness or pathology, but a vital if neglected component of leadership in organizations. In the literature on leadership, organizational change, and educational reforms, the neglect and significance of emotion are being recorded simultaneously (Beatty, 2000; Fineman, 2000; Hargreaves, 1998; Hochschild, 1983; Maddock & Fulton, 1998). None of this literature, however, deals with emotions and leadership in the context of higher education or, specifically, matters of race and leadership in divided societies. The business and organizational literature still tends to focus on the management of other people's emotions, normally employees (Green & Butkus, 1999). The education literature focuses almost exclusively on the emotional labor of teachers (Hargreaves, 1998). What about deans? What about deans of faculties of education? What about Black deans? What about Black deans in White universities? I begin this writing, therefore, with both a positive impression of the small but growing literature on emotions and a recognition of its limitations.

In describing the process of educational change and the emotions of deanship, I focus on problems of race and gender and their interaction with institutional leadership. I show how correlates of institutional culture — such as authority, *beleefdheid* (politeness), silencing, and the construction of insiders and outsiders — constrain and instruct leadership action. I demonstrate how language functions as a powerful political instrument for restraining change. I conclude by arguing that leadership in such contexts requires constant emotional balancing, even as the task of change is relentlessly pursued.

The methodology employed in this study rests on recordings of critical incidents in my life as dean over a three-year period (July 2000 through March 2003) as dean of the faculty of education at the University of Pretoria, South Africa's largest residential university, with about 40,000 residential students and an additional 10,000 students in distance education programs. This record of events has been composed from direct observation of daily events, participation in meetings, interviews with faculty members, and the reading of university policies in relation to institutional practices.

Creating Initial Zones of Comfort and Authority

With the vice principal, I walked into a meeting of department heads chaired by the acting dean. All White, all men, all Afrikaners. They jumped to their feet to greet me. I encouraged the meeting to continue and left after a few minutes to survey my new office. The meeting with my secretary was most uncomfortable. She was in a state of panic, jumping around as the vice principal introduced me. For a senior Afrikaner woman who had served several White, conservative deans, this must have been most traumatic. Now I was alone, and I knew I had to break the tension. I called her in and encouraged her to tell me how she would like the office organized, and asked how I could best support her in her role as the dean's secretary. Gradually, we both relaxed. In those moments, I realized that I would have to initiate grounds for any *toenadering* (coming together, meeting to reconcile) with my colleagues by creating a nonthreatening, nonracial space in which they would feel free to talk, work, and live with their new dean. But my historical commitment to "servant leadership," while workable within the Black university I had just served as dean and vice principal, created emotional and political dilemmas in this White university. Seared into my consciousness as a young boy, I remember watching my father wash the floors in homes of rich White people in Cape Town, working as, in the language of those days, a servant. If I remained true to my commitments and values as a dean, servant leadership would mean sacrificing my time, energy, and emotions for the sake of my colleagues. On the other hand, this was risky and could be interpreted as the Black dean "knowing his place" and being willing to continue servitude in this White institution. I decided to take the risk, but with a high degree of alertness to any possible misinterpretation of my service commitments. Thus, in my interviews with each staff member, I made the point I had made more comfortably in other places: *I am here to serve you.*

During those individual interviews, and in the typical slog of meetings facing an administrator, I realized that to a large extent my fears about the acceptance of my authority as dean were unwarranted. At this university, unlike any other I had worked in, the dean was regarded as a great and formidable authority figure. I found that I was not expected to discuss things; I was expected to pronounce on things. The unbridled power of this university's administration and the efficiency of this cultural system was light-years away from the University of Durban, Westville, where I had worked as academic leader for six years.

A typical example of the cultural differences between the two university environments occurred when I was called on to chair a selection committee for a new faculty member. The selection panel included the union representatives of the academic staff and senior faculty. I listened to the discussions and tried to summarize individual positions around the table in order to formulate a proposal that reflected the consensus of the panel. After a majority of the panel agreed on a candidate, I asked one more time if this person's name could be forwarded to "admin" for appointment. The panel agreed. Then a senior professor caught me completely off guard. "Despite all this," he said, "at the end of the day it is your decision as dean as to whom you would appoint." I was stunned. The question ran through my mind: Why have a committee? I stayed with the majority decision.

My conversations with individual colleagues constituted the richest form of "data" on the institution, on the deanship, and on the possibilities for change. One of my standard practices as dean has been to meet with faculty members to inquire about their current rank as academics, their career goals, and the support they required from my office to attain their personal goals. The interviews were difficult, as colleagues struggled to open up with this stranger in their midst, a Black dean asking probing personal questions about their careers. At the same time, most of my colleagues really appreciated what they said was "the first time ever" that they were asked about their intellectual goals and what they required from the dean to make these goals happen in their lives.

Gradually, my colleagues opened up. Women academics were remarkably consistent as they recollected stories of abuse at the hands of former deans and department heads. A typical story was the following:

> I disagreed with the dean in a meeting. He called me aside and told me that that was the last time I would ever disagree with him again. He also told me that my career was over, and that while he was dean I would never get [a] pro-

motion. Final. I was destroyed, and I learned that you never, ever disagree with your dean.

If this confidence represented one voice among many, I would have considered the possibility that the colleague in question was a difficult person or that the dean in question had had a bad day. But I heard stories like these over and over again, in various forms, during those interviews. I tried to contain my anger at this devastating abuse of women academics (all of them White Afrikaner women). I realized that this was a systematic attack on women, which helped explain why there had never been a woman as dean or department head in this faculty of education's century of existence. It explained the relentless Dutch-Calvinist logic of the Afrikaners, in which the man was responsible to God and the woman to the man, "in subjection." It explained why women simply did not speak in any of the initial faculty meetings until I insisted on such participation. It explained the phenomenon of Afrikaner patriarchy.

Race, Gender, Distance, and Emotion

But there was another revelation that came through during these interviews with women faculty — the difficulty of dealing with a Black dean in private conversations about careers. The White women, with notable exceptions, were very uncomfortable in this private space. They did not appear relaxed, and they sat far away from me at the table. I noticed the distance and discomfort. I searched for explanations even as I conducted the interviews, trying as hard as possible to create a comfortable and relaxed atmosphere. It struck me that this was probably the first time in their entire lives, shaped and molded by apartheid, that my female colleagues had ever occupied space alone in a room with a Black male adult figure, who also happened to be their senior authority in the faculty. All those racist myths, I thought, about pure White women being ravaged by a Black man must have left indelible marks on the consciousness of these colleagues. I realized, in those moments, that the struggle would have to be fought on both sides of the table. My own anger at what I perceived to be a racial and gendered distancing had to be managed, and their fears about racial and gendered stereotypes had to be overcome.

Trust was to become the essential ingredient in relationship-building. I had entered a microcosm of the real-life cauldron of racial reconciliation after apartheid, something that was difficult, messy, emotional, and unpredictable. It certainly lacked the glamour and elegance of Nelson Mandela's celebrated autobiography, *Long Walk to Freedom*, or the triumphant mood of the myriad of publications on the South African "miracle." In my first nine months at the University of Pretoria, it was women academics who gradually began to open up, to share, and to commit to a vision of transformation in which I made it clear that women and Black academics would be readily affirmed in my tenure as dean.

My relationship with Afrikaner men was very different. Some of them simply did not show up for the interviews, despite repeated attempts by my secretary to schedule these meetings. After about a month, this got to me, and I suspected that there might be real racial dilemmas faced by these White men (no more than five) in discussing what inevitably were personal and revealing topics. I decided to call them myself and insist that they show up immediately for the planned interviews. I did not want to use that tone as a dean, but I believed that this situation, bolstered by my intuitive sense that race was the problem, justified my insistence.

The men, with few exceptions, did not open up during those interviews. They were "fine." The fact that they were not publishing was not because they did not know how to do research, but simply because there was no time. My job, I was told, was simply to provide the space and the resources, and they would "get on with the job." It was as simple as that. These interviews were probably the most difficult for me. It was here that I realized that huge emotional and political chasms had to be crossed. The men across the table had all done military service, under compulsion, for the apartheid state. Some, I noticed from their curricula vitae, were captains in the apartheid military. Others were members of a secret society of White men, the Afrikaner *Broederbond*.[2] I had hated these institutions — the visible and the secretive — as my political awareness developed while I was an undergraduate student on the politically charged campus of the University of the Western Cape. Later, as a young teacher in the volatile townships of the rural and urban Western Cape, I witnessed the viciousness of the apartheid machinery in the daily lives of Black people. Now I suddenly felt these emotions awakened as I tried to cross racial chasms in the face of, at best, the quiet hostility of the faculty members. Within months and with my encouragement, some of these reluctant men left the faculty of education, either on early retirement or resignation. They were not going to change, and I was not going to allow them to stagnate; a simple and decent way of dealing with this was for them to leave. Gradually, but after a much longer time than with the women, several of the Afrikaner men also opened up and became centrally involved in the administration of the faculty of education.

From Beleefdheid to Openness

With both Afrikaner men and women, there was another serious impediment to faculty transformation, something called beleefdheid. It is a strange Afrikaans word that probably means politeness, but carries with it a sense of hypocrisy — polite to the extent of being dishonest. The institutional culture, I observed, was averse to public conflict.

How did this problem express itself during my efforts to democratize the faculty of education? After undertaking a strategic review of the strengths and limitations of the faculty, I presented a detailed report to a full meeting of all academic and administrative staff, together with an action plan. The report contained some dramatic, wide-ranging proposals for action, including a one-year forced sabbatical for eighteen young academics to give them exposure to the best universities in the world, and a series of steps to build a more diverse faculty that affirmed Black and women colleagues.

There was, after an hour of presentation, not a single word of critical feedback from this packed meeting. In fact, the few who spoke said simply that "this was fine." I realized there was a problem. I would never know how well or badly I was doing as dean because beleefdheid insists that you do not confront anyone, tradition requires that the dean must be right, and past experience suggested that disagreement with authority could terminate a career. The only opposition I received to my action plan was my suggestion that the portraits of those four patriarchs should come down. But it came in the form of an anonymous letter slipped under my door. This puzzled and infuriated me. I encouraged and looked forward to challenge and criticism, but not the cowardice of anonymous correspondence. I sent the word out on the online bulletin board that such notices were unacceptable in a democracy. At the next heads of department meeting, I bemoaned the fact that the only criticism, though couched in a very *beleefd* manner, was delivered under my door. Halfway through my lecture, the former acting dean raised his hand and confessed, "It was I."

I now was even more determined to change the culture of the faculty by encouraging greater openness. I used the faculty online bulletin, called *Opforum*, to list some provocative ideas for change in the hope that it would stimulate discussion. Nothing happened. I noted this silence on *Opforum*. Very apologetic comments started to come from younger academics, but at least there were grounds for dialogue. I did not evaluate those comments or counter proposals, but simply allowed much of the dialogue to flow. Several comments from the older academics were intensely angry and awkward, representing the opposite of direct, intelligent engagement. It was as if after decades of being shut up, their words were not coming through in the constrained yet challenging manner typical of rigorous academic exchange. I accepted that it would take time to modify these angry outbursts into the kind of critical, informed dialogue that remained riveting in style and content. As new faculty joined from the outside, *Opforum* became a regular site for expressing ideals, for engaging new policies, for challenging the dean.

Faculty Leadership within the Broader Institution

It is one thing trying to change a faculty within a university; it is another matter when the entire institution is steeped in a top-down, authoritarian culture that reinforces and replicates this negative behavior across the campus. The most troubling event in which I participated as a dean at the University of Pretoria was my first senate meeting, the senate being a universitywide decisionmaking body. About 165 persons attended — mainly White, male Afrikaners. A thick agenda appeared; in less than an hour, the meeting was rushing to a close. The chairperson, a fine scholar and a graduate of *Tukkies*, had done what his predecessors had done before: simply list an item and make a decision.[3] There was no discussion, and even when discussion was called for, the audience knew not to engage. One of the issues on the agenda concerned the restructuring of the faculty of veterinary sciences. Although drastic cost-cutting measures and possible staff losses were on the horizon, there was still no serious discussion. I raised my hand and asked, "What is the educational rationale for such a decision in the vet school?" I explained that while the financial rationale was clear, the senate, being the highest academic decision-making body in a university, had an obligation to ask questions about the academic basis for faculty decisions. I was clearly out of order, and I sensed that immediately from the silence that followed. There was an awkward fumbling as the chair and the dean of the veterinary school scrambled for explanations outside of the financial calculus that had come to determine so much of what universities in South Africa (and the rest of the planet) do under conditions of managerialism, markets, and globalization. I was tolerated with polite answers. Then something else completely unexpected happened.

A young Afrikaner actuarial scientist, apparently buoyed by this unexpected questioning in the hallowed halls of the senate, started to raise his own series of questions about the restructuring. To put it mildly, he was eaten alive. He suffered a series of aggressive counter-punches from the leadership of the institution. To his credit, he refused to back down. I got the distinct impression that the reason this young professor was so aggressively treated was that he was supposed to know better; he was one of the *volk* and should have known his place in an authority-driven culture where knowledge, wisdom, and the final word rested with his superiors. I could be tolerated as the ignorant outsider — the Black dean who, if challenged, would raise inevitable racial questions about White aggression in this cathedral of Afrikanerdom. This experience, more than any other, made me realize how faculty-based transformation can be impeded and constrained by institutional inertia with respect to critical issues of dissent, democracy, and affirmation.

Black Dean, Public Intellectual

Curiously, as the number of Black academics increased in the first nine months of my deanship, race was seldom mentioned as a problem within the faculty. In fact, it appeared as if the senior staff who stayed were quite eager to appoint Black academics in some of the departments. But the problem of race did surface once in an unforgettable experience. I had always regarded myself as a public commentator on education policy issues and a public critic of racism in any society. So it appeared perfectly natural that when I was asked by a left-wing Dutch journal to write and comment on race and racism six years after apartheid, I would write about my personal observations and experiences. I wrote about the persistent attacks on Black people by White farmers, about the (Black) CNN reporter and her husband who had just been attacked by White policemen, about racial slurs I tolerated every day in the suburbs of Pretoria, about Black children segregated within classrooms of allegedly desegregated schools, and so forth. When the article appeared, in Dutch, I placed the journal on the reading room table where guests waited to see the dean. Shortly thereafter, two of my senior colleagues, both Afrikaner men, came to see me. They had read the article. They were offended by what I had said about Afrikaners. The picture, one colleague insisted, was "one sided" and did not talk about the wonderful things happening among races in the country. Afrikaners were portrayed in a negative way. I was told, politely, that the article needed to be "balanced."

I was left surprised and slightly off balance. I explained that public writing was a matter of personal perspective, that every case cited in the magazine was authentic, that my goal was not to add to the literature on "the South African miracle," and that I write what I like. It was the first and the last time that race ever surfaced in a discussion during my deanship. That article was circulated to all the principals of Afrikaans high schools in the area: Everybody now had a view of the Black dean. I realized then that race and racism, neatly packaged and stored away by reconciliation politics and institutional beleefdheid, must be put on the table for frank and honest discussion. As in so many parts of South Africa, we had not worked through the emotions and experiences of racism in ordinary life, in established institutions, in schools or universities or bars or churches. This unfinished business could come back to haunt us.

The Language of Leadership: When Is It Race? When Is It Language?

If race was not the obvious and explicit dividing line in the faculty, the problem of language certainly had potential to derail transformation. I had not understood, until I came to Tukkies, how deep, sensitive, and entrenched the issue of the Afrikaans language was to the university community, its alumni, and to language activists on the outside. The *laager* was drawn on the language issue by language politics on the outside and changing language demographics on the inside.[4] The minister of education made it clear that, historically, Afrikaner universities were using language (that is, the Afrikaans language) to limit access to non-Afrikaans language speakers (that is, mainly Black students). On the other hand, the changing language demographics within some Afrikaans universities had raised alarms in Afrikaner cultural circles and among prominent academics.

At the University of Pretoria, for example, the most dramatic shift in student demographics was not in terms of race, but in terms of language. By

2001, the sharp increase of English-speaking students (a large proportion of whom were White) on the campus had approached 50 percent, with the university now forced to offer more and more classes in English, in addition to those traditionally offered in Afrikaans. In the faculty of education, this problem was whispered about in the corridors and tearoom but, as usual, seldom directly with the dean. Only once did a senior colleague raise the complaint — as if it were not his own — "*dat die plek verengels*" (that the place is being Anglicized). What he meant was that the increasing number of Black and non-Afrikaans-speaking staff (I had also recruited White English speakers as part of my broad-based strategy for diversity) had changed the language of communication in the faculty. I decided early on not to address the language issue directly, but to allow the changing staff composition to create the new language policy. At some point, of course, the language problem was bound to erupt. And it did so in a most gentle manner.

I was chairing a faculty meeting in which a number of policy issues were being decided on — though not language. The participants in the meeting made various comments and offered feedback almost entirely in Afrikaans; occasionally there were comments in English. I used both languages, though mainly English, at this meeting. An additional problem was that the documentation for the meeting had been written only in Afrikaans. Toward the end of that meeting, in a calm but deliberate way, a Black South African academic, recruited from her graduating doctoral class at Michigan State University, stopped the meeting with these comments, "I am a new member of staff. I am really trying to participate in this meeting and to make a contribution to the faculty of education. But I am finding this very difficult because all the documents and communication are in Afrikaans. I appeal to you to consider those of us who do not understand Afrikaans." A sympathetic silence fell on the meeting, largely because of the kind and gentle manner in which the point was made. I decided not to lead the response from the chair, and to see what happened. Senior colleagues in the room insisted that, as a practical matter, documentation should be produced in both languages and one even insisted that (also as a practical matter) our meetings should be conducted in English only when non-Afrikaans speakers are present. The proposal on dual-language documentation received enthusiastic body-language responses; the English-only meetings, perhaps less so. But this interruption was perhaps the single most important change in the cultural and language direction then taken in the life of the faculty of education.

The language problem will not go away as easily, as this episode might suggest. Since then, I have participated in several national and media-inspired debates on the future of Afrikaans. I still hear quiet grumbling, especially among older staff, about the loss of status of Afrikaans in the life of the faculty. I still wonder why the debate on Afrikaans in the twenty-first century remains so deeply mired in the history of Afrikaner-English struggles, ongoing since at least the 1890s. And I have realized that, despite being a Black dean, my growing competence in Afrikaans creates access to people and politics that I would not have enjoyed without this simple but powerful device.

My most important challenge as dean, though, came in my relationship with the principals of Afrikaans schools. Soon after I arrived, I reorganized the annual School Principals' Symposium, an annual meeting of school leaders from the traditionally White schools around the university. The invitation list was broadened so that the symposium would include a more diverse grouping of principals, including those from the Black schools around Pretoria. In addition, a Black jazz ensemble consisting of former street children was hired to perform the music. The two speakers at the symposium were both English-speaking, from Australia and the United States. I did not realize that this reorganization would cause dissension in the ranks of the Afrikaans principals. As was the custom at the university, none of these complaints reached my office directly — the discontent was shared with my senior colleagues and with the marketing division of the University of Pretoria. Another source of discontent was the concern expressed among some of the school principals that the place was being Anglicized. Indeed, the marketing brochures and the new website appeared only in English. To make matters worse, a member of my staff had sent one of the principals an invitation — in English! The discontent that followed was, again, not raised with me directly but with my colleagues. But not with the Black dean. How was this issue to be approached? These tensions had potentially serious repercussions for the faculty of education.

The school principals sent messages, again indirectly, that they would advise their students against registering at the University of Pretoria since it no longer represented the language and cultural interests of Afrikaans speakers. They would rather redirect their students to the Potchefstroom University for Christian National Higher Education, or to the Rand Afrikaans University, or even to Stellenbosch University in the Cape. This would be disastrous for undergraduate education, since Afrikaans families were the only ones in South Africa that still sent their children to study to become teachers (and ministers). Students from Black families simply had not found teaching attractive as a profession, a perception fueled by violence in schools, retrenchments of teachers, negative images of teaching reinforced by politicians, and the popular television series *Yizo Yizo*, which portrays constant incidents of rape, murder, and dysfunction in township schools. In a very real sense, therefore, the future of the faculty depended on the steady recruitment and enrollment of White, Afrikaans-speaking students. But I did not act on the basis of either veiled threats from the Afrikaans schools (as taxing as this was emotionally) or because of a narrow financial interest in the sustainability of the faculty of education (as attractive as this was strategically). I decided to act on the basis of a simple principle, namely, that all universities belong to all South African students — and that included Afrikaans speakers. My role as dean, therefore, was to ensure that Afrikaans speakers felt as comfortable at the University of

Pretoria as any other language group, and I would do my best to ensure this. I started visiting each principal of the Afrikaans high schools, to introduce myself, to present the faculty's commitment to that school, and to inquire as to how our service could be better rendered to the Afrikaans-speaking community of schools. It would be part of a broader set of visits to Black and English-speaking schools.

The anxiety about Afrikaans will continue in my relationship with schools, for it is only generated in part by what the faculty of education does. These concerns are nested within the broader actions of the university itself, as well as the political machinations of government officials who often use the language issue for symbolic "point scoring" in the face of a declining number of Black students passing high school and entering university. But the relationship between a faculty of education and its "feeder schools" demonstrates the emotional dilemmas of a Black dean in powerful ways. On the one hand, I had to recognize the privileged and protected role afforded Afrikaans in the past century, often at the expense of indigenous African languages; on the other hand, I had to promote a public position that encouraged a broader language inclusiveness — even for White Afrikaans speakers. It was often difficult to constrain my own emotions and feelings about language injustice in South Africa (after all, I speak Afrikaans because I was forced to under apartheid). As a dean, these constraints on my emotions have been very difficult to manage, especially when I have felt that language was being used as a proxy for race. In particular, I became concerned that some insiders and outsiders described language as the primary problem of institutional transformation when it was actually the changing racial demographic that really unsettled them.

Black Outsider, White Insiders: Negotiating Authority

If the rules of the game in institutional life were based simply on open and fair participation by all persons, regardless of color, then my life as a dean would be relatively easy. I realized that after I left a room of all-White administrators, I could not always be assured that what was agreed among us would stand after consultation with fellow *broeders* (brothers). It struck me time and again that I was, and for the foreseeable future would be, an outsider.

My outsider status became especially clear when the minister of education decreed that the college of education (Pretoria Teachers College) be incorporated into the university as part of the newly restructured higher education system. The decision by the government to close or incorporate more than 100 colleges was motivated by reports that the quality of teacher preparation at most of these institutions was very poor; that these colleges, as artifacts of apartheid, were irrationally distributed across regions of the country to serve previous racial and ethnic communities; and that the colleges were over-producing teachers at a time when teacher rationing was being pursued to reduce the salary bill to the national government.

Until 2001, colleges were part of the provincial education departments and were therefore regarded, in legal terms, as "a provincial competence." Incorporation would mean that colleges would lose their status (and existence) by becoming part of a university (or technikon) and, therefore, would be classified as "national competence" under direct authority of the minister of education. Before my arrival in July 2000, the University Council and the College Council had already agreed on incorporation for reasons that made rational sense: The two institutions, both White and Afrikaner, had long relationships of working together, they were within a 10-minute drive from each other, and the cultural fit, of course, was perfect.

It was evident to me that the agreements reached before my arrival had several flaws. For example, in letter and spirit, the agreement anticipated the wholesale transfer of staff from the college into the university and, for most of them, into the faculty of education. This created three problems. First, there was a competency problem, since most of these staff were not trained to do university-level teaching and research. Second, there was an equity problem in that the majority of college staff were White and simply bringing them into the university would further hinder the goal of building racial diversity in the faculty of education. Third, there was a financial problem in that the traditionally small lecturer-to-student ratios in a college meant that if the college was reconfigured into a university, the faculty of education would be seriously overstaffed, given the university tradition of one lecturer teaching large undergraduate classes. This meant that as a consequence of the incorporation process, of the ninety-odd staff, only about fifteen to twenty would make the selection process.

Time after time, when I met the university administrators, they not only appeared to understand the problem as I sketched it but they vigorously supported my proposal for taking less staff. I initially was buoyed by the fact that my senior colleagues supported me on this matter. But as soon as I left their offices, the senior college administrators would march in and change the substance of our agreement. Initially I thought I should relent a little, since these processes are always political and involve serious horse-trading among stakeholders. But later it really frustrated me that I could not understand why my seniors would agree with me so vociferously, and then change the agreement. It was only much later that I understood my disadvantage. These were colleagues who had worked together for many years, as broeders, and had forged cultural, linguistic, social, and political ties that were firm and loyal. They attended the same church, served on the administration of the same rugby and sports clubs, and shared *braais* (barbeques) and fishing trips. In addition, their children knew and married each other. My proposals disturbed those racial and cultural ties of the fraternity. Once I realized what was going on, I tightened my proposals for staffing, refused to back down, and sent some strongly worded correspondence to my administration. I am told by several sources that as the position of the Black dean became clear, there were some nasty scenes in which traditional loyalties, racial loyalties, and cultural loyalties were questioned. I understood then, in graphic terms, how the institutional rules were culturally written in ways that exclude some and include others. I also realized that leadership required assertion that challenged those rules, or else the transformation of White universities would remain an illusion of the political class and, more importantly, an impediment to greater inclusiveness.

Black Dean: Afirmative Action Appointment?

Dealing with the university administration and staff was one kind of experience; dealing with students was a different emotional challenge in the deanship. The challenge in the undergraduate class was that more than 95 percent of the students were White, and of this group, almost all were Afrikaans speakers. The reverse was true of the postgraduate class. I have always enjoyed working with students, which explains why I have always taught a class, regardless of whether I was dean or vice principal. One day, a young staff member asked me whether I would do a guest lecture for her class in comparative education. She mumbled something about my need to meet students and her awareness of the fact that I appeared to be shielded from them. What happened next, seconds before I took the podium, rendered me speechless.

The senior faculty member for comparative education had also decided to attend the class, along with other (I suppose) curious members of the academic staff — since I could not believe they had an interest in the role of symbolic politics in comparative education. The senior colleague introduced me to the students, displacing (by custom and invitation) the person who invited me. She said:

> This is our new dean. Now normally when one meets someone like this, we think of affirmative action and that such a person came in because they are Black. Well, I wish to assure you that this is not the case with this man; he studied at Stanford and is a prolific researcher, and widely respected. You may even have seen him on television. So I introduce to you Professor Jansen.

Until that point, I had decidedly not thought of myself in relation to affirmative action. Now that my colleague had raised the question, I suddenly felt aware of the argument that those bright, White eyes in front of me might very well see me as a special treatment candidate. Even if they did not, the seeds for such thought had been planted among students in this, my maiden lecture. For the first time in my life, I started a lecture not knowing quite what to say. As is so often the case, I had to submerge these emotions for later reflection and get on with the job. I would like to think that the students in that lecture were soon made to forget that this was the dean, or that he was Black, or that he came in through the back door. However, I could not be sure.

Asserting Personal and Professional Authority

Another incident I wish to draw on in my emotional journey as dean in a historically Afrikaner university concerns my relationship with the academic community outside of the faculty of education. I experienced two strains in this relationship with the broader campus. One strain was a strong expression of support for changing the faculty of education. Many of the "education" initiatives on campus, I found, had proceeded as if there was no faculty of education. I pondered whether the law school would allow a major discussion on legal issues to be chaired and led by the medical school or the education faculty. This isolation of the faculty of education, I was told repeatedly, was a result of our own doing. People on the campus felt that education was aloof, outdated, inward looking, and, quite simply, a nonentity in the educational life of the campus. The historical attachment to "fundamental pedagogics," an Afrikaner variant of Dutch phenomenology with a particularly conservative bent, was referred to in derisory terms on the campus. To this group of people, the new dean could rescue education and create new synergies with other faculties and departments. The second strain was a strong expression of hostility toward my leadership within the campus. I noted that there were several senior colleagues on parts of the campus who were decidedly unfriendly, even challenging, of the new dean. Two episodes come to mind.

The first episode occurred when a senior colleague from administration came to instruct me on how to submit annual faculty reports. There was no discussion, simply a statement of "this is what I want you to do." I have always reserved judgment, in initial contacts of this sort, as to whether this was a racist attitude or simply the kind of authoritarian style that this group of people used in communication. However, I perceived this as an aggressive approach by a colleague. In this case, I assumed that both could be true and asked him to leave my office. It was the first time that I "snapped" and let down my emotional guard with fellow colleagues from another part of the campus.

Sometimes my emotions are provoked by a very different kind of encounter that on the surface appears friendly but may carry with it a particularly venomous racism. One of the deans insisted on greeting me with the phrase "my friend." In another time and place, this might be regarded as a genuine, sincere effort to make a new person feel welcome. But this was South Africa, and I had witnessed countless times how in a group where the Black person was a minority, a typical White male greeting would acknowledge everybody else by their first names or titles, and then turn to the Black person with the line, "my friend." It was a distinctly patronizing, offensive practice among White males in South Africa. I have never in my life inside South Africa heard a White man introduce himself to another White man in such terms. The first time my fellow dean used the term I let it slide, not ready so early on to really challenge this provocative racialized practice. The next time, however, I stopped, and in a large audience made it very clear that he would never again address me as his "friend" — in part since I hardly knew him, and in part because I had a name. He never did this again.

Taking the Message More Broadly

My most vivid recollection of the University of Pretoria was in a public lecture. The university holds a regular series of lectures on "innovation," and this typically involves some high-tech motivational speech on the growing significance of science and technology on campus and in the world. I was asked to present and entitled my talk, "Why Tukkies Cannot Develop Intellectuals." I knew this was putting the ideological cat among the long-rested Tukkies pigeons. I also knew that this was a platform to address a broader set of concerns about institutional transformation, such as racism, sexism, authoritarian practices, and their suffocating effect on the development of intellectuals. I seriously thought I would be disinvited, given the title alone. I prepared a written paper, something I seldom do for campus talks or school presentations, because of the time that this takes when you have three or four such invitations every week. But I wanted to think through my experiences and record them, since I hoped the talk could really chip away at the core of authoritarian practices and beliefs that continued to keep the University of Pretoria from becoming a genuinely humane environment for Afrikaner women, Black people, and any person who dared to hold themselves as different from the dominant, White, patriarchal, "Christian" culture. I expected few people to show up for this lecture. The senate hall was packed beyond my expectations.

I argued that intellectuals develop under one of two conditions: severe repression or genuine democratic conditions — neither of which existed at the University of Pretoria. I inquired whether Tukkies had ever publicly acknowledged how its laboratories were used as research sites for the apartheid scientific and military establishments. I suggested that "the only thing worse than being Black at Tukkies was being a woman." For while there was historically a symbolic point at which Black South Africans could claim to have been free, such a moment had never materialized for Afrikaner women. I reported on incidents of student abuse in our authoritarian system and the hypocrisy of religious cover for what we do. I demonstrated that our institutional commitment to change was narrow and instrumentalist, and at odds with building a culture of innovation in which ethics, politics, and values would become the steering mechanisms for moving toward an open, diverse, and democratic learning culture. There was sustained and intense applause. Speaker after speaker acknowledged most of what had been shared as accurate; there were accolades and encouragement. Several noted that this was the first time in their twenty or thirty years that an event like this had ever happened on campus. I did not expect this. My goal was to rattle conceptual and ideological cages, not to be praised.

This was a turning point in my own emotional disposition toward Tukkies. In those moments, I realized that in this large university there was a critical mass of scholars with an acute understanding of the cultural and ideological problems weighing down on the institution — problems that stood in the way of a broader transformation of the University of Pretoria. I also understood, toward the close of the event, that being a Black dean held distinct advantages. I could see and respond to institutional problems from a position that few other colleagues shared. It was an emotional high point, for I sensed the possibility not only of change, but of transformation.

Reflections on Race, Method, Emotions, and Deanship

My initial objective was simply to record my life and experiences as a Black dean at the University of Pretoria. I did not intend to publish this material, in part because I was uncertain of its external and internal reception. As I started to discuss the material with friends inside and outside the faculty, there appeared to be a genuine interest in reading and engaging the experiences represented in this article. With the passage of time, it also became easier for me to talk about these often sensitive human emotions and institutional experiences. What started as a personal and private set of reflections gradually became a public and professional matter. The last objective of this article, therefore, is to describe the complex and difficult process of institutional transformation from records of personal observation and through the lens of human emotions.

In my conceptual frame I place my life, as it were, on the line. I open up to the emotional challenges and struggles of being a Black dean in a White university. I try to show that actions in the deanship are not simply rational and technical decisions, but deeply emotional and political decisions. I demonstrate that these emotions emerge from and are shaped by the very real and recent context of apartheid, with its dual horrors of racial oppression and economic exploitation. I try to shake off innocence by showing that as dean I am not immune to intense personal struggles with change and commitment in the context of a historically White university, or to organizational culture as it shapes and sustains racial and gendered attitudes among staff and students. I have tried not to present either myself or the people I work with as "emotionally anorexic" (Fineman, 1993, p. 9) but as people living through and expressing the real dilemmas, uncertainties, contradictions, failures, and successes of a changing institution and a changing country seven years after the legal termination of apartheid. In declaring my methodological point of departure, I present moments of emotional withdrawal or "backing up," perhaps even silence, but also moments of emotional assertion, perhaps even aggression.

On the one hand, therefore, I am implicated in Hochschild's (1983) disturbing observation that "this [emotional] labor requires one to induce or suppress feelings in order to sustain the outward countenance that produces the proper state of mind in others" (p. 7). On the other hand, I also express moments that Sergiovanni (1992) labels as

> leadership by outrage . . . the practice of kindling outrage in others [that] challenge[s] the conventional wisdom that leadership should be pokerfaced, play their cards close to their chest, avoid emotion, and otherwise hide what they believe and feel (p. 130).

This kind of writing also raises, of course, the issue of ethics. Is it right, in the first place, to write other people's stories? I think this is fairly common and, in the case of people living, it is good methodological and ethical practice to consult them. But this is relatively easy in cases where the stories told are positive ones about personal achievements, such as Reddy's (2000) life histories of Black South African scientists, or heroic struggles such as Lather and Smithies's (1997) account of North American women living with HIV/AIDS. But what if, as in this case, the stories are less celebratory of individuals or even an institution, as captured in this narrative built around critical incidents? I believe that in both cases, but especially the latter, it is important to share the draft writings with the individuals or incidents written about, not only to inform them about the narrative but also to secure their advice and comment in improving or sharpening the story of changes and continuities in a faculty of education. In addition, I have tried not to mention names of specific individuals or list the dates of specific events. At the same time, I believe it is critical to bring into open dialogue the kind of writing and reflection that challenges the status quo, whether in political or methodological terms, as part of an ongoing process of transforming not only how we practice education, but also how we think about and experience it.

The research context for reflection on race, emotion, and the deanship is a very turbulent one. The University of Pretoria, as should by now be clear, is a historically White university with roots in Afrikaner history, politics, and language. It is not only South Africa's largest residential university, but also its wealthiest. It has benefited from leadership by a particularly entrepreneurial vice chancellor with a strong personality and a keen insight that has helped the University of Pretoria enjoy a credible reputation after apartheid. In his terms, the university had to become "internationally competitive and locally relevant." Yet, in a memorable phrase, he recalls that "while I might have turned the ship around, it still drifts in the same direction."[5] He has made firm if not sufficient commitments to challenging the racial privileges of the University of Pretoria. He hired three Black deans and one (Afrikaner) female dean. He invested considerable resources in attracting Black doctoral and master's students. And, he has made "employment equity" one of the focal points for change during his tenure. Despite all these actions, he has not been able to transform qualitatively and substantively the cultural capital with which power is sustained at lower levels in the university. By this I mean curriculum changes, changes in staffing at departmental levels, and changes in the overall institutional culture and practice.

South African universities are beginning to realize that simply changing the structures of an institution is one thing; changing the cultural essence of a university is a completely different challenge. This reflective essay shifts the emphasis from the structural and organizational to the personal and individual; from policies declared to practices experienced; from official intentions to everyday life; from behavior to emotions. At the same time, the narrative in this essay shows the interplay between the individual and institutional levels of university life.

Studies on the interaction between race and gender in institutional contexts are virtually unknown in South African educational and social research. This narrative not only describes the different roles between White men and White women in relation to the Black dean, but also the changing roles of these three groups as the project of faculty restructuring proceeded. Afrikaner women had a stronger sense of new "space" for their academic advancement through various policy messages from the dean's office. Afrikaner men, for whom ascendancy to departmental headship, and the deanship, was almost a rite of passage, clearly felt a sense of loss in the new deal. What requires further research and reflection in this context is the role of institutional culture in Afrikaans universities as yet another variable in determining gender-race interactions with the Black dean over time (Jansen, 2005). Such a narrative would have to take into account the various traditions served by Black universities, White English universities, and the White Afrikaner universities as outlined in the historic address of Professor Jakes Gerwel in 1987 on the occasion of his inauguration as vice chancellor of the University of the Western Cape in Cape Town, South Africa.

There is still very little written on the complex ways in which race, gender, culture, and history come together to define the possibilities and the limits of change. In this respect, I am very conscious of the fact that while race has been privileged in the account of life inside Tukkies, I am also clear in the narrative that gender is a critical factor in institutional life. The people most threatened by the changes in South Africa, and at the University of Pretoria, are White Afrikaner men. Time after time I was told as dean that the changes undertaken in the faculty in fact disadvantaged men. And this was true. For over 100 years women never became department heads in the faculty of education, and now male ascendancy was no longer inevitable. I had announced, several times, that the next dean would be a woman and that 2000 was the last year that there would be no woman as department head. Young and middle-aged men, in particular, were especially distraught that they now had to compete on an even slate with women. Whereas men previously were almost guaranteed top positions, this was now dependent on a fair and equal process that was also committed to affirming women. In this regard, the writings of Cameron McCarthy and others (McCarthy & Crichlow, 1993) offer powerful starting points for understanding the relational terms between Black and White women academics in universities.

In looking back on this written account of my experiences as Black dean, I hope to have made several marks on the growing literature on leadership in education. First, I hope to have shown that in leadership research, context matters. It is the broader context of apartheid, and how it was resolved, that enabled this kind of leader to emerge (I would never have held such a position under apartheid) and that required this kind of leadership to build and then bring together an increasingly diverse faculty. It is not, however, enough to assert that context matters; I hope this narrative shows how context shapes and constrains decisionmaking within the deanship.

Second, I hope to have broken through the decidedly ethnocentric character of research on leadership that holds Western norms and trends as the standard against which to judge particular kinds of leaders and leadership styles. For example, I am not at all sure that Western disillusionment with heroic leaders is applicable in a context that enabled Nelson Mandela to emerge and in which there is little cynicism with, in fact even expectation of, strong and visible leaders. Third, I hope to have shifted the focus from a voluminous literature on school leadership to the relatively sparse research terrain on academic deans as leaders.

Fourth, I hope to have created windows for viewing leadership not as a simple technical, rational, and logical frame approached through a toolbox of finite techniques, but as a complex political and emotional process in which the outcomes are not always predictable and measurable. Finally, I hope I was able to lay the groundwork for further studies on leadership under conditions of social transition. In the context of South Africa's negotiated political settlement, this essay shows that transformative leadership inevitably involves living with and balancing a set of tensions: the tension between affirmation and inclusion, between retention and restitution, between caring and correction, between accommodation and assertion, and between racial reconciliation and social justice.

Notes

1. The vice principal in South Africa is equivalent by rank to a vice president in a North American university.
2. There were often two ways to know that one was a part of this secret society. First, colleagues would volunteer this information and even list this association on their curriculum vitae. Second, it was generally known that no senior position in the academic, corporate, or political world could be attained without Broederbond membership.
3. The University of Pretoria started as the *Transvaalse Universiteits Kollege* (Transvaal Education College), with the acronym TUKS and the affectionate reference, Tukkies.
4. The laager refers to the ways the Afrikaners, during the great movement (or great trek) from the Cape colony into the interior during the nineteenth century, would

draw their ox wagons into a circle to defend against an attacking enemy. The word has come to take on symbolic meaning to refer to any defensive or inward-looking behaviors of those calling themselves Afrikaners.

5. Johan van Zyl, former vice chancellor, in private conversation with the author.

References

Beatty, B. R. (2000, December). *Emotion matters in educational leadership.* Paper presented at the Australian Association for Research in Education Annual Conference, Sydney, Australia.

Fineman, S. (1993). *Emotions in organizations.* Thousand Oaks, CA: Sage.

Fineman, S. (2000). *Emotions in organizations* (2nd ed.). Thousand Oaks, CA: Sage.

Green, T. B., & Butkus, R. K. (1999). *Motivation, beliefs and organizational transformation.* Westport, CT: Quorum.

Hargreaves, A. (1998). The emotions of teaching and educational change. In A. Hargreaves, A. Lieberman, M. Fullan, & D. Hopkins (Eds.), *International handbook of education change, part one* (pp. 558–575). Dordrecht, Netherlands: Kluwer Academic.

Hochschild, A. R. (1983). *The managed heart: Commercialization of human feeling.* Berkeley: University of California Press.

Jansen, J. D. (2005). The color of leadership. *Educational Forum, 69,* 203–211.

Lather, P., & Smithies, C. (1997). *Troubling the angels: Women living with HIV/AIDS.* Boulder, CO: Westview/Harper Collins.

Maddock, R. C., & Fulton, R. L. (1998). *Motivation, emotions and leadership: The silent side of management.* Westport, CT: Greenwood.

Mandela, N. (1995). *Long walk to freedom: The autobiography of Nelson Mandela.* Randburg, South Africa: Macdonald Purnell.

McCarthy, C., & Crichlow, W. (Eds.). (1993). *Race, identity and representation.* New York: Routledge.

Reddy, J. (2000). *Life histories of Black South African scientists.* Unpublished dissertation, University of Durban Westville, South Africa.

Sergiovanni, T. (1992). *Moral leadership: Getting to the heart of school leadership.* San Francisco: Jossey-Bass.

"I Was Born Here, but My Home, It's Not Here":

Educating for Democratic Citizenship in an Era of Transnational Migration and Global Conflict

THEA RENDA ABU EL-HAJ

For Palestinian youth living in the United States in this era of *intifada* (the Palestinian uprising against the Israeli occupation) and post–September 11 politics, navigating everyday life in schools and communities is often a difficult task. The Palestinian youth with whom I have been conducting research for the past three and a half years negotiate their way through a school environment in which they are frequently framed by pervasive and pernicious public discourses and practices that render their communities invisible, save for one dominating image — that of "terrorist." The stories that these youth tell of everyday encounters with the equation Arab = terrorist range from the absurd to the frightening. One ninth-grade boy was sent to the school office for discipline when his pronunciation of "tourist" was misheard as "terrorist" — a misapprehension that took a legal challenge to have it expunged from his permanent record. With some frequency, peers accuse Palestinian youth of carrying a bomb, and these unsubstantiated taunts often lead to unwarranted searches of bags and lockers. One teacher told a girl who was wearing a *hijab* (the headscarf worn by some observant Muslim women) that she looked "like a disgrace in that thing," while another teacher threatened a girl with a disciplinary sanction if she did not remove hers — a threat that was painful even though it was not carried out.

At moments, conflicts arise between Palestinian (and other Arab) students and their teachers and non-Arab peers because of significantly different perspectives on global politics. Lamia, a high school junior, had recently moved back to the United States after living in the occupied West Bank for eight years. One afternoon, she arrived at the school's Arab student club visibly upset. She related to the group that she had been sent to the disciplinary office earlier that day after an argument with her teacher over a map of Asia, in which the western half of the continent was missing. Lamia recalled:

Harvard Educational Review Vol. 77 No. 3 Fall 2007, 285–316

> I look at [the map] and asked him, "What happened to Palestine?" He said, "Palestine is not a thing." So I felt mad. . . . So I told him, "What do you mean it's not a thing?" He said, "It's not a thing, so I don't want to hear anything about it." I looked behind him and saw a big map on the wall. I said, "Why don't you point out on the map where it says Palestine?" I thought he was going to say Israel, but he didn't say Israel. So I just gave him a chance to say something. Just that it exists. Not even a thing! So he ignored me. I said, "You want me to get up there and show you?" He said, "No, forget about it. I said it's not a thing, and that's it." I said, "Look, I came from Palestine, and you're saying it's not a thing. Then you need to tell me, where did I come from?"

Lamia's outrage that a teacher would deny the existence of her homeland may partly be anger born of his refusal to acknowledge the experience of having lived most of her years in the occupied West Bank. However, it is also a sign of the deep aspirations that she, as well as her peers and community, have that one day they will behold an independent state of Palestine. It signals their sense of belonging to a national community that exists beyond the borders of a recognized nation-state. Many of the Palestinian youth in this study have experienced similar encounters with teachers who refuse to acknowledge both the legitimacy of their aspirations for an independent state and their everyday experiences living under Israeli occupation in the West Bank. Unfortunately for Lamia and many of her peers, these encounters often ended, as it did in her case, with disciplinary sanctions.

In this article, I focus on the complex and contradictory ways that Palestinian American youth from one immigrant community are positioned by others and position themselves in relation to notions of citizenship and national belonging at this particular historical moment. Moreover, I examine school as a key context within which these young people grapple with these complex identities and affiliations. Three key concerns frame my argument. First, in concert with a growing number of scholars (Hall, 2002, 2004; Levinson, 2005), I am concerned that existing frameworks for understanding the education of immigrant youth in the U.S. do not adequately account for the relationship between education, citizenship, and nation formation. Second, while examining how a community of Palestinian American youth construct their national and citizenship identities in relation to two imagined national communities (Anderson, 1983/1991; that of the United States, especially as they encounter it inside schools, and that of Palestine, as they experience it in their families and community), I explore the complex push-pull dynamic that these youth endure. On the one hand, through everyday discourse and practices inside their schools and communities, Palestinian youth experience their positioning as outside the "imagined community" of the U.S. nation, framing them as "enemies within." As a result, they struggle to feel a sense of belonging to the nation in which they hold citizenship. On the other hand, these Palestinian American youth view their U.S. citizenship positively in terms of legal and political rights and economic access. Yet, they tie their national identities — their sense of where they belong — to a Palestinian homeland.

Finally, I look to the experiences and perspectives of these youth to consider how democratic citizenship education, especially as it is practiced inside public schools, must change in order to account for the dynamic nature of belonging in this era of transnational migration, as youth are positioned and position themselves in relationship to multiple imagined communities. Educating immigrant youth for substantive inclusion in society — the capacity to participate fully and contribute meaningfully — depends on helping them develop a sense of belonging and the tools for civic engagement within *and* across the boundaries of the nation-state in which they reside.

Education and Nation Formation

Scholars of immigrant education have sought to explain factors that contribute to groups' differential patterns of incorporation into the U.S. economy and society and the variability in their academic achievement. They focus on issues such as cultural, national, and religious identities (Ramos-Zayas, 1998; Sarroub, 2005); sociohistorical trajectories (Ogbu & Simons, 1998); and the institutional processes of schooling through which youth come to take their place in the racialized hierarchy of the nation (Lee, 2005; Lopez, 2003; Olsen, 1997; Valenzuela, 1999). Globalization and the transnational nature of contemporary immigration raise new questions for the study of education (Suárez-Orozco, 2001). The prevalence today of transnational communities suggests the limitations of nation-states as organizing boundaries for people's personal and political sense of belonging (Castles & Davidson, 2000; Suárez-Orozco, 2001; Yuval-Davis, Anthias, & Kofman, 2005). Hall (2004) argues that most studies of immigration have investigated the processes of assimilation and acculturation for immigrant youth, ignoring the processes of nation formation at work in schools and society. She criticizes research that, in defining culture in terms of group beliefs, traditions, values, and identities, focuses analyses of immigrant acculturation around questions of how they preserve or adapt these "cultural" practices in their host country. Such analyses reify the nation and nationalism, rather than explore the cultural politics through which national belonging is negotiated in relationship to immigrant communities. This can compromise immigrant students' capacities to participate as engaged and empowered members of their new society.

Hall (2004) suggests that the extent to which immigrant communities can be assimilated depends in part on the symbolic creation of the nation as an imagined community. This idea of an imagined community references the ways that nations are ideologically constructed and reconstructed through discourse (e.g., media, public debates) and political practices (e.g., state policies, civil rights movements) as the boundaries of belonging are negotiated over time in relation to different groups of people (see Anderson, 1983/1991). Racially and/or ethnically oppressed groups within modern nation-states, for example, have had a tenuous relationship to this imagined community, being symbolically framed as less than the ideal citizen or as perpetual foreigners (see, e.g., Hall, 2002; Ladson-Billings, 2004; Olsen, 1997; Ong, 1996). Importantly, the symbolic construction of an imagined community — of who truly belongs to the nation-state — is closely related to how people are differentially positioned to exercise a range of rights that facilitate their capacities to participate fully and on an equal basis in the social, political, cultural, and economic spheres of the nation-state (Castles & Davidson, 2000; Yuval-Davis et al., 2005).

Imagined communities can also reflect a sense of national belonging common to people who are struggling for a nation-state, as is the case, for example, with Palestinians. Immigrants are often navigating their sense of identity and belonging in relation to multiple national communities. Thus, considering immigrant incorporation as intimately interwoven with practices that regulate both the physical and the imagined borders of the nation suggests a need to understand how immigrant communities are positioned and position themselves in relation to various national identities (Ong, 1996; Yuval-Davis et al., 2005). In addition, we must examine how this positioning regulates immigrants' capacity to mobilize rights and resources that facilitate participation in the economic, social, cultural, and political spheres of the nation in which they now reside. Schools play an important role in the construction of the symbolic boundaries of the nation — in constructing who is and is not a member of the nation — and in the provision of resources with which immigrant youth learn to belong to and navigate their new society.

In the post–Cold War era, Palestinian and other Arab and Muslim youth living in the United States and other Western nations face a particular form of exclusion from the imagined community of these countries (Abu El-Haj, 2006). With the end of the Cold War came the rise of a new ideology that posited Islam as inimical to Western values and "culture" (see especially Huntington, 1996; Lewis, 2002; and for critiques, see Mamdani, 2004; Said, 2001). Today, members of Muslim communities in Western nations are racialized in ways that position them as "enemies" to all that the West is seen to stand for, such as democracy, secularism, and women's rights. The speed with which Muslim, Arab, and South Asian communities across the United States were attacked and harassed after September 11, 2001, reveals the consequences of such positioning and the vulnerable place these communities occupy in the public's imagination of the nation. In important ways, since September 11, there has been a redrawing of the symbolic boundaries of the U.S. nation to include (if partially and conditionally) African American, Latino, and East Asian communities, while positioning Arabs, South Asians, and Muslims as true outsiders (Volpp, 2002).[1] State-directed policies that create a new category of people who are excluded from accessing the rights and protections usually afforded to citizens, or even those guaranteed by international law, have contributed to this symbolic redrawing of boundaries (see Akram & Johnson, 2004; Moore, 1999; Murray, 2004; Volpp, 2002). It is against these contemporary politics of nation formation that Arab American youth from immigrant communities must forge their citizenship identities.

Research and the Community Context

This article draws on data from a multisite ethnographic study of Palestinian and other Arab youth that I have been conducting for the past three and a half years in a large U.S. city.[2] Here I focus on data gathered from one site — a neighborhood high school. The youth with whom I work at this school are members of a relatively small Palestinian Muslim immigrant community living in the city.[3] A majority of their families comes from the same village in the occupied West Bank. The first member of the community moved to the United States in 1908, and the subsequent economic and political struggles of life under Israeli occupation, which began in the 1960s and intensified throughout the 1980s and 1990s, drove many more families to migrate to the United States. Here, for the most part, members of these families own small businesses (e.g., grocery stores and food trucks) or work as sales clerks and managers in family-owned and other local businesses. Income generated in the United States is used to support family members who have remained in the West Bank.

The Palestinian youth in this research are all U.S. citizens; however, most are also transnational migrants. Many of them were born in the United States but spent the majority of their childhood years in Palestine, often living with their mothers and extended families while their fathers worked in the United States. Members of this community move back and forth between the United States and Palestine for both short trips and extended periods of time. However, the inception of the second intifada in 2000 made daily life in the West Bank arduous and dangerous, and many families returned to the United States.

My relationship with this group of Palestinian youth grew out of an invitation from a local Arab American community organizer. It was his hope that, as a Palestinian American and an educator, I could help address some of the conflicts and tensions that had arisen in several schools across the city in the wake of September 11. The students in this study attend Regional High, the largest high school in the city.[4] With a student population of around 3,500, the school can feel overwhelming and chaotic. The Palestinian group is small compared to the school's other racial and ethnic groups. However, the Palestinian youth manage to find each other between classes and during off periods, often retreating to the school library to hang out in a relatively quiet space. According to school district statistics for the 2003–2004 school year, White students represent the largest racial group (approximately 1,400 students); Black students make up the second largest (approximately 1,000 students);

Hispanic and Asian/Pacific Islanders are the next largest groups (approximately 500 in each group); and American Indians comprise a small minority (six students). The school district does not record statistics on Arab students; they are classified, in accordance with the federal guidelines, as White. Administrators and students estimate that there are around one hundred Arab students enrolled in the school at any given time. Approximately 20 percent of the student population qualifies for free or reduced-price lunch.

My initial contact with Regional High was in response to the administration's request for help after several racial fights broke out between Palestinian and Russian immigrant students. As the community organizer and I met with Palestinian parents and young people to discuss these fights, stories emerged about feeling alternately invisible and persecuted within the school. Some felt that Palestinian boys, in particular, were being disproportionately disciplined, suspended, and expelled because racialized images of Arabs as terrorists framed these male students as threats. Although some students acknowledged a genuine effort on the part of the principal and a few other administrators to reach out to their community, myriad experiences with peers, teachers, and the school's disciplinary team had fostered a difficult and often hostile school climate that they felt they had little power to change.

In the fall of 2003, upon hearing these stories from students and families, three Arab American colleagues and I joined Anne Larson — a Regional High teacher and peace activist who had worked hard to be an ally to Palestinian and other Arab students — to form an Arab youth group in the high school. Of my three Arab American colleagues, one was the founder of a local Arab American community arts organization, another was a college student who was a member of the local Palestinian community and was working as an AmeriCorps volunteer for an Arab American community organization, and the third was a law student at a nearby university. As we all worked with the high school students and developed our program, I also acted as a researcher and collected data about our project.[5] Our aim in forming this group was to create a space in which Palestinian youth could share their knowledge, experiences, and stories using a variety of media (writing, photography, and video) to communicate with a broader public.[6] This work has been presented at youth film festivals, local community events, and teacher workshops. Attendance at youth group meetings ranged from as few as three students to as many as thirty; typically, we had six to eight committed attendees. Over the next three years, we explored the limited and limiting images of Palestinians and Arabs in contemporary media and political discourse; we discussed social and cultural issues within the Arab American community; we shared stories of discrimination and acts of kindness inside and outside of schools; we examined histories of immigration; we watched documentary and fictional films about Palestine; and finally, working with a video artist, some of the youth produced short films that served as counter-stories to the dominant media images of Palestinians as terrorists.

Throughout this time, I documented these meetings as part of my research. At the same time, as I got to know students, I invited them to participate in a larger research study through extended individual interviews. In addition, I invited four students (two male and two female) to be focal participants for this research. These four students were chosen for more intensive participation because they were representative of the range of ways the youth negotiated transnational identities and their schooling. A research assistant and I followed these students through their school days and, on some occasions, to community and family events. We also conducted extensive interviews with their teachers and with key administrators in the school. In the following sections, I draw on field notes and student interview data to examine the complex and multifaceted perspectives these youth expressed in relation to these national and citizenship identities. These perspectives illustrate how the youth work to construct a sense of belonging in relation to their transnational community, their status as U.S. citizens, and their routine positioning as enemy outsiders to this nation, especially inside their school.

Discourses of Citizenship and Belonging

Samira began a self-description by saying, "I am from Palestine." A sixteen-year-old junior when we first met, Samira was born in the United States, and, with the exception of one brief visit as a toddler, she had not spent time in Palestine. Nonetheless, her life experiences within her family and community engendered in her a powerful and profound Palestinian national consciousness. Samira, like other Palestinian youth with whom I work — both those who have and have not spent significant time in Palestine — articulated what is for her a complex relationship between the ideas of citizenship and national belonging. These youth acknowledged that their U.S. citizenship was legally important, but they identified as *being* Palestinian, as belonging to an imagined community that is engaged in a struggle for liberty and an independent nation-state (for a historical perspective, see Khalidi, 1997).

Being Palestinian

To a person, the youth I interviewed stated that they were Palestinian. Although a few, like Samira, had lived their entire lives in the United States, the majority lived transnational lives, moving back and forth between their homes in the United States and their villages in what they usually referred to as the *bilaad* (homeland) or *Falisteen* (Palestine). Khalida was born in the United States, but she lived in the occupied West Bank for seven years before returning to the United States as a teenager. Her description of her national identity resembled that of many other students:

> I don't think of myself as both. I only think of myself as Arab — a Palestinian, actually. Most people ask me, "You're a Palestinian American?" I told them,

> "No, just Palestinian." Then they start getting stupid about it: "And then how do you know English?" I'm like, "No, I'm American Palestinian. I just want to be a Palestinian."

Khalida's words — her hesitance and multiple clarifications — indicate the complexity of forging identities that are culturally produced at the nexus of multiple, intermingling systems (Hall, 2002). She simultaneously acknowledges ("I'm American Palestinian") and rejects an identity that is *both* American and Palestinian. Khalida's discourse suggests that being Palestinian American is fraught with tensions and can involve a fractured rather than a hybrid or even hyphenated sense of identity for these youth.

Adam, who lived a majority of his eighteen years in his family's West Bank village, distinguished between *being* Palestinian and *having* U.S. citizenship. "I'm an Arab, Falistini [Palestinian] Arab. I got an American citizen[ship]. I was born here, but my home, it's not here." Adam's identification as a Palestinian seemed more fundamental and less negotiated than Khalida's, and it was tied to his connection with a "home" in Palestine. A majority of the youth in this study, including Khalida, felt that their home was in Palestine. Adam and many of his peers spoke of being Palestinian as an essential quality, one that was inherited at birth. Zena, a seventeen-year-old senior who had lived her entire life in the United States, said, "I always say I'm Palestinian no matter what, because that's where my mom and dad and all our ancestors are from."

Being Palestinian was also explained in reference to a notion of an "authentic" cultural identity: the belief that there are particular immutable cultural practices that represent authentic ways of being Palestinian. The parameters defining this authenticity, however, were a source of constant debate among the youth. To Zayd, the distinction was clear:

> To be a Palestinian, you're an Arabic speaker. You follow the customs. You go up to the Friday prayer. It's either that or you go to the coffee shop. It's one of the two. You go do prayer. You go to the coffee shop. You just do the customs.

For Zayd and his peers, these "authentic" Palestinian customs were inextricably intertwined with religious and gendered practices. Friday prayer, as well as other religious practices — such as fasting during Ramadan and strict guidelines for relations between males and females — offered key markers of Palestinian identity that were, for Zayd and his peers, inextricably linked with Islam. Zayd's reference to the coffee shop — a segregated space in which Arab men gather to discuss everything from business to families to politics — also highlighted gender distinctions in everyday practices that were not restricted to religious norms.

For Zayd, the distinction between being Palestinian and being American often entailed perceiving sharp differences between the cultural practices of the two groups. Asked about what makes someone an American, Zayd replied:

> You don't have to be a citizen. To be an American is to do the things they do here. You see something on TV and you do like them. You become, as they say, Americanized. Most of [the girls], they're from a new age, not like the old age where they don't go to school. I'm saying there's no problem with going to school. But I'm saying they have it in their head where they're not cooking for their man. They're not doing this, not doing that, and "I'm going to do this if they want it or not" . . . their thinking is Americanized. It's not like that in our background, our culture and stuff.

As Zayd explains, *being* American, rather than indicating one's citizenship status, reflects both everyday practices (e.g., women not cooking for men) and ways of thinking that assert independence, particularly for the girls and women in the community. In line with a familiar pattern among some immigrant communities, the regulation of female bodies and sexuality offered the most obvious site for producing a culturally authentic identity for these youth and their families (Abu-Lughod, 1998; Yuval-Davis & Werbner, 1999; Yuval-Davis et al., 2005).

This authentic gendered identity was hotly contested, as girls and boys in the afterschool club continually debated what it means to *be* Palestinian. The boys in the group supported restrictive roles for girls in public spaces. For example, male members of the afterschool club threatened to withdraw from performing the *debke* (a traditional folk dance) at the school's multicultural fair if the girls insisted on dancing in public, and a few of the girls in our group had to battle their brothers for permission to stay after school to participate in our activities. Most of the male students also believed that wearing a *mendeel* (another word for a hijab) was a religious and/or cultural requirement of Islam. Among the girls, there was much more disagreement about appropriate gender roles. Some girls defended their right to dance in public, while others viewed public performance as unacceptable for religious and cultural reasons. Similarly, some believed girls should wear a mendeel and others did not. Importantly, although girls within the community made different decisions about public performances or religious dress, they all defended the choices they made as being compatible with acceptable cultural and religious identities and practices.

These debates reveal that although these Palestinian students describe the existence of an authentic cultural identity, the parameters of that identity reflected the processes of cultural production — that is, these youth are constructing variable ways of being Palestinian within and through everyday practices that draw on their experiences living within and across multiple communities and national spaces. In addition, even as youth define, contest, and negotiate their national identities through everyday practices that are flexible, evolving, and reflective of multiple cultural influences, they construct Palestinian and American identities as dichotomous (for similar observations of British Sikh youth, see Hall, 2002).

Although ancestry and cultural authenticity were key aspects of how the youth in this research defined what it meant to be Palestinian, these were not the only, or even the most important, aspects of carving out a Palestinian identity. In large part, their strong national identification emerged from the experiences that many of these youth and their families had while living under Israeli occupation. Khalida, who had asserted her desire to be only Palestinian, explained her feeling, saying, "Most of the reason I feel that way is because Palestinians suffered a lot. And they're still suffering, actually." Her knowledge of this suffering came from her seven years of residence in the West Bank. Zayd described how his identity as a Palestinian emerged when, as an early adolescent, he returned for two years to his family's village in Palestine: "Before I went to my country I didn't look into [being Palestinian] at all. I went back home and then I seen three people die in front of me, and it was a big change." Zayd reported being politicized by witnessing the shooting of peaceful demonstrators and by being subject to numerous curfews, and he returned to the United States with a different sense of himself as a Palestinian Arab. He defiantly contrasted conditions in Palestine with the commonly perceived threats of city living in the United States: "I'm from the West Bank. Do you know what the West Bank is? You know? It's like [here in this city] there are thugs that steal from people. You know, I'm from the West Bank, around people throwing a missile at you." In contrast to Zayd's family home, the village where a majority of these youths' families came from was, according to their reports, relatively free from daily confrontations with the Israeli army. Nevertheless, all the youth who had spent time in the West Bank spoke of the harsh conditions of the occupation, including restricted movement, house searches, confrontations with soldiers at the checkpoints, and a crippled economy.

Whether shaped by their experiences in Palestine or not, the strong national and cultural connection to Palestine that all of the youth expressed was maintained and reinforced through the practices of everyday life in the United States. As part of a close-knit community that was mostly related by birth or marriage, these young people spent their in-school and out-of-school hours in each other's company, rarely interacting with peers or adults who were not family members. Some recent immigrants spoke almost exclusively in Arabic, and even those who were completely comfortable speaking English shifted seamlessly between the two languages. Late spring marked the start of the wedding season, and weekends were often taken up with many nights of festivities that included up to one thousand relatives and friends. In many ways, these young people felt they were part of an extended village. Girls, for example, often remarked how quickly news of their activities, especially rumors about impending engagements, reached their relatives in the bilaad.

The students' connection to a kind of transnational village was amplified by their nationalist longing for an independent state. Palestinian youth expressed a strong sense of belonging to a state that is not yet recognized or independent. This became apparent from the first activity we undertook in our afterschool club. Drawing on Islamic art forms, each participant decorated one tile to represent her- or himself. These tiles were then assembled into a mosaic that was bursting with symbols of Palestine. The Palestinian flag and the Dome of the Rock appeared frequently, and some tiles showed the word "Palestine" written in Arabic calligraphy or the black-and-white checkered *kafiyya* (headscarves) that are symbols of the resistance movement.[7] These youth also consistently displayed these symbols of Palestinian national identity on their clothes, backpacks, keychains, and jewelry.

These symbols represented the ways that Palestinian youths' lives were constantly informed by their yearning for an independent national state, and it reflected their community's ongoing efforts on behalf of this ideal. They attended local and national peace rallies and, through Arabic media sources and books shared by older relatives, they kept themselves informed about the Israeli-Palestinian conflict. Relatives, community members, and those youth who had lived in Palestine shared stories about living under occupation. Families and individual young people contributed to charitable causes that support education and medical care for Palestinian youth in the Occupied Territories and in refugee camps in Lebanon, Syria, and Jordan. Families hosted Palestinian youth from the West Bank and Gaza as they underwent medical care in the United States for wounds sustained in the conflict. Thus, through their everyday practices in the United States, these families continually constructed and sustained a Palestinian national consciousness, a deep connection to their home villages in Palestine, and aspirations for a future independent national state.

The experiences of these Palestinian youth illustrate the complexity of negotiating national identities and civic and political participation in contemporary times. Transnational migration, supported by modern transportation and communication technologies, has yielded more opportunities for youth and families from immigrant communities to maintain affiliations with and ongoing participation in multiple nation-states, even as they move temporarily or permanently across the boundaries of nation-states (Louie, 2006; Ong, 1999). For this Palestinian transnational community, border-crossing has not diminished a sense of national belonging or the longing for a nation-state; they maintain a strong connection to the imagined community of their "homeland" (see Louie, 2006; Maira, 2004). Thus, modern citizenship entails a contradiction: While the technologically enabled flow of goods, information, and people across borders weakens the salience of nation-states, the idea of belonging to a national community maintains a strong hold on the imagination (Yuval-Davis et al., 2005).

U.S. Citizenship as a Privileged Legal Status

Transnational communities, then, raise questions about the nature of citizenship in contemporary times. Citizenship, rather than being linked to a shared national identity, is increasingly connected to civil, social, cultural, and political rights that afford people the possibility of participating effectively in society (Castles, 2004; Castles & Davidson, 2000; Soysal, 1994). The youth in this study speak explicitly about this uncoupling of national and citizenship identities. They identify strongly with a diasporic Palestinian community, but they distinguish this sense of national belonging from their U.S. citizenship status and the particular rights it affords. U.S. citizenship is considered a privileged status, highly valued for the economic, political, civil, and social rights it offers youth and their families.

Perhaps the most important function of citizenship (and legal residency) for these youth is to facilitate economic opportunities that are unavailable "back home" to Palestinian families, due to the harsh conditions of the occupation. Adam dreamed of a future in which he could "go back home," but he argued that the current conditions in Palestine made this impossible in the near future:

> Back home in this time, it's hard to find a job. And it's hard to go to school. Over here you're free. You can do whatever you want. And we own two stores, and we're working. We're getting money, and we're sending money back home.

Samira viewed her privileged citizenship status in terms of the responsibility it entailed to family members in Palestine:

> For me and other Palestinians living in the United States of America, I think that there is . . . a big reason why my family and me are living here. And while we are living here, we are supporting those in Palestine. I have relatives who live there, and my dad is working here in America, and he's taking the money and sending it to Palestine in order for them to pay their bills or get food or clothes and everything else. So over here I feel it is our duty to work and, you know, help out the people over there because over there right now, there are no jobs.

U.S. citizenship affords Adam, Samira, and other Palestinian families the right to work and earn money with which to support their families in the West Bank, who face extreme financial hardship from living under military occupation. Thus, like many transnational immigrants who are driven to migrate from their homelands because of political and economic conditions, these Palestinian families look to the U.S. nation-state as a place to realize various social rights, such as the right to work and opportunities for education (Castles & Davidson, 2000), while working on behalf of and maintaining a connection to those "back home."

Palestinian youth also pointed to social rights (especially the right to an education) as important features of residing in the United States. Social rights reference a broad range of rights that guarantee citizens minimum standards for economic security, well-being, and social inclusion, such as the right to work, equal educational opportunity, and entitlements to health and other welfare services (Abowitz & Harnish, 2006; Castles & Davidson, 2000). Many students said they had experienced, or were aware of, how difficult it was to get an education in Palestine because of the frequent closure of schools. Others spoke positively about some aspects of U.S. education, contrasting the stricter, more traditional schooling system in Palestine with the more relaxed atmosphere in U.S. schools. Some of the girls noted that there were more opportunities in the United States for them to finish high school and attend college. A majority of the students spoke about their parents' desire for them to obtain professional training, even though most of these students were not academically well-prepared by their high schools and either did not pursue higher education or entered community colleges with little aspiration to finish a four-year degree.

Khalida pointed to important social rights in the United States that did not exist to the same extent in Palestine:

> In a way, I feel comfortable here because we have a lot of rights here; for example, child abuse. A lot of people abuse their children there and no one can do anything about it. And where I live [in Palestine] there is no source of medical attention, no hospitals, no clinics. We have to transfer and take transportation about 15–20 miles away from where we live just to get medical attention and medical help. And now with the checkpoints it takes even longer. So a person can die just on the way there. And here every other county, not a county, just a neighborhood, there's a clinic or a hospital or somewhere you can go. That's the only difference.

Khalida contrasted positively the social services available in the United States to the lack of comparable services in the occupied West Bank. Even with the erosion of the welfare state in the United States, the guarantee of social rights here far exceeds those in the occupied West Bank. For Khalida, these positive experiences did not outweigh her deep desire and preference to return to Palestine. Asked what being American meant to her, she replied, "It is just a place I was born. If I had the option, if it was up to me, if I had the option to choose between living here and living in Palestine, I'd go back there." Khalida knew the struggles of life under occupation; however, she missed the small village where she felt "more comfortable" and known. Despite this desire, Khalida and her family felt they did not have an option to return given the current conditions in the West Bank. From their stories it is clear that this Palestinian community, like many other transnational communities, was compelled to emigrate by the unequal global distribution of social, economic, political, and civil rights.

Exercising what Ong (1999) calls "flexible citizenship," transnational communities mobilize social, political, and economic resources across national borders to respond to shifting political and economic conditions (see also Maira, 2004). Moreover, U.S. citizenship provides a basic civil right denied many Palestinians: the right to move across borders. For the community with whom I work, U.S. citizenship facilitates travel to and from their village in the

West Bank. Zena, a seventeen-year-old senior, put it this way: "As an American citizen, you have the right to go and come back and do whatever you please. It gives you more respect, I think." Zena's words suggest that holding U.S. citizenship is both a legal permit that allows border-crossing, as well as a source of some degree of respect and protection from the routine harassment that many Palestinians have experienced at borders across the globe. Importantly, the power of U.S. citizenship is linked to U.S. and other Western nations' global dominance in that this citizenship affords members greater economic, political, and civil rights than those of many other nations.[8]

Border crossings hold a particular place in Palestinian consciousness. Rashid Khalidi (1997) writes:

> Borders are a problem for Palestinians since their identity — which is constantly reinforced in myriad positive and negative ways — not only is subject to question by the powers that be, but is also in many contexts suspect almost by definition. As a result, at each of these barriers which most others take for granted, every Palestinian is exposed to the possibility of harassment, exclusion, and sometimes worse, simply because of his or her identity. (pp. 1–2)

The borders of nation-states have separated Palestinian people from their places of birth and from their family members. Many Palestinians carry no citizenship, only travel documents issued by Israel, Egypt, or Lebanon that list them as stateless Palestinians and allow them limited mobility across national borders (Khalidi, 1997). Even Palestinians who do carry the citizenship of some nation-state, including that of the United States, are often treated differently at borders. They may be granted more respect, as Zena suggests, but they are not guaranteed freedom from harassment or exclusion, as exercising their right to move across borders is often accompanied by increased surveillance, harassment, or questioning, such that their freedom of movement is constrained and racialized.[9] Nevertheless, these Palestinian youth were well aware that U.S. citizenship offers them relative freedom that Palestinians typically lack to traverse borders. These border crossings highlight the contradictory nature of the modern era: Amidst global flows of people, information, technologies, and products, nation-states maintain a strong central role in regulating and maintaining their borders (Soysal, 1994; Yuval-Davis et al., 2005).

These young people also described the importance of U.S. citizenship in terms of other freedoms that involved their political, civil, and social rights (see Castles & Davidson, 2000). Some students referenced access to a legal system (through which, for example, they could attempt to contest unfair school expulsions) and the right to vote as valued freedoms that they and their relatives in Palestine struggled to exercise under the conditions of the occupation. At our first afterschool club meeting following the 2004 U.S. presidential election, Adam was thrilled about having voted for the first time, despite his disappointment that his candidate was not chosen. Another student, Leila, appeared well schooled in the rights and responsibilities of citizenship, which she had learned through civic education in school (Abowitz & Harnish, 2006). She explained:

> You have to feel some connection [to the United States], because you were born here and . . . you carry citizenship from here. So you're considered a citizen of the United States of America. So if you're considered a citizen, you have to commit to your duties toward the United States. . . . Every vote counts. Every voice can be heard, like they say. And to me, being a citizen, registering to vote, is important because like they have all the bulletins, "Register to vote because your voice could be heard." Every voice could be counted. One vote could make a difference. . . . So, once I turn 18, I'm going to register to vote.

To a greater degree than many other Palestinian youth, Leila articulated a sense of connection to the United States because of her citizenship and expressed a commitment to fulfilling the traditional roles and obligations that citizenship entails. However, her words (here and elsewhere in her interviews) suggest hesitation and a tenuous relationship with this nation-state: "You carry their" — she broke off, and then continued — "you carry citizenship from here." Thus, her words, as well as those of other Palestinian students, presented a view of U.S. citizenship as a possession that she carried rather than an identity she inhabited.

These Palestinian youth drew a distinction between citizenship and a sense of national belonging ("having" citizenship versus "being" Palestinian). At times they spoke of the United States in terms that highlighted their position as outsiders: They described "living in *their* country" and "carrying *their* citizenship." However, they also donned the protective cloak of their citizenship to argue for the important rights that U.S. citizenship afforded them. They continually discussed and negotiated the shifting boundaries between "ours" and "theirs," between "being American" and "being Palestinian." The distinctions these young people make between national identity and citizenship suggest the ways modern citizenship is a complex affair for those defined as outsiders to the imagined national community. On the one hand, modern democratic citizenship has increasingly been defined around a set of rights that is not circumscribed by membership to particular ethnic, racial, or religious groups; these rights are, rather, due all individuals by virtue of universal human rights. On the other hand, in the United States and other multicultural states, the boundaries of national belonging and the rights that follow from this belonging are being shaped by the politics of immigrant incorporation and those of the "global war on terror" (Castles & Davidson, 2000; Hall, 2004; Soysal, 1994; Yuval-Davis et al., 2005).

Everyday Conflicts over the Politics of Belonging

The boundary that Palestinian youth draw between citizenship and national belonging was not constructed solely as a consequence of their transnational connections to Palestine. It was negotiated at the highly charged border of everyday interactions in the United States with peers and authority figures within their school, as well as in the community at large. The youth with whom I work often seemed thankful that their families had remained relatively unharmed after September 11, 2001, especially in light of the widespread attacks on Muslim, Arab, and South Asian communities across the country (Ahmed, 2002; Ibish, 2003; Volpp, 2002). However, the many stories they shared about family members harassed in their neighborhoods and other public places, "random" stops by police officers, and confrontations with teachers and fellow students reflected how frequently they were positioned outside the imagined community of the nation.

Some of the youth feared that the privileges of citizenship were tenuous for members of their community. In the aftermath of September 11, some worried that their communities might be rounded up en masse or expelled from this country. Many knew the history of Japanese internment during World War II and discussed the possibility that Arab Americans might face a similar fate. Adam often reminded others that in contrast to Palestine, there was a working legal system in the United States that they could use to protect their rights, yet he did not completely trust this system. In fact, he had arrived home one afternoon to find Secret Service agents searching his house; his mother, confused and terrified, was unable to communicate with the agents since she did not speak English. Apparently, the school district's central office had called the Secret Service after the school had reported that Adam's brother, Ibrahim, had threatened to kill the president. According to the brothers and other Arab students who were present, the alleged incident occurred in an ESL class in the midst of an argument about the U.S. occupation of Iraq. Some non-Arab students referenced recent revelations about the Abu Ghraib prison torture and several kidnappings and assassinations of foreigners in Iraq. They taunted Arab students, accusing Arabs of being prone to violence. Arab students argued for a different perspective on the war. The Arab students reported that Ibrahim (who was still struggling with English proficiency) responded to these taunts by asking the group how they would feel if one of their important leaders (their "big ones" in Arabic) were killed.

The teacher waited several days to report the incident to the dean's office; according to her very different account, Ibrahim was reading a newspaper in the back of her class when he announced that he would like to kill the president. It was following the teacher's report — several days after the alleged threat occurred — that the school suspended Ibrahim and called the school district's central office for safety, which reported the incident to the Secret Service. Ultimately, a school district judge who hears disciplinary appeals found credible Ibrahim's account of what happened. However, Ibrahim was not allowed to return to his high school because he had publicly stated he would "get" the person who had snitched on him; he was transferred to a disciplinary school for his senior year.

This experience, along with the detention of many Arabs after September 11, 2001, and the Iraqi occupation, created a context of uncertainty that made Adam worry, "Maybe they're going to kick all Arabs from America. Go back home!" For Adam and some of his peers, contemporary politics and policies raised questions about their membership in the American polity and their capacity to exercise full citizenship rights. Importantly, the incident with the Secret Service points to the connection between schools and those contemporary state policies that circumscribe the lives of Arab American communities (see Akram & Johnson, 2004; Moore, 1999; Murray, 2004; Volpp, 2002).

School was the primary site within which these young people confronted their status as national outsiders and enemies. Palestinian students faced myriad conflicts with their peers. Zayd recounted how fellow students tried to incite fights with Arab youth immediately after September 11, 2001:

> They would say, "Oh, you come to this school thinking like it's over? You're going to bomb the towers and then sit here? Get the hell out of this school. Dirty animals." And then that would start a fight.

Students reported that the taunt of "terrorist" followed them for years after September 11. Fights were not uncommon in the aftermath of such name-calling. Several students told of former friends whose families forbade their sons and daughters to continue relationships with Arabs after September 11.

For these students, the most painful stories were those that related a perceived betrayal by some of the adults in the community. For instance, Khalida described the day she decided to stop wearing the hijab:

> A student came up to me and she told me, "Why did you take off your head covering?" She didn't know what it was called. "Is it because you didn't want people to know you were a terrorist?" And we were in a classroom and the teacher heard her, but the teacher didn't say anything. And I couldn't do anything because I was all mad about it because the fact is that the teacher didn't care about what was going on, and she didn't even try to stop the student from discriminating in her class against others.

Many students felt that some teachers challenged racist comments by students directed at other communities but ignored those that were made about Arabs. Samira, for example, stated:

> The majority of people that work in our schools, they're not going to stick to your side. When somebody makes a racial comment about Arabs, the teachers, they don't do anything. But then when somebody makes a racial comment about Whites or Blacks, you're suspended or kicked out of the school. Well, why didn't that other person get kicked out when they made a racial comment about me?

Many Palestinian students felt that the school's official policy of "zero tolerance for intolerance" offered their community little to no protection.

More serious still were the stories of teachers' harassment of Arab students. A teacher asked Zayd, "Are you planning the next 9/11?" Several students told me that one of their history teachers was very hostile to Palestinian national aspirations. Zayd described a conversation with this teacher about the Israeli-Palestinian conflict: "He just started saying, 'All the Palestinians deserve to die' and 'they're all dogs . . . they're like animals.'" At the start of the U.S. invasion of Iraq, one Palestinian student came to our afterschool club deeply upset after she witnessed a teacher tell an Iraqi boy, "Go back to where you come from."

Students' sense of peril and betrayal was reflected in their discussions of a persistent rumor that these students believed to be true. Khalida recounted, "There was actually once a meeting in the school trying to have all the Arab students [kicked] out. Ms. [teacher's name] told me about it, and she named a couple of teachers that were involved in that meeting that were trying to get all Arab students out of this school." Although the veracity of this particular story was difficult to confirm, it is important to note that many students believed it to be true. Another story I heard suggested that the sense of insecurity and lack of trust that many of these Palestinian youth felt in the school community was not unwarranted. Several administrators, including the principal, told me that on September 11, 2001, one teacher came into the principal's office and demanded that he "round up all the Palestinians." The principal was appropriately shocked and outraged by this behavior and retorted, "Should I put a target on their backs too?"

Interestingly, in the face of hostile teachers who singled out Arab students as outsiders to the nation, these Palestinian students sometimes called upon their U.S. citizenship in order to assert their rights as insiders. For example, Samira, Zena, and Leila reported an argument with a teacher who had called them pigs (for eating in class). Samira said that when they confronted him, he yelled at them, "I know how the men in your country treat you. I've been to your country twice already. If you talked to your family member like that he would smack you across the face." The girls were shocked, and Samira said that she retorted, "This is our country. What country did you visit?"

These stories reveal the ways in which Palestinian American students' complex and often fractured sense of national belonging is negotiated in school and community contexts in which they continually encounter "Americans" who, drawing on racialized nationalist discourses of belonging, position Arabs as dangerous outsiders and enemies. While it is important to note that these Palestinian American students had numerous positive experiences with teachers and peers, it was the repeated negative ones that are implicated in the fracturing of Palestinian and American identities. In schools, the politics of nation formation — the processes of defining who belongs and does not belong to the imagined national community — are played out in everyday practices, and these practices help structure the parameters of inclusion for Palestinian and other immigrant youth (Hall, 2004).

Pledging Allegiance to What?

The experiences of being positioned as outsiders — as suspect terrorists — in turn raised questions and conflicts for the Palestinian students about how to position themselves in relation to the nation. This uncertainty was especially evident in their complex debates about (and actions in reference to) the daily ritual of standing and reciting the U.S. Pledge of Allegiance, a ritual that took on heightened significance within the school after September 11, 2001. Whereas these Palestinian students almost universally agreed they would not pledge the flag, they argued among themselves about whether to stand during this ritual. Some, like Khalida, refused to participate entirely. She explained her decision:

> There was an assembly and the teacher told us to stand up for the Pledge of Allegiance. And that day I was really feeling lazy and not wanting to. And the teacher comes up to me. She says, "Okay. You need to stand up for the pledge." I told her I didn't want to. She was like, "Are you American or are you not American?" I told her, "Yes. I am living in America." She was like, "Exactly. You are living in America, so you have to stand up for the Pledge of Allegiance." And I refused to. . . . It was in December 2002 when it happened, and after that I never stood up for the Pledge of Allegiance. There's a lot of things in the Pledge of Allegiance . . . for example, "with liberty and justice for all." There isn't always justice for everybody. That's like one thing the United States don't have, that's justice.

Khalida's refusal to stand during the Pledge of Allegiance may have begun as an act of laziness, but upon her teacher's insistence that standing for the pledge was a requirement of "living in America," it quickly became a politicized choice. She connected her refusal to stand for the pledge to her critique of the U.S. myth of "justice for all."

Khalida explained her distrust of American justice in relation to a large fight between a group of Russian boys and a group of Palestinian boys that had occurred soon after September 11, 2001. She argued:

> For example, in the fight that happened between the Russian group and the Arab group at Regional High, well, the fight happened between both of them. They both got into the fight, but the only ones that had to pay were the Arab students.

Khalida and other Arab students often referenced this fight and the resulting suspensions as symbolic of a pattern of discriminatory disciplinary actions. From the school's perspective, these suspensions were justified because although many Russian and Arab boys were involved in this fight and several were injured, one Russian boy was hospitalized; his assailants were the students who were suspended. However, Khalida, along with other Arab youth and several of their parents, felt strongly that, in this case, both the Russian and Arab boys had been responsible for the fight; they also believed that, in general, the Arab boys were disciplined more harshly because of discriminatory practices of the school's disciplinary team.[10] Importantly, Khalida's perception of a discriminatory climate against Arab students, particularly in a post–September 11 school climate, made a mockery of the claim for "liberty and justice for all" and led her to refuse to participate in the routine morning ritual of pledging the flag.

Zayd took a different stance on the pledge and adopted a leadership role among the Arab students, urging them to stand during the ritual:

> I make sure that when I'm there, [the Arabs] stand during the Pledge of Allegiance. If you don't want to say it, don't say it. But stand out of respect. We are Arabs, and it's after 2001, after September 11th. Just stand up or they are going to talk against us. It's better for us. They are going to say, "Okay. We're the better people." Unlike a lot of other people that are just too lazy to get up. We get up. We just stand through the thing, but we're not going to salute it.

Zayd viewed standing for the Pledge of Allegiance as an important public act through which Arab students could show respect for Americans and improve their image in the larger school community. Seeking to gain ground as "the better people," Zayd acted to challenge the exclusionary boundaries that delineate Arabs as outsiders/enemies.

Leila argued for standing as a sign of respect and as a mark of her connection to her U.S. citizenship:

> You were born in America. You have an American passport. In the auditorium, when they get up to pledge allegiance to the flag, most of the Arab students, they sit down. To me, that's rude, disrespectful to the American flag. Disrespectful to the country we're living in today. They stay sitting down, like, "Oh, I'm not going to respect the American flag." Just get up. Stand up. Look at the flag. You don't have to say the pledge. You're just looking at the flag and having the respect toward the people that are standing. So, as for respecting the United States, it's a big thing. To me, I respect where I live. I'm glad to be Palestinian. And I'm proud to be Palestinian and a Muslim and an American citizen, you could say.

For Leila, it is the country — in which she lives and carries citizenship — that is due respect. Leila named multiple sources of identification (being Palestinian, Muslim, *and* a U.S. citizen) as sources of pride and so expressed less conflict than most of her peers about the relationship between her multiple identities. Her words represented a moment of possibility in which these multiple identities were not fractured, but existed comfortably next to one another. At the same time, Leila's stance toward the pledge was complicated. Though she stood out of respect and was one of the few Arabs who recited it, she also stated, "I say it even though I don't mean it from the heart."

Speaking about the pledge, Samira also revealed a complex relationship to her citizenship identity:

> We're sitting in the auditorium full of Americans in the morning. When we get up and Americans look at us, and they're like, "Oh my God. She's wearing

> a mendeel, and she's standing for our flag." Even though I'm not saying the Pledge of Allegiance, I stand up as a matter of respect toward those people. I love when they look at me, especially those teachers and they're like, "Look. She has respect toward herself and others because she's standing up for our flag." Even though it is my flag, too, because I'm living in the United States of America. I don't [feel] that it's my flag, but the truth is, you're a U.S. citizen, so it's your flag.

Samira imagined that other students and teachers viewed her as a visible outsider because she wore a mendeel; by standing for the pledge, she hoped to seed another image of Arab Muslims than the one she believed they held. At the same time, Samira explored her insider/outsider status as a citizen: She was conflicted about her relationship to this flag that was hers by virtue of her citizenship but that evoked no emotional connection. Samira, it should be recalled, was one of the few students who had spent her entire life in the United States. However, as a Muslim and a Palestinian, she felt a tension and separation from "Americans" — a difference between residing in and belonging to the nation. Yuval-Davis, Anthias, and Kofman (2005) argue that belonging is a "thicker concept" than citizenship: It is a social connection that is created, to some extent, through experiences of inclusion or exclusion. For Samira and many of her peers, school experiences provoked an ongoing tension between their citizenship status and their sense of not belonging to — of being positioned outside of — the community of Americans.

For Samira and other Arab students, this decision to stand, but not to pledge, was also related to questions of global politics. Samira argued that standing for the pledge was a sign of respect for the "American people"; however, she feared that saying the pledge would signal support for U.S. foreign policy, such as the war in Iraq. She stated:

> I feel like they're pledging for — there are the American troops in Iraq killing Arabs. So when I think about it, it's like me praying for the troops to kill more Arabs. That's how I think of pledging to the flag.

Samira was deeply conflicted about whether pledging to the flag was a sign of supporting the war in Iraq and, as such, condoning the killing of Arabs. Khalida, who refused even to stand for the Pledge of Allegiance, also cited U.S. foreign policy as a large part of the reason for her actions. Khalida cited U.S. support for the Israeli occupation as a critical reason she did not want to pledge allegiance to the United States. She also said she felt confused about whether paying taxes in the United States indicated complicity in the occupation, given the level of U.S. financial support to Israel. These conflicted feelings suggest that the demand for allegiance to a single nation-state may be anachronistic in an increasingly transnational world, one in which people often have a complex, multilayered sense of belonging.

These students' conflicts in relationship to the daily ritual of pledging allegiance illuminate the everyday practices of schooling that are involved in ongoing processes of nation formation. These processes work to create stark boundaries between American and Arab identities. These fault lines of national allegiance were heightened by the political climate of the Bush administration's global war on terror. President George W. Bush's declaration after September 11, 2001 — "You're either with us, or you're with the terrorists" (Bush, 2001) — fostered a climate in which dissent from national foreign policy, particularly among Arab American communities, may be suspect.

Importantly, after September 11, schools across the nation participated in generating a resurgence of nationalist and patriotic sentiment (see Westheimer, 2006). The senate in the state in which Regional High is located passed a law requiring that students and teachers in all schools (public and private) recite the Pledge of Allegiance every morning. This law was immediately challenged and could not be enforced, pending the judgment of the courts. Despite the U.S. Supreme Court's ruling that affirmed students' and teachers' rights to refuse to say the pledge (*West Virginia State Board of Education v. Barnette*, 1943), Arab students at Regional High reported being disciplined for their refusal to stand for the ritual. Anne Larson, the teacher with whom I worked, also refused to participate in the pledge on religious grounds; she was called to task by her principal, even though, as she pointed out, she had a protected right not to say the pledge.

Regional High was implicated in other ways in the production of patriotism, nationalism, and ideological compliance with U.S. policies, particularly by encouraging students to support the military and the war in Iraq. For example, posters in the hall displayed pictures of former students serving in Iraq and asked students to make contributions to send them provisions. Some teachers asked students to buy yellow ribbons in support of the war. Under No Child Left Behind's requirements that open schools to military recruitment, recruiters hosted a free but mandatory lunch for faculty to instruct them on how to help with these efforts.

However, some teachers resisted the nationalist fervor to line up behind U.S. foreign policy in Afghanistan and Iraq. Anne Larson was an outspoken voice for peace, and she also actively supported Arab students, sponsoring the afterschool club and defending them against unjust disciplinary actions. An English teacher who ran the newspaper staunchly defended the right of a Palestinian student to publish a poem that proved controversial in the broad school community for its defense of Palestinian national aspirations. Another social studies teacher sponsored a group for students opposed to the war in Iraq, a risky and controversial move, given the school climate.[11] Although these teachers were important allies for Palestinian students, they could not shield these students from a school climate in which they were positioned as not belonging to this nation, even as these students were called upon to participate in exercises signaling patriotic commitment to the United States.

The distinction that Palestinian American students make between their citizenship status and their national affiliation — their sense that they *are*

Palestinian but *carry* U.S. citizenship — is critically bound up with contemporary processes through which the imagined community of the U.S. nation is being created and negotiated. The strong affiliation that these young people maintain with Palestine is related not only to their community's aspirations for an independent nation-state — that is, their involvement with the imagined community of Palestine — but is also a reflection of their experiences of exclusion from the imagined community of the United States.

Belonging in a Transnational World

The United States, like many other nations across the globe, is confronted with a new tension. Recent migration patterns across porous borders have changed the demographics in such a way that many people now residing in the country have multiple national affiliations. At the same time, a rise in nationalist sentiment has led to increasing demands by some to fortify the borders against undocumented migrants who are seen to threaten national security and the jobs of U.S. workers. Following the events of September 11, the United States, the United Kingdom, and other Western nations have engaged in fierce debates and soul-searching about the extent to which Muslim immigrant communities do (and should) experience a primary sense of belonging to the nation-state in which they reside.

As debates rage about whether Muslim values and practices are compatible with Western democracy, little attention has been focused on exclusionary policies and practices that position immigrant Muslim communities precariously inside these nation-states (Yuval-Davis et al., 2005). In a post–September 11 climate, Arab and other Muslim communities are often burdened with the threat that maintaining multiple affiliations and dissenting from U.S. foreign policy jeopardizes their inclusion in the American polity. At the same time, state policies and practices, along with the discursive construction of Arabs and Muslims as threatening outsiders, work to weaken a sense of belonging within those communities. It is, however, precisely a strong sense of belonging, along with conditions for substantive inclusion in a society, that enables new immigrant communities to fully exercise their rights and responsibilities as citizens (Castles & Davidson, 2000; Yuval-Davis et al., 2005).

Importantly, the Palestinian American students constructed and negotiated a complex, multilayered sense of national belonging, one that was more encompassing than, and at times inclusive of, their citizenship status. Practicing what some researchers term flexible citizenship (see Maira, 2004; Ong, 1999), these young people were deeply tied to the political movement for an independent state of Palestine, even as they appreciated the privileges that U.S. citizenship affords in terms of economic, social, and political rights. To some extent they leveraged the rights and privileges of U.S. citizenship to maintain their physical and emotional connection to their family and village in Palestine, and to support, through economic and political action, the Palestinian struggle for freedom and justice. These youth were anything but civically disengaged.

At the same time, it would be a mistake to misread their relationship to U.S. citizenship as merely a utilitarian one. Certainly, many of the youth with whom I work wrestled with their sense of belonging to the U.S. nation — a struggle that was inextricably linked to the ways that they, as Arabs and Muslims, have been pushed outside of the boundaries of belonging and care in the context of the post–September 11 political landscape. However, in important ways they often called upon their status as Americans to challenge exclusionary discourses and practices. Through everyday actions, they confronted teachers and peers, calling to task their racialized assumptions about Arabs and Muslims. They exercised their rights to due process to challenge, for example, unjust disciplinary actions, persisting even though they were rarely successful. They called upon a right to free speech to offer alternative perspectives on U.S. policy in the Middle East, with full knowledge that, given the current political climate, the consequences of expressing these alternative views were potentially dangerous, as confirmed by the Secret Service's visit to Ibrahim's home. Through our afterschool club, several youth made short films directed at countering the public image of Palestinians as terrorists; these films continue to be screened in various public venues. The youth with whom I work, then, confronted — persistently, albeit sometimes tentatively — exclusionary discourses and practices that often position their communities not only outside the nation, but outside the bounds of human concern. Through their words and actions, these young people endeavored to make visible peoples and communities too often rendered invisible (Muslim women, Palestinians, Iraqis, and so forth) in the U.S. public imagination. In doing so, they pushed against dominant and dominating public ideologies of U.S. nationalism and patriotism.

Implications: Educating for Democratic Citizenship in an Era of Transnational Migration

Transnational communities are changing the demographics of the United States and other modern nation-states. Communities that bridge the boundaries of nation-states challenge us to rethink what belonging and citizenship mean in our times. These new transnational immigrant communities pose particular challenges for public education. Practitioners concerned about educating immigrant youth for citizenship and democratic participation must hold fast to a vision of schools as sites from which to strengthen immigrant youths' sense of belonging. As the primary institutions through which immigrant youth encounter the state, schools play a key role in shaping citizenship and democratic participation. As global migration trends are dramatically reshaping the demographics of the U.S. and other countries, we face a critical need for public education to recommit to this important purpose. How can the experiences of the Palestinian youth in this study help educators think about what it means to teach youth to become active, engaged participants in the social, civic, and political spheres within and across the boundaries of the nation-state? This research suggests concrete implications for the kinds of discourse communities we must create within classrooms; however, it also suggests a need to shift our conceptual frameworks for citizenship education in schools in ways that engage questions of identity and inequality, and that educate youth for social change.

Educators must build classroom communities that foster students' and teachers' capacity to speak and listen respectfully across differences in values, beliefs, perspectives, politics, and so forth. There is, of course, nothing new about this idea, which is central to the practice of democratic education (Abowitz & Harnish, 2006; Gutmann, 1987), and the pedagogical tools are available for engaging in and learning from difficult conversations (Parker, 2006; Parker & Hess, 2001). Yet none of the students in this study reported curricular opportunities in which educators helped students explore and discuss the very events that positioned Arabs and Muslims as threatening outsiders to the United States.[12] The reasons for this curricular silence about September 11, the wars in Iraq and Afghanistan, and the Israeli-Palestinian conflict were likely due to a complex set of factors; however, at the very least, we must work to ensure that educators have the knowledge, commitment, time, and resources to develop classroom communities in which youth are taught the skills and dispositions needed to listen across differences. With such a commitment we could imagine that for Palestinian youth, as well as for many other youth whose knowledge is similarly silenced or dismissed, schools may become more inclusive sites that help to build diverse, democratic citizens.

A second implication of this work is that educating youth for democratic participation also demands rethinking the frameworks of K–12 citizenship education to directly engage questions of identity and belonging and to consider how these influence individuals' capacity for substantive inclusion in society. Abowitz and Harnish (2006) point out that the dominant frameworks for citizenship education in schools tend to focus on civic literacy (teaching facts about U.S. history, government, and geography), patriotic identity, and teaching the liberal virtue of tolerance through learning the skills and dispositions necessary for deliberation, cooperation, and decisionmaking. These foci, however, fail to take up the fundamental challenges to citizenship education posed by new immigrant communities, as well as historically marginalized groups.

Educating youth for citizenship and civic participation must challenge universal, abstract notions of citizenship that focus on legal status, and instead foreground the different ways that people are positioned in relation to the resources necessary for full participation in the social, political, and economic spheres. Inside schools, this means at the very least radically transforming the social studies curriculum, which is the traditional site for citizenship education. Youth need opportunities to critically examine models of citizenship that call for assimilation to an unexamined idea of "American" identity or that celebrate cultural pluralism while leaving unexamined the structural inequalities of our society that are related to people's differential access to social, civil, political, cultural, and economic rights (Castles & Davidson, 2000). Indeed, this differential access has been and continues to be substantively related to the discursive construction of "American" identity. At different times, and in various ways, members of racially/ethnically marginalized groups have been simultaneously perceived as less than fully American and have been structurally excluded from accessing their rights as members of this society to full economic, social, cultural, and political participation.

For Palestinian American youth, the failure on the part of a majority of their teachers to question and explore critically the ways that Arabs and other Muslims are being framed as enemies and outsiders to this nation, and the consequences this positioning has for their families, contributed to the youths' conflicted sense of belonging to this society. However, it is not only Palestinian or other Muslim immigrant youth who struggle with this question of belonging — many youth from racially/ethnically subordinated communities also have described a contradiction between the idealized notions of citizenship and democracy they are taught in schools and the historical and contemporary experiences of their communities that belie those idealizations (Ladson-Billings, 2004; Rubin, 2007). Citizenship education should engage youth in the study of the complex, contradictory, and uneven promises of U.S. citizenship to help youth understand how belonging — *being American* — has been, and continues to be, constructed in ways that deny some groups, citizen and immigrant groups alike, rights that would guarantee their substantive inclusion into this society. Citizenship education that helps youth reflect critically on the relationship between citizenship, identity, and rights could help young people construct a sense of belonging that draws on what Renato Rosaldo (1994) has called cultural citizenship — "the right to be different and belong in a participatory democratic sense" (p. 402). Rather than viewing group affiliations as potentially in conflict with American identity, as did the Palestinian youth in this study, the experiences and knowledge forged within different communities can serve as a site from which young people can, following a long tradition, challenge this nation to live up to its stated ideals.

Importantly, the rise of transnational communities also requires that we redefine citizenship in ways that acknowledge that people increasingly hold multilayered affiliations across the borders of this nation. It is not enough for citizenship education to examine how rights and resources are distributed in relation to differentially positioned racial/ethnic groups within the boundaries of the United States. Transnational communities, like those of these Palestinian American youth, suggest that people residing in one nation-state may see themselves as belonging to the imagined communities of other nations, and as a result of this sense of belonging they may be affected by, and struggle for, the rights of people living elsewhere. For an increasing number of young people, transnationalism shapes their identities, political sensibilities, and capacity to participate both in this society and on a global stage. The commitment to and engagement with transnational issues must not be taken as a sign of disloyalty or a problem for citizenship, but as an opportunity to help all of us think about rights and justice across national borders. Rather than viewing multiple national affiliations as a threat to social incorporation, we might consider transnational communities as an important source of new visions of identity and belonging, and as a resource for engaging with alternate perspectives on local and global issues.

A final implication of this research is that educators need ways of helping young people imagine being a democratic citizen that is distinguishable from, and larger than, their national identifications. Focusing our efforts on teaching young people to participate actively in the social, economic, cultural, civic, and political spheres offers possibilities for developing their commitments to the local and the global community. It means educating youth to confront structural inequalities and to organize for social change locally and globally. For example, youth in this study sought ways to speak out and engage the local community, challenging the images of their family and community. They also worked to contribute productively to Palestinian society. They found these opportunities in out-of-school spaces, rather than within the school's citizenship education curriculum. The Arab afterschool club at Regional High, for example, offered youth an important alternate space in which they could explore and speak back to the exclusionary discourses they were encountering in their schools and communities. Educators often work in out-of-school sites to promote youth civic engagement (see, e.g., Flores-Gonzalez, Rodriguez, & Rodriguez-Muniz, 2006; Kwon, 2006). I argue that transforming citizenship education inside public schools to offer youth the opportunity to investigate injustice and inequality and work for social change would support students as they develop a strong sense of social belonging and civic commitment (see, e.g., Rubin, 2007; Torre & Fine, 2006). Participation and engagement, rather than a sense of national identification, may in the end prove a stronger base for developing active citizens.

This is a critical time to reinvigorate public school commitment to citizenship education in ways that engage with diversity, conflict, and structural inequalities that know no national borders. Despite the alarming statistics about the resegregation of public schools, they remain one of the few sites in which youth come together across the many communities that constitute our global village. As educators, this feature of public schooling offers us a key opportunity to engage youth with conflicting perspectives on local and global conditions. Discussing cosmopolitanism, philosopher Anthony Appiah (2006) suggests the path to "living together as the global tribe we have become" (p. xiii) depends on "the simple idea that in human community, as in national communities, we need to develop habits of coexistence: conversation in its older meaning of the word, of living together, association" (p. xix). Importantly, Appiah argues that the point of encouraging conversation across our differences is not so much to persuade others to change their minds; rather, he argues, change happens because habits and practices change as we engage with the experiences and ideas of others over time. Admittedly, it may be too much to count on the expansive possibilities of discussion as a tool for educating for democratic participation. However, creating opportunities inside schools in which youth and their teachers interact with each other in meaningful work and talk may be a critical first step for building engaged, diverse democratic publics that can engender a more just and peaceful future for our world.

Notes

1. This partial inclusion must be understood, however, to be mainly symbolic, as subordinated racial communities continue to be marginalized and oppressed.
2. This research was supported by a National Academy of Education/Spencer Foundation Postdoctoral Fellowship.
3. According to the demographic count of the local Arab American community organization, there are approximately ten thousand Arabs and Arab Americans living in this city of approximately 1.5 million residents. Palestinians comprise over half of this Arab community. The organization's demographic count is significantly higher than that of the U.S. Census Bureau, which lists the number of residents claiming Arab ancestry at 5,119. It is difficult to get exact demographic figures for residents of Arab origin. Undocumented immigrants and migration back and forth between the United States and countries of origin contribute to inaccuracies in accounting for the exact number of Arabs residing in the city. In addition, although the 2000 U.S. Census included a question about ancestry on its long form, which was only given to one in six families, it did not recognize Arabs as a specific ethnic group (http://www.census.gov/prod/2003pubs/c2kbr-23.pdf). According to the Census Bureau, 19 percent of respondents did not respond to the ancestry question at all.
4. The names of the high school and participants in this research have all been changed to protect confidentiality.
5. Over the course of this research project, I played multiple roles in relation to these young people. This research was enhanced greatly by my various roles as a mentor, organizer, and researcher, as I was able to engage the youth in many conversations and activities that explicitly addressed and interrogated all of our assumptions about identity, nationality, culture, and citizenship.
6. Although this group was formed as an Arab American youth alliance, the majority of the Arab population in the school is Palestinian, and it was these youth who gravitated to the meetings.
7. The Dome of the Rock is the golden-domed Islamic shrine in Jerusalem that houses the rock from which Muslims believe the Prophet Muhammed ascended to heaven.
8. In recent years, the exercise of civil rights, particularly for Muslim residents of the United States has been eroded, especially in the post–September 11 era (Akram & Johnson, 2004; Moore, 1999; Murray, 2004; Volpp, 2002).

9. My thanks to Doris Warriner for pointing out this contradiction.
10. In the spring of 2002, a local community organizer and I held a meeting with parents and students to discuss their concerns about these disciplinary patterns. Parents and students pointed, for example, to numerous cases of Arab boys suspended for verbal, not physical, arguments, and they stated that eleven boys (out of approximately forty Palestinian students) had been suspended or transferred out of Regional High during the 2001–2002 year. Because the school has no way to disaggregate disciplinary data for Arab students, it was not possible to verify the accuracy of the community's perception of a disproportionate number of disciplinary actions against Arab students, especially the boys. My data contain many examples of students being written up or suspended for actions that may be indicative of fear and suspicion of Arab youth.
11. None of the Palestinian students were involved in this group. This teacher taught Advanced Placement courses and, with one exception, none of the Palestinian students knew her.
12. Teaching about all of the Middle East was considered such a hot topic in the school district that, in 2005, the director of curriculum gave an interview to a local paper in which she declared that the school district purposefully did not teach any topics about the modern Middle East.

References

Abowitz, K. K., & Harnish, J. (2006). Contemporary discourses of citizenship. *Review of Educational Research, 76,* 653–690.

Abu El-Haj, T. R. (2006). Race, politics and Arab American youth: Shifting frameworks for conceptualizing educational equity. *Educational Policy, 20,* 13–34.

Abu-Lughod, L. (1998). Feminist longings and postcolonial conditions. In L. Abu-Lughod (Ed.), *Remaking women: Feminism and modernity in the Middle East* (pp. 3–31). Princeton, NJ: Princeton University Press.

Ahmed, M. (2002). Homeland insecurities: Racial violence the day after September 11. *Social Text, 72,* 101–115.

Akram, S. M., & Johnson, K. R. (2004). Race and civil rights pre–September 11, 2001: The targeting of Arabs and Muslims. In E. C. Hagopian (Ed.), *Civil rights in peril: The targeting of Arabs and Muslims* (pp. 9–25). Chicago: Haymarket Books.

Anderson, B. (1991). *Imagined communities: Reflections on the origin and spread of nationalism.* New York: Verso. (Original work published 1983)

Appiah, A. (2006). *Cosmopolitanism: Ethics in a world of strangers.* New York: W. W. Norton.

Bush, G. W. (2001). Address to a joint session of Congress and the American people. Available at http://www.whitehouse.gov.news/releases/2001/09/20010920-8.html

Castles, S. (2004). Migration, citizenship and education. In J. A. Banks (Ed.), *Diversity and citizenship education: Global perspectives* (pp. 17–48). San Francisco: Jossey-Bass.

Castles, S., & Davidson, A. (2000). *Citizenship and migration: Globalization and the politics of belonging.* New York: Routledge.

Flores-Gonzalez, N., Rodriguez, M., & Rodriguez-Muniz, M. (2006). From hip-hop to humanization: Batey Urbano as a space for Latino youth culture and community action. In S. Ginwright, P. Noguera, & J. Cammarota (Eds.), *Beyond resistance! Youth activism and community change: New democratic possibilities for practice and policy for America's youth* (pp. 175–196). New York: Routledge.

Gutmann, A. (1987). *Democratic education.* Princeton, NJ: Princeton University Press.

Hall, K. D. (2002). *Lives in translation: Sikh youth as British citizens.* Philadelphia: University of Pennsylvania Press.

Hall, K. D. (2004). The ethnography of imagined communities: The cultural production of Sikh ethnicity in Britain. *Annals of the American Academy of Political and Social Science, 595*, 108–121.

Huntington, S. P. (1996). *The clash of civilizations and the remaking of the world order.* New York: Simon & Schuster.

Ibish, H. (2003). *Report on hate crimes and discrimination against Arab-Americans: The post–September 11 backlash.* Washington, DC: Arab American Anti-Discrimination Committee.

Khalidi, R. (1997). *Palestinian identity: The construction of modern national consciousness.* New York: Columbia University Press.

Kwon, S. A. (2006). Youth of color organizing for juvenile justice. In S. Ginwright, P. Noguera, & J. Cammarota (Eds.), *Beyond resistance! Youth activism and community change: New democratic possibilities for practice and policy for America's youth* (pp. 215–228). New York: Routledge.

Ladson-Billings, G. (2004). Culture versus citizenship: The challenge of racialized citizenship in the United States. In J. A. Banks (Ed.), *Diversity and citizenship education: Global perspectives* (pp. 99–126). San Francisco: Jossey-Bass.

Lee, S. J. (2005). *Up against Whiteness: Race, school and immigrant youth.* New York: Teachers College Press.

Levinson, B. A. U. (2005). Citizenship, identity, democracy: Engaging the political in the anthropology of education. *Anthropology and Education Quarterly, 36*, 329–340.

Lewis, B. (2002). *What went wrong? Western impact and Middle Eastern response.* New York: Oxford University Press.

Lopez, N. (2003). *Hopeful girls, troubled boys: Race and gender disparity in urban education.* New York: Routledge.

Louie, V. (2006). Growing up ethnic in transnational worlds: Identities among second-generation Chinese and Dominicans. *Identities: Global Studies in Culture and Power, 13*, 363–394.

Maira, S. (2004). Imperial Feelings: Youth culture, citizenship and globalization. In M. M. Suárez-Orozco & D. B. Qin-Hilliard (Eds.), *Globalization: Culture and education in the new millennium* (pp. 203–234). Berkeley: University of California Press.

Mamdani, M. (2004). *Good Muslim, bad Muslim: America, the Cold War and the roots of terror.* New York: Pantheon Books.

Moore, K. M. (1999). A closer look at anti-terrorism law: *American-Arab Antidiscrimination Committee v. Reno* and the constructs of aliens' rights. In M. W. Suleiman (Ed.), *Arabs in America: Building a new future* (pp. 84–99). Philadelphia: Temple University Press.

Murray, N. (2004). Profiled: Arabs, Muslims and the Post–9/11 hunt for the "enemy within." In E. C. Hagopian (Ed.), *Civil rights in peril: The targeting of Arabs and Muslims* (pp. 27–68). Chicago: Haymarket Books.

Ogbu, J., & Simons, H. D. (1998). Voluntary and involuntary minorities: A cultural-ecological theory of school performance with some implications for education. *Anthropology and Education Quarterly, 29*, 155–188.

Olsen, L. (1997). *Made in America: Immigrants in our public schools.* New York: New Press.

Ong, A. (1996). Cultural citizenship as subject making: Immigrants negotiate racial and cultural boundaries in the United States. *Current Anthropology, 37*, 737–751.

Ong, A. (1999). *Flexible citizenship: The cultural logics of transnationality.* Durham, NC: Duke University Press.

Parker, W. C. (2006). Public discourses in schools: Purposes, problems and possibilities. *Educational Researcher, 35*(8), 11–18.

Parker, W. C., & Hess, D. (2001). Teaching with and for discussion. *Teaching and Teacher Education, 17*, 273–289.

Ramos-Zayas, A. Y. (1998). Nationalist ideologies, neighborhood-based activism, and educational spaces in Puerto Rican Chicago. *Harvard Educational Review, 68*, 164–192.

Rosaldo, R. (1994). Cultural citizenship and educational democracy. *Cultural Anthropology, 9,* 402–411.
Rubin, B. C. (2007). "There's still not justice": Youth civic identity development amid distinct school and community contexts. *Teachers College Record, 109,* 449–481.
Said, E. W. (October 22, 2001). The clash of ignorance. *The Nation,* (pp. 11–13).
Sarroub, L. K. (2005). *All American Yemeni girls: Being Muslim in a public school.* Philadelphia: University of Pennsylvania Press.
Soysal, Y. N. (1994). *Limits of citizenship: Migrants and postnational membership in Europe.* Chicago: University of Chicago Press.
Suárez-Orozco, M. M. (2001). Globalization, immigration, and education: The research agenda. *Harvard Educational Review, 71,* 345–365.
Torre, M., & Fine, M. (2006). Researching and resisting: Democratic policy research by and for youth. In S. Ginwright, P. Noguera, & J. Cammarota (Eds.), *Beyond resistance! Youth activism and community change: New democratic possibilities for practice and policy for America's youth* (pp. 269–286). New York: Routledge.
Valenzuela, A. (1999). *Subtractive schooling: U.S.–Mexican youth and the politics of caring.* Albany: State University of New York Press.
Volpp, L. (2002). The citizen and the terrorist. *UCLA Law Review, 49,* 1575–1600.
West Virginia State Board of Education v. Barnette. 319 U.S. 624 (1943).
Westheimer, J. (2006, April). Politics and patriotism in education. *Phi Delta Kappan, 87,* 608–620.
Yuval-Davis, N., & Werbner, P. (Eds.). (1999). *Women, citizenship and difference.* London: Zed Books.
Yuval-Davis, N., Anthias, F., & Kofman, E. (2005). Secure borders and safe haven and the gendered politics of belonging: Beyond social cohesion. *Ethnic and Racial Studies, 28,* 513–535.

I would like to thank my colleagues, Patricia Buck, Meira Levinson, Beth Rubin, Ellen Skilton-Sylvester, and Doris Warriner, for their careful, detailed, and provocative responses to earlier versions of this article. I presented some of the ideas in this article at the American Anthropological Association Meetings in 2005 and 2006. I am grateful to Michelle Fine, Kathleen Hall, Bradley Levinson, and Ray McDermott for their generous and challenging comments as discussants for those papers. I thank the Editorial Board of the *Harvard Educational Review* for their thoughtful and focused feedback on earlier versions of this manuscript.

PART TWO

New Forms of Education Amidst Conflict

PART TWO

Introduction

As *Reforms of Education Amidst Conflict* reveals, educators, students, and community members can use existing educational institutions to enact societal change. By working within the system—altering the current schools and school systems—these actors use educational spaces to negotiate layered political identities, imagine new social orders, and enact, transmit, or resist ideologies. The within-the-system approach, however, is not the only route to educational change within violent conflicts. Stakeholders have also adopted processes *outside* the system, offering educational programs and institutions that exist beyond the establishment. We focus on these approaches in the second part of this volume. Like the educational reforms explored in the first part of this volume, new forms of education can also incite broad political and societal shifts, engender resistance, and promote peace, although, again, not without complication and compromise.

This section explores the many ways that students, educators, and communities work around or beyond existing schooling systems to promote political and social transformation. Authors describe a variety of approaches to and experiences with creating new educational opportunities and methods in response to conflict. These practices include those designed to preserve and promote the knowledge and culture of marginalized groups, as well as efforts to create new educational systems featuring alternative curricula, broader access, or improved educational equity.

We open this section with an examination of two underground schools. The first, by Hanna Buczynska-Garewicz, describes the creation of a clandestine "flying" university in Poland, established to resist the constraints of a restrictive state and to provide a liberating curricular alternative to the government-controlled system of higher education. Clandestine schooling was also embraced by Jews in the Warsaw Ghetto, as Susan Kardos documents, and served as sites and symbols of defiant opposition to Nazi oppression and genocide. While the "flying university" offered alternative forms scholarship to those allowed in the state university, the Ghetto schools provided the only education for ghettoized Jews and served to sustain the threatened Judaic culture. These underground institutions, operating in defiance of oppressive governments, offered alternative sources of knowledge, revived suppressed ideologies, and sustained endangered communities.

The next two articles highlight the efforts of fledgling governments to establish educational systems. The first, an interview with former Palestinian education leader Khalil Mahshi, reveals the structural and social challenges—including limited resources and partial public support—faced by officials creating Palestinian schools and educational opportunities during and after Israeli occupation. This discussion highlights the unexpected potential benefits of building educational systems in the context of conflict; here, community-based education, initially a form of resistance to Israeli occupation, garnered greater support than more conventional, official systems. David Tyack then examines the opportunities and challenges involved in the post-conflict codification of a new national educational ideology. He describes the differing educational philosophies of key American political figures following the Revolutionary War, exploring their efforts to reconcile the need for social order and unity with the pluralistic principles of the new United States.

Continuing of the exploration of the promise and limitations of insurgent educational change, the section concludes with attempts to build new systems that expand educational access. Asgedet Stefanos examines the efforts of the newly independent Eritrean government to create an educational system that included girls and women, part of a national effort to promote educational equity as well as economic productivity. She tracks the disillusionment of Eritrean women, whose early hopes soured over time and led them to conclude that their educational options were greater during, rather than after, the conflict. Authors Fernando Cardenal and Valerie Miller then explore the Nicaraguan National Literacy Crusade, a program that applied military tactics to teach literacy to thousands of people in remote and impoverished communities throughout the country. The campaign established reading and writing as a pillar of the nation's response to wartime inequity, foreign domination, and military repression and its plans for liberation.

Together, these articles shed light on the complicated negotiations involved in creating new educational sites and systems in the service of advancing political aims or ensuring peoples' survival. As in *Reforms of Education Amidst Conflict*, we see that leaders pursue educational change to promote their political agendas and values, and to introduce new ideas and ways of living together in the world. Regardless of where educational change originates, the articles in this collection reveal the power of schooling in wartime—whether used intentionally or unintentionally; whether created to promote conflict or peace; whether designed to preserve cultures and peoples or destroy communities and identities. No educational stakeholder in a global community is untouched by these processes.

The Flying University in Poland, 1978–1980

HANNA BUCZYNSKA-GAREWICZ

Towarzystwo Kursow Naukowych*

We the undersigned bring the *Towarzystwo Kursow Naukowych* (Society for Academic Studies) into being. By taking this initiative, we express our wish to respond to the recently awakened aspirations of Poland's students and young intellectuals to broaden, enrich, and complement their knowledge. These aspirations are particularly striking in the realm of the social sciences and the humanities. They result from the need to understand the historical period and the society we live in, as well as from the desire for self-knowledge. Both this intellectual quickening and its motivations form a phenomenon that is extremely valuable to society. After all, creative and independent civic attitudes cannot be formed if people do not search for the truth about the world and about themselves. Forming these attitudes requires not merely the attainment of professional competence—however indispensable it may be—but also an understanding of the whole of society's life. What is needed is a solid knowledge of the historical roots of all dimensions of the present. There is no place in the world today where the educational system is able to satisfy these needs. The educational system serves pragmatic purposes by favoring increasingly narrow specialization both in teaching and research. This results in a dangerous disintegration of culture into instrumental and cognitive layers, a separation that is harmful to both pursuits. Another result is the transformation of an intellectual into a performer of tasks; he does not participate in their formulation and is not even able to sensibly participate because his narrow professional specialization makes him unable to realize the consequences of those tasks. This potential danger is made more acute by the structure of political power in our country. All this brings harm to our society, to its culture and learning. Those who are hurt most are the young people: they try to satisfy their needs by undertaking self-education initiatives. The shortcomings of official education and the political and ideological restrictions on learning have been known and criticized for

*This declaration was originally published in *Biuletyn Informacyjny KOR* in Warsaw and reprinted in March 1978 in *Kultura*, a Polish journal published in Paris. The translation was done for *HER* by Stanislaw Baranczak, Alfred Jurzykowski Professor of Polish Language and Literature, Harvard University.—ED.

Harvard Educational Review Vol. 55 No. 1 February 1985, 20–33

centuries. In an effort to remedy this situation, societies have been creating institutions and forms of education and self-education outside the official educational system. In this respect, the history of Polish learning and education has a splendid tradition of numerous educational associations: the flying university, the guidance for independent study, or, in the interwar period, the Polish Free University. Aware of this tradition, as well as of our present needs, we declare our initiative. Our purpose is to help anybody who wishes to increase his or her knowledge through self-education. We wish to offer—within the limits of our capacity—our counsel, knowledge, and assistance in teaching and research to anybody who would like to approach us. The curriculum board, appointed by us, will take the responsibility for the quality and scope of this program, its methods and direction, and its freedom of discussion and exploration. During the academic year, the nucleus of this activity will be the work of self-education groups that will study selected problems in history, sociology, economics, literature, philosophy, and pedagogy. The classes are open to anyone free of charge. The participants are students, graduates of virtually all fields, and lecturers who work without remuneration. Despite the fact that taking part in self-education does not provide the student with any special privileges and does not offer a diploma, the interest among the young is remarkable, confirming the existing social need for this kind of activity. We undertake our initiative as a result of our conviction that an action of this kind is urgently needed today. Further developments of this initiative will depend on its acceptance by the students themselves, as well as on the support of the society as a whole.

— *Warsaw 22 January 1978*

Stephan Amsterdamski, Stanisław Baranczak, Władysław Bartoszewski, Władysław Bienkowski, Jacek Bocheński, Marian Brandys, Alina Brodzka, Hanna Buczynska-Garewicz, Tomasz Burek, Andrzej Celinski, Mirosława Chamcowna, Bogday Cywinski, Izydora Dąmbska, Roman Duda, Kornel Filipowicz, Wacław Gleichgewicht, Michał Głowinski, Antoni Golubiew, Joanna Guze, Stanisław Hartmann, Aleksander Hauke-Ligowski, Maria Janion, Aldona Jawłowska, Jerzy Jedlicki, Jakub Karpinski, Adam Kersten, Jan Kielanowski, Andrzej Kijowski, Tadeusz Kowalik, Waldemar Kuczynski, Władysław Kunicki-Goldfinger, Edward Lipinski, Jan Jozef Lipski, Hanna Malewska, Marian Malowist, Tadeusz Mazowiecki, Adam Michnik, Halina Mikołajska, Zygmunt Mycielski, Irena Nowakowa, Severyn Pollak, Stanislaw Rodzinski, Barbara Skarzanka, Irena Sławinska, Adam Stanowski, Julian Stryjkowski, Jan Jozef Szczepanski, Zdzisław Szpakowski, Wisława Szymborska, Marek Tabin, Karol Tarnowski, Adrzej Tyszka, Henryk Wereszycki, Andrzej Werner, Krzysztof Wolicki, Władysław Wołoszyn, Maria Wosiek, Jacek Wozniakowski, Adam Zagajewski, Czeslaw Zgorzelski, Tadeusz Zipser.

An underground university in Poland arose in response to the Polish political and social situation in the late 1970s. the *Latajacy Uniwersytet* or the "flying university," as it became known, was designed as a clandestine quasi-institution to provide an independent education in a totalitarian state. Although it was small and short-lived—existing only two years and involving about sixty professors and writers with no more than 500 students—its significance surpasses the boundaries of its small community. The experience of the flying university can contribute to the solution of many problems in contemporary academic communities.

The main goal of the clandestine university was to provide free academic instruction irrespective of the petrified bureaucratic systems of power and all political and pragmatic impacts. Generally speaking, it was an attempt to revive the ideal of academic freedom and it is this fact which gives the flying university its universal significance. In Poland today, the university is less free than in many Western countries, and bureaucratic and political pressures have a tremendous influence on research and teaching. However, the problems of academic independence are present everywhere and are of universal importance. Thus the Polish experience takes on universal meaning.

The Polish clandestine university can not provide any detailed pattern for educational action in other countries. Each action must depend on the surrounding historical context and must be highly individualized; what is good for one country might be absurd in another. Nevertheless, the Polish experience may reveal one general truth: scholars can and should defend academic freedom by building new, independent communities that reach beyond the limits of established formal political and social structures. This sort of communication and collaboration, free of bureaucratic intrusion, may in the long run save the idea of academic freedom. Quite often the simple fact of disobedience to the existing bureaucracy has the power to revive old values.

Since the end of World War II, Polish higher education has been dominated by state universities ruled by a special ministry of education. Members of the office are appointed by the government and approved by the Polish Communist Party. Currently there are over thirty universities in Poland, only one of which is private. Before the war there were thirteen state and five private universities. This ratio is quite typical of higher education in Europe, where the majority of universities are state-run. The concept of a state university with full scholarly autonomy and great academic freedom is a cornerstone of European education. The contemporary form of this concept arose in nineteenth-century Germany and still functions well for education and research in Europe. However, one must remember that the idea of an autonomous state university is a product of liberal state ideas, and such an institution can only exist in a liberal democratic state. In a totalitarian or dictatorial state there is no room for such an institution. The experiences of Nazi Germany and of East European countries—in particular, Poland, Czechoslovakia, Hungary, and East Germany—prove this. The distinctive character of this type of European university is that the state provides the bureaucratic structure and finances but does not intervene in research or teaching. Full freedom of instruction—by which I mean the freedom of the faculty to decide what is taught, how it is to be taught, and who will teach it—constitutes the essence of a liberal university. Furthermore, a free university enrolls students, regardless of their political views. In other words, the idea of an autonomous state university assumes that the state is liberal itself, at least to some extent, and has no interest in restricting academic freedom. The liberal state is seen as a guardian of academic freedom, promoting and guaranteeing the free scholarly functioning of the university. When the state is totalitarian, the idea of the autonomous state university disappears. In this article, I would like to discuss several events in Poland which resulted from the distortion of the traditional idea of the autonomous university and from the violation of academic freedom. A discussion of the situation of the Polish universities between 1883 and 1919, 1940 and 1945, and since 1945 may help in discerning what the totalitarian distortion of the idea of university means.

The official status of the university in Poland has not changed radically since World War II. Owing to the new ideological and totalitarian character of the state, however, its actual functioning is severely hampered and its freedom seriously endangered. The state has taken two ideological positions regarding the university. First, the state reasons that, since it provides the university's finances, it has a right to make decisions about all academic problems—in effect, making the university simply an object of governmental policy. The university's financial dependency on the state has become subjugation by the state, resulting in the loss of a vast part of the university's academic autonomy. Second, since Poland is at present clearly an ideological state that openly promotes and promulgates Soviet Marxist ideology, all educational institutions, by definition, become instruments of the state's ideology and politics; education is identified with ideological indoctrination.

The combination of financial dependency with ideological and political subjugation defines the present position of the university in Poland. The state intervenes in everyday academic life and decides upon most academic questions. The most crucial aspect of this intervention involves state control over university personnel. All professors and teachers are government employees, which gives the state the opportunity to supervise and control their public political opinions and activities; all new appointments are decided by the state, and all university authorities, such as rector, dean, and chairman, are appointed by the state. This last control was modified somewhat during the Solidarity Year 1981, when Polish scholars were granted a regulation that university administrators would be appointed only from a select group of candidates chosen by the faculty. However, in 1982, following the December 1981 imposition of martial law in Poland, the government started to restrict this privilege and refused to appoint many of the newly elected rectors; instead, the government nominated its own candidates.

A faculty's freedom to choose its own members is an integral part of academic freedom. In liberal countries this freedom is sometimes curtailed, but in Poland it is simply not recognized. Under the state's ideology, academic qualifications are of secondary importance. Even student enrollment is politically controlled, and young people cannot be admitted to the university if their records are politically suspect. Other restrictions of academic freedom include the state control of all teaching programs and curricula and the censoring and limiting of scholarly research and writing. Of course, not all disciplines are equally affected by this ideological and political supervision. Some, such as the majority of the sciences, are restricted mainly by the state's control over new faculty appointments. The situation in the humanities and social sciences is much worse. According to official doctrine, the humanities are "ideological disciplines" and the purpose of teaching them is not education but indoctrination.

In spite of all these difficulties, Polish universities survive more or less as academic institutions, trying to perform independent scholarly research and to provide a decent education. Moreover, many Polish scientists and scholars continue to contribute to the international academic world. This survival is primarily due to the long and strong tradition of independent scholarship in Poland, and to the fact that the values of freedom and independence are deeply rooted in the consciousness of Polish intellectuals. This tradition contributes to the strong reaction against the loss of autonomy in the state universities by many professors. It also helped in the founding of the clandestine university in 1978 in Warsaw and Cracow. This university was formally named *Towarzystwo Kursow Naukowych* (TKN), or the Society for Academic Studies, and known also as the flying university. Both names have been used before and have important historical connotations, bound up as they are in Poland's political history. Clandestine education in Poland began in the nineteenth century and is part of Poland's national history. This is of great importance for an understanding of the flying university of 1978. Without a deeply rooted tradition, the TKN would not have so immediately received such broad and strong social support or exerted such a powerful moral influence on the entire Polish academic world.

After Poland lost its independence as a result of partitions in the eighteenth century, national survival and preservation of cultural identity became principal concerns.[1] The educational situation was different in the various parts of Poland; it was better in Galizia under the Austro-Hungarian rule but much worse in the western sections of Poland belonging to Prussia and in the eastern sections which became part of Russia. Under Prussian and Russian rule, teaching in Polish was prohibited. The Polish people's most urgent need was to preserve Polish as the medium of instruction and to teach the language and literature in elementary and secondary schools. The new activities of home education and self-education were born and numerous groups and societies organized and promoted clandestine education in an effort to preserve Polish cultural identity.

At the university level, the development of clandestine education occurred for many of the same reasons. To understand the desire to have a university one has to remember that in independent Poland, before the partitions, there was a strong tradition of academic teaching. The oldest Polish university, the Jagiellonian University, was founded in Cracow in the fourteenth century. In Wilno the university was established in 1578, and it was begun in Lwow in 1661.[2]

In Krolestwo Kongresowe, however, under Russian domination, all attempts to have a legally functioning Polish university failed. In 1818 the Royal Warsaw University was established but it functioned only until 1831 when, after an uprising, the Russians closed it and prohibited any further activity.[3] In 1862 an attempt was made to create a university called *Szkola Glowna Warszawska* or the Main School in Warsaw but it only survived until 1869 when it was abolished. Under these conditions the idea and the tradition of free clandestine academic education was born and the constitution of underground universities was established. These universities came to be called flying universities because they had no campuses, land, or buildings, and to avoid persecution, each class meeting was held in a different private apartment.

The original flying university existed in Warsaw from 1883 until 1905. At that time, the need for academic instruction in the eastern part of Poland belonging to Russia was very strong. The flying university began as a system of small self-education groups secretly meeting in private apartments. The teachers were the outstanding Polish professors who had been dismissed from Warsaw University when it was closed.[4] The flying university grew quickly, reaching a peak between 1887 and 1890, when its numerous groups supported a systematically organized web of lectures and seminars. There were curricula, syllabuses, final examinations, and diplomas. Students paid a small tuition, though some poor people attended free of charge, and professors received a small honorarium.[5]

Because of difficult conditions for instruction, self-education was emphasized; unlike a regular university, students had to learn more by themselves and less from teachers. This situation produced a new and very interesting type of textbook, better suited for self-education groups. The self-educational textbook was an encyclopedia of a particular subject that included a complete bibliography and instructions on how to study the subject. These books were published in numerous copies and were present in a great many homes.[6]

The flying university in the 1800s promoted two important educational ideas. First, it raised the question of democratic mass education, holding that the opportunity to learn should not be determined by social status and that education should be available to everyone. Second, it emphasized the education of women. The flying university created the first opportunity for academic studies for women in Warsaw and the eastern part of Poland, a great number attended classes, and about three thousand women received diplomas between 1883 and 1905.[7]

In 1905 the flying university became publicly known as the TKN[8] and was a semilegal organization partially recognized by the government, but it functioned with an even greater range of activities than allowed by its official status. In reality, it was a fully functioning university, but because such universities were prohibited by the Russian authorities, it claimed formally to be only a scholarly society.[9] Consequently, by necessity the clandestine character of the teaching was partly preserved.

This TKN functioned in Warsaw as a university divided into four departments: science, humanities, mathematics, and agriculture. In 1916 the faculty of the TKN created the Institute of Education, a special school for teachers. In the academic year 1906–07, the humanities department had 700 students; mathematics and science had 600. In 1906, 16 professors made up the humanities faculty; by 1912, the number had risen to 25; and by 1919, its last year of activity, the faculty numbered 45. The science and mathematics faculty grew from 14 in 1906, to 20 in 1912, to 39 in 1919. The total number of professors between 1905 and 1919 in the TKN was about 300, and the average yearly enrollment was 2,500.[10] Women constituted 69 percent of the student body. The TKN finished its activity in 1919 when Poland regained its independence and several new state universities were established.[11] However, the Society did not disappear totally but became a free private university named *Wolna Wszechnica.*

The tradition of clandestine education in Poland also includes the academic education that was carried on during World War II, when the universities in Warsaw, Cracow, and Lwow functioned as networks of small underground groups and provided an opportunity for young people to carry on their studies despite the closing and banning of Polish universities by the Germans.[12]

Historically, the relationship between teaching and courage has been part of the Polish concept of education. During both of these periods, 1883–1919 and 1940–1945, involvement in the clandestine universities was extremely dangerous. One could compile a long list of names of people who were severely punished for their teaching; stories of their exile to Siberia or imprisonment are numerous. And during the Second World War, teachers as well as students took the risk of being killed or sent to a concentration camp. Because of this danger, a pattern of the courageous teacher was born. Courage is now understood as an essential virtue in a teacher, so much so that the Polish people believe that one who is not courageous cannot be a good teacher. Furthermore, because clandestine students were endangered as well, all involvement in the educational process gained a particular moral approval from a broad spectrum of the public. This approval continues in contemporary Poland, deeply rooted in the clandestine educational activities of the nineteenth century.

To educate oneself and to teach others has always been considered a national and moral obligation in Poland. Since the partitions in the 1800s, the question of education has never been ethically neutral. While the emphasis in the nineteenth century was on the preservation of language and the national tradition, the ethos included all academic education. Only by reaching the highest standards of education could the Polish resume their partnership with the European academic tradition.

In January 1978, a group of sixty-one Polish intellectuals, including thirty-seven professors and fifteen writers, continued the tradition of independent thinking and research and established a clandestine university in Warsaw named for its predecessor, the TKN. The main function of the new TKN was to provide lectures and seminars, to publish scholarly writings, and to stimulate research. The group was composed of professors active at state universities or in research institutions like the Polish Academy of Science and Humanities, of former professors who had recently lost their teaching positions for political reasons, and of some distinguished writers and artists. Their first act was the publication of a declaration in the clandestine press to explain the ideals and goals of the TKN as well as to announce a series of public lectures.[13] The state authorities responded immediately with reprisals: the first lecturer was arrested, and the apartment where the lecture was to be held was occupied by the police.[14] Various acts of repression against all sixty-one persons who signed the declaration occurred soon after. It was then clear that the lectures and teaching would have to be clandestine and that these activities would continue to evoke repression against professors and students. The structure of the underground university reflected this knowledge: teaching was conducted in small groups, the time and place of each lecture or seminar were secret and were communicated by person-to-person contact. The Society had no permanent meeting place, rather, the lectures moved from one private apartment to another, thereby earning again the name flying university.

Since some broader publicity was necessary, the names of professors and course subjects were published in the clandestine press, which at that time was flourishing in Poland. In large cities such as Warsaw and Cracow, the publicity functioned quite well and the clandestine university became almost immediately known and discussed among many students at the state universities. This made it possible for students to get in touch with the clandestine teaching professors and "enroll" in classes. Since student anonymity was strictly recommended to avoid repressions against them, there was no formal registration and no list of students' names. There were also no grades, no final exams, and no diplomas. These features resulted in an entity that is best described as a combination of nineteenth-century coffeehouse and eighteenth-century French salon rather than a bureaucratically functioning institution. University students were most often the students at the flying university. Almost all students led a double life: an official one at Warsaw University and a clandestine one at these other courses. That was one of the reasons why student anonymity was so strictly recommended—otherwise the official status of many students would have been endangered. In particular, the rector of Warsaw University was especially eager to dismiss any student who was accused of contacts with clandestine teaching. Some high school students attended clandestine lectures as well.

The TKN never pretended to provide a complete academic education. The goals of the flying university were to offer a system of additional courses in the humanities rather than to totally replace the state university. To replace the state university was not only impossible but probably not necessary. What was really needed was supplementary instruction in the humanities and social sciences that had political and ideological impact and where the distortions of official propaganda were extremely severe.

Some professors, like the students, combined their official and clandestine lives, but the major difference was that the professors' names were publicly announced. There was a practical and moral reason for this. First, the students wanted to know who the teachers were; without a name the scholarly status of a person remains hidden. Second, clandestine teaching was a kind of civil disobedience designed to provide a moral standard. All this activity took place in a highly idealistic atmosphere. As a consequence, the teachers were punished for their civil disobedience by being forbidden to publish or by having their passports revoked; some were dismissed from their official teaching positions, others were arrested and beaten.[15]

In order to explain the activity of the flying university, the three principle motivations for its creation must be understood. All of them were closely related. The first involved the need to inquire, discuss, and teach subjects which were excluded from the state university. There were many such excluded topics in Poland: for historians, excluded topics are contemporary Polish history and the history of Polish-Russian relations; for philosophers, any subject which goes beyond the limits of Soviet Marxism and the materialist interpretation of the history of philosophy; for students of literature, all Polish literature written in exile; and for sociologists, many aspects of social life.

Since the existence of "areas of darkness," a term used to describe prohibited topics or interpretations in the state university's curriculum, was the primary impetus for the founding of the flying university in 1978, I would like to analyze this phenomenon in more detail. These areas of darkness are a result of the ideological nature of the state. According to the official state policy, the humanities and the social sciences have essentially an ideological function which is either for or against socialism and, therefore, for or against the state; neutrality is impossible. Without denying the possible ideological character of these disciplines, I would like to analyze what happens when they are seen exclusively in an ideological light.

Political control has the greatest effect on the study of the contemporary history of Poland. The list of distortions and falsifications of Polish history made by official propaganda seems endless. For instance, there is an official doctrine concerning the origins of the present regime, and all facts which contradict it are not allowed to be published.[16] Some names and facts cannot be mentioned at all; others are essentially misinterpreted or may appear only in the context of severe criticism. For example, the Nazi-Soviet agreement—that is, the Ribbentrop-Molotov pact—can never be mentioned in any publication passing through state censorship. According to Polish history textbooks, many real events never occurred. Thus, one method of political pressure on historians is the exclusion from publication of particular facts. Many names from recent history are also neglected; some significant Polish politicians cannot be mentioned at all, while others can be mentioned only very briefly and with critical commentary. What is banned for publication is banned for teaching as well. According to all official curricula and syllabi, professors of history at universities and in schools must teach this censored history as fact.

Another method of political control involves changing the proportion of facts. For example, the present ruling Communist party claims that it was a leading political power in Poland from 1919 to 1939. Before the Second World War, however, Communists were a tiny group, and the Polish workers' movement was dominated by the Socialists in the Polish Socialist Party. This controversy produces an entire field of falsehoods, prohibitions, and limitations. Another topic that is distorted in a similar way concerns the Western allies during World War II. The official version neglects the links between Poland and England and the existence of a Polish government-in-exile based in London, and emphasizes the significance of Polish-Russian relations. Similarly, when the case of Polish resistance during the war is analyzed, the small amount of Communist guerilla activity is emphasized, while the overwhelmingly powerful underground ruled by the Home Army and linked with the London government-in-exile is ignored. Many other subjects are distorted in the same way. Not only are some facts denied in the official history, and the balance of their significance changed, but some very particular interpretations are also imposed. Consequently, almost every attempt to publish a decent book on contemporary Polish history produces a fight with state censorship. Many writers have at least partly succeeded but many compromises have had to be made.

This situation has created a deeply felt need for a good history book. There is an excitement about history in Poland, but it is rather difficult to get a good book dealing with contemporary Polish history. When something is published, even in a very large edition, it is sold out in a few hours.

National history was always an important topic in Poland; especially during times of partitions, teaching and learning national history was a sort of patriotic duty. Moreover, it was sometimes risky and required heroism. History was a very important part of keeping the national identity, and in contemporary Poland it has preserved its crucial position. So, all falsifications, restrictions, and misinterpretations are felt as particularly painful. The "hunger for history"—there is no exaggeration in calling this yearning a hunger—is especially strong among the young. The older generations know a lot about the recent past from their own experience or from the memories of their parents, but students have a strong desire for tradition and national history. And the state university cannot feed their hunger.

Plainly, then, an obvious task of the clandestine university was to provide accurate instruction in contemporary Polish history. The lectures and seminars were focused on the areas of darkness. History courses were the most popular with students. A second task was to evaluate the official curricula in history instruction and to reveal all distortions and falsifications. A special working group of historians within the flying university was formed for this critical project. In addition, the TKN inspired several research projects in contemporary Polish history, and a few were published by the underground publishing houses. The TKN also sponsored several doctoral dissertations in the areas of darkness. In only two years a great deal was accomplished.

Underground teaching also made some impact on the state university. For the first time, the official teaching was openly challenged, with the main challenge coming from the students themselves. They became more critical and started to put pressure on official instruction. In this way, the immediate impact of the underground university was enormous, despite the relatively small number of clandestine students; it influenced indirectly the entire student population. The whole situation of state teaching was changed, particularly as students questioned the monopoly and credibility of the state university. All of this was possible only because of the distinguished historians among the clandestine teachers.

The situation in philosophy was somewhat different but also difficult. Philosophers are not harmed as much by censorship as historians because they deal with much more abstract concepts. Their work, however, is under more ideological pressure. Whether in their teaching at state universities or in their publications, philosophers are expected to study only what is known as "Marxist philosophy." According to the official point of view, philosophy is a class ideology that is either proletarian or bourgeois, which simply means that the former should be promulgated and the latter undermined. Officially, there is no room left in philosophy for independent scholarly studies. According to the state university curriculum published by the ministry of education, which decreed what was obligatory for all teaching faculty, instruction in philosophy is defined as an indoctrination of Marxism. It is important to point out that "Marxism" here means a version of Soviet Marxism, that is, a combination of dialectical and historical materialism with some elements of the history of philosophy added. It includes very few of Marx's works and excludes all contemporary Western Marxist writing, such as that of Marcuse, the Frankfurt School, or French Marxists. Fortunately for the state of the discipline in Poland, philosophers there tend to be very disobedient people; only their civil disobedience can save philosophy in contemporary Poland.

There is a strong tradition of philosophical thinking in Poland that motivates the powerful resistance of philosophers against the state's ideological pressure. Philosophy flourished while Poland was independent between the two world wars. At that time, the center of Polish philosophic scholarship was the Jan Kazimierz University in Lwow where Twardowski's school was born and gave rise to Polish logic. Another influential school of thought was phenomenology, which was brought to Poland by Roman Ingarden, a student of Husserl and himself a prolific scholar. Catholic philosophy was also important and strong during this period. Logical positivism, phenomenology, and Catholic philosophy still have a great impact on philosophy in Poland. Before World War II, instruction in philosophy in high schools and universities focused on logic and the art of argumentation. Philosophy had a respected position in Polish academia, as it brought together several distinguished and world-renowned minds.[17]

As a consequence, the process of destroying philosophy, which began the moment its ideological function was stressed, has been going very slowly. The past generation's leaders in Polish philosophy have died, but their influence is still very much alive. The current generation of professors, for the most part, knew their predecessors and experienced the high standards of instruction in philosophy that they had maintained. It seems obvious, then, that philosophy would appear among the subjects taught at the clandestine university.

There are no particular areas of darkness in philosophy; rather, the whole discipline is in darkness. The main battlefield is the method and the way of thinking. So, the task delineated by the TKN was to regain philosophy's academic character rather than contribute to its ideological status. This was attempted by teaching philosophy as a radically critical way of thinking and as an art of analysis and interpretation. This approach was very appealing to students who were disgusted with the type of indoctrination they encountered in their official classes.

Some areas in philosophy are more prone to ideological impact than others. Political and social philosophy are most affected and are thus the least independent areas, although moral philosophy and ethics are often repressed as well. Logic is the least affected. Consequently, there was also an attempt made by the flying university to give instruction in moral philosophy. A course was taught in phenomenological ethics and Max Scheler's axiology, for example.

Another subject frequently taught at the clandestine university was Polish literature. Since the end of World War II, Polish writers have been divided between those in exile and those living in Poland. There are two important aspects of this situation. First of all, it happened that the most distinguished contemporary Polish writers lived in exile and that the most significant works of literature were written outside of Poland. Among the most famous are the names of Witold Gombrowicz and Czeslaw Milosz. Secondly, emigrants had never been published in Poland; state censorship banned even the mentioning of their names. People in Poland were thus deprived of the best recent works in Polish literature. Only a very few copies of publications written in exile were available in the country. This produced real social anger. The underground publishing houses[18] started to print thousands of copies of exiled literature, and interest in it was rapidly growing. The most hungry were students, and the TKN initiated several lectures and classes in this area. People met secretly to read Gombrowicz's plays and Milosz's poems. The founders of the flying university included several writers, many of whom were already blacklisted in Poland. Their writings also were read, discussed, and studied. The very existence of this new underground audience stimulated them to write more and to discuss several important topics banned from contemporary Polish history. In this way, interest in history and the growth of independent, uncensored writing developed together.

The whole system of prohibitions in history, philosophy, and literature left vast unexplored areas in the important domains of human thinking. However, prohibition, as always, evokes two different reactions: fear and attraction. It raises considerable interest in the areas of darkness and the need to explore them increases. For professors and students it was exactly this need which provided the main motivation for participation in the flying university—to say what is unspeakable in the system of censorship, to teach, to learn or to publish what is restricted.

The second motivation involves the social aspect of this intellectual restriction: a number of disobedient scholars and writers have been punished by dismissal from their teaching positions. In Poland, all appointments for academic positions, not only at the rank of professor but even at the level of teaching assistant, must be approved by party authorities, who conduct special political and ideological screenings of every candidate. Someone who is under suspicion is not allowed to enter the university, and people who are later suspected of disobedience are dismissed. This system of restriction and repression produces a group of intellectuals who are unemployed and ready to join protest action, and to teach or publish clandestinely. In the 1970s, as the result of several political activities undertaken by intellectuals, unemployed professors were particularly numerous. Thus an ever-increasing process was set in motion as intellectuals dismissed from their university posts joined the political protests.

The third motivation behind the flying university involved a similar situation among the students. As a result of the careful political and ideological screening of students, there were numerous young people dismissed from or never admitted to the university in the late 1970s. Just as the unemployed intellectuals had needed to teach, the rejected students needed to learn, and these two groups came together easily.

In Poland in the late 1970s, then, there were areas of darkness (subjects and interpretations prohibited by the state, with censorship of scholarly research, publication, and teaching), a relatively large group of unemployed or underemployed intellectuals, and young people looking for good and decent instruction and education.

The combination of these factors produced the flying university, the main goals of which were to explore the unexplored domains of the social sciences and the humanities, teach what was restricted or banished from the official university, and provide some new publications.[19] The flying university did not cover all intellectual problems but focused its scholarly and educational activity on the areas of darkness. That was the reason why its teaching function was intended to supplement the official, state university instruction. Its purpose was to teach what was prohibited and to correct what was falsified. Moreover, it provided those who had lost their academic positions at Warsaw University an opportunity to teach and to talk with students and a chance to publish their own writings. And finally, it would produce a new intellectual elite by giving a better education to its students. Each of these goals was partially realized in the mere two years that the university was functioning.

Poland of 1978–1980 was a country of social discontent with a growing civil rights movement. In the fall of 1980, this situation produced Solidarity, a trade union, which in a few months became the most influential social organization and radically changed the balance of power in Poland. As a result, the government became more flexible, and new hope for some very needed changes arose among the people. The intellectuals and scholars started to press the authorities for more academic freedom. A new rector of Warsaw University, who was much more liberal than the previous one, invited TKN professors to present their lectures openly and legally on the campus of Warsaw University. In October 1980, the first public lecture was presented in Auditorium Maximum by a senior professor and famous economist, Edward Lipinski. It was a significant and joyful event that had a symbolic meaning. It seemed that it was time to change a clandestine activity into an open one; to teach the "unspoken" at the normal universities. Several professors who had previously been dismissed from their teaching jobs returned to work at Warsaw University. In this new situation, the TKN general assembly decided to dissolve the flying university.

The time of hope did not last long. A year later, on December 13, 1981, martial law in Poland was imposed, the Solidarity movement destroyed, and a more rigid and severe political regime introduced. Thousands of civil rights activitists, among them many TKN professors, were detained.

Notes

1. Norman Davies, *God's Playground: A History of Poland* (Cambridge, Eng.: Oxford University Press, 1981).
2. Z. Skubala-Tokarska and Z. Tokarski, *Uniwersytety w Polsce* (Warszawa, 1972).
3. See S. Askenazy, *Uniwersytet Warszawski* (Warszawa, 1905); S. Kieniewicz, Dzieje Uniwersytetu Warszawskiego (Warsawa, 1981); and A. Kraushar, *Siedmiolecie Szkoly Glownej Warszawskiej* (Warszawa, 1933).
4. J. Mackiewicz-Wojciechowska, *Latajacy Uniwersytet* (Warszawa, 1883). The most famous professors of this flying university were J. W. Dawid, A. Dygasinski, P. Chmielowski, L. Krzywicki, S. Posner, Z. Heryng, and W. Nalkowski.
5. S. Sempolowska, "Latajacy Uniwersytet," *Spoleczenstwo,* 11 (1908).
6. S. Michalski and A. Heflich, wyd. [eds.] *Poradnik dla Samoukow;* J. Jelenski, *O samopomocy w ksztalceniu* (Warszawa, 1873); and A. Dygasinski, *Jak uczyc sie i jak uczyc innych* (Warszawa, 1889).

7. J. Hulewicz, *Sprawa wyzszego wyksztalcenia kobiet w Polsce w wieku 19-tym* (Krakow, 1939).
8. The creation of TKN was announced in the *Gazeta Polska* on 13 November 1905.
9. *Towarzystwo Kursow Naukowych—Dziesieciolecie Wszechnicy Polskiej* (Warszawa, 1917).
10. Z. Skubala-Tokarska, *Spoleczna rola Wolnej Wszechnicy Polskiej* (Warszawa, 1967).
11. H. Kiepurska, "TKN, 1906–1915," W[in]: *Inteligencja Polska pod zaborami,* R. Czepulis-Rastenis (Warszawa, 1978).
12. See *Z dziejow podziemnego Uniwersytetu Warszawskiego* (Warszawa, 1961). *Ne Cedat Akademia: Kartki z dziejow nauczania w Uniwersytecie Jagiellonskim, 1939–1945* (Krakow, 1975); A. M. Zarebowie, wyd. [ed.] *Alma Mater w podziemiu* (Krakow, 1964).
13. The text of the declaration is translated and reprinted at the beginning of this article.
14. All harassment and persecution was reported in the issues of *Biuletyn Informacyjny KOR,* the main clandestine publication; see also *Komisja Helsinska w Polsce: Dokumenty w sprawie bojowek SZSP,* which can be found at the Harvard College Library, Bibliography of Solidarity, Microfiche No. FMP 62.
15. In Poland all publications, including academic journals, are censored by the state censorship office. It was very easy, therefore, for the authorities to forbid all TKN members to publish their writing. They were forced in this way to publish only in the underground publishing houses. Furthermore, the state blacklisted *all* TKN members and deprived them of their passports, making travel abroad impossible. A list of the cases where passports were refused was published in *Kultura,* November 1979. Frequently, professors were arrested just before their classes and detained for a short time so that they would have to miss their lectures.
16. See *Czarna Ksiega Cenzury PRL* (London: Aneks, 1977).
17. For example, Kazimierz Twardowski, professor of philosophy at Lwow University; Kazimierz Ajdukiewicz, professor of philosophy at universities in Lwow and Warsaw; Tadeusz Kotarbinski, professor of philosophy in Warsaw; Jan Lukasiewicz, professor of philosophy in Warsaw and Dublin; Roman Ingarden, professor of philosophy at Jagiellonian University; and Alfred Tarski, Jan Salamucha, and others.
18. The best known was NOWA publishing house and publications produced by Glos.
19. TKN started to sponsor and publish a series called *Zeszyty Nuakowe;* a review of the first volume appeared in *Kultura,* May 1980. Published were the following issues: T. Burek, *Jaka historia literatury jest nam dlzis potnebua?* (NOWA, TKN: Warszawa, 1979); S. Amsterdamski, T. Kowalik and K. Wolicki, *Plotka a monopol informacji* (NOWA, TKN: Warszawa, 1981); and *O czym myslec nie lubiny?* (NOWA, TKN: Warszawa, 1981).

"Not Bread Alone":

Clandestine Schooling and Resistance in the Warsaw Ghetto during the Holocaust

SUSAN M. KARDOS

Throughout the most trying times in their history — dispersions, forced conversions, state-sponsored massacres, exclusion, discrimination, and mass migration — the Jews have maintained their commitment to education and organized schooling.[1] But no time was more desperate for the Jews than the years of the Holocaust in World War II Europe, and no attempts to sustain education and organized schooling were more poignant than those that occurred secretly and at great peril in the Warsaw Ghetto.

Central questions about the role of education emerge from the stories of the clandestine schools, which were maintained at a time when life for the Jews was shadowed by death and despair: Why have schools? What is schooling for? Should schools prepare students for the future, provide for the present, or preserve the past? For whom should schools be organized — for individuals, for communities, or even for whole cultures? These questions are important to ask — in the United States and around the world — as critics challenge the importance of schooling and wonder about the purpose or relevance of schools as they currently exist. Historians, critical theorists, economists, psychologists, and social scientists have written extensively about the implicit and explicit purposes of schools, highlighting shifting objectives within particular historical or social contexts.[2] One set of answers to the questions posed above can be found in the story of the underground schools in the Warsaw Ghetto. It is a story not only of organized schooling, but also of resistance. It is a story of how schools can be used for individual survival, community continuity, and cultural endurance.

This article examines how the Jews of the Warsaw Ghetto used clandestine schooling to resist Nazi intentions to erase them from the world — not only to eradicate them person by person and community by community, but also to eradicate their entire culture — indeed, their entire history. I first describe the multiple forms of clandestine schooling within the underground

Harvard Educational Review Vol. 72 No. 1 Spring 2002, 33–66

network and explain how the schools originated, and then discuss the diversity of schools run by house committees, soup kitchens, orphanages, youth movements, religious groups, and private citizens. I analyze the multiple purposes these schools served, arguing, first, that organized schooling can be characterized as a present-oriented form of resistance, which aided the Warsaw Ghetto Jews in their daily struggles against hunger, chaos, and inhumanity. Organized schooling also served as a future-oriented form of resistance by providing a sense of hope in otherwise desperate and uncertain conditions. Finally, I argue that, for the Jews of the Warsaw Ghetto, clandestine schooling was a form of resistance that was at once past, present, and future oriented. Using examples of curricular content and the activities of the Jewish youth movements in the Ghetto, I maintain that, through the collective action of organized clandestine learning, the Warsaw Ghetto Jews were able to defy the objectives of their oppressors and resist historical and cultural annihilation.[3]

The Warsaw Ghetto

The bomb craters that pockmarked the Polish landscape in September 1939 gave testimony to the three-week *Blitzkrieg*, or lightning war, that befell the country when the Germans attacked. The Nazis immediately issued anti-Jewish decrees and, within a year, walled in a 100-square-block area of the city to form the Warsaw Ghetto. The equivalent of one-third of Warsaw's population, between 400,000 and 500,000 Jews,[4] was squeezed into 2.4 percent of the total area of the city.[5] The original purpose of the Ghetto was to seal off the Jews completely from Poland's economic and cultural life.[6] Initially, although the Jews were fired from all public service jobs, prohibited from being hired by companies owned by non-Jews, and barred from social places such as libraries, theaters, and railroads, they were still permitted to enter and exit the Ghetto. However, on November 15, 1940, all twenty-two entrances to the Ghetto were sealed, and Jews were no longer permitted to leave.[7] In his diary entry for this date, Adam Czerniakow, leader of the *Judenrat* (the Jewish Council governing the Ghetto), wrote, "I was ordered to have 10 of our militiamen posted at each of the street exits from the ghetto by 7 A.M. tomorrow. . . . [Members of the Jewish leadership council] are to block with barbed wire a number of streets which have not been walled up."[8] Two days later he wrote in his characteristically concise style, "November 17, 1940 — Sunday. At the boundaries of the ghetto the *Ordnungspolizei* [German order police]. Throngs of Jews pass by with bared heads."[9] Thus the purpose of the Ghetto shifted. While it was initially intended to humiliate and separate the Jews completely from the rest of the city's population, it now became a means by which to suffocate them, as food was scarce and disease was rampant.

Tens of thousands died of starvation and typhus. In 1941, 43,000 Jews died in the Ghetto; more than 27,000 perished in the first half of 1942, preceding the first mass deportation.[10] For the rest the Ghetto served as a waiting area for those who were later transported to the Treblinka death camp. Although it seems the death rate would have decimated the Ghetto population, the constant influx of Jewish refugees from other provinces kept it crowded. On January 20, 1942, high-ranking Nazi officials met at the Wannsee Conference in Berlin, where they decided to implement the "final solution of the Jewish question" — the extermination of all European Jewry.[11] This decision had immediate consequences for the remaining Ghetto inhabitants; mass deportation to Treblinka began on July 22, 1942. Like much of Nazi-occupied Europe, the Ghetto was rapidly and systematically transformed as part of the grander Nazi objective of the total eradication of Jewish culture and history from the world.[12]

There was nevertheless a sense among the Jews in the Ghetto, at least before they knew of the death camps, that they were glad to be sequestered, "sheltered from harm's way,"[13] and under the direct rule of a Jewish Council rather than the Nazis.[14] Despite the harsh and restrictive decrees issued against the Jews, the random violence and humiliation perpetrated against them, the desperate living conditions, the corruption of the Ghetto police, and the harsh criticism of the Judenrat, the Warsaw Ghetto was the site of an "extraordinary and intense intellectual life."[15] Clandestine religious groups, schools, reading circles, lectures, dramatic programs, and orchestras thrived in the Ghetto.[16] The underground press was strong and integral, particularly the several dozen illegal youth publications that analyzed political issues, outlined educational tasks, urged passive resistance to the Nazis, and laid the foundation for what was to become an armed uprising.[17] The Bundist youth publication *Yugnt Shtime* (*Voice of Youth*) declared:[18]

> The very expression of apathy indicates submission to the enemy, which can cause our collapse morally and root out of our heads our hatred for the invader. It can destroy within us the will to fight; it can undermine our resolution . . . and because our position is so bitterly desperate, our will to give up our lives for a purpose more sublime than our daily existence must be reinforced. . . . Our young people must walk with heads erect.[19]

The youth groups in the Ghetto were responsible for many social, cultural, and political activities and were largely responsible for leading the highly organized and heroic armed Warsaw Ghetto Uprising, which began on April 19, 1943. The Nazis had originally planned to liquidate the Ghetto in three days; however, the Ghetto fighters — mostly from the ranks of the youth groups — defended the Ghetto for five weeks.[20]

. . . Not Bread Alone

While the last and most dramatic story of the Warsaw Ghetto is the uprising, many other forms of resistance were taking place in the Ghetto before the armed revolt. One of the most important arenas of individual and collective resistance was the clandestine school network. When one considers the harsh living conditions of the Ghetto's inhabitants, particularly the children, one wonders why, though expressly prohibited, organized schooling happened nonetheless. In the face of such despair, why did teachers consent to teach and students to learn? An anonymous essayist writing in the Warsaw Ghetto posed a series of similar questions: "Why should one study at all, when uncertain of the day and the moment, with no prospect of to-morrow, not knowing where one shall be, whether one shall eat and what? — How can one, in these circumstances, think of educating children?" This essay, one of many found after the war,[21] sought to answer the question, "What propels youth to schools and learning and bids parents to squeeze out the last penny in order to provide their children with some education, *not bread alone* [author's emphasis]?"[22]

The Jews of the Warsaw Ghetto faced multiple struggles. There was the personal daily struggle against hunger, disease, poverty, overcrowding, and the possibility of deportation, which was intensified by the struggle to maintain a sense of dignity, normalcy, and hope in the face of brutal inhumanity. Then there was the community's struggle to stay organized and cohesive and to maintain social services, political organization, religious life, and governance within the Ghetto walls. Finally there was the broader struggle against historical and cultural eradication and, ultimately, against complete, collective annihilation.

That the Jews of the Warsaw Ghetto enthusiastically organized a variety of forums in which teachers could teach and students could learn illustrates how teaching and learning can be individually and collectively liberatory. Even in the darkest circumstances, teaching and learning can provide participants with the possibility of social and self-determination by transcending the moment and serving as the lifeline between hopelessness and hope.[23]

CLANDESTINE SCHOOLS IN THE WARSAW GHETTO: MULTIPLE FORMS, MULTIPLE ORGANIZING GROUPS

Most schooling for Jewish children ceased when the Nazis bombarded Warsaw in September 1939, destroying school facilities. Although the Nazis prohibited schooling for Jews, some schools stayed active for a few months until the last building at 55 Okopowa Street was taken over by the Nazis.[24] From the beginning of the occupation, the Judenrat continually pressed the German authorities for permission to reopen schools. As early as November 1939, then again in December, and once more in May 1940, Adam Czerniakow wrote in his diary about the need for schools. With the exception of some official vocational courses, the requests of the Jewish leadership proved fruitless, and on October 11, 1940, Czerniakow wrote, "There have been rumors that, because of fear of epidemic, Jewish schools will remain closed."[25]

Poetry class in the Warsaw Ghetto, 6–8 Gesia Street. Yad Vashem Photo Archives, courtesy of United States Holocaust Memorial Museum Photo Archives.

Despite the fact that teaching and learning were perilous acts for Jews in occupied Poland, they persisted. Mary Berg was a teenager from Lodz who fled with her family to Warsaw. She continued her education in Warsaw in a small study circle with teachers and other students from Lodz. On July 12, 1940, she commented in her diary about the proliferation of study groups "in cellars and attics" around the city.[26] She then wrote, "Two . . . schools were discovered by the Germans sometime in June; later we heard that the teachers were shot on the spot, and the pupils had been sent to a concentration camp near Lublin [Majdanek]." Berg went on to describe the "special intensity and warmth" that the grave situation engendered:

> The teachers put their whole heart and soul into their teaching, and all the pupils study with exemplary diligence. There are no bad pupils. The illegal character of teaching, the danger that threatens us every minute, fills us with a strange earnestness. The old distance between teachers and pupils has vanished, we feel like comrades-in-arms responsible to each other.[27]

After the Warsaw Ghetto was sealed off in November 1940, the Nazis continued to forbid the Jews from operating schools for the estimated thirty to forty thousand school-age children who were confined there.[28] Nevertheless, clandestine "children's corners" and kindergartens were in operation; elementary classrooms operated in conjunction with public kitchens; an active network of study groups thrived; religious education persisted; and, in whatever ways possible, youth groups continued their flourishing pre-war intellectual and political activities. Extensive private tutoring, a few clandestine high schools, and hundreds of *komplety* ("complements," or study circles) also existed.[29] Vocational training[30] and university-level programs were offered as well. At their peak, five hundred students were enrolled in medical courses that employed famous lecturers from the Jewish medical faculty of Warsaw University and Krakow University.[31]

These clandestine educational activities in the Warsaw Ghetto engendered the same sort of atmosphere that Mary Berg described. In oral testimony given in 1991, Vladka Meed, a teenage youth movement member, underground activist, and Ghetto survivor, recounts experiencing a similar atmosphere while listening to lectures with other members of her youth group:

> I was a young girl . . . and it was at the time of starvation and typhoid and hunger and constantly peril in the Ghetto, but nevertheless . . . lectures took place in many places and in many houses during the Ghetto period, and the young people used to go there, and they were asking questions. . . . I . . . remember the atmosphere, the elevation, being together with the people and talking about the writer and the character.[32]

The intensity and warmth Berg described was felt by teachers as well. Teacher Ana Natanblut wrote about conversations she had with her friend, researcher and teacher Fanny Boymberg, who was later murdered in Treblinka:

> She gave lessons about her beloved subjects, Latin and history, from early in the morning until late at night. And after all the lessons, she would spend time discussing the material with her female students. She especially worked on old Greek texts and wrote articles, but she also derived pleasure from her discussions with her students, and she used to say that she had never had such joy from her teaching as she had in the Ghetto.[33]

During the second year in the Ghetto, from the fall of 1941 through the summer of 1942, the Judenrat was able to secure permission from the German authorities to open primary schools for no more than five thousand Jewish children. Nevertheless, most clandestine educational activity in the Ghetto continued until the end.

Origins of Schools

The political organization within and outside the Ghetto was composed of complex authority structures, both above- and underground. The loci of authority that were primarily centralized outside the Ghetto — but ultimately determined much of what happened in it — included the occupying German army, the various Nazi forces, the general government of occupied Poland, and the Polish underground. An equally complicated authority structure existed inside the Ghetto. Some groups, such as the Judenrat and the Jewish Police, were recognized by the Germans, while many others were not. Despite the arrests and the flight of Jewish political leaders eastward, some of the organized leadership of the pre-war Jewish community was reestablished in the Ghetto upon its creation.

The sociopolitical structures in the Ghetto created a climate that enabled the clandestine schools to be formed. The youth movements, Ghetto organizations such as Jewish Self-Help and CENTOS (The Jewish Society for the Care of Orphans), cultural organizations such as YIKOR (Yiddish Culture Organizations) and *Tecumah* (dedicated to the "revival" of the Hebrew language), religious organizations, the Judenrat, professional educators, and private Ghetto citizens were all responsible for promoting organized clandestine schooling in the Ghetto.

German education policy in Poland was part of the overall Nazi effort to destroy the intelligentsia (both Polish and Jewish) in the occupied territories; thus, education in occupied Poland was severely restricted for both Poles and Jews. However, once the Jews were ghettoized, the Nazis showed little interest in their political and social activities. An *Oneg Shabbat* essay, entitled "A Preliminary Study in Teaching People During the War," includes an account of the German policy toward schooling during the occupation of Poland.[34] According to the essay, the Germans initially considered dealing with clandestine schools a waste of time because, ironically, they did not see the schools as threatening their primary interest in "demoralizing the masses in order to destroy . . . Jewish culture that is so 'dangerous' to humanity."[35] Therefore, a strong network of underground schools developed in the Ghetto's earliest days.

Clandestine Schooling

House Committees, Soup Kitchens, and Orphanages

House Committees (known also as Building Committees) in the Ghetto organized themselves to provide care and education for small children in "children's corners" and gardens. In the summer of 1941, approximately 4,500 children were under the care of 164 children's corners. Natan Koninski, a teacher and *Oneg Shabbat* contributor, wrote that the youngsters in the children's corners benefited from "competent instructors" and the "company of their peers." The children "spend their time in playing and in games, in learning songs, in exercise, and in listening to interesting stories and instructive talks." According to Koninski, while some children's corners had formally qualified kindergarten teachers, others were taught by lay women or older youth from the apartment houses.[36] For instance, Benjamin Meed, a youth group member, was asked by the elders of his House Committee to help with the children. The program he organized for approximately thirty children included teaching them early literacy skills and Polish songs, and distributing soup.[37]

CENTOS organized soup kitchens and day-care centers, which also provided children with clandestine education. In March 1944, after the liquidation of the Ghetto, Emmanuel Ringelblum (historian, educator, and organizer of the *Oneg Shabbat* Archives) and Adolf Berman (director of CENTOS) made a desperate attempt to report to the world about the activities, events, and tragedy of the Warsaw Ghetto in a communiqué to the Jewish Scientific Institute in New York City. Writing from their hiding places in Warsaw after their escape from the Ghetto, they described many things in the Ghetto, including cultural and educational endeavors. They reported, "Under the mantle of children's kitchens and CENTOS centers, there were formed a network of illegal schools of various ideologies" representing various political, religious, and educational philosophies.[38]

Indeed, in November 1941, teacher Natan Koninski wrote of secret schools fronted by CENTOS kitchens:

> In some kitchens systematic school instruction has now been conducted for a year. Children, grouped according to age and mental development, learned regular school subjects on the basis of a continuous, regular curriculum. Several kitchens conducted the schooling according to the ideological programmes of pre-war times. Thus children were taught the Yiddish or Hebrew languages, studied History of the Jews, [and] literature. Every opportunity was taken to arrange public functions and produce plays or have a convention devoted to Yiddish and Hebrew writers, such as Peretz or Bialik. In kitchens as, for instance, the one at Prosta Street 8, or Nowolipki 68, normal, regular school lessons were maintained and children were getting, apart from the meals, also the so very needed food for the intellect.[39]

Not all kitchens had carefully organized schools; some offered only half-day care programs for the needy and for refugees from all over Poland, and some children were just too ill or malnourished to participate in the programs. Koninski reports that CENTOS ran thirty-five kitchens, boarding houses, and day houses that were responsible for feeding 35,000 homeless, refugee, or otherwise desperate children.[40]

Because of disease and starvation, and because the Warsaw Ghetto was a repository for Jewish refugees from all over Poland, orphans abounded there. Many orphanages organized schooling for their children, but none is more famous than that established by Dr. Janusz Korczak. Korczak, an author and educator, is well known for his child-centered educational philosophy, his commitment to and respect for children, and his final march with his orphans to the deportation site.[41] The orphanage, which existed in Warsaw before the war and later moved into the Ghetto, was set up with a student-run system of justice to which all children and adults were accountable. When the orphanage was moved into the Ghetto, many more children were taken in, and members of the Jewish intelligentsia had jobs as cooks and cleaners as they hid from the Germans. Survivor David Kochalski describes the education program in the orphanage and the access he and the other children had to "all the intelligentsia, teachers, professors, doctors, [and] psychologists . . . who were hiding." He explains, "It was something like a university. . . . We had terrific lectures on everything. . . . All the boys would sit down and . . . every other night another professor would start teaching us."[42]

Having just performed a play, Korczak's children were dressed in costumes when the Nazis arrived to deport them on August 5, 1942. Although only the children were to be deported, Korczak and his assistant, Stefania Wilczynska (Madame Stefa), went with them, marching in lines behind a big green flag carried by one of the boys. This green flag was similar to the one carried by King Matt — the protagonist in one of Korczak's children's stories, *King Matt the First* — as he led a "peaceful crusade" of the children of the world in the name of peace, justice, and an end to all wars. And just as the boy-king is led through the street in chains in the final scene, so too were Korczak and his children led to their demise.[43]

Survivor Erwin Baum remembers his own experience living in Dr. Janusz Korczak's orphanage during the war. Baum had escaped from the Ghetto to get bread the day before Korczak, Madame Stefa, and the rest of the two hundred children were deported. On his way back to the orphanage he came across a woman wailing, "They took the children! They took the children!" Baum ran to the *Umschlagplatz* (assembly point), where the trains deported Jews to Treblinka, and he watched Korczak argue with a soldier, apparently insisting on going on the transport with the children. Baum tried to go too, but was waved away by a German soldier who reprimanded him, "You are not a Jew, get away from here." Baum was left alone with his last hope taken away. He was left to wonder, "What am I going to do without him? How am I going to survive without him?" Fifty-eight years later he says of Dr. Korczak, "I would gladly give half my life for him."[44]

Youth Movements

In the Ghetto, the youth movements established urban *kibbutzim* (communes) in buildings where they conducted intellectual activities, opened high schools, and sponsored lectures and study groups. A Ghetto inhabitant wrote of the youth in *Oneg Shabbat:* "It is no exaggeration to state that the only environment in which political movement still pulsates with life, in which the will to act has not utterly failed and in which action actually takes place — is that of the youth."[45] Emmanuel Ringelblum lectured before a seminar run by a youth group and described his experience in his journal: "When I looked into the glowing faces of youth thirsty for knowledge, I altogether forgot the war [ravaging] the world. The seminars were held directly opposite the [post of the] German sentry who guarded the Ghetto gate . . ."[46] While this is just one small example of the ways in which youth movements valued and actively participated in education, their boldness and defiance illustrate the daily risks the students and teachers took in order to engage in teaching and learning.

Youth movement members who lived in the kibbutzim were able to sustain an active political, cultural, and intellectual life, while maintaining the primary focus on "the teaching of the youth movements' traditional ideologies and values."[47] Survivor Leah Silverstein, one of approximately twenty youths who lived in the kibbutz run by the Zionist youth group *HaShomer HaTzair* (The Young Guardian), describes it as an "oasis in the terrible Ghetto." She remembers: "In the evenings and on *Shabbat* [Sabbath], we used to gather and [have] discussions and . . . presentations by all kinds of literary men who used to come to the kibbutz. So we were politically and intellectually active, in spite of terrible conditions that existed in the Ghetto."[48]

Youth movement members were trained by the youth group leadership as cultural workers and lecturers by attending seminars on political, sociological, historical, and literary subjects. They then traveled to different buildings and repeated these lectures. Vladka Meed was one such youth lecturer. She explains that the purpose of the lectures was to elevate the people, and that the lecturers, who were "proud to belong to this group" of cultural workers, were very "serious about [their] mission."[49]

Societies in the Ghetto other than the youth movements sponsored a wide range of educational and cultural activities. With the help of the residential Building Councils and the Self-Help Organization, the Yiddish cultural organization YIKOR and Tecumah, which was dedicated to the revival of the Hebrew language, held literary meetings and readings in those buildings after curfew.[50] The importance of such activities is represented in an *Oneg Shabbat* essay, which called for an increased number of accessible cultural events in the Ghetto. The author wrote:

> It seems that the present is the worst period in our history. One of the most important tasks in this, our time, is the preservation of spirit in our community. We must undertake everything possible . . . so that our struggle (or rather our wrestling for daily bread) does not exhaust the last, remaining vital force in our nation.[51]

Study Circles, Gymnasia, and Religious Study

In an *Oneg Shabbat* essay entitled "A Preliminary Study in Teaching People During the War," the author, writing about high school–aged children, described clandestine study groups composed of a teacher and a small group of students, which met approximately twelve hours a week for a low tuition fee. The study groups were organized either through private teachers, private citizens, or through the youth movements of political organizations. In the winter of 1940–1941, there was a sharp rise in the number of study groups and the number of students.[52] By 1941 the study groups numbered in the hundreds.[53]

Soon after the formation of the Ghetto, the Jewish teachers began to actively form clandestine study groups, both to earn money and to address what they perceived to be the need for schools, since a large number of Jewish youth at all levels were being deprived of an education. An *Oneg Shabbat* essayist wrote that, in December 1939, "feeling the pinch of necessity, teachers began vigorously to organize youth — mostly without the participation of former headmasters. . . . They came into contact with former students with relative ease and offered them the only feasible option — a clandestine study group composed of former students."[54] There was no shortage of teachers, as discussed in the *Oneg Shabbat* essay "The School System": "We have far too many well-qualified teachers, and an equal or higher number of new candidates. Add to this, that each graduate from secondary education, and each student in more advanced schools, tries hardest to enter the profession due to lack of other sources of income."[55] "A Preliminary Study in Teaching People During the War" reported that in the Ghetto "youngsters study diligently and often show great interest in the course of their work" and "the teachers work very hard and with exceptional honesty, though their material situation is extremely difficult."[56]

This activity, at first economically motivated, was later motivated by other forces as well. Vladka Meed remembers:

> People were going on in the most difficult situations and holding on to life as human beings. . . . Our neighbor . . . in the Ghetto was selling pieces of bread . . . outside of the building of our house . . . and looking out if a German patrol is not passing because in her apartment above us, her daughter was giving lectures to children . . . a small illegal school. This woman did not even think that she is the hero and her daughter didn't think that she is the hero, but they were conducting illegal classes for children, knowing that if a German patrol will . . . catch them, they will be right away not only arrested but also killed. And this is the way people lived.[57]

Joseph Kutrzeba, who came to the Ghetto from Lodz at the age of fourteen, explained that his parents wanted him to continue with his education "no matter what [the] conditions." His father was a prominent teacher, musician, and composer in Lodz, and after the family's arrival in the Ghetto, his father's colleagues, also teachers, organized themselves and their students "almost right away" into komplety. He was part of a study group with two girls, two other boys, and "excellent professors, some of whom were Ph.D.'s."[58] He describes the degree of secrecy under which these classes took place:

> Secrecy was most important . . . so we would meet almost every day somewhere else. . . . And before we entered the courtyard, each one of us . . . walked back and forth to make sure that nobody is following [us]. And [we] prearranged knocks on the door. When we studied, there were no manuals so [we] just [had] the professor's memory and written notes. We always had a game of dominos or chess ready in the event someone knocked on the door. Hide the books! And

> immediately we're just sitting playing the game. So secrecy was very very important because nobody trusted anybody.[59]

He studied "virtually the whole array of high school subjects except those requiring labs" in his clandestine study group, including history, geography, Polish literature ("the great Polish masterworks"), beginning English (which he "adored"), Latin, literature, math, and Hebrew. According to Kutrzeba, the teachers were "stunning" and the education was extremely high quality: "The two years in the Warsaw Ghetto sunk in very deeply. To this day, I know the Latin that was taught."[60]

Study circles were not the only means by which older children could be schooled. The Hebrew *gymnasia* (secondary schools) served students associated with the Zionist *Tarbut* movement, which was a cultural and educational movement dedicated to modern Zionism and the Hebrew language.[61] The youth group *Dror* (Freedom) established a gymnasium in the Ghetto in August 1940 that was based on their ideology of Labor Zionism. At first it was organized for its own members, but it came to include nonmembers as well. Thirteen teachers taught 120 students a traditional curriculum, including Hebrew, Yiddish, Bible studies, singing, art, Jewish history, French, and German, which was replaced with English in the second year of the school's existence.[62]

Religious education also persisted. For example, the religious boys' schools *Yesodey HaTorah* (Foundations of the Torah) and the religious girls' schools *Beis Yaakov* (House of Jacob) reopened soon after the bombardment ended. At their peak, in 1941, forty-six boys' classes employed 132 teachers and four girls' classes employed sixteen teachers at these schools. Eight full *Yeshivot* — religious high schools — were also in operation under the same auspices, serving a total of 3,500 students.[63] In addition to the Yiddishist schools, religious Zionist schools run by the *Mizrachi* (Spiritual Center) organization were also in operation. Finally, many religious youths studied privately with Rabbis, such as the thousand orthodox children studying as part of the "'Patronage' of Torah" study groups established by Rabbi Meshulam Kaminer.[64] On March 18, 1941, Emmanuel Ringelblum described a religious study scene in his journal:

> There's an apartment in a Jewish courtyard where traditional studies are secretly going on. The door of the apartment is opened only to the password (one knock). When you come in, you see a large group of Talmudic students sitting over their studies.[65]

Sanctioned Schools

After a great effort, the Judenrat secured a modest concession from the Nazis and was granted permission to open a small number of sanctioned early primary schools in the Ghetto. On September 5, 1941, Judenrat leader Adam Czerniakow wrote tersely in his diary:

> In the morning at the Community. I am not getting any answers to a number of my letters [to the authorities]. Among other requests I submitted one for authorization of Children's Month. At last permission was given today for opening the elementary schools. I summoned a commission at once and we held a meeting.[66]

Despite the difficult circumstances, the Jewish School Commission saw continued schooling as a necessary investment in the Jewish community's future. By October 1941, six official schools were operating in the children's shelters; by the end of that school year, nineteen were in operation, some of which had previously been underground classes.[67] Meanwhile, the komplety and other covert education activities continued to function separately and clandestinely. In a letter dated December 15, 1941, addressed to possible donors, a special committee of The Patronate of Jewish Cultural Activities in Warsaw articulated the purpose of the organized schools: "Friends and people concerned must now create about the school, and on behalf of it, the right social atmosphere conducive to a healthy education of the Jewish child, for the sake of the future. . . . We must create what is necessary. This is our duty."[68]

According to Ana Natanblut, a school commission member and teacher, it was the dream of Abraham Wolfowicz, chair of the commission, to "create a unified Jewish school on a democratic basis with a particularly national color."[69] The commission decided that "in all the types of schools, the program should be constructed on a Jewish theme and for the most part teach in Yiddish and Hebrew, depending on the type of school."[70] However, despite the official sanction, day-to-day terror in the Ghetto caused even these schools to have a furtive and perilous aspect to their operation. Czerniakow wrote in his diary about a speech he gave on December 21, 1941, at an official ceremony honoring the Judenrat-sponsored schools: "Somebody reported to the authorities what went on at our school ceremony. The work of a well-known scoundrel."[71]

Despite this peril, Natanblut described the sanctioned schools as places of "celebration" that elicited the same intense devotion from students and teachers as the clandestine schools:

> It was truly crowded and cold and there were no textbooks, but there was an atmosphere of work. The moral climate was uplifted . . . and there were no bored teachers or bored students. One's heart would fill with joy and pride when they came to visit a school, and after an interruption of two years time, we once again experienced a true school, with true classes with boards and benches and children learning with a violent desire. People sensed a celebration in the schools.[72]

While the desperate conditions in the Ghetto persisted and Jews were silently dying of hunger and disease, the cultural and educational work of the community still continued. Abraham Wolfowicz found solace in the fact that the schools were taking the first steps "to unite the fragmented Jewish people" despite the fact that the schools actually represented quite different political, philosophical, and religious ideologies.[73] Natanblut further found teachers to be vital in any attempts to overcome the desperation and despair in the Ghetto. She wrote:

> In the days of fear, when the sword of Damocles was hanging over everyone, when hunger and epidemics were our daily bread, when we were sinking into depression because of all of this, the teachers made the effort to build such a school system that shimmered with all the colors of the rainbow in the darkness that had fallen so heavily upon us.[74]

Indeed, Czerniakow commented in his diary on the contrast between the teachers and the desperate conditions under which they taught. On January 20, 1942, he wrote:

> I inspected 4 types of our primary schools. Where the teachers are idealists, the conditions from the educational point of view are . . . satisfactory. On the other hand, in general, the classrooms, corridors, and staircases are very dirty.[75]

By the end of the 1941–1942 school year, the only officially recognized school year in the Ghetto, the nineteen official schools that were fully or partially operational enrolled 6,700 pupils.[76] This number does not include the thousands of students engaged in clandestine study groups, Torah study, and children's corners.[77]

As late as July 5, 1942, less than three weeks before the start of the *Aktion* — the catastrophic deportation of Jews from the Warsaw Ghetto — Czerniakow wrote in his diary about an organized student presentation he attended: "A program was offered by 600 boys and girls from elementary schools. From among the performers I invited to sit at the stand with me a little girl who was made up as Chaplin (great applause)."[78] That, however, was to be among the final joyous occasions for most of the students, their teachers, and even Czerniakow himself.

The Aktion

On July 22, 1942, two and one-half weeks after the joyous moments that the Judenrat leader described in his diary, the Aktion began. Eliminating Warsaw Jewry was another step in the Nazi goal of making Europe *Judenrein* — cleansed of Jews. On that day, Czerniakow was asked by the German authorities to sign a deportation order that would include children. Strongly committed to the Ghetto children but powerless to save them, Czerniakow committed suicide the next day.[79] The Aktion continued for the next seven weeks, until an estimated 265,040 Jews were transported to Treblinka, where most were gassed to death.[80] More than ten thousand Ghetto Jews died or were killed during the Aktion; some (about 11,580) were sent to a *Dulag* (transit camp), from which they were transferred to one of a number of forced labor camps; and some (about 8,000) escaped to the Aryan side of Warsaw.[81] The Ghetto was in chaos; sanctioned schools and other institutions ceased to exist, and the remaining inhabitants were afraid to be out on the streets. After the mass deportations, the Ghetto population was decimated; a mere 55,000 of the 350,000 who were there on July 22 remained.[82] Escapees brought word of mass killings at Treblinka back to the Ghetto, and by the end of August the remaining Jews of Warsaw knew they were doomed to die.[83]

Over the next few months, however, the remaining CENTOS members and teachers organized approximately ten children's clubs in building courtyards with secret passageways between them to avoid getting captured on the streets. Private teachers continued with their komplety as well. Natanblut remembers the gatherings of teachers that took place during this time:

> They did not give in. [Teachers] began to gather weekly in the evenings. Saturday nights and sometimes on Friday nights we would gather in one of the apartments and sit on beds, boxes, windowsills, on the few chairs. In the light of the smelly carbide lamps we would listen to a talk, a recitation, a political bulletin, participate in a discussion, sing together. We would not talk about those things that were looming over us. We would come here to strengthen ourselves. . . . The entire remnant of teachers began to come. . . . They brought together memories of the school, common interests and common pain.[84]

Despite the continuation of these educational activities, the Aktion marked a monumental shift in all aspects of Ghetto life. In response to the devastation caused by the mass deportations, and within a week of the first one in July, youth movement representatives, many of whom were active in the Ghetto's educational and cultural life, focused their attention on forming the Jewish Fighting Organization. This group would ultimately be responsible for the organized, active revolt against the Germans and their plans for the final liquidation of the Warsaw Ghetto.[85]

WARSAW GHETTO SCHOOLS: MULTIPLE PURPOSES

Why Education?

The questions remain: Given the perilous nature of the activity and the grim conditions in which it was undertaken, why did organized schooling thrive in the Ghetto? What was the purpose of the teaching and learning? The existence and vibrancy of the schools in the Ghetto is particularly remarkable, given the fact that many children became the sole supporters of their families, working as peddlers or in shops. Many children needed to smuggle, beg, or steal food, and school took them away from these survival activities.

It seems that for the Jews in the Warsaw Ghetto, organized schooling in its multiple forms served as a form of resistance that is oriented simultaneously to the past, present, and future. It contributed to individual survival, not only as a means through which to supply food to the hungry (as in the soup kitchens, children's corners, and orphanages), but also as a way to help children and their teachers resist dehumanization and hopelessness by maintaining normalcy and humanity, which seeded hope for the future. Organized schooling also helped the Ghetto society resist decay by sustaining its social, cultural, and political organizations and maintaining community cohesiveness, thus providing a vehicle through which the Jews could resist cultural and historical eradication. They were able to sustain and continue a vibrant cultural, intellectual, and spiritual life, which — within the context of the immediacy of the situation — used a reverence for the past to look toward the future.

Hunger, Normalcy, and Humanity: A Present Orientation

In one sense, organized schools were oriented toward meeting the immediate needs of the children and the community. It was, after all, the paramount goal of soup kitchens to distribute soup and of orphanages to care for orphans. Similarly, in his *Oneg Shabbat* essay, Koninski and others wrote that study circles kept the youth off the streets and provided a livelihood for unemployed, destitute teachers.[86]

An anonymous writer in *Oneg Shabbat* asked, "What propels youth to schools and learning and bids parents to squeeze out the last penny in order to provide their children with some education, not bread alone?"[87] Implicit in this question is the fact that children and adults sought to overcome the immediate, terrible conditions in the Ghetto not only with the essential food and sustenance, but also with teaching and learning. This essayist claims that study, although its practical value might be "questionable," somehow enabled students to persevere in the face of demoralization:[88]

> The Jew, with all his faults, was known for one laudable passion, the one that has kept him from forgetting spiritual life even in the worst, bleakest moments of his life. This passion, the primordial and untamable, keeps swelling in the Ghetto from day to day in inverse proportion to available facilities. It grows despite logic, in defiance of daily events. . . . The young yearn to study on their own, without external spur, not thinking of gain or immediate and future benefit. . . . This phenomenon, in such contrast to the general bestiality, brutalization and demoralization, is the source of power that enables one to persevere, to overcome difficulties and to keep trying and disregarding dangers. . . . The risk . . . is real, not imaginary; . . . the ultimate value, is questionable.[89]

Ghetto survivor Joseph Kutrzeba also described how learning provided students escape from brutalization and entrée into a "different," more normal world. He stated simply, "I wanted to go to school and my parents wanted me to." He recounted that after his komplety lessons he would go to his job for three or four hours a day, delivering telegrams to earn money for his family, and then do homework in the evening: "There was terror and starvation and hunger . . . and yet, for us kids, it was, in a way, it was a salvation. Because what else are you going to do?" He posed this same question later in his testimony — "What do you do with kids under these terrorizing circumstances?" — and then described the role school played: "At least they enter[ed] for a few hours a day into a different world."[90] Survivor Leah Silverstein echoed the idea that children went to school not only for immediate salvation from a brutal and demoralized existence, but also to actively fight daily apathy and despair. "In terrible times," she said, "and in life-threatening situations, study was the one thing to hold on to. Otherwise you just think about hunger. It is a sort of relief."[91] She further described how the sense of normalcy was maintained:

> There were a lot of activities, you know. People, first of all, all the youth organizations were very active. In addition to this . . . people were trying to hang on to . . . the way of life that they had before they came to the Ghetto and to a certain extent, they succeeded in it. There were . . . cultural organizations. Of course, schooling even was going on in a clandestine form because you were not allowed to have open schools. But schools were existing, . . . even high schools and elementary schools, even universities.[92]

Debórah Dwork, Holocaust historian and chronicler of children's experiences in it, explains how critical it was for the children to maintain some sort of normalcy in an otherwise chaotic and devastated life:

> As we have seen so often before, to go to school, to persevere with one's studies, was a basic tenet of childhood. It was an essential activity that embodied the principal of normality: life would go on, there would be a future after this madness. . . . Many children wished to continue to learn and in extraordinary circumstances they did so.[93]

Chaim Kaplan, another *Oneg Shabbat* contributor, also commented on the drive to maintain some sense of normalcy when he wrote in his diary in 1942 about nursery schools and about older children having lessons, songs, games, stories, and exercises in urban gardens. He wrote, "In short, [schooling was] an arrow in the Nazis' eyes! The arteries of life do not stop pulsing."[94]

Jews also showed their desire to be connected with the world outside the Ghetto and to be counted among the living. The oppressive decrees, the monstrous wall surrounding the Ghetto, the prohibitive travel edicts, and the economic and social separation between the Jews and the rest of Warsaw were unequivocal signals that the Nazis wanted to sever all links between the Jews and the outside world. Holocaust historian Israel Gutman explains:

> The hermetic isolation from human society at large also influenced the quality of life. The Jews of Warsaw felt segregated and abandoned, and the motivations that usually direct a group that strives to be counted among the components of a standard human society disintegrated completely in the Ghetto. There is deep significance to the fact that the Jews were uncertain of what awaited them at the hands of the Nazis. . . . The edicts followed one after the other and left the pub-

> lic in a state of continuous anxiety, which left no time or strength to concentrate on or analyze affairs from a broad or forward-looking perspective.[95]

In the midst of this despair, study was a way for Jews to connect with the living world outside the Ghetto and resist being demoralized and dehumanized. Hundreds of study circles were held in which students took exams and received grades, and Gutman writes that students were "enthusiastic about their studies, which were a kind of link with the great and free world outside."[96] Places such as Janusz Korczak's orphanage brimmed with educational and cultural life. Survivor David Kochalski remembers the humanizing impact that life in the orphanage had on him: "What they tried to do in this orphanage, they tried to make human beings out of us under the worst circumstances, because inside we were like an island. Outside it was hell, a real hell."[97]

Youth group member and Ghetto survivor Ben Meed connects the drive to maintain normalcy through education as a type of "spiritual resistance," that is, "not giving the enemy what he wants," which was "to break you morally, then with hunger, then with disease. And then they want to kill." For Meed the motivation to teach the children came from the desire to "help the children be normal, to be as close as possible to a *life which was,*" even though "it's very difficult under the conditions of hunger to be normal." When he taught young children, Meed felt "the singing of the children to be spiritual resistance."[98]

The Ghetto as a "Transient Episode": Hope for the Future

While organized schooling helped some Warsaw Ghetto Jews resist their demise by providing for some of their immediate needs, including normalcy and dignity, there was also a sense that, through their participation in normal activities such as schooling, they could suspend their current state of being, accept the horrors of the Ghetto as a "transient episode," and look completely toward the future.[99]

In his 1997 study of spiritual resistance in the Ghettos and camps, Joseph Rudavsky explored the notion of resistance within the framework of the Jewish conceptions of *Kiddush HaShem* (the sanctification of G-d), usually through martyrdom, and *Kiddush HaHayyim* (the sanctification of life) through living a righteous and joyful life. Rudavsky links the Jews' struggle to maintain normalcy with their struggle for human dignity and hope for the future:

> [The Jews] resolved to conduct their lives not as hunted victims but as human beings who hoped to see a better future, or if they could not survive the war, then at least make the Germans understand that though they might succeed in killing the Jews, they would not succeed in divesting the Jews of their human dignity. The Jews knew that their end might be *Kiddush HaShem,* the sanctity of martyrdom, but while they lived they would implement in their daily activities the age-old principle of *Kiddush HaHayyim,* as they lived meaningful lives, Jewishly and otherwise. They would strive to educate their children, to continue

> their Jewish studies, to observe their religion, and even to carry on the Zionist struggle for the Jewish Homeland as if the Ghetto were just a transient episode. Scholars of Jewish law would continue to study and teach; poets, composers, and writers would not permit ghetto life to throttle their creativity, and artists would record the ghetto experience on paper and canvas for future generations.[100]

Joseph Kermish, Holocaust historian and editor of the published *Oneg Shabbat* Archives, further explains this forward-looking stance as passive resistance that grew out of a struggle for normalcy and connectedness to the outside world:

> One of the most interesting and important features of the passive resistance of the Jews in the Ghetto — that struggle so stubbornly and persistently kept up in the will to overcome and carry on — was to maintain a life on a certain cultural standard and to keep up that level in spite of the frightful isolation from the external world; it was marked by great care devoted to providing for a future generation of professional intelligentsia, and by the buildup of a wide network of courses and teaching facilities for higher professional and academic education.[101]

Marian Malowist, a young high school teacher and pedagogue, wrote about the factors that induced Jewish youth to study during wartime, stating that "youth fears it might go astray and wants to accomplish something useful. It expects that the war will end successfully; and then, it will be relatively easy, after having studied in the clandestine study-circles, to obtain a proper school certificate."[102] He posited that youth had some sense of their future that motivated them to study. This was, of course, before the first escapees brought eyewitness accounts from the death camps back to the Ghetto. Ghetto students were further motivated by the promises they received from Polish authorities, at least at first, that their educational certificates and diplomas would be valid after the war.[103] The many students and teachers who stayed engaged in their work based their actions on the hope that the nightmare of the Ghetto would pass.

Explanations based on the hope that a better life would come are inextricably connected to explanations that schooling enabled Warsaw Ghetto Jews to maintain a sense of normalcy and human dignity. However, the many dimensions of the purposes of organized schooling are only fully understood in the context of a discussion of how the Jews collectively used organized schooling as a way to resist historical and cultural obliteration, and how this resistance is at once past, present, and future oriented.

Resistance to Cultural and Historical Eradication: Past, Present, and Future

By prohibiting assemblies of people, religious observance, cultural symbols, celebrations, meaningful work, genuine self-rule, artistic expression, and education, the Nazis sought to snuff out Jewish history and culture in the Warsaw Ghetto and in the world forever. Yet the Jews defied prohibitive edicts by learning, teaching, and sustaining their culture clandestinely, thus realizing the emancipatory possibilities of education. Despite the peril and horrors experienced daily by Ghetto inhabitants, the Jews were able to keep some social, cultural, and political institutions relatively intact. As a result, some semblance of community cohesion was maintained amidst the chaos. Organized schooling in particular served to keep children, adolescents, and adults involved daily in organized community life.

Warsaw Ghetto Jews — students, teachers, parents, and other community members who helped organize and support the various forms of organized teaching and learning — acted collectively to resist cultural and historical annihilation by keeping these very things vibrantly alive in schools, study circles, and youth activities. One example of how the Jews, in their darkest hours, used a reverence for their past to light their future is found in the explicit and implicit content of the curricula of the clandestine schools. Another example is the role the youth movements played in the educational, cultural, and political life in the Ghetto and in their primary role in staging the armed Warsaw Ghetto Uprising.

Curricular Content

Students in clandestine elementary classes and in study circles learned geography, history, math, literature, and Yiddish culture. A document titled "An Outline of Pedagogical Activity in the Alimentation Points on Karmelicka Street 29, Nowolipki Str. 39, and Krochmalna Str. 96" offers insight into the aims of three elementary schools operating out of soup kitchens.[104] In one section, "The Aims of Our Work," the first of eight aims reads, "We strive to turn Alimentation Points into centers to succeed pedagogically and influence children."[105] Other aims included paying attention to the spiritual life of the child, fostering interest in several academic subjects, providing an emotional outlet, implanting a love of and devotion to the Yiddish language and culture, as well as teaching hygiene, cooperation, good behavior, and punctuality. Another section of the document, "Manners of Operation," described such activities as singing, poetry recitation, song enactments, acting out fables, as well as telling or reading certain "suitable tales and literary works." For example, the younger children studied *Pinocchio, Robinson Crusoe,* biblical stories, Greek myths, and tales by Yiddish authors Y. L. Peretz and Sholem Aleichem. The older children also studied stories by these Yiddish authors and by Sholem Asch, as well as novels such as *Uncle Tom's Cabin.*[106]

While these schools clearly had multiple aims, great importance was placed on studying Jewish history and Yiddish literature and culture.[107] According to Yiddish literature scholar Sol Liptzin, literary greats Y. L. Peretz and Sholem Aleichem are purported to be the "awakeners" and "comforters" of Yiddish-speaking Jewry.[108] Where Peretz "stimulated Yiddish creativity and weaned Jewish youth from perilous assimilationist tendencies," Aleichem "brought to light the inner dignity and moral grandeur" hidden beneath the "apparent submissiveness" of the persecuted Eastern European Jews.[109] Peretz, himself a Warsaw native, created simple characters who lived hard lives but were rewarded in this world and in heaven for their piety and self-sacrifice. His works often included a mystical character who symbolized "unexpected help that may come to those who are worthy of extraordinary assistance because they retain faith in fundamental justice that must prevail in heaven and on earth."[110] Aleichem's characters suffered the daily trials of a difficult life, but they exhibited not only an indefatigable will to survive, they did so nobly and heroically, with joy and humor. Liptzin says of Aleichem, "His is a laughter through tears, a stoic humor that surmounts all obstacles and disappointments."[111] Aleichem taught Jews how to "seek liberation from pain in jest" and how to "retain inner dignity and humaneness in a undignified world."[112] Because of their hopeful orientations, Peretz and Aleichem seem appropriate curricular choices for Warsaw Ghetto children. Similarly, in addition to early literacy and daily living skills, children in children's corners and orphanages learned stories, songs, poems, and plays with Jewish historical or cultural themes. Likewise, in addition to their secular subjects, students in study circles and the gymnasia also studied subjects with Jewish historical and cultural relevance.

According to scholar Joseph Kermish, education planners in the Ghetto "aspired to fill their education with the highest humanistic ideals in view of a 'brighter, better future.'"[113] Teacher Ana Natanblut's description of the celebrations put on by the sanctioned schools in honor of the coming of spring in 1942 illustrates the importance of humanistic ideals to the Ghetto educators:

> The Polish school at Gesia 9 presented a performance about how children of different peoples and races loved each other and through this, furthered the brotherhood of all people. The children approached a lonely orphan girl, bringing her presents, joy and love. Each group of children in the presentation sang and danced and dressed in its own way. National differences were not watered down — but that didn't evoke mistrust, but the opposite, more interest and connections with others.[114]

The performances had "deeply ideological content."[115] The school at Nowolipki 68 combined the songs and poems of Yiddish writers such as Chaim Nachman Bialik and Abraham Reisen into a medley as a "march of victorious spring which envelops the world despite the fact that at the beginning, the earth is sunken in ice and the evil winds howl."[116] Natanblut describes the impact these performances had on their audiences:

> The impression was unearthly, either because of the allegorical content which awakened the deepest feelings, be it with song, with the appropriate verses, with

> beautifully colored costumes, with decorations, or with the play of light and the rhythm of dance.[117]

The Warsaw Ghetto children experienced a profoundly relevant curriculum that was drawn from their Jewish literary tradition and was ideologically charged. This curriculum, as well as religious education, reveals how schooling served as a means through which Ghetto Jews kept their history and culture alive day-to-day and secured its future by instilling it in their youth.

Youth Movements

The youth movements served a similar function through their involvement in educational, cultural, and political activities in the Ghetto. Even before the war, education and political socialization were at the center of Jewish youth group activities, since the groups were youth divisions of predominantly Zionist political and ideological organizations. Holocaust historian Israel Gutman explains that between the two wars "political education in the youth movement did not consummate with commitment only to an ideological line; the dominant foundation of this education was a yearning for radical change — in the existing state of affairs, the nature of the Jew as a human being, and the fate of the Jewish people."[118] In the trying times of Ghetto incarceration, education was an essential means of ensuring the continuation of the movement and its ideology. Though diverse in particular ideologies — including socialist, communist, cultural, or religious — youth groups were united in their belief "that there is going to be a better world," as survivor and youth group member Benjamin Meed stated.[119] These movements were all oriented toward creating a new society based on Jewish ideals, and they believed that their pioneering efforts would come to fruition in the Land of Israel. Moreover, this future orientation had at its heart a reverence for the Jews' historical, cultural, and political past. Indeed, in the Warsaw Ghetto, the youth movements were at the forefront of resistance that took the form of education, cultural events, the underground press, and ultimately the Warsaw Ghetto uprising.

The youth movements took an active role in preserving culture and used organized education to do so. According to Gutman, the youth movements put great emphasis on the spiritual and cultural aspects of their role for two main reasons. First, they feared that the poverty and other Ghetto conditions would permanently damage the psyche of the youth, which they assumed was precisely the aim of the Nazis. In May 1941, the youth organization HaShomer HaTzair's underground paper *Neged HaZerem* (*Against the Current*) published a call for youth leadership and a look toward the future:

> The poverty and total economic deprivation will pass when political conditions change, but the people will not recover from their decline if our youth are blemished and decadent; for only we, the youngsters aged thirteen to eighteen today, are destined to lead the Jewish masses to a different, better future.[120]

Second, the youth movements assumed that in the near future they would be called upon to lead their people, so they had to prepare themselves for the task under the difficult conditions of the Nazi occupation.[121] The September 1941 issue of the Bund youth division's *Yugnt-Shtime* read:

> Our rulers are mistaken in thinking that a draconian prohibition, an official stamp, can nullify cultural values that have been acquired over tens and hundreds of years. . . . We, the working youth of the people, must assume the task of initiating and directing the cultural and educational endeavor among children and youth . . . otherwise our cultural movement among the youth is in danger of spiritual decline. . . . We must exploit the period of calm to prepare for missions that are sure to come.[122]

It is no wonder that, more than any other group, the youth movements were poised to take leadership roles in many areas of Ghetto life. According to Gutman, the youth groups met the demand for a flexible and adaptable kind of leadership that could cope with trying circumstances and could adjust to the changing leadership needs of the Ghetto community. The youth group leadership was thus able to fill the vacuum left by the large numbers of Jewish political and intellectual leaders who fled Warsaw for the East. Gutman claims that it was the youths' "daring, sensitivity to social injustice, and a willingness to sacrifice [that] advanced the young into the roles they were destined to assume."[123] They were, indeed, fiercely ideological and idealistic.

The underground press was a particularly important forum for education, culture, and resistance for the youth groups. Of the nearly fifty underground publications that appeared in the Ghetto at various times in either Polish, Yiddish, or Hebrew, approximately two-thirds were sponsored by the youth movements.[124] In addition to analyzing Ghetto concerns, the youth papers "presented surveys of innovations in science, book reviews, profiles of famous personalities . . . and columns devoted to educational issues raised by the war."[125] They also included editorial columns and information about the political, cultural, and educational activities of the particular sponsoring movement. According to historian and archivist Joseph Kermish, the underground press

> promoted resistance, kindled its readers' spirits, invigorated their will-power, shaped their character, and served as a light to guide their way. It considered its main task to be that of fighting demoralization and despair; it therefore aroused the suffering youth to seek knowledge. Its pages faithfully reflect the youth's growing interest in books, and mainly in serious ones.[126]

Through the underground press, the youth movements served the important function of keeping members of the Ghetto community informed and connected with one another, but they also served the special function of keeping the youth group members closely connected to the various groups' ideals and to one another. Survivors from the youth movements speak passionately about their affiliations with their groups; for example, HaShomer

HaTzair member Leah Silverstein attributed members' strength and ability to survive to the "deep moral principles . . . acquired in the youth organization." She credited the youth movements with giving them a purposeful aim in life. Silverstein explained, "We had this aim, and we were instilled in good humanistic principles, and in a time of crisis they came to our rescue."[127] Joseph Kutrzeba, a HaShomer HaTzair member for nearly two years, explained simply, "It gave the kids something to believe in."[128] In her analysis of the Polish Zionist youth movements and resistance through education, Erica Nadelhaft writes that the groups offered the youth "an alternative society filled with idealism, learning, and mutual aid and respect" that stood "in opposition to the deterioration of life in the Ghetto and the general decline in moral values."[129]

The youth movements clearly seemed to be hopeful about the future as well. Nadelhaft maintains that

> continuing to educate the young in spite of Nazi prohibitions was thus a form of resistance for the youth movements. They believed that in order to safeguard both the physical and the spiritual existence of Jewish youth they must continue to be active intellectually and culturally. . . . They realized that the Nazis' attack on education was a deliberate attempt to destroy the Jewish people from within, and they acted purposefully and forcefully to counter the blow.[130]

In the days before the Jews of Warsaw found out and recognized that they were doomed to die, they actively worked to avoid becoming demoralized. Survivor Vladka Meed, a youth group member, attributes these actions to her belief that resistance was a reactive response to the particular kind of oppression perpetrated by the oppressor. A community that is resisting, she explains, does so in different ways depending on what the enemy puts before it. Meed says that "resistance was [a way] to hold on to culture and history so that the spirit should not be crushed."[131] Thus, the youth groups not only continued their political activities, but also took on a wide range of social and cultural services.[132] Their members found themselves organizing cultural and educational events, attending and delivering lectures, teaching and caring for younger children, and being part of a vibrant intellectual community that revolved around not only political ideology but also Jewish history, culture, and language.

As an expression of humanity and liberation, education stood in direct resistance to Nazi attempts to dehumanize the Jews of the Warsaw Ghetto and historically and culturally obliterate them. The youth groups stood at the head of this resistance. Because of the strength of their affiliations, their connectedness with one another, and their commitment to issues regarding the "nature of the Jew as a human being and the fate of the Jewish people,"[133] the youth movements were able to unite in collective defiance, first by sustaining this rich intellectual and cultural life and, ultimately, by armed struggle. Leah Silverstein attests that "it was a determination among our group, they are not going to take us alive."[134] After the mass deportations began, escapees and scouts came back to the Ghetto with confirmation of mass killings. It was then that activities of resistance evolved into plans for revolt. Some students and teachers, both secular and religious, continued their studies, but the attention of the Ghetto underground turned toward armed struggle and the formation of the Jewish Fighting Organization.

From Resistance to Revolt

A connection can be traced from the political and cultural underground activities in the Ghetto, including the clandestine schools, to the formation of the Jewish Fighting Organization (ZOB).[135] After the mass deportations began, leaders of the Ghetto underground began to meet and lay plans to form the ZOB. The organization's leadership came from the ranks of the youth movement leadership and was commanded by HaShomer HaTzair member Mordechai Anielewicz. In the weeks and months that followed the Aktion, the Jewish Fighting Organization dug trenches, built bunkers, printed leaflets, drew maps, trained members, and smuggled weapons and explosives into the Ghetto. A second Aktion in January 1943 took the Ghetto Jews by surprise. They revolted with small street battles and resistance from within the buildings, but five thousand Jews were deported nonetheless. Still, Nazi attempts to quickly assemble eight thousand deportees were thwarted; some Germans were killed, and the fighting galvanized the resolve of the fighters and of the remaining Ghetto population.[136] On April 19, 1943, German forces armed with weapons and artillery marched into the Ghetto to complete the final liquidation of Warsaw's Jews. They were surprised by the organized, formidable uprising staged by the Jewish Fighting Organization. A poorly armed, ragged collection of about 750 fighters, mostly under the age of twenty-five, successfully fought off German forces from April 19 to May 16, 1943, when the fighting stopped and the Ghetto burned.[137]

Gutman credits clandestine education with having had a part in the successful organization of the armed uprising by the way it

> played a decisive role in the struggle by keeping together a united cadre of people who maintained and cultivated social norms and values during a desperate time. Thanks to the protracted existence of the movements in the underground . . . a consolidated and reliable nucleus stood at the disposal of the Jewish Fighting Organization.[138]

Vladka Meed maintains that "during all the years of the Nazi occupation, resistance took place," but that "in different times, it had different forms."[139] The uprising was the culmination of many smaller acts of resistance, including teaching and learning, and was only possible because of the "inner preparation to stand up against the enemy" created and maintained in clandestine schools, study groups, and in youth group lectures, cultural organizing, and political activity. She explains that in the three years prior to the Uprising, the Jews were preparing and organizing, and the groups that would rise to lead the Jews in revolt stayed "a part of the people" in a grassroots way. While other ghettos showed passive or spiritual resistance, none was able to organize the kind of armed revolt executed by the Jews of Warsaw. Meed attributes this to the fact that "in Warsaw, the ZOB and the underground leadership had a closer relationship with the Ghetto people at a critical time."[140] The Ghetto leadership — both the sanctioned and the underground — was tied into important community organizations, including schools. Furthermore, the youth group leadership was strong and committed. Vladka Meed explains:

> We, the youth, were taken over. We realized that this is an important mission we have to do. Not only for ourselves, but we had a certain idealism. And it was idealism that brought the Uprising. The majority of the organizers and fighters were from the organized youth, and we were raised in justice, humanity, and the belief in mankind.[141]

She added, "But when it comes to deciding our destiny about death, *we* decide in our own way."[142] The clandestine schools of the Warsaw Ghetto helped to provide students, teachers, and the organized community with power, hope, and a sense of humanity. They also served to develop unified group associations and to continue the processes of political socialization, which prepared the youth of the Warsaw Ghetto to lead the best organized and most heroic Jewish armed revolt in the history of the Holocaust.

CONCLUSION

Clandestine schooling helped the Warsaw Ghetto Jews, especially the youth, not only to cling to a sense of normalcy in an abnormal and horrific situation, but also to resist dehumanizing social, political, and physical forces bearing down on them day to day. Schooling also helped them maintain hope for the future. Clandestine schools helped the Jewish community stay organized and cohesive and, by ensuring the continuity of Jewish cultural and historical education, enabled the Jews to resist Nazi attempts at their cultural and historical obliteration. Moreover, the resistance — in its multiple forms and with its multiple purposes — was led by the strength, resolve, and idealism of the organized political youth groups. Ultimately, these groups provided an even greater and more heroic form of organized youth leadership. In her study on Jewish youth groups and resistance through education, Erica Nadelhaft writes:

> Through their educational programmes, cultural events, social-welfare programmes, and other activities, the youth movements were able to preserve their vitality and strength despite the overpowering demoralization and deterioration of ghetto life. Their ability to enclose themselves in their own spiritual world, to cling stubbornly to values and norms of behaviour in spite of all, and their

> refusal to acknowledge moral decay gave them the strength and determination to survive under Nazi rule. Members remained compassionate, loyal, and above all, human. It was because of this determined and courageous effort that, when the time for armed resistance came, there existed a united, organized, and morally responsible body of young people willing to make a stand.[143]

For the Jews in the Warsaw Ghetto, schooling promoted resistance in multiple ways. In clandestine schools some Jews (both students and teachers) found relief against hunger, discord, and dehumanization. By aiding in children's and teachers' daily struggles to stay healthy and alive, by providing a sense of normalcy, and by instilling a sense of power and dignity, clandestine schools facilitated participation in a present-oriented resistance. Clandestine schools also facilitated a future-oriented resistance. Teaching and learning are inherently hopeful acts, and the Jews in the Warsaw Ghetto engaged in these acts with a desperate, pleading nod toward the future and the lives they hoped to reclaim when the dark days of the Ghetto were over. As teachers taught and students learned, Ghetto Jews were also engaged in a form of resistance that was at once past, present, and future oriented. They were resisting not only their individual demise and communal decay but also their cultural and historical annihilation. By committing themselves to a curriculum that was built on a shared sense of history, culture, and Jewish nationalism, education in the Warsaw Ghetto became an act of collective defiance. Hersz Wasser was a *Po'alei Zion* (Zion Workers) youth group member and the *Oneg Shabbat* Archive secretary. In an *Oneg Shabbat* essay describing the mission and work of YIKOR, Wasser described its "popular university," which offered Saturday morning lectures on current Jewish topics to hundreds of Ghetto residents. He made an explicit link between education, Jewish culture, and resistance. He wrote, "The intent of the lectures was not just to deepen the interest in science, Jewish history or sociology, but also to strengthen the sense of national dignity and the will to offer resistance."[144]

This story of the clandestine schools in the Warsaw Ghetto during the Holocaust reveals one answer to the essential question, What is schooling for? Survivor accounts woven together with archival evidence bring to life the ways in which schooling can be a form of resistance. This is a story of the relationship between school, community, and culture. It is also a story of courage and heroism — of students and their teachers learning and teaching together in the shadows of despair.

Notes

1. See, for example, Deut. 27:1–8, 31:12–13, found in *Tanakh: A New Translation of the Holy Scriptures According to the Traditional Hebrew Text* (New York: Jewish Publication Society, 1985); Abba Eban, *My People: The Story of the Jews* (New York: Random House, 1968); Chaim Potok, *Wanderings* (New York: Alfred A. Knopf, 1978); Raphael Patai, *The Jewish Mind* (New York: Charles Scribner's Sons, 1977).

2. See, for example, John Dewey, *Democracy and Education* (New York: Free Press, 1916); Lawrence A. Cremin, *The Transformation of the School: Progressivism in American Education 1876–1957* (New York: Vintage Books, 1961); David B. Tyack, *The One Best System* (Cambridge, MA: Harvard University Press, 1974); Patricia Albjerg Graham, "Schools: Cacophony about Practice, Silence about Purpose," *Daedalus, 113,* No. 4 (1984), 29–57; Paulo Freire, *Pedagogy of the Oppressed,* trans. M. B. Ramos (New York: Continuum, 1970); bell hooks, *Teaching to Transgress: Education as the Practice of Freedom* (New York: Routledge, 1994); Alfred N. Whitehead, *The Aims of Education and Other Essays* (New York: Free Press, 1929); Amy Gutman, *Democratic Education* (Princeton, NJ: Princeton University Press, 1987); Richard J. Murnane and Frank Levy, *Teaching the New Basic Skills: Principles for Educating Children to Thrive in a Changing Economy* (New York: Free Press, 1996); James P. Comer, *Waiting for a Miracle: Why Schools Can't Solve our Problems — And How We Can* (New York: Dutton, 1997).
3. It is important to study and understand the Holocaust in terms of the horrific images that comprise it; however, it is also important to resist these images as the only ones. There are also stories of courage, heroism, and resistance, and I seek to illuminate them and move them to the foreground. While this article purports to tell a story of resistance and heroism in the face of Nazi tyranny, it is perhaps also the story of my own resistance to forgetting, to silence, to dehumanization, and to hopelessness.
4. See, for example, Nora Levin, *The Holocaust: The Destruction of European Jewry 1933–1945* (New York: Schocken Books, 1973), p. 208; Israel Gutman, *The Jews of Warsaw 1939–1943: Ghetto, Underground, Revolt,* trans. I. Friedman (Bloomington: Indiana University Press, 1982), pp. 62–65; Anonymous, 1941, "The Jewish Quarter in Warsaw, ARI/PH/10a-2-3," in *Selected Documents from the Warsaw Ghetto Underground Archives, "O.S." Oneg Shabbath* (henceforth *O.S. Archives),* ed. J. Kermish, (Jerusalem: Yad Vashem, 1986), p. 146.
5. Levin, *The Holocaust,* p. 207; I. Gutman, *The Jews of Warsaw,* pp. 60, 62–65; Anonymous, "The Jewish Quarter in Warsaw," p. 146.
6. I. Gutman, *Jews of Warsaw,* pp. 15, 21, 31; Levin, *The Holocaust,* p. 208.
7. Nehemia Titelman, "Setting Up a Closed Ghetto, PH/33-1-8," in Kermish, *O.S. Archives,* pp. 143–145; I. Gutman, *Jews of Warsaw,* p. 48; Levin, *The Holocaust,* p. 208.
8. The *Judenrat* was the Jewish Council, established by the Nazis to receive and implement their dictates. The Council, composed of twenty-four Jewish members, was led by Adam Czerniakow.
9. "Bared heads" refers to the requirement that Jews remove their caps in deference to German guards.
10. Levin, *The Holocaust,* p. 230; I. Gutman, *Jews of Warsaw,* pp. 64–65. See also Ruta Sakowska, "The Warsaw Ghetto," in *The Warsaw Ghetto: The 45th Anniversary of the Uprising.* (Poland: Interpress, 1988), p. 10; "Cable Between Warsaw, London, New York, Tel Aviv, 16 March 1941," trans. L. Silverstein. From the Sikorski Collection, Archives of the YIVO Institute for Jewish Research, RG 493, Folder 174 #1394.
11. "The Wannsee Protocol, Minutes of Discussion 20 January 1942," in *The Holocaust: Selected Documents in Eighteen Volumes, Volume 11: The Wannsee Protocol and a 1944 Report on Auschwitz by the Office of Strategic Services* (New York: Garland, 1982), pp. 18–32.
12. I. Gutman, *Jews of Warsaw,* p. 65.
13. Levin, *The Holocaust,* p. 207.
14. Levin, *The Holocaust,* pp. 206–207; I. Gutman, *Jews of Warsaw,* p. 66.
15. Levin, *The Holocaust,* p. 225. See also Debórah Dwork, *Children with a Star: Jewish Youth in Nazi Europe* (New Haven, CT: Yale University Press, 1991), p. 159. In "Origins of the Education Problems in the Ghetto," *Yad Vashem Bulletin,* No. 12 (December 1962), p. 28, Joseph Kermish describes the intellectual and cultural life in the Ghetto as "filled with a deep spirit of Jewish creativity."

16. "Letter from Adolf Berman and Emmanuel Ringelblum in Warsaw to Jewish Scientific Institute in New York, March 20, 1944," trans. S. Chazen, G. Weiss, and W. Weiss. From the Sikorski Collection, Archives of the YIVO Institute for Jewish Research, RG 493, Folder 180 #1573. See also Joseph Rudavsky, *To Live with Hope, To Die with Honor: Spiritual Resistance in the Ghettos and Camps* (Northvale, NJ: Jason Aronson, 1997); Shimon Huberbrand, *Kiddush Hashem: Jewish Religious and Cultural Life in Poland During the Holocaust*, ed. J. Gurock and R. Hirt, trans. D. Fishman (New York: Yeshiva University Press, 1987); Levin, *The Holocaust;* I. Gutman, *Jews of Warsaw;* Kermish, *Selected Documents from O.S. Archives.*
17. Levin, *The Holocaust,* p. 228; I. Gutman, *Jews of Warsaw,* pp. 144–154.
18. The *Bund* was the Jewish Socialist Democratic Party.
19. Joseph Kermish, "The Underground Press in the Warsaw Ghetto," vol. I, pp. 104–105, as quoted in Levin, *The Holocaust,* pp. 228–229.
20. Levin, *The Holocaust,* p. 352; See also Israel Gutman, *Resistance: The Warsaw Ghetto Uprising* (Boston: Houghton Mifflin, 1994).
21. To understand better the complex political and power structure in the Ghetto, to illuminate the network and organization of underground schools, and to access commentary on clandestine schooling and other cultural events, I relied on the essays and documents of the *Oneg Shabbat* Archives (also known as the Ringelblum Archive), written, compiled, and buried by inhabitants of the Warsaw Ghetto in 1943, under the direction of historian and educator Emmanuel Ringelblum. Of the three collections of materials that were hidden in canisters in the Ghetto during the war, only two were found, one in 1946 and one in 1950. The third, containing material on the underground Jewish Fighting Organization, has never been recovered.

    The *Oneg Shabbat* (Joy of Sabbath) archives, located at the *Yad Vashem* museum in Jerusalem, contain many documents including essays, research surveys and reports, monographs, biographical portraits, announcements, underground periodicals, letters, and materials belonging to the underground organizations. *Oneg Shabbat* was initially intended to be an organization for scientific research, in the tradition of the Vilnius YIVO (Institute for Jewish Research), in which Ringelblum was active before the war. This tradition included interdisciplinary research combining history, sociology, and economics. *Oneg Shabbat* researchers collected data using surveys, questionnaires, guided interviews, and ethnographies that aimed to document the impact the war was having on the Jewish community. Materials were written and collected by an ideologically diverse group of community leaders, economists, educators, and other experts in relevant fields, many of whom came from the ranks of the youth group leadership. Because the compilation of the *Oneg Shabbat* archives was an underground activity, many of the documents are unsigned and undated. The documents I used have been published in a collection called *Selected Documents from the Warsaw Ghetto Underground Archive "O.S." ["Oneg Shabbath"],* ed. Joseph Kermish, trans. M. Z. Prives, Y. Kirshbaum, J. Karsch, S. Katz, L. Reznikoff, E. Shaul, and V. Brown (Jerusalem: Yad Vashem, 1986).
22. Anonymous, "The School System, ARI/74," in *O.S. Archives,* p. 501.
23. This concept of "transcending the moment" was first introduced to me in a personal communication with Eileen de los Reyes, Harvard Graduate School of Education, December 16, 1997.
24. Ana Natanblut, "Shuln in Varshever Geto," trans. P. Parsky, *YIVO Bleter* III, No. 2 (Winter 1947), p. 173.
25. Czerniakow, *Warsaw Diary,* p. 206.
26. Mary Berg, *Warsaw Ghetto* (New York: L. B. Fischer, 1945), pp. 32–33, quoted in Dwork, *Children with a Star,* pp. 181–182.
27. Berg, as quoted in Dwork, *Children with a Star,* p. 182.

28. "The School System," in *O.S. Archives,* p. 501. See also Dwork, *Children with a Star,* p. 201.
29. "The School System," in *O.S. Archives,* p. 503. See also I. Gutman, *Jews of Warsaw;* Dwork, *Children with a Star;* Natanblut, "Shuln in Varshever Geto," p. 173.
30. The *Judenrat* was permitted by the Nazis to open vocational schools for children and adults so that these trained Jews could then work in factories or industries in direct support of the German regime. In addition to the many vocational training activities organized, "the council did not hesitate to deceive the Germans and ran a comprehensive program of [regular academic] classes, including even university-level courses, under the guise of vocational training." I. Gutman, *Jews of Warsaw,* p. 83.
31. Kermish, *O.S. Archives,* p. 460. See also "The School System," in *O.S. Archives,* pp. 513–514.
32. Interview with Vladka (Fagele Peltel) Meed, Transcript of Oral History Interview, 1991, Courtesy of United States Holocaust Memorial Museum (USHMM) Department of Oral History, RG-50.030*153.
33. Natanblut, "Shuln in Varshever Geto," pp. 173–174. See also Genia Silkes, "Letter: Children-Heroes in the Days of Fire, Paris, April 21, 1950," trans. H. Agus, Archives of the YIVO Institute for Jewish Research, RG 1187, Box 3, Folder 39.
34. Anonymous, "A Preliminary Study in Teaching People During the War, PH/13-2-4," in *O.S. Archives,* pp. 468–469.
35. "A Preliminary Study in Teaching People During the War," in *O.S. Archives,* p. 471.
36. Natan Koninski, "The Profile of the Jewish Child, ARI/47," in *O.S. Archives,* p. 389.
37. Interview with Benjamin Meed, February, 29, 2000, New York City.
38. "Letter from Adolf Berman and Emmanuel Ringelblum in Warsaw to Jewish Scientific Institute in New York, March 20, 1944," YIVO Archives. See also Dr. Hillel Seidman, 1943, *The Warsaw Ghetto Diaries,* trans. Y. Israel (Southfield, MI: Targum Press, 1997), Diary Entry October 1, 1942, pp. 142–144.
39. Koninski, "The Profile of the Jewish Child," in *O.S. Archives,* p. 385.
40. Koninski, "The Profile of the Jewish Child," in *O.S. Archives,* p. 385.
41. See Janusz Korczak, *Ghetto Diary* (New York: Holocaust Library, 1978); Betty Jean Lifton, *The King of the Children: The Life and Death of Janusz Korczak* (New York: St. Martin's Griffin, 1997); Larry Brendtro and Denise Hinders, "A Saga of Janusz Korczak, the King of Children" (Essay Review), *Harvard Educational Review, 60* (1990), 237–276.
42. Interview with David Kochalski, Transcript of Oral History Interview, 1994, Courtesy of USHMM Department of Oral History, RG-50.030*001.
43. Brendtro and Hinders, "A Saga of Janusz Korczak," p. 245.
44. Interview with Erwin Baum, Transcript of Oral History Interview, 1994, Courtesy of USHMM Department of Oral History, RG-50.030*016.
45. Anonymous, "Jewish Youth in Warsaw in the War Years," in *O.S. Archives,* p. 516.
46. I. Gutman, *Jews of Warsaw,* p. 141.
47. Erica Nadelhaft, "Resistance through Education: Polish Zionist Youth Movements in Warsaw, 1939–1941," in *Poles, Jews, Socialists: The Failure of an Ideal,* ed. A. Polonsky, I. Bartal, G. Hundert, M. Opalski, and J. Tomaszewski (London: Littman Library of Jewish Civilization, 1996), p. 227.
48. Interview with Leah Silverstein, Transcript of Oral History Interview, 1996, Courtesy of USHMM Department of Oral History, RG-50.030*363.
49. Interview with Vladka Meed, February, 28, 2000, New York City.
50. I. Gutman, *Jews of Warsaw,* p. 129.
51. Anonymous, "A Call for the Establishment of an Organization for 'Moral Supply in the Warsaw Ghetto,' ARI/88," in *O.S. Archives,* p. 456.
52. "A Preliminary Study in Teaching People During the War," in *O.S. Archives,* p. 472.

53. Kermish, "Origins of the Education Problems in the Ghetto," p. 31.
54. "A Preliminary Study in Teaching People During the War," in *O.S. Archives,* p. 470.
55. "The School System," in *O.S. Archives,* p. 505.
56. "A Preliminary Study in Teaching People During the War," in *O.S. Archives,* p. 473.
57. Interview with Vladka (Fagele Peltel) Meed, Transcript of Oral History Interview, Courtesy of USHMM.
58. Interview with Joseph S. Kutrzeba (Fajwiszys), February, 12, 2000, Rego Park, New York.
59. Interview with Joseph S. Kutrzeba (Fajwiszys), February, 12, 2000.
60. Interview with Joseph S. Kutrzeba (Fajwiszys), February, 12, 2000.
61. Rudavsky, *To Live with Hope,* pp. 52–53.
62. Rudavsky, *To Live with Hope,* pp. 52–53; Nadelhaft, "Resistance through Education," p. 228.
63. Seidman, *Warsaw Ghetto Diaries,* pp. 305–306.
64. "'Patronage' of Torah Study-Groups," in *O.S. Archives,* p. 417; Seidman, *Warsaw Ghetto Diaries,* p. 306.
65. Emmanuel Ringelblum, 1942, *Notes from the Warsaw Ghetto,* ed. and trans. J. Sloan (New York: McGraw-Hill, 1958), p. 138.
66. Czerniakow, *Warsaw Diary,* p. 206.
67. I. Gutman, *Jews of Warsaw,* p. 84. See also "The School System," in *O.S. Archives,* pp. 506–507.
68. "The Patronate of the Jewish Cultural Activity in Warsaw, ARI/217," in *O.S. Archives,* p. 463.
69. Natanblut, "Shuln in Varshever Geto," p. 174.
70. Natanblut, "Shuln in Varshever Geto," p. 174.
71. Czerniakow, *Warsaw Diary,* p. 312.
72. Natanblut, "Shuln in Varshever Geto," p. 180.
73. Natanblut, "Shuln in Varshever Geto," p. 182.
74. Natanblut, "Shuln in Varshever Geto," p. 182.
75. Czerniakow, *Warsaw Diary,* pp. 317–318.
76. I. Gutman, *Jews of Warsaw,* p. 84.
77. I. Gutman, *Jews of Warsaw,* p. 84; Natanblut, "Shuln in Varshever Geto," p. 180; "'Patronage' of Torah Study-Groups, ARII/104," in *O.S. Archives,* pp. 417–418.
78. Czerniakow, *Warsaw Diary,* pp. 374.
79. Czerniakow, *Warsaw Diary,* pp. 385; Dwork, *Children with a Star,* p. 173.
80. I. Gutman, *Jews of Warsaw,* pp. 197, 213.
81. "The Aryan side" is a common reference to what lay on the other side of the Ghetto walls, namely communities devoid of Jews.
82. I. Gutman, *Jews of Warsaw,* p. 213.
83. Anonymous, 1942, "The Destruction of Warsaw, II/198," in *O.S. Archives,* pp. 701–703; Anonymous, 1942, "Reminiscences of a Treblinka Escape, ARII/295," in *O.S. Archives,* pp. 710–716; Gutman, *Jews of Warsaw,* p. 223.
84. Natanblut, "Shuln in Varshever Geto," p. 185.
85. I. Gutman, *Jews of Warsaw,* p. 236.
86. Koninski, 1941, "The Profile of the Jewish Child," in *O.S. Archives,* pp. 371–373, 386; "The School System," in *O.S. Archives,* p. 505; "A Preliminary Study in Teaching People During the War," in *O.S. Archives,* p. 468.
87. "The School System," in *O.S. Archives,* p. 501.
88. "The School System," in *O.S. Archives,* p. 502.
89. "The School System," in *O.S. Archives,* pp. 501–502.
90. Interview with Joseph S. Kutrzeba (Fajwiszys), February, 12, 2000.
91. Interview with Leah Silverstein, February 9, 1998, Silver Spring, MD.

92. Interview with Leah Silverstein, Transcript of Oral History Interview, Courtesy of USHMM.
93. Dwork, *Children with a Star*, p. 180.
94. Chaim A. Kaplan, *Scroll of Agony*, quoted in Dwork, *Children with a Star*, p. 189.
95. I. Gutman, *Jews of Warsaw*, p. 115.
96. I. Gutman, *Jews of Warsaw*, p. 95.
97. Interview with David Kochalski, Transcript of Oral History Interview, Courtesy of USHMM.
98. Interview with Benjamin Meed, February, 29, 2000.
99. Rudavsky, *To Live with Hope*, p. 39.
100. Rudavsky, *To Live with Hope*, p. 39.
101. Kermish, *Selected Documents from O.S.*, pp. 458–459.
102. Marian Malowist, 1942?, "Youth and their Education in the Ghetto, ARI/38," in *O.S. Archives*, p. 497.
103. "The School System," in *O.S. Archives*, pp. 501–502, 509.
104. Anonymous, "An Outline of Pedagogical Activity in the Alimentation Points on Karmelicka Street 29, Nowolipki Str. 39, and Krochmalna Str. 96, PH/5-4-3," in *O.S. Archives*, pp. 474–475.
105. "An Outline of Pedagogical Activity in the Alimentation Points on Karmelicka Street 29, Nowolipki Str. 39, and Krochmalna Str. 96," in *O.S. Archives*, p. 474.
106. "An Outline of Pedagogical Activity in the Alimentation Points on Karmelicka Street 29, Nowolipki Str. 39, and Krochmalna Str. 96," in *O.S. Archives*, pp. 474–475.
107. Among the most important aims was teaching students critical hygiene lessons to help them avoid typhus in the disease-ridden Ghetto.
108. Sol Lipzin, *A History of Yiddish Literature* (New York: Jonathan David, 1985), p. 56.
109. Lipzin, *A History of Yiddish Literature*, p. 56.
110. Lipzin, *A History of Yiddish Literature*, p. 62.
111. Lipzin, *A History of Yiddish Literature*, p. 68.
112. Lipzin, *A History of Yiddish Literature*, p. 68.
113. Kermish, "Origins of the Education Problems in the Ghetto," p. 29.
114. Natanblut, "Shuln in Varshever Geto," p. 181.
115. Natanblut, "Shuln in Varshever Geto," p. 181.
116. Natanblut, "Shuln in Varshever Geto," p. 181.
117. Natanblut, "Shuln in Varshever Geto," p. 181.
118. I. Gutman, *Jews of Warsaw*, p. 133.
119. Interview with Benjamin Meed, February, 29, 2000.
120. *Neged HaZerem*, 13/2, Yad Vashem Archive, Underground Press Division, as quoted in I. Gutman, *Jews of Warsaw*, p. 142.
121. I. Gutman, *Jews of Warsaw*, p. 142.
122. *Yugnt-Shtime*, II (September 1941), Yad Vashem Archive, Underground Press Division, as quoted in I. Gutman, *Jews of Warsaw*, p. 142.
123. I. Gutman, *Jews of Warsaw*, p. 133.
124. I. Gutman, *Jews of Warsaw*, p. 152.
125. I. Gutman, *Jews of Warsaw*, p. 153.
126. Kermish, "Origins of the Education Problems in the Ghetto," p. 32.
127. Interview with Leah Silverstein, Transcript of Oral History Interview, Courtesy of USHMM.
128. Interview with Joseph S. Kutrzeba (Fajwiszys), February 12, 2000.
129. Nadelhaft, "Resistance through Education," pp. 218–219.
130. Nadelhaft, "Resistance through Education," p. 229.
131. Interview with Vladka Meed, February, 28, 2000.
132. I. Gutman, *Jews of Warsaw*, p. 121.

133. I. Gutman, *Jews of Warsaw,* p. 83.
134. Interview with Leah Silverstein, Transcript of Oral History Interview, Courtesy of USHMM.
135. I. Gutman, *Jews of Warsaw,* p. 144; "Resistance through Education," pp. 212, 221. See also Interview with Vladka Meed, February, 28, 2000; Interview with Leah Silverstein, February 9, 1998, Silver Spring, MD.
136. I. Gutman, *Jews of Warsaw,* pp. 311–313.
137. I. Gutman, *Jews of Warsaw,* pp. 364–440. See also Levin, *The Holocaust,* pp. 317–361; Simha Rotem, *Memoirs of a Warsaw Ghetto Fighter,* trans. B. Harshav (New Haven, CT: Yale University Press, 1994); Vladka Meed, *On Both Sides of the Wall,* trans. S. Meed (Washington, DC: Holocaust Library in Conjunction with the United States Holocaust Memorial Museum, 1993); Azriel Eisenberg, ed., *Witness to the Holocaust* (New York: Pilgrim Press, 1981), pp. 393–410.
138. I. Gutman, *Jews of Warsaw,* p. 144.
139. Interview with Vladka Meed, February, 28, 2000.
140. Interview with Vladka Meed, February, 28, 2000.
141. Interview with Vladka Meed, Transcript of Oral History Interview, Courtesy of USHMM.
142. Interview with Vladka Meed, Transcript of Oral History Interview, Courtesy of USHMM.
143. Nadelhaft, "Resistance through Education," p. 231.
144. Wasser, Hersz, 1942, "Yiddish Culture Organization 'YIKOR,' Warsaw Ghetto 1940–1942," in *O.S. Archives,* p. 444.

This project has truly been a community effort. Above all, I owe my deepest gratitude to the survivors who gave generously of their time and of themselves to tell me their stories and to critique my retelling. They are Leah Silverstein, Saul Horn, Vladka Meed, Rachel Gurdus, Benjamin Meed, and Joseph S. Kutrzeba (Fajwiszys). Second, I am indebted to the translators and those who helped me find them. I am grateful to the research staffs, archivists, and volunteers of the United States Holocaust Memorial Museum, Washington, DC, and the YIVO Institute for Jewish Research in New York City. Many thanks also to Richard F. Elmore, Leslie Santee Siskin, and Patricia Albjerg Graham, who respectively spurred the conception of this project, encouraged the big ideas, guided the methodology, and saw it through to the end. Finally, thanks to colleagues, friends, and family who believed in the importance of this project and in my ability to complete it. In particular they are Neal Brown, Robert R. Carson, Jr., Dr. David J. Cowen, Alana Feiler, Hillary Johnson, Lesley Nye, and Heather G. Peske. I am also grateful to Adriana Katzew and Tere Sordé Martí, of the *Harvard Educational Review,* for their passionate work on this article.

This article is dedicated to the martyrs and heroes of the Warsaw Ghetto, whom I have come to better understand, to admire, to long for, and to love. It is especially dedicated to the youngest victims — to the students — and their teachers, who learned and taught together in the shadows of despair. They knew that to be counted among the living they needed each other, their history, and their culture. Not bread alone.

An Interview with Khalil Mahshi

In 1989, the Harvard Educational Review *published "The Palestinian Uprising and Education for the Future" by Khalil Mahshi and Kim Bush. In that article, Mahshi and Bush reviewed Palestinian education from the time of the Ottoman Turks until the late 1980s. They documented that throughout history, Palestinians were educated within systems imposed by outsiders. Mahshi and Bush argued that an already contentious relationship with Israel was exacerbated by the combination of an Israeli civil and military authority and a Jordanian educational curriculum. The first* intifadah *(uprising), which began in December 1987, challenged the Israeli occupation and its imposed institutions. During this time period, educational establishments in the West Bank and the Gaza strip were subject to frequent closures by Israeli military authorities, forcing Palestinians to reexamine their current system of education and to look for both short- and long-term alternatives.*

Given these conditions, Mahshi and Bush argued that the first intifadah was a catalyst for educational change in Palestine. They examined different models of education that were developed when schools in the Palestinian territories were forcibly shut down by the Israeli military: United Nations Relief and Works Agency schools in refugee camps in the West Bank, Gaza, Jordan, Syria, and Lebanon; private schools; Popular Committee schools; and neighborhood schools. They also analyzed several initiatives created by and for Palestinians during that time: informal, community-based education methods; alternative modes of instruction such as home-learning packets, which did not require the school structure but still used the existing system and textbooks; and long-term planning that conceived of education as nation-building. Mahshi and Bush argued that the intifadah created a giant educational laboratory and challenged conservative educators to start afresh. Finally, they outlined a pioneering project, Education for Awareness and Involvement, that they believed contained the beginnings of a new Palestinian curriculum that would connect school and community and shift the focus from end-of-school examinations to student-centered pedagogy.

By articulating the challenges of Palestinian education clearly, Mahshi and Bush encouraged debate among educators in Palestine and the international educational community about the future of Palestinian education. In the more than fifteen years since their article was published, the debate on Palestinian education has flourished. And much has changed. Khalil Mahshi served as the director-general of international

Harvard Educational Review Vol. 76 No. 1 Spring 2006, 64–79

and public relations for the Palestinian Ministry of Education and Higher Education and is now a senior program specialist with the International Institute for Educational Planning at the United Nations Educational, Scientific, and Cultural Organization (UNESCO) in Paris. Preceding the Palestinian elections of January 2006, and given both Mahshi's extensive experience and his close relationship with Palestinian education, the Harvard Educational Review *took the opportunity to interview him. On December 1, 2005, two members of the* HER *Editorial Board spoke with Mahshi about the legacy of the first Palestinian intifadah and the current state of Palestinian education. Mahshi — who asked us to call him "Khalil" — emphasized the subjective nature of his observations and the complex role of commenting on the work of colleagues who are still engaged in the difficult work of building an education system. Khalil describes the changes that have taken place in the education of Palestinians since he and Bush wrote "The Palestinian Uprising and Education for the Future," and he outlines lessons from this development process that are applicable globally to the building and rebuilding of education systems in the face of occupation, resistance, and conflict.*

We are excited to speak with you, Khalil. We would like you to start by describing the educational situation in the West Bank and Gaza since the publication of your and Kim Bush's 1989 HER *article, "The Palestinian Uprising and Education for the Future." What is the current status of the education system from preschool to higher education, including the kinds of alternative and community-based forms of education that you describe in that article?*

Community-based education existed at the time we wrote the article because Palestinian schools were ordered closed by the Israeli military authorities. And so the community created alternatives to the closed schools. Since then, the situation has changed significantly. There is now a Ministry of Education and Higher Education in Palestine. There are two regions of Palestine — the West Bank and Gaza. Palestine is still not an independent state, [but] there is some sort of autonomy, self-rule. And, therefore, there is a Ministry of Education, which manages education at all levels. The system is managed by one ministry in both regions, the West Bank and Gaza, but in East Jerusalem, the Palestinian Ministry of Education doesn't have full control.

So, now is the time to develop education — it has been for a while — because there is a Ministry of Education. But you have to keep in mind that [Palestine] is not an independent state. There are [therefore] some constraints, and the constraints have to do with the resources that are available to the Palestinians to develop their system of education. If it were an independent state — with a good tax collection system working and good external relations in terms of trade, export and import, and free movement within the country and across borders — maybe its revenues would improve and there would be more financial resources to develop education and more freedom to develop human resources. The constraints also relate to the Palestinians being carefully watched by the donor community and the international community at large in terms of what curriculum they develop, what textbooks they write, and what they include in the curriculum and the textbooks. This is the time to develop Palestinian education but not with total freedom.

In 1989, you wrote of "a future when a Palestinian system of education can be developed." How did the system of education that exists now, which is managed by one Ministry of Education, develop from the community-based forms you described in the article?

After the Oslo agreements between Israel and the Palestine Liberation Organization [in 1993], there was a decision to establish the Palestinian Authority.[1] Therefore, a number of ministries had to be established. In late August of 1994, a minister of education was appointed and, immediately after that, a core group of ten people were contacted to set up the ministry. I was one of them.

We started from scratch. We were lucky in the sense that the minister and the deputy minister who were appointed at that time — Yasser Amro and Naim Abu Hommos — wanted people who were professional educators and professional workers. He went for people who were professionally trained and who were experienced in their own fields, so it was appointment of people based on merit. These ten people created a number of departments within the ministry. You can guess most of these departments: teacher training, human resources, curriculum development, planning, financial matters, management of field offices, international relations, etc.

One clear relationship between popular education as we described it in our 1989 article and the [establishment of the] Ministry of Education is that the people who were appointed to lead the process were people who were known for their activity in education and education-related fields.

The other aspect that relates to popular education is that from the very beginning of the work of the Ministry of Education, a decision was made to involve "stakeholders," to involve the community in the work of the ministry, in giving opinions and in participating in decision-making related to the development of education.

What would you say is the legacy of the first intifadah, which began in 1987, and the impact on Palestinian education of a continued Israeli presence in the West Bank and Gaza?

There are two kinds of impacts, in my view. One is a positive impact. When you have occupation, you have resistance; and when you have resistance, you have defiance, and you have room for initiative, and you have room for creativity. You have room for being daring and defying. People may disagree with me, but I think a positive impact of occupation is the spirit of defiance by the occupied, by the people under occupation.

This is what was reflected in popular education: It was an act of defiance. Maybe we did not manage to cover the curriculum during the repeated closure of schools; maybe we did not give quality education. But it was an act of defiance that was translated through the process of popular education, which meant that *both* the teachers and the students were highly motivated. The whole community was highly motivated to be part of the education process.

In normal circumstances, the students are not as motivated to be part of the education process. They feel the process of schooling is some sort of homework, it is some sort of burden, which wasn't the case during popular education. Nobody forced anybody to go to school. The students would come because they wanted to come, because they were defying. And nobody forced teachers to come; [the popular education teachers] were not being paid, [and] it was also an act of defiance on the part of these "teachers."

This spirit is not the same any more. We're back to schooling. We're back to forcing students to come, and parents forcing their children to go, and teachers have to go because it's their job. Some go because they like it, but not the majority.

The negatives are many. As you know, Palestine is still not independent. We hope it's on its way to becoming a state. The situation on the ground since the first intifadah, in a sense, has worsened. Notably the separation wall, the Israeli separation wall, is causing many problems in terms of movement of Palestinians, whether students or teachers, and therefore is negatively impacting education.

Also, part of the negative legacy of the first intifadah is that schools were ordered closed. There was popular education, but it never could cover the same amount of work and quality of work that normally schools would cover. Therefore, academic quality in the Palestinian territories dropped. And we are still suffering, as Palestinians, from this dropping of quality. Quality became worse, and those who graduated from schools during the first intifadah are now teachers and managers and doctors; I think the quality of these people in terms of their knowledge and skills [is] worse than their predecessors. Therefore, this is affecting the whole society. And we are still suffering from that.

What is the legacy of the first intifadah for young Palestinians who did not experience this time and for their education today?

Young people now have not been directly affected by the first intifadah, but their teachers have been. Their teachers were then students, so the quality [of teaching], in my opinion, is not as good as it would have been if we didn't have the closure of schools during the first intifadah and punishment by denying the Palestinians formal schooling, not only at school level but also at university level, for long periods of time.

I think that one of the lasting effects is that during the period of the Israeli occupation — which still, in a sense, in one form exists in the Palestinian territories — Palestinians were denied [the chance] to teach about their own society and to develop a national identity. This is one of the priorities of the present system of education, which is being expressed through the kind of curriculum that is being developed, and the focus on activities related to national identity. When you're denied something that is important to you, you really work hard to get it done. This is what you see happening now in the Palestinian education system.

It is done through the curriculum, which is teaching now about Palestine, about Palestinian culture. You can see it also in extracurricular activities, which focus on folkloric dance, on Palestinian music, on Palestinian literature. You see it in many flags raised as well, which the Palestinians couldn't do before. You couldn't raise a Palestinian flag. You would be imprisoned if you did.

You describe the first intifadah as "the opportunity of a lifetime" for education and describe the changes in thinking around education that resulted from this period of struggle. Have there been other periods of intense change that have added or magnified the legacy of the first intifadah, as you have just described it?

The only intense change was the setting up of the Palestinian Authority and, therefore, the establishment of a Ministry of Education and, very importantly, the development of a Palestinian curriculum. This is the first time in history that the Palestinians have had an opportunity to develop their own curriculum and to write their own textbooks. This is very important; I cannot overemphasize it. It is something which Palestinians always craved: they wanted to be in control of what their children study in schools and not to be denied certain topics or certain subjects or certain textbooks or parts of textbooks.

How has the development of the curriculum and the textbooks taken place?

The development of a Palestinian Curriculum Development Center was a joint venture between the Palestinian Ministry of Education and UNESCO [United Nations Educational, Scientific, and Cultural Organization]. It started [in October 1995] with funding coming through UNESCO from Italy, where UNESCO would provide the technical support to set up a Palestinian Curriculum Development Center under the Ministry of Education. At the beginning of its work, the ministry involved academics from outside the ministry to lead the process of establishing the curriculum center and of reviewing the existing textbooks — the Jordanian [textbooks] in the West Bank and the Egyptian [textbooks] in Gaza — in preparation for putting together the elements of the curriculum and the syllabuses and, later, the textbooks.

How would you describe the implementation of the new curriculum and the introduction of the new textbooks in schools?

The Ministry set a time frame to develop the curriculum and to produce the textbooks.[2] This year, they are in the final stage. [The curricula and textbooks from Jordan and Egypt that were used in the West Bank and Gaza respectively] were replaced in stages by the Palestinian curriculum and Palestinian textbooks, two grades at a time each year, and this is the final year. After this year, [all of the] textbooks would have been replaced by Palestinian ones. And while the replacement is taking place, review of the new Palestinian textbooks is happening every year, and partial rewriting is also happening.

Just anecdotally, what do you hear from your friends or family or on the street in terms of sentiment about this new curriculum and new textbooks?

I think people are still thrilled that we can write our own textbooks based on our own curriculum. But, there are divergent views. If you ask a certain number of intellectuals in the Palestinian community, they would tell you that the textbooks and the curriculum are not up to their expectations. If you ask others, [they] would be elated simply by the fact that it is our own textbooks written by ourselves, not by others, and that we have full control of — almost full control of — what we have in these textbooks.

How you can create a consensus is the difficult question. How can you create agreement on what is to be changed and how it is to be changed and what is our common vision? It's a very difficult question — how do you create a common vision? This is why the ministry wanted to involve, as much as possible, the community in its own internal discussions about the curriculum. And [the Curriculum Development Center] has done so: town meetings, focus group meetings, interviews with leading figures, and consultations with academics and technicians. [There has been] a whole process of getting views on what is to be done, and how, and the content and how it is to be taught. Whether everything has been translated into an action plan by the ministry is the question. I think most of it has. Whether everybody is satisfied, I'm sure not. There are many people who are *not* satisfied. They would like to have better results. And each person defines what "better" is. So it's a big process. I don't think there is full satisfaction with what the ministry has done. You hear criticism, but this is natural.

You talk about the possibility that occupation creates for generating resistance. How would you describe the role that education plays in generating this resistance?

Education creates resistance by clarifying what the harmful effects of occupation are and by reinforcing the sense of community. Occupation is very harsh on individuals, but it is less harsh on people if they stick together. There is strength in being together even under harsh measures, like closure of schools. Take the first intifadah as an example. When [our schools] were ordered closed, if we each sat at home and taught our own children, we wouldn't have a strong sense of defiance and resistance as much as we would have when we [engaged in] the popular education movement. We got together as a community. We felt we were being collectively punished and we had to respond collectively — not individually, not within family units. And, therefore, in that sense occupation created resistance, created defiance, created elements of innovation, created elements of creativity to respond to these collective punishment measures.

You make a distinction between the kind of change that can happen at the individual or family level and the change that happens with large-scale involvement. What role do you think education currently plays in shaping Palestinians at an individual level, and what role it might play in larger-scale change?

Education is now trying to create a national sense of identity with elements I have described earlier. And I think it is also trying to attempt change at the individual level by creating ability to self-learn. In my view, [education in Palestine] has not yet succeeded in creating enough ability to have self-learning happen so, in that sense, education still has to go some way in Palestine. Education has to go a *long* way, really, before it allows the individual to [experience] self-learning, to [develop] self-confidence. Self-learning and learning by doing lead to active involvement in the learning process, to mastery of skills, and to a sense of ownership of knowledge. When involved, one feels that one has been productive and has made significant accomplishment. Production, accomplishment, mastery, and ownership are basic ingredients of self-confidence.

If there is self-confidence amongst Palestinian youth, it is not thanks to schools so far. It is more thanks to the culture of resistance that has been created within the Palestinian community and which is still taking place. The Palestinian community is still struggling to get independence, and the youth have played an important role in resistance. They have always led resistance, all through the various stages of occupation and resistance to occupation. The credit [for developing self-confidence] is not really to formal schooling, it is to the broader sense of education that happens mostly outside schools. It also happens partially within schools, but not *mainly* inside schools.

What implications does the second intifadah, that began in September 2000, have for how you think about the first intifadah, particularly related to the situation of education?

I did not live through the whole period of the second intifadah because I left a few months after it started. But from what I have witnessed first hand, the first intifadah was more of what we call "intifadah." Let me qualify this: Intifadah is an uprising. The meaning of intifadah is "shaking off." And people wanted to shake off Israeli occupation; they wanted to get rid of Israeli occupation. And what was different about the first intifadah, is that it was really popular, in the sense that everybody was involved. In the second intifadah, I felt that people were not as involved. This is a major difference: Many people felt detached from the second intifadah, in contrast to the first intifadah. The young people were involved, but not all others to the same extent.

And I think the second intifadah missed a lot of the creativity of the first intifadah, including related to education. But you have to keep in mind that during the second intifadah there *was* a Ministry of Education, there was a Palestinian system of education, a Palestinian *management* of education. So we did not have the need to have popular education because schools were not ordered closed by the military. (In certain areas they were, but not a blanket closure of all institutions like what happened during the first intifadah.) So, the second intifadah was less popular in terms of participation by the people. It was less demanding on our creative abilities. I think the first intifadah was a *real* intifadah, in the sense of popular participation; the second intifadah was marked by less participation and more use of violence and armed means of resistance.

You've stated why the kind of popular education that existed during the first intifadah doesn't exist in the current context. Are there other kinds of popular education that do need to exist today that may be slightly different in form but somewhat similar in intent?

I'm sometimes hesitant when we use [the word] "education." I clearly differentiate between education in the broad sense and schooling. Although I'm interested in formal schooling and I've always worked for formal schooling, I see its limitations in terms of educating people for life after school. In that sense, popular education related better to the daily life of students, to their community. During the popular education period, daily life and issues of the community come into the teaching and learning process. Now there is more of a separation between this kind of relevant education and the kind of schooling that students get that is more formalistic, more bookish.

I think popular education does not exist any more. There are attempts at broadening the education of students and even university students through some activities that the community initiates here and there, basically through NGOs [nongovernmental organizations]. But the level of involvement by the community is not the same. The community has not pursued activity in education because it is not expected to. At the time when we had popular education, schools were closed. Now schools are open and Palestinians are managing education — not the Israeli military any more. And so the community feels that education is in good hands.

You note that one of the challenges during the first intifadah was building and sustaining ties between schools and communities. Have there been efforts to create these links since that time?

Yes, the ministry tried to create better parents' associations; they have encouraged the process, but it was up to schools to do that. If you're asking me whether there are now stronger links between the school and the community as compared to the time when we didn't have any such mechanisms, yes, there *are* stronger links. If you are asking me whether I'm satisfied with the link between the school and the community, I would say, not really. I would have liked to see more participation on the part of the community in the life of the schools and the schools in the life of the community.

I've recently visited Egypt and, at the face value of it, I was impressed to see that the Egyptian Ministry of Education has decreed the creation of boards of trustees for each school, involving parents, teachers, and the principal or the director of the school himself or herself. Most importantly, this decree has given more authority to the community representatives on that board of trustees to make decisions on how the school operates, its budget, its future plans, its yearly plans. This hasn't happened in Palestine. Schools are still strongly governed by the Ministry of Education. I would like to see more school-community links in many respects, including the creation of decision-making governing boards. There should be a clearer direction toward giving more decisionmaking power to the community.

When you worked as director-general of international and public relations for the Palestinian Ministry of Education in Ramallah from August 1994 to January 2001, it was clearly a different time from when you wrote the article in 1989. When you were with the ministry, what was your vision for education of Palestinians?

Very different times, but my personal vision remained the same. You see, at the Ministry of Education I was in charge of external relations, which meant really two things. It meant fundraising and liaising to the external world to get support for starting the development process of education. But since at that time we did not have a plan for the development of education, I had to inject my own vision. But also to make sure that the vision of my other colleagues who started the Ministry of Education was incorporated.

So my personal vision, as reflected in the article of 1989, is, first, to engage the students in active learning. They should be active in their own learning — if you want the jargon, student-centered approaches to teaching and learning. Second, [they should] learn about their situation, about their country. Third, [they should] strengthen their Palestinian identity because the Palestinian identity was not being reinforced by the curriculum or by formal teaching. They were denied the right to study about Palestine, and they were denied the right to reflect about the situation in Palestine. Fourth, I had as part of my vision to relate school education to the world of work — to production, to employment, to skill development for production. Fifth, my vision incorporated an element of participation in decisionmaking by students, relating to their education and their future life. Finally, my vision included an element of values—important values which would make it possible for people to live together, to work together, to build a healthy society, and to be open to the world, not to be enclosed. Because when you're reinforcing a national identity sometimes you become chauvinistic, and that wasn't part of my vision.

In your article, you noted some of the challenges and some of the promises of Education for Awareness and Involvement.[3] *Has it been developed, changed, implemented, or studied further since 1989?*

The Education for Awareness and Involvement captured most of my vision for education. But it's not only *my* vision — it's the vision of many people like me who worked in the education field in Palestine, who believed in a more progressive form of education. By more progressive, I mean more relevant, with clearer values that relate to the development of society, and incorporating things we learn from the outside world into our own education. Education for Awareness and Involvement encapsulated these elements.

The crux of Education for Awareness and Involvement is the teaching process itself, the teaching and learning process. In order to translate the philosophy of Education for Awareness and Involvement into action, you need teachers who would not lecture at students. You need teachers who would animate, who would incite, who would facilitate discussion and action on the part of students. You need to have *active learning* inside the classroom.

Active learning is the opposite of rote learning. Unfortunately, if you look at Palestinian schools nowadays, you see lecturing going on, based on the textbooks only. If you wanted to see active learning — in the sense of not bookish, academic, and lecturing methods — I don't think you would see many cases. And this is, I think, where the whole process of changing the system from the formal schooling/rote learning system into an active learning system centered around the child hasn't really happened.

Why? Because the teachers are not capable of doing that. They need to be equipped with better skills and they need to be freed from working toward preparing students for exams. The system of examinations is negatively impacting on our education system, most importantly what we call the *Tawjihi*, which is the matriculation exam at the end of twelve years of schooling. It still decides the future of students. As long as this is the most important aspect of schooling in Palestine, teachers and students will all work toward the same thing: passing the exam. And all other aspects of good schooling and good education will become subsidiary to that.

One of the contradictions that you noted about the first intifadah was the development of what you called a "culturally dependent mentality" and the idea of a tension between people wanting to go back to a predictable life versus an excitement about creating a new society. Does this tension continue to play itself out today?

Yes, the tension still exists. But now the tension is partially due to the fact that a new element is coming in: the Internet, globalization at large, the influence of the outside world on each community and each country. This is part of the new tension, tension brought about by external factors that are trying to create homogeneity of cultures. This is now the new tension: being part of the outside world, part of the international community, aspiring to become an independent state, and, therefore, being on equal footing with other countries and other nations, yet at the same time preserving our own culture, our own identity. This is not unique to the Palestinians.

How do the media and technology affect education of Palestinians today, especially in this era of globalization?

This is a positive development in the Palestinian schools. There have been serious attempts by the Ministry of Education to include media, very specifically, computers and the use of the Internet in schools. A few months ago they also initiated a major project together with the Ministry of Communication and the information technology businesses in the West Bank and Gaza to introduce more computers and more use of the Internet in the schools. This is very different from the popular education we were talking about, but it is a positive development in the direction of the vision that you asked me about, which is bringing knowledge about the world into the classroom.

I mentioned this opening up to the world as one of the elements of the vision that I and others had. I think this is happening through the Internet. Whether all schools would be able to have this accessibility to the Internet is still a question, but I think it is moving in that direction.

Why is it so important for education to help open up the world for Palestinians?

Palestine is very small. It doesn't have many natural resources. The best resources that Palestinians have are human beings. If our children are not knowledgeable about the world, if they cannot compete for income generation in this more globalized world, then it will be tough on the Palestinians economically. We will not have many sources of income. Our sources of income [need to be] more or less based on providing services and value addition to certain services, for instance, computer technologies, development of software. These all depend on our people and our human resources.

We have highly competitive neighbors: Israel, next door, is well advanced in terms of computer technology, information technology, and it's well advanced in terms of providing services, like tourism. Jordan is moving up in this direction. So the two most immediate neighbors are relatively advanced. We have the potential. But if we are enclosed, if we are not open to learning and to incorporating what we learn from other countries and from the world at large, we will be behind. And we cannot afford to be behind.

What do you think the role of peace education is within popular education?

The concern of the popular education movement was resistance to occupation. In resistance to foreign occupation you have an element of peace-building, because peace cannot be built by dominating and being dominated. Lasting peace is built between two equally free parties. In that sense, resistance itself was part of peace-building and peace education, since it aspired for freedom for the Palestinians on equal footing with the Israelis.

There isn't really an element in the present curriculum that is clearly called "peace education." This is one of the points of contention about the Palestinian curriculum, whether they should be teaching more clearly about Israel as a neighbor or not. That's a very sensitive issue that has always been a matter of heated debates and discussions within the Palestinian community itself, and between the Palestinian community and the Ministry of Education on the one hand and Israel and other parties on the other hand.

There isn't an element of peace education clearly defined as such within the Palestinian curriculum, and there wasn't within the popular education movement during the first intifadah. But you find many activities in Palestine, and also in Israel that relate to peace education at the level of trying to create mutual understanding and reconciliation. These activities have recently become more difficult — after the second intifadah and after the restriction of movement of Palestinians by the Israelis, with the separation wall and with putting up checkpoints. Before, Palestinians were able to move more freely between the West Bank and Gaza and Israel, and, therefore, to communicate, meet, have dialogue, debates, and joint activities with Israelis, which I would put under peace education at large. Now it has become more difficult and a little bit frustrating.

Currently, you work as a senior program specialist with the International Institute for Educational Planning at UNESCO. Has your vision for the education of Palestinians changed since you stepped out of a government role and started working for UNESCO? How do your experiences in Palestinian education shape your work around the world?

I think in all countries where I work, I aspire for the same thing. If a country needs support, we give it support. This is the role of UNESCO and the role of the UN. In my work, I focus on helping ministries of education based on my experience in Palestine, which was a very rich experience. I was lucky to be there when the Ministry of Education was created. How many people get the chance to start a Ministry of Education from scratch? I think very few around the world.

I go to areas or countries where there has been either conflict or a situation of emergency. [These are places where] a Ministry of Education didn't exist, or existed but stopped functioning — the case of Afghanistan, for instance, or places where there is civil war. I help ministries build capacity for planning and for quality improvement, which means I focus on their departments of planning, creating them, helping ministries develop them, and then helping ministries focus on what is important. After they achieve or start achieving access, what is important is the *quality* of education. Access to and quality of education are major, and a third element that is major is proper management.

I'm lucky to have been given the opportunity to keep believing in the same things I believed in, to keep having the same vision, and to be working to help countries that need assistance to realize this kind of vision.

What are some of the challenges Palestinians face now with respect to short-term and long-term educational planning?

In a short period of time, the Palestinians have managed to create a well-functioning Ministry of Education. There are people who are not satisfied with the kind of curriculum or the quality of the textbooks, but I think, in general, the creation and the functioning of the Ministry of Education in Palestine has been a success story. And this is a great achievement: to start a ministry from scratch and, in a matter of ten years, to achieve what the Ministry of Education has achieved by developing a Palestinian curriculum, by managing schools, by building more schools (many more schools are being built), by getting everybody to school, by keeping salaries going, by creating a planning department and formulating a five-year plan and finishing the implementation of this plan, and entering the process of formulation of the second five-year plan. If you compare it with what other countries that have been independent for so long are doing, it is a major, major achievement. So in that sense I feel that the Palestinians have to be congratulated, especially the Ministry of Education.

The challenge is a challenge of having quality education; it's not only a challenge of bringing students to school. [Access] has been achieved, more or less, by the Ministry of Education and by the Palestinians at large. It's not only the ministry — we have to give credit to the community at large for supporting education. People give land to build schools on; people give money to build schools; people donate money to schools for planning purposes; people volunteer their time to support schools. It's the community at large: people giving of their time and energy to offer ideas and to come to meetings. It's a vibrant process. It could have been better, all of us can aspire for better, but it's a good process.

Now, as I said, the challenge is a challenge of having quality education. And by quality education, I go back to the same point: students learn freely and with relevant education, rather than bookish education, rather than just rote learning, rather than just a process of preparation to pass exams. This is still a problem in Palestinian education. Education requires us to build confidence in students, confidence to think, confidence to create, confidence to learn by themselves, and not to be slaves to books and to exams.

How do you assess whether education is of good quality or not? It's really by affecting change inside the classroom, and this is where teachers become important. It is the challenge of transforming the teaching methodology, the teaching methods that are used nowadays by teachers. It's creating teachers who are self-confident themselves, to create, to innovate, to facilitate the learning of students. This is the basic challenge, in my view, for Palestinian education at large.

How do you see the education of Palestinians in 2015, the target year for reaching the Millennium Development Goals?

In terms of millennium goals, the Palestinians are very close to achieving comprehensive basic education: All children who should be in schools *are* more or less in schools, both male and female. So in terms of access to primary or basic education, the Palestinians don't have a problem. There are still a few children not attending or dropping out of education, but I think the record shows improvement. By 2015, I don't think the Palestinians will have a problem in terms of access to education if they go on doing what they are doing now, in terms of building schools and classrooms.

In terms of preschool, [access to which is also one of the Millennium Development Goals], it's a challenge. The percentage of the population group in preschool is around 35 percent. There is a long way before achieving comprehensive preschooling, and I don't think it's realizable by 2015. Preschool is provided not by the government; it's provided by the community, and NGOs, and I don't think they will be able to provide 100 percent preschooling.

In terms of equity, I think the Palestinians *are* achieving equity between males and females, and providing education for the poor is not a problem in Palestine. Everybody goes to school.

In terms of quality, this is the challenge — what kind of quality of education are we providing, and can we provide better quality in the way *I* defined it? Again, people may differ on definition. [By quality] I mean self-learning, I mean confidence, I mean inculcation of values that will keep the community cohesive, and opening up to the world. I think quality is the major challenge when it comes to the Millennium Development Goals.

What changes do you expect for education in the aftermath of the Israeli military withdrawal from Gaza?

I don't see any major change as a result of withdrawal from Gaza. My hope is that Gaza will sincerely be open to the outside world, which is not yet certain. Less than two weeks ago [November 2005] the border point between Gaza and Egypt was opened, seemingly under Palestinian control, with the presence of European observers and with remote observance by Israel. I'm hoping that this will be an opportunity for Gazans to lead a more normal life [with the possibility for freedom of movement] and, therefore, this would introduce some new demands on education. Otherwise, I don't see a major change happening in the education system because of the Israeli withdrawal from Gaza. I think people misinterpret the withdrawal of Israel as full independence, which is not yet the case.

What role has education — within the kind of culture of resistance that you've described — played in your life and your development as an educator and an activist?

Education, first of all, has helped me create awareness. I'm not talking only about formal schooling because I am also one of the products of schooling under occupation. I have learned through the broader networks of education: youth movements, political parties, meetings. I was one of the people who were open to and also took initiatives to meet with Israelis; this is also part of my broader education.

[These experiences] created a new sense of resistance. You resist to not only to overcome your enemy; you resist to be on equal terms with who is presently your enemy, so that you are partners to peace later on. And, therefore, you are not trying to defeat your enemy. You are trying to make your enemy come to terms with the fact that we both have to coexist and hopefully cooperate within our region. This kind of education I did not get from my schooling days, or from my university days. It came as a result of being involved in political activities, being involved in community-related activities, in voluntary work for the community, in NGOs, and also being part of the attempts of Palestinian peace activists and Israeli peace activists to get together and to work together. I think this has broadened my view of what we are trying to achieve: a two-state solution and not to defeat Israel. The purpose is not to defeat Israel. The purpose is to achieve peace.

Is there anything else you wanted to add, Khalil?

Yes. One thing. You're asking me about Palestinian education and about Palestinians maybe because I'm Palestinian and I happened to be there at that moment in time [the first intifadah], and wrote this article [in the *Harvard Educational Review*]. I was proud that the person I wrote the article with was not a Palestinian. He was an American, which brings me to my point. I believe in good education for all children, not only for Palestinian children. This is why I am really lucky to be working at the International Institute for Education Planning, which puts me in a position to be assisting other countries and other ministries of education, not only the Palestinian Ministry of Education, to realize better quality education for *all* children.

And this is what I was, in a sense, missing in Palestine. I've always worked for Palestinian education and in Palestine, but I felt that before being Palestinian and before being of a certain religion, I'm a human being. I think this is why I kept insisting on opening up to the world; this is more important than being of a certain nationality and carrying a certain flag or working in a certain country. We should insist that we are all human beings who have much more in common than we have differences. And, therefore, we should learn from each other and we should help each other. Our work in one part of the world should help us learn lessons that we can use in other parts of the world, with adaptation, of course.

Therefore, I do not want to give the impression that Palestinians are behind or ahead of others; it's a process that is happening all around the world to various degrees. It's a process of change. And it's a process of creating a common understanding of what works and what doesn't work, and a sharing of experiences. The Palestinians have contributed to this learning process by providing this model of popular education during part of their history, during the first intifadah. If this popular education experiment has ended, it has ended because it wasn't needed any more. But we have to learn from it. We have to keep remembering *why* we started it and what we aspire to have and to keep feeding that learning into formal education systems, not only the Palestinian system but other education systems as well.

Notes

1. Text of the agreement is available online at http://www.yale.edu/lawweb/avalon/mideast/isrplo.htm.
2. See http://www.pcdc.edu.ps/clarification_III.htm for more information on this process.
3. Education for Awareness and Involvement was a pilot project initiated in 1985 in six private schools in the West Bank. It focuses on five key elements of educational transformation: active learning; vocational training; career exploration; study of the Palestinian situation; and building ties between school and community.

Forming the National Character: Paradox in the Educational Thought of the Revolutionary Generation

DAVID TYACK

I

"Most of the *distresses* of our country, and of the *mistakes* which Europeans have formed of us," Benjamin Rush wrote in 1786, "have arisen from a belief that the American Revolution is *over*. This is so far from being the case that we have only finished the first act of the great drama. We have changed our forms of government, but it remains yet to effect a revolution in our principles, opinions, and manners so as to accomodate them to the forms of government we have adopted. This is the most difficult part of the business of the patriots and legislators of our country." In much the same spirit Noah Webster called for an "ASSOCIATION OF AMERICAN PATRIOTS for the purpose of forming a NATIONAL CHARACTER."[1] Self-consciously, many Americans of the revolutionary generation sought to construct the artifact of American nationality.

As successful revolutionaries, Americans tried to conserve and consolidate their gains. Just as the Puritans had feared failure in their errand into the wilderness, so many leaders in the early Republic, charged with a deep sense of destiny, masked a dark vein of anxiety by assertive nationalism. A number of them believed that history demonstrated that republics were as evanescent as fireflies on a summer evening, that Europe was conspiring to wreck the new nation, that internal disorders and factions were threatening to shatter the republican community.

The age-old problem of balancing order and liberty haunted intellectuals of the revolutionary generation. Was it possible to stabilize freedom and preserve republican principles? Where along the spectrum from tyranny to anarchy would Americans find the proper synthesis of ordered liberty? "We daily see matter of a perishable nature rendered durable by certain chemical operations," observed Rush. "In like manner, I conceive, that it is possible to ana-

Harvard Educational Review Vol. 36 No. 1 Spring 1966, 29–41

lyze and combine power in such a way as not only to increase the happiness, but to promote the duration of republican forms of government far beyond the terms limited for them by history, or the common opinions of mankind."[2] One means of doing this was schooling.

Educational theorists of the period were concerned mainly with constructing institutions, not tearing them down. They stood at an opposite pole from Rousseau, who sought to extricate Emile from a corrupting society. Three writers expressing a common concern for education but representing different shades of opinion on the function of schooling were Thomas Jefferson, Noah Webster, and Benjamin Rush.[3] As devout libertarian, Jefferson feared a new absolutism. In his "Bill for the More General Diffusion of Knowledge" he warned that "experience hath shewn, that even under the best forms [of government], those entrusted with power have, in time, and by slow operations, perverted it into tyranny. . . ." The Federalist Webster, conservative compared to Jefferson, worried that republican government might prove anarchical. "The United States are in no danger of monarchy or the aristocracy of hereditary estates and offices," he said. "But these states will always be exposed to *anarchy* and *faction,* because these evils approach under the delusive but specious guise of *patriotism.*" Rush, more concerned about preserving freedom than Webster, but alarmed at centrifugal forces in American society, wrote that Americans "understood perfectly the principles of liberty, yet most of us were ignorant of the forms and combinations of power in republics."[4]

Thus from the educational theories of Jefferson, Rush, and Webster emerged definitions of the republican American. Not content with unconscious and haphazard socialization provided by family, political meeting, press, and informal associations, not trusting in the "givenness" of political beliefs and institutions, these men sought to instruct Americans deliberately in schools.[5] Having fought a war to free the United States from one centralized authority, they attempted to create a new unity, a common citizenship and culture, and an appeal to a common future. In this quest for a balance between order and liberty, for the proper transaction between the individual and society, Jefferson, Rush, and Webster encountered a conflict still inherent in the education of the citizen and expressed still in the injunction to teachers to train students to think critically but to be patriotic above all. Hence proceeded a paradox from their search for ordered liberty: the free American was to be, in political convictions, the uniform American. In Jefferson's case the paradox became sharpest in his insistence on a type of political sectarianism at the University of Virginia. It emerged in Rush's demand that children should be made "republican machines" despite his opinion that government was a "progressive" science. And Webster not only desired political orthodoxy but grew alarmed at any deviation of free Americans from a common cultural standard. As a result, in differing degrees, they saw conformity as the price of liberty.

II

Negatively, they defined Americanism as the rejection of European ideas and institutions. Even while Jefferson enjoyed the sophisticated life of Paris, he praised American innocence, just as Franklin had posed in France in his fur cap as nature's own philosopher. America had no feudal tradition, no encrustation of illiberal institutions, no corrupt and gothic history to live down. America's newness was its greatest asset. To the extent that monarchical customs lingered in the United States, its citizenry had to cultivate the art of forgetting.[6]

A pervasive fear of European contamination persuaded the Georgia legislature to pass a law in 1785 disbarring its residents from civic office for as many years as they had studied abroad (if sent overseas under the age of sixteen). George Washington advocated a federal university so that American youth would not need to go abroad for higher education and run the danger of "contracting principles unfavorable to republican government." He believed that such an institution would assimilate "the principles, opinions, and manners" of Americans: "The more homogeneous our citizens can be made in these particulars, the greater will be our prospect of permanent union. . . ." Jefferson argued all his life against the policy of educating Americans abroad:

> Cast your eye over America: who are the men of most learning, of most eloquence, most beloved by their country and most trusted and promoted by them? They are those who have been educated among them, and whose manners, morals and habits are perfectly homogeneous with those of the country . . . the consequences of foreign education are alarming to me as an American.[7]

The "perfectly homogeneous" American, then, must be educated at home. Further, he must study American textbooks. For America to use the textbooks of the Old World, Noah Webster wrote in the preface of his spelling book, "would be to stamp the wrinkles of decrepid age upon the bloom of youth and to plant the seeds of decay in a vigorous constitution." Instead, he urged, America must "prevent the introduction of foreign vices and corruptions . . . promote virtue and patriotism [and] . . . diffuse an uniformity and purity of language. . . ."[8] The same impulse which drove Joel Barlow to write his patriotic epic the *Columbiad* and Philip Freneau his republican poems, and Charles Wilson Peale to paint American themes, impelled textbook writers like Noah Webster and Jedediah Morse to exalt American language, geography, and history. Students should study America first and last. Education must be a republican *paideia,* an all-out effort to Americanize through the schools, the press, the pulpit, the work of the artist, the courtroom, the political assembly—by all the means of shaping character and intellect.

Noah Webster inculcated uniformity in spelling, pronunciation, and political and economic principles. "However detestable personal pride may be," he declared, "yet there is a national pride and a provincial, that are the noblest passions of the republican patriot. . . . For my own part, I frankly acknowledge, I have too much pride not to wish to see America assume a national character." His textbooks were the chief weapon of his campaign for nationalism; in them he sought to homogenize the language "by demolishing those odious distinctions of provincial dialects which are the subject of reciprocal ridicule in different States," to instruct in patriotic principles by a judicious selection of speeches of representative leaders, and to hasten the flowering of American literature.[9] In his essay "On the Education of Youth in America" Webster observed that

> our national character is not yet formed; and it is an object of vast magnitude that systems of Education should be adopted and pursued, which may not only diffuse a knowledge of the sciences, but may implant, in the minds of American youth, the principles of virtue and of liberty; and inspire them with just and liberal ideas of government, and with an inviolable attachment to their own country.

Only American teachers should be employed, skilled in "prepossessing the mind with good principles." As soon as the American child "opens his lips, he should rehearse the history of his own country; he should lisp the praise of liberty, and of those illustrious heroes and statesmen who have wrought a revolution in her favor."[10] Benjamin Rush agreed with Webster's policy of transforming American statesmen into demi-gods. Though he had not admired Washington's leadership during the war, he concurred with a friend who thought it wise to tell less than the full truth about the founding fathers: "Let the world admire our patriots and heroes. Their supposed talents and virtues by commanding attention will serve the cause of patriotism and of our country."[11]

III

Rush stated in its most unequivocal form the paradox that the *free* American was the *uniform* republican. Whereas heterogeneous colonial education largely perpetuated existing differences in society, Rush proposed "one general, and uniform system of education" which would "render the mass of the people more homogeneous, and thereby fit them more easily for uniform and peaceable government." Webster, Rush and Jefferson believed that education must be systematic, useful, and uniformly republican in aim. The only social agency capable of creating such an educational system was the government, whether state or national. "I consider it as possible to convert men into republican machines," declared Rush.

> This must be done, if we expect them to perform their parts properly, in the great machine of the government of the state. That republic is sophisticated with monarchy or aristocracy that does not revolve upon the wills of the people,

> and these must be fitted to each other by means of education before they can be made to produce regularity and unison in government.[12]

Benjamin Rush was explicit about the republican duties this public education must inculcate in the young:

> Let our pupil be taught that he does not belong to himself, but that he is public property. Let him be taught to love his family, but let him be taught, at the same time, that he must forsake and even forget them, when the welfare of his country requires it. He must watch for the state, as if its liberties depend upon his vigilance alone, but he must do this in such a manner as not to defraud his creditors, or neglect his family. He must love private life, but he must decline no station, however public or responsible it may be, when called to it by the suffrages of his fellow citizens. He must love popularity, but he must despise it when set in competition with the dictates of his judgement, or the real interest of his country. He must love character, and have a due sense of injuries, but he must be taught to appeal only to the laws of the state, to defend the one, and punish the other. He must love family honor, but he must be taught that neither the rank nor antiquity of his ancestors, can command respect, without personal merit. He must avoid neutrality in all questions that divide the state, but he must shun the rage, and acrimony of party spirit. He must be taught to love his fellow creatures in every part of the world, but he must cherish with a more intense and peculiar affection, the citizens of Pennsylvania and of the United States. I do not wish to see our youth educated with a single prejudice against any nation or country; but we impose a task upon human nature, repugnant alike to reason, revelation and the ordinary dimensions of the human heart, when we require him to embrace, with equal affection, the whole family of mankind. He must be taught to amass wealth, wants and demands of the state. He must be indulged occasionally in amusements, but he must be taught that study and business should be his principal pursuits in life. Above all he must love life, and endeavor to acquire as many of its conveniences as possible by industry and economy, but he must be taught that this life 'Is not his own,' when the safety of his country requires it.[13]

The tone of Rush's catalog of duties, his statement that the student "is public property," is reminiscent of a poem, "The Solution," which Berthold Brecht wrote after the uprising in East Berlin:

> After the rising of June 17,
> The Secretary of the Writers' Union
> Had leaflets distributed in the Stalin-allee
> In which you could read that the People
> Had lost the government's confidence,
> Which it could only regain
> By redoubled efforts. Would it in that case
> Not be simpler if the government
> Dissolved the people
> And elected another?[14]

Rush was far more definite about republican behavior than about republican beliefs. When he turned to the principles which must be impressed upon the pupil, he simply declared, "He must be taught that there can be no durable liberty but in a republic, and that government, like all other sciences, is of a progressive nature. The chains which have bound this science in Europe are happily unloosened in America."[15] This grandiose trust in the "progressive nature" of political science, coupled with a desire to use the schools to homogenize the citizenry, created an illusion of consensus which sometimes obscured actual political bias. The result could be indoctrination disguised by the sense of "givenness" of American political ideas and institutions.

Rush, Jefferson, and Webster shared a common eighteenth-century faith in the diffusion of knowledge, a trust expressed in almost all the early American state constitutions. In *Sketches of American Policy* Webster contended that "A general diffusion of science is our best guard against the approaches of corruption, the prevalence of religious error, the intrigues of ambition and against the open assaults of external foes."[16] "Enlighten the people generally, and tyranny and oppression of body and mind will vanish like evil spirits at the dawn of day," wrote Jefferson, arguing that "the diffusion of knowledge among the people is to be the instrument" of vast progress. All three agreed in theory that elementary instruction of all classes was more important than higher education of an elite. Jefferson and Rush believed that it was wise to disenfranchise the illiterate.[17] None of them, however, wrote in detail about what kind of political knowledge should be diffused.

In his bill for education in Virginia, Jefferson wrote that every teacher should "give assurance of fidelity to the commonwealth," but he did not specify the curriculum for the common people beyond the three R's and history. In *Notes on the State of Virginia,* he commented that young children, too immature for religious inquiries, should have their minds "stored with the most useful facts from Grecian, Roman, European, and American history."[18] Later he indicated what sort of history was most "useful" when he tried to have an expurgated and liberalized version of Hume's history taught at the University of Virginia. He feared that if Americans read the Tory Hume, they would slide into Federalist doctrine. Thus he approved the policy of the editor who "gives you the text of Hume, purely and verbally, till he comes to some misrepresentation or omission . . . he then alters the text silently, makes it say what truth and candor say it should be, and resumes the original text again, as soon as it becomes innocent, without having warned you of your rescue from misguidance."[19] Like Rush, who wanted a romanticized view of the founding fathers taught to instill a uniform patriotism, Jefferson wished to diffuse only knowledge which would produce homogeneous—and Whig—political views. Dialectic, the clash of factions, the battle of opinions in the "progressive science" of government had no place in the schoolroom.

Both Webster and Rush believed that the teacher should be an absolute monarch. "The government of schools . . . should be *arbitrary,*" wrote Rush. "By this mode of education we prepare our youth for the subordination of laws, and thereby qualify them for becoming good citizens of the republic. I am satisfied that the most useful citizens have been formed from those youth who have never known or felt their own wills till they were one and twenty years of age. . . ." Instruction in the principles of government became indoctrination: witness the "Federal Catechism" which Webster appended to the 1798 edition of his *American Spelling Book* in which he told children of the advantages of republicanism and the defects of monarchy, aristocracy, and democracy.

There were, indeed, ambiguities in this notion of diffusing knowledge. Webster wrote in 1796 that public information would correct the evil of faction, maintaining that when the people "*understood* public affairs, they *will not do wrong*." But in his conservative old age he lost this trust:

> . . . the opinion that intelligence in the people of a country will preserve a republican government must depend for its accuracy on the fact of an intimate or necessary connection between *knowledge* and *principle*. It must suppose that men who *know* what is right will *do* what is right; for if this is not the general fact, then intelligence will not preserve a just administration nor maintain the Constitution and laws. But from what evidence can we infer that men who *know* what is right will *do* what is right? In what history of mankind, political or ecclesiastical, are the facts recorded which authorize the presumption, much less the belief, that correct action will proceed from correct knowledge?[20]

IV

Webster, Rush and Jefferson never succeeded in convincing their countrymen of the need for a uniform system of public elementary education, though Webster did reach the rising generation through his textbooks (over 20,000,000 copies of his speller alone were sold by 1829). Their conception of the political role of education also emerges clearly in their ideas about the proper education of leaders, most notably in the case of Jefferson, who founded the University of Virginia in his old age, fulfilling a life-long ambition. While he advocated primary education on abstract principles, higher education was an intensely personal matter; in effect he was trying to institutionalize his own self-education.[21]

All of the first six Presidents of the United States urged the creation of a national university to prepare an elite. Benjamin Rush even suggested that Congress pass a law "to prevent any person [thirty years after the founding of the university] being chosen or appointed into power or office who has not taken his degree in the federal university." Rush believed that such an institution could be a place "where the youth of all the states may be melted (as it were) together into one mass of citizens. . . ."[22]

In his bill of 1779 "For the More General Diffusion of Knowledge," Jefferson had sketched a plan for the selection and education of a natural aristocracy which would supplement but not supplant the aristocracy of birth and wealth. He designed a rigorous system to select these natural aristocrats for scholarships—"raking a few geniuses from the rubbish" he called it. The majority of students in the grammar schools and at William and Mary would continue to be the sons of planters and professional men who had long enjoyed a near monopoly of formal education.

Jefferson believed that the people could be divided into two major groups, the "laboring and the learned." Consequently, the educational system had two tracks. The laboring class needed but the three years of elementary schooling in which the basic precepts of republicanism were to be inculcated along with the three R's. The learned class was composed of those destined for the professions and the wealthy, who "may aspire to share in conducting the affairs of the nation. . . ."[23] His scholarship boys, the few students of talent and virtue raked from the rubbish, constituted the natural aristocracy. One of Jefferson's remarkable assumptions was that the electorate would select his natural aristocrats for office, along with the "unnatural" aristocrats, of course, who had looked on office as their expected prerogative in colonial times. Such an assumption would soon be outmoded in the shifting style of political leadership to come in the Jacksonian period. It was a normal carryover, however, from the paternalistic pattern of political power in pre-war Virginia. Although his proposal to reform William and Mary did not succeed, Jefferson returned in later years to his earlier desire to found a true university in Virginia.

In common with most of the educational theorists of the revolutionary generation, Jefferson did not operate on egalitarian principles of leadership. Like Rush, who proposed the remarkable plan of an interlocking directorate of the federal university and the federal government, he believed that the education of the guardians was of consummate importance. They must think and act correctly, for the fate of the state was in their hands. Thus it is revealing to examine Jefferson's practical role in his one successful educational reform, the founding of the University of Virginia, a role in which he appears as the high priest of political sectarianism.

Religious sectarianism in higher education was, of course, no new phenomenon. Harvard, William and Mary, and most of the other colonial colleges had been founded to prepare orthodox ecclesiastical and political leaders. It was precisely this sectarian cast of William and Mary which had most disturbed Jefferson about his alma mater and had impelled him to attempt unsuccessfully to render it a secular institution in 1779.[24]

Passionately anti-clerical, Jefferson declared a lifelong war against religious bigotry. Like many other eighteenth-century liberals, he acquired a profound distaste for theology and what he called "metaphysics," choosing instead to interpret Christianity as a humanistic moral code. He edited the Gospels in a new and improved Jeffersonian Bible, culling the genuine sayings of Christ from the spurious "as easily distinguishable as diamonds in a dunghill." A zealous advocate of tolerance, he prided himself on Virginia's Bill for Establishing Religious Freedom. He opposed the establishment of any church, contending "That to compel a man to furnish contributions of money for the propagation of opinions which he disbelieves and abhors is sinful and tyrannical . . . truth is great and will prevail if left to herself. . . ." To the end he remained consistent and forceful in his defense of religious liberty, and claimed that he "never attempted to make a convert, nor wished to change another's creed."[25]

About theology the doctrinaire libertarian cared little, but political ideology was another matter. It is here that Jefferson's rigid liberalism became apparent, and nowhere more so than in his work as founder of the University of Virginia. To Jefferson, political principles separated people into camps almost as distinct as the split between the regenerate and the unregenerate for the Puritan. "The Division into Whig and Tory is founded in the nature of men," he wrote; "the weakly and nerveless, the rich and corrupt seeing mere safety and accessibility in a strong executive; the healthy, firm and virtuous, feeling confidence in their physical and moral resources, and willing to part with only so much power as is necessary for their government. . . ."[26] Obviously, American leaders must be Whigs.

Religious or philosophical heresies did not matter, but political heresy did. In 1811 Jefferson wrote that "the eyes of the virtuous all over the earth are turned with anxiety on us, as the only depositories of the sacred fire of liberty, and . . . our falling into anarchy would decide forever the destinies of mankind, and seal the political heresy that man is incapable of self-government."[27] In his study of *Jefferson and Civil Liberties: the Darker Side,* Leonard Levy contends that Jefferson was convinced that "the great American experiment in self-government and liberty was in nearly constant danger. He completely identified with that experiment, to the point that an attack on him or on the wisdom of his policies quickly became transmuted in his mind as a threat to the security of the tender democratic plant." Just as the revolutionary generation had earlier feared the taint of European monarchical maxims, so the liberal Jefferson came to fear that future leaders would be contaminated by Federalist doctrine.[28]

Jefferson had given a libertarian charter to the University of Virginia, proclaiming that it "will be based on the illimitable freedom of the human mind. For here we are not afraid to follow the truth wherever it may lead, not to tolerate any error as long as reason is left free to combat it." But when the time came to hire the faculty, he wrote to James Madison, "In the selection of our Law Professor we must be rigorously attentive to his political principles." He insisted on the importance of finding an orthodox advocate of states rights republicanism, for

> It is in our seminary that the vestal flame is to be kept alive; from thence it is to spread anew over our own and the sister States. If we are true and vigilant in our trust, within a dozen or twenty years a majority of our own legislature will

> be from one school, and many disciples will have carried its doctrine home with them to their several states, and will have leavened thus the whole mass.

"Seminary," "vestal flame," "disciples," "doctrine," "leavened thus the whole mass"—what are these terms if not the vocabulary of the sectarian? In a letter to an ally in the legislature, Jefferson spoke of "the political holy charge" which the university would transmit to the students.[29]

Not content with loading the political dice by selecting an orthodox professor, Jefferson also insisted that the lay Board of Visitors prescribe the textbooks:

> There is one branch in which we are the best judges, in which heresies may be taught, of so interesting a character to our own State, and to the United States, as to make it a duty in us to lay down the principles which are to be taught. It is that of government. . . . It is our duty to guard against the dissemination of such [Federalist] principles among our youth, and the diffusion of that poison, by a previous prescription of the texts to be followed in their discourses.[30]

Jefferson's prescription of texts meant to a Federalist Virginian such as Chief Justice Marshall, who favored a strong central government, that he was being compelled by the state to contribute money for the propagation of opinions which he disbelieved and abhorred. If the true test of tolerance is to permit heresies about which one cares deeply, then the Virginian Federalists might appear greater libertarians than the man who "swore eternal hostility to tyranny over the minds of men."

V

Perhaps no one saw more clearly than Benjamin Rush that a new field of sectarian battle was emerging after the Revolution. "We only change the names of our vices and follies in different periods of time," he wrote. "Religious bigotry has yielded to political intolerance. The man who used to hate his neighbor for being a Churchman or a Quaker now hates him with equal cordiality for being a Tory."[31] Indeed, as Rush himself demonstrated in his own comments on "republican machines," it was difficult to be a consistent libertarian in a nation striving to articulate and inculcate liberal republican principles.

The United States was a great experiment. Earnestly, Jefferson, Rush, and Webster worked to make it succeed. Experience could give no guarantee that citizens would be loyal to the principles and institutions which made them free; yet, at the same time, only if individuals could dissent with impunity from the most fundamental convictions of society would they know that they were indeed free. From this clash of necessary consensus and of freedom to dissent stemmed the paradoxical nature of the educational theories of the three intellectuals. Determined to preserve the heritage of the Revolution, to unify the nation, and to inculcate proper principles of government, they advocated a kind of republican indoctrination, hoping that the ensuing enlightenment would bring a salutary uniformity. But freedom implies intellectual diversity and open choice, even with respect to the most basic political values. "Even what is best in America is compulsory," Santayana would later observe, "the idealism, the zeal, the beautiful happy unison of its great moments."

Notes

1. *Letters of Benjamin Rush,* ed. Lyman H. Butterfield (Princeton: Princeton University Press, 1951), I, 388; Allen O. Hansen, *Liberalism and American Education in the Eighteenth Century* (New York: MacMillan Co., 1926), p. 237; Harry R. Warfel, *Noah Webster: Schoolmaster to America* (New York: MacMillan Co., 1936), p. 285.
2. Benjamin Rush, *A Plan for the Establishment of Public Schools and the Diffusion of Knowledge in Pennsylvania, to Which Are Added Thoughts upon the Mode of Education, Proper in a Republic* (Philadelphia: Thomas Dobson, 1786), p. 23.
3. In his *Liberalism and American Education* Hansen discusses a number of other, less-familiar American educational writers, including Robert Coram, James Sullivan, Nathaniel Chipman, Samuel Knox, and Samuel H. Smith. These men, as well as Jefferson, Rush, and Webster, disagreed on a number of details in their plans of education, but almost all agreed that schooling should have a predominately political aim: to unify the nation. Rush Welter analyzes the educational views of some of the other founding fathers in *Popular Education and Democratic Thought in America* (New York: Columbia University Press, 1962), Chap. ii.
4. *The Papers of Thomas Jefferson,* ed. Julian P. Boyd (Princeton: Princeton University Press, 1950), II, 526–27; *Letters of Noah Webster,* ed. Harry R. Warfel (New York: Library Publishers, 1953), p. 140; Harry G. Good, *Benjamin Rush and His Services to American Education* (Berne, Ind.: Witness Press, 1918), p. 198–99.
5. For the concept of the "givenness" of American political values see Daniel J. Boorstin, *The Genius of American Politics* (Chicago: University of Chicago Press, 1953), Chap. iii; for an analysis of "Political Experience and Enlightenment Ideas in Eighteenth-Century America" see Bernard Bailyn's essay in *The American Historical Review,* LXVII (January, 1962), p. 339–51.
6. Carl Van Doren, *Benjamin Franklin* (New York: Viking Press, 1938), p. 631; on the importance of America's lack of a feudal tradition see Louis Hartz, *The Liberal Tradition in America: an Interpretation of American Political Thought Since the Revolution* (New York: Harcourt, Brace, 1955), Chap i; Hansen, p. 61.
7. *A Documentary History of Education in the South Before 1860,* ed. Edgar W. Knight (Chapel Hill: University of North Carolina Press, 1950), II, 4, 17, 21–22; Boyd, VIII, 636–37.
8. Warfel, *Noah Webster,* p. 60.
9. Warfel, *Noah Webster,* p. 53–59; also see Noah Webster, *An American Selection of Lessons in Reading and Speaking* (Hartford: Hudson & Goodwin, 1789), preface.
10. Noah Webster, *A Collection of Essays and Fugitive Writings on Moral, Historical, Political and Literary Subjects* (Boston: I. Thomas and E. T. Andrews, 1790), pp. 3, 17–21, 23, 25.
11. Good, p. 61.
12. Rush, pp. 14, 27.
13. Rush, pp. 20–22.
14. As quoted in Martin Esslin, *Brecht: The Man and His Work* (Garden City: Doubleday & Co., 1960), p. 191.
15. Rush, p. 22–23.
16. Noah Webster, *Sketches of American Policy,* ed. Harry R. Warfel (New York: Scholars' Facsimiles and Reprints, 1937), p. 28.

17. *The Writings of Thomas Jefferson,* eds. Andrew Lipscomb and Albert E. Bergh (Washington, D.C.: Thomas Jefferson Memorial Ass'n, 1903), XIV, 487; James B. Conant, *Thomas Jefferson and the Development of American Public Education* (Berkeley: University of California Press, 1963), p. 11; Good, pp. 194–95: John C. Henderson, *Thomas Jefferson's Views on Public Education* (New York: G. P. Putnam's Sons, 1890), p. 31, *passim;* for an excellent essay on the relation of Jefferson's political and educational ideals see Gordon C. Lee, *Crusade against Ignorance: Thomas Jefferson on Education* (Teachers College, "Classics in Education," No. 6 [New York: Teachers College Bureau of Publications, 1961]), pp. 1–26.
18. Boyd, II, 527–30, III, 251–53.
19. Leonard W. Levy, *Jefferson and Civil Liberties: the Darker Side* (Cambridge: Harvard University Press, 1963), p. 146; Herbert B. Adams, *Thomas Jefferson and the University of Virginia* ("U. S. Bureau of Education, Circular of Information," No. 1, 1888 [Washington: U. S. Government Printing Office, 1888]), pp. 141–42.
20. Rush, p. 24; Warfel, *Letters,* pp. 140, 479; Noah Webster, *The American Spelling Book . . .* (Boston: I. Thomas and G. Andrews, 1798), pp. 154–56.
21. On the failure of these schemes for public education see Bernard Bailyn, *Education in The Forming of American Society* (New York: Vintage, 1963), pp. 45–47, 112–14; Warfel, *Webster,* p. 71; *Early History of the University of Virginia as Contained in the Letters of Thomas Jefferson and Joseph C. Cabell,* ed. Nathaniel F. Cabell (Richmond: J. W. Randolph, 1856) reveals the extent of Jefferson's day-by-day involvement in establishing the University; see also Roy J. Honeywell, *The Educational Work of Thomas Jefferson* (Cambridge: Harvard University Press, 1931), Chaps. v–ix.
22. Butterfield, pp. 494, 388; Good, pp. 177–78; on the project of a national university see Edgar B. Wesley, *Proposed: the University of the United States* (Minneapolis: University of Minnesota Press, 1936).
23. Lipscomb and Bergh, XIX, 217–21.
24. Honeywell, pp. 205–10; Robert M. Healey, *Jefferson on Religion in Public Education* (New Haven: Yale University Press, 1962), pp. 229–30.
25. Lipscomb and Bergh, XII, 390; Adrienne Koch, *The Philosophy of Thomas Jefferson* (New York: Columbia University Press, 1943), Chap. iv; Boyd, II, pp. 545–46; Healey maintains, pp. 225–26, that Jefferson was unwittingly sectarian in his religious views (as well as in his political opinions) since he tried to inculcate a generalized "religion of peace, reason, and morality"—in itself, and by exclusion of opposing positions, a form of sectarianism.
26. Lipscomb and Bergh, X, 319.
27. Lipscomb and Bergh, X, 319; XIII, 58.
28. Levy, pp. 167, 149–57.
29. Lipscomb and Bergh, XII, 456; XV, 314; Healey, pp. 196–201.
30. Cabell, 339; for more sympathetic interpretations of Jefferson's actions than Levy and Adams presented in the works cited above, or than I have given here, see Arthur Bestor, *The Restoration of Learning: a Program for Restoring the Unfulfilled Promise of American Education* (New York: Alfred Knopf, 1955), pp. 427–432, and Adrienne Koch, *Jefferson and Madison: The Great Collaboration* (New York: Oxford University Press, 1964), pp. 275–79. It is only fair to observe, as Levy does, (p. 157) that "the law school was no more partisan than its Northern counterparts, and the University of Virginia, as a whole, was as free as any institution of higher learning that had been established in the nation."
31. Butterfield, p. 295.

Women and Education in Eritrea: A Historical and Contemporary Analysis

ASGEDET STEFANOS

In 1961, the Eritrean people launched a national liberation struggle in response to Haile Selassie's unilateral incorporation of Eritrea as part of Ethiopia. In 1970, a group of Eritrean activists formed the Eritrean Peoples Liberation Front (EPLF), which became the predominant organization to shape and forge the war of liberation. This struggle was enormously successful in mobilizing and uniting the Eritrean people. In 1993, against great odds and without the sponsorship of a major world power, Eritrea gained its national independence. Early on, the EPLF asserted that the liberation struggle must take the form of a national democratic revolution and took steps to establish forms of democratic organization in the liberated areas.[1] In addition, the EPLF claimed that there was an interrelated need for both national independence and an egalitarian social revolution and that the former could not be attained without pursuing the latter. In 1974, the EPLF made a major decision to admit women into its ranks and to mount a comprehensive series of policies to foster women's emancipation[2] in the society as a whole.

During the contemporary period (1961–1997), Eritrea and Eritrean women have been undergoing massive social changes. This article explores whether and to what extent Eritrean women have been achieving emancipation, and, if so, what role education has played in that process. It assesses the changes that have occurred for women in the realm of education, during the armed struggle and after national liberation, by examining systems of schooling and learning opportunities — both formal and nonformal — available to women, curricula and pedagogical methods, and supports to promote the EPLF's stated goal of gender equity in education.[3] This assessment of women and education in contemporary Eritrea draws from the policies, programs, and commentary of Eritrea's political leadership and, in addition, from the perceptions and experiences of a diverse sample of Eritrean women, who were interviewed in 1983 and 1997. In a Third World society, particularly one undergoing major social change, the impact of education on women can be

Harvard Educational Review Vol. 67 No. 4 Winter 1997, 658–688

grasped only in the context of evaluating conditions in other realms of their lives, including family life, the economy, and politics.[4] Consequently, this article analyzes these other spheres, particularly when developments within them have affected how women have responded to educational reforms.[5] In addition, it discusses whether the dynamics of the revolutionary process itself have facilitated or burdened the political leadership's campaign for gender equity in education and women's capacity to pursue opportunities for schooling and learning.

The analysis of women and education in Eritrea during the contemporary period needs to be situated in a broader historical context. Accordingly, this article provides an overview of the general social condition of Eritrean women and the forms of learning and degree of educational access available to them in both the period of pre-colonial traditional society and the eras of Italian (1889–1941) and British (1941–1952) colonialism.

Women and Education in Eritrea in Traditional Society and Under Colonial Regimes

Before and during colonialism, Eritrean women's status was severely subordinate in educational and sociopolitical spheres. However, Eritrean women's dependent position was not static. Depending on the particular contradictions posed by changing socioeconomic and political conditions, women created spaces for themselves within the existing structures to gain some degree of cultural and social autonomy and self-determination.

The history of women's education in Eritrea demonstrates that broad social factors and specific developments in education that were relatively emancipatory for men — liberating them from natural, social, or ideological restraints — often have had quite different, and even opposite, effects upon women. These disparities between women's and men's experience were rooted in the social forces that systematically created obstacles for women's educational equity.[6] For example, under the Italian colonial regime of the 1940s, Eritrean women, in contrast to men, did not significantly partake in the educational and economic expansion of the period.[7] Those women who found access to learning and urban employment got locked into the informal sector of the economy, turning domestic duties into economic activities. A major reason for the separation of the sexes in education was the colonialists' disregard for women and for their productive capacity. This stance reinforced the prevailing indigenous system of gender inequality in education.[8]

Eritrean Women and Education in Traditional Society

In traditional Eritrea,[9] women's status was established within two distinct semi-feudal socioeconomic systems — agricultural and pastoral — and two conservative religious value systems — Coptic and Muslim.[10] For both sedentary highlanders and pastoral semi-nomadic lowlanders, the family was a crucial unit of learning and cultural activities.[11] The family was hierarchical, patrilineal, and authoritarian, with strict sexual and generational divisions of labor.[12]

Traditional formal education was established for religious purposes. Secular education can be generally characterized as informal and nonformal education. Traditional learning patterns reflected the agricultural and pastoral life of Eritrea, and were suited to the needs of the people; education fitted the young for their roles in communal life. Skills and crafts were handed down, along with traditions, customs, and knowledge of the complex system of rights and duties that ordered the society. Education was usually rounded-off by initiation ceremonies or "regimental" training, marking the young person's entry into full adult status. Thus, traditional Eritrean education was functional and utilitarian with respect to the social and economic roles women and men were called upon to fill.[13]

Religious education, controlled by the Coptic Church for the Christian highlanders and by the Mosque for the Muslim lowlanders, tended to buttress the political and social preeminence of men. The aim of this education was to prepare males for religious vocations and, in a few cases, for secular occupations that required literacy. Clerical authority was supportive of the upper-rung social groups and conservative in its view of women's place in society. Theological schooling for girls was not deemed worthwhile because women were always excluded from the ecclesiastical hierarchy and from temporal duties of governance in their communities. The majority of Eritrean women remained nonliterate.

Girls received much of their education from their mothers, who focused on the "sacramental" duties associated with being a wife and mother. Women's exclusion from public roles and the strict sexual division of labor determined that girls needed to learn skills directly connected to household management, child care, and health care. The early training of either Christian highland or Muslim lowland girls also focused on a limited range of religious activities and the social codes of "proper" family relationships. They learned to be courteous and subordinate, and to defer to males, even those younger than themselves. They came to expect that, once they became matriarchs, they in turn would accrue power and status over younger female household members.[14]

Within the family, women were given chief responsibility for household management. At the young age of five or six, daughters began to assume an array of tasks, such as caring for siblings, gathering firewood, carrying water, milking sheep and goats, pounding dried grains for brewing, and churning milk into butter. Women also learned various crafts, including spinning cotton, weaving baskets, and decorating household items and their homes.[15]

Early marriage meant that most girls would leave their homes before becoming of significant labor value to their families. The future bride was selected by the groom's parents with an eye to the continuity of the family's lineage (bearing male heirs) and proper household management. Girls often married well before puberty, as early as ten to twelve years of age. Once married, the young bride acquired further training under the tutelage of her mother-in-law.

In the predominantly agrarian society, women participated actively in the economic sphere. Eritrean Highland women were essential to the economy, farming the land along with men. They cleared acreage, weeded, harvested, winnowed, tended livestock, and ground grain into flour. Despite their active economic role in agricultural production, Highland women's status was subordinate to men's within the rural economy. Men were the sole owners of agricultural produce, and the fruits of their wives' and daughters' labor was their undisputed property. Men made unilateral decisions in the distribution of surplus produce and had total control over formal bartering transactions.

By contrast, female labor was not necessary among the nomads, who raised only cattle, and women were under significant subjugation. The constant movement of the family in search of pastures meant an isolated and rough existence for women. They were totally secluded and covered up while traveling on camel back, and then restricted in a small tent at a temporary campsite where they prepared the family meal, pushing it under the tent for the men of the family to eat. These nomadic women's activities consisted of building the frame of the hut and staying out of sight in it except to care for small children, while men moved around freely with their cattle and sat in the open air socializing with other men. The complex interaction of ecological necessity and Islamic religious laws resulted in a stark asymmetry between the sexes.[16]

Eritrean Women and Education during Colonialism

Eritrean educational institutions under Italian colonialism had a pattern of deliberate exclusion of females and sex-differentiated schooling. Beginning in 1889, the Italians introduced a capitalist economy, heavy taxation, and expropriation of land, which increased pressure on men and women alike. When men migrated to cities, women were left behind in the rural areas.[17] Usually only males were employed in the cash crop plantations and in mines and urban factories. Thus, women were excluded from the cash economy and were dependent on men.

Under both Italian (1889–1941) and British (1941–1952) colonialism, there was no effort to educate or develop the skills of women, since it was considered unnecessary to secure political domination and economic exploitation. In addition, Western patriarchal conceptions of acceptable sex roles contributed to different educational opportunities for boys and girls.[18]

Italian colonialism brought limited modern education to Eritrea — male Eritreans received education up to a fourth-grade level.[19] A handful of state vocational schools were established to train boys as noncommissioned officers, artisans, clerks, male nurses, and plantation workers. There were also Catholic and Protestant missionary schools, which largely excluded females, that were designed primarily to garner Eritrean converts, and only secondarily to train subalterns for the colonial administration.[20] Post-primary education was minimal, since the Italians were concerned that higher education might inculcate in Eritreans an anti-colonial outlook.[21] After almost sixty years of Italian colonization in Eritrea, only a small, predominantly male segment of the population could claim rudimentary schooling,[22] and only a minority with "assimilated status"[23] were given the opportunity to pursue their education.

Generally, the British were less stringent than the Italians in restricting educational opportunity. They oversaw a notable expansion of schools in villages and towns. The rewards of schooling were visible, and Eritreans' desire for education increased rapidly. They began to enter white-collar professions as teachers, lawyers, entrepreneurs, and newspaper reporters, fervently taking advantage of the new educational programs. Nevertheless, these limited educational opportunities were largely reserved for males.

Both the secular and missionary educational systems constructed by the Italians and British shared characteristic features of colonial education. They negated Eritrea's history and culture and claimed that history began with the civilizing presence of colonialists.[24] Placing no value on Eritrean customs and institutions, they introduced European standards of behavior and general outlook into the educational system. This pedagogical bias was the "de-Africanization of nationals."[25]

In the shift from traditional to colonial education, two factors remained constant: females were generally denied access to formal schooling, and educators sponsored deliberate patterns of sex-differentiated roles. Education, even literacy, was not considered useful for women as they performed their daily tasks.

The few schools established for girls were run by missionaries. Curricula focused on general literacy education and on subjects that upheld the stereotypical role of women, with home economics as the principal subject. The schools' curricula included domestic duties such as sewing, embroidery, and cooking. Learning these skills constituted a girl's vocational education and socialized her to become an industrious and obedient woman.

A major component of missionary schools for girls was the promotion of converts and implanting religious principles in Eritrean families by turning girls into Christian wives and mothers. While most Eritrean women had little or no chance for wage-earning, schooling for girls was valued by all because it could provide a better opportunity for securing husbands who had good educational and economic standing. An unmarried educated and/or Christian woman's choices were limited to joining a convent and working within a missionary structure as a single woman. Some women married fellow male converts or evangelists.

In large part, Italian and British rule exacerbated Eritrean women's economic subjugation and reinforced their exclusion from education. Increased economic activity in the urban areas and Italian land confiscation brought a migration of Highland men out of the rural areas. This shift of men from working on farms to work on cash crop plantations and in mines and urban factories placed additional pressure on women in the rural areas.

Women, who never were property owners, were also excluded from the cash transactions and technical innovations of the modern sector, since only Eritrean males engaged in business activities. This exclusion also increased women's economic marginality. Colonialists' cultural prejudice and patriarchal biases led them to ignore Eritrean women. Not having access to wage employment, women could not learn the new skills that paid jobs offered. Thus, conservative Western conceptions of gender roles and capitalism's sexual division of labor were grafted onto existing traditional features of Eritrean women's subordination. The result often combined the worst elements of these diverse forms of gender inequality.

When women moved to the urban areas that arose with colonialism, job opportunities for Eritreans in the modern sector were far broader for males than for females, and jobs were stratified by gender. In the colonial hierarchy, the Eritrean women held the lowest position — the few girls who had access to training and skills were only prepared for household labor and for the humbler occupations in the modern sector.

In the early Italian colonial period, most families lived apart — men in the cities and towns close to work, their wives and children in the villages. The wives lived on their husbands' remittances, together with whatever subsistence farming they could muster. Normally husbands visited their homes once or twice a year, usually around planting and harvesting season to work on the family plot. Many male workers found this a double burden and ceased returning to their villages, yet continued to send money to their spouses. Many men lived with other women in the city and thus became even more estranged from their wives in the countryside.[26] Some married women in the villages led a miserable and lonely existence under the control of their in-laws. They were mostly viewed as misfits and treated as lowly workers. They were expected to raise their children and to wait indefinitely for husbands who often never returned.

Unlike other European colonialists, the Italians left the traditional family code untouched. Accordingly, abandoned women had no legal recourse. However, the contradictions between the traditional and colonial economic systems inadvertently created possibilities for women. In response to their men's departure to plantations and the city, some women left their villages and went to cities looking for jobs. Also lured to the city were those few women who did not conform to the social norms of the traditional village and were viewed as outcasts — widowed women, women without dowries, and divorced women. The city offered these women wider horizons and a certain freedom to start a new life. Some entered the informal market of brewing, handicraft, selling foodstuffs, and laundry work, while others gradually worked their way into agricultural industries.

By the 1940s, some women began to enter light industrial sectors such as textiles, matches, and coffee factories, where they were paid lower rates than men and endured long hours and harsh treatment. Despite discriminatory wages and unhealthy working conditions, urban employment gave women an alternative to marriage and a chance to earn their own money. Some created opportunities for themselves by turning domestic labor into an economic activity, serving in Italian households as maids, cooks, and nannies. They boarded with Italian families and supported their parents, siblings, and extended families with their wages. Many of them decided to forego marriage in order to lift their family members from poverty, expecting that in old age they would be supported by one of the many relatives they had helped.[27]

Existence in the city enabled some Eritrean women to exercise greater control over their social lives and their choice of male partners. Among these were a group of females who owned and ran bars. While a number of them offered sexual favors to Eritrean and Italian male customers, most were respectable small business women who garnered extraordinary independence and were notable figures in the urban social milieu. They resisted the sexual advances of colonialists, and later on, many actively contributed to the national liberation movement. Generally, the urban areas provided anonymity and a certain measure of autonomy for women who were escaping the control of extended families and the village. It provided women with a rare opportunity to reinvent themselves. Sharing similar experiences, women residing in cities created networks and solidarity amongst themselves. The majority of these women were nonliterate.

Women and Education in Eritrea during the National Liberation Struggle and after Independence: Policies and Programs

An examination of both the traditional period and the eras of Italian and British colonialism indicate that education was undervalued and constricted and that Eritrean women in particular were greatly impeded in pursuing schooling and all forms of learning. The contemporary period (1961–1997), which commences with the launching of the war for national liberation, represents a radical departure in that educational resources have been greatly expanded, and there has been a significant break with the longstanding prohibition against women pursuing educational opportunities.

Education was viewed by political leaders as integral to the national liberation struggle, and is currently valued by policymakers as a core element of nation-building. In the view of both the EPLF and the government, the broad educational arena relates to both formal and nonformal learning; to efforts at consciousness-raising, including those that occur outside of schools; and to all opportunities for building skills. The design of and strategy for education is linked to a larger social vision that is egalitarian, responsive to the interests of peasants and workers, independent, oriented to self-reliance, and able to mobilize effectively all human and material resources.

Educational goals and objectives that were pursued during the liberation struggle have been adopted and expanded by the post-independence government. The broad educational strategy has a range of core components. First, there has been an effort to highlight Eritrea's history and heritage, and thereby eliminate the colonized mentality. Second, education has been designed to expose elements of the traditional culture that retard social and economic transformation, such as disdain for certain vocations, religious zealotry, and superstition.[28] There is an emphasis on training people in the scientific method in the study of both nature and society. There is a commitment to ensure that education engages and is accessible to the vast majority of people, rather than to a small, highly specialized elite. Accordingly, nonformal schooling has been given equal status to formal learning; both are seen as critical to developing the resources of the independent nation. In addition, the curriculum is anti-elitist; all subject areas highlight the everyday experiences encountered by students and are rooted in the concrete challenges of local life. The cleavage between mental and manual labor is seen as a false dichotomy that promotes an undesirable divide between exalted thinkers and denigrated laborers. Accordingly, the educational system combines learning with productive work. The pedagogical approach promotes active learning and collective cooperation. Teachers are encouraged to play a role in designing educational materials and to act as co-learners with, rather than transmitting agents to, their students. A great deal of emphasis is placed on peer learning, and students are involved in shaping educational experiences.[29]

In the mid-1970s, the EPLF recognized the need to engage the full and active participation of Eritrean women in the liberation struggle. With this recognition came a commitment that has continued beyond independence to establish educational equity between the genders. Education was recognized as crucial in transforming women and enabling them to redefine their private and public roles. It has been a critical avenue for developing the consciousness of a newly emancipated woman, for disarming the objections of men and mothers, and for providing skills that permit females to operate on an equal footing with males in the reconstruction of Eritrean society.

The strategy for integrating the masses of women into a new educational system included combating the material and attitudinal barriers to access.[30] A fundamental obstacle was the parental view that a girl's only goal was to prepare for and succeed in getting married and that female education was an unnecessary frill or, worse yet, a costly distraction. Aside from notions about male superiority, there was an economic basis to parents' opposition to education for girls: the need for children to help with the persistent demands of domestic and agricultural labor. While some parents anxiously ceded time for schooling to sons, they stiffened when it came to daughters. The EPLF recognized the need for an intensive political education campaign in the liberated areas to confront parental resistance to female education. In mass gatherings and individual meetings, the EPLF's political activists explained to elders and parents the value of making education available to all young people. They noted that gender discrimination in schooling undermined the liberation effort and sometimes sternly criticized those who withheld education from their daughters. The cadres organized communal assistance for those families who relied on their daughter's extra hands, and the school calendar was often planned to minimize interference with periods of peak agricultural activity.

However, once access to education was established in the countryside, girls often lagged behind in their school work, and their dropout rate was high. Parents would often turn up to retrieve their daughters for work "because something unexpected had come up."[31] During the national liberation struggle, the EPLF was not able to block fully such parental interference, but it did work to accelerate its ability to help village girls to move to base areas to pursue their education.

The EPLF's Revolution School, established in the base area in 1980, became a site for advancing approaches to education that promoted female emancipation and reduced male chauvinism. It attempted to combat sexual stereotyping in its structure, methods, and curriculum. At the Revolution School, girls and boys were equal partners in all aspects of school life. Both boys and girls engaged equally in academics, gymnastics, maintenance, cooking, fetching water from the well, and building construction.[32] The integration of both genders into all school activities was considered essential to ensure that girls were able to experience fully an emancipatory environment and to participate in new learning and training opportunities.

In contemporary educational settings, curriculum materials include new images of women, such as handling tools or military equipment.[33] School texts discuss women's relationship with family, their work outside the home, domestic chores, and parenting, eliciting discussion on the value of women's work and their place in society. They note women's achievements in the revolution, including their new roles as combatants, teachers, mechanics, and engineers.

There is little systematic statistical data to measure the impact of the EPLF's campaign to give girls access to school. A 1987 EPLF report indicated that 40 percent of Revolution School students were female — an extraordinary increase from girls' almost total exclusion from schooling.[34] However, there is little doubt that the Revolution School benefited from the singular energy and control applied to it by the Front, and that its achievements on behalf of girls were not representative of schooling throughout the liberated territories or the country as a whole.

With independence, the new government took on the massive responsibility of education throughout the nation and of developing an expanded educational system that continued to promote female emancipation. The preeminence of education as the means to advance national reconstruction and development was upheld. The Ministry of Education's policy guidelines committed the government to compulsory basic education, including instruction in local languages, and eventually ensuring universal access to schooling.[35]

Other Realms: Alternative Venues for Learning by Women

The EPLF and the post-independence government have launched a multiprong attack on impediments to women's emancipation. This campaign goes beyond reshaping the educational system to engage and be accessible to females. Substantial interventions have occurred in economics and politics, and, to a lesser degree, in the domain of family life. In each of these arenas, interventions from above have opened up a range of opportunities for women to develop consciousness, acquire new knowledge, and pursue skills once unavailable to them. The contemporary leaders of Eritrea view education and learning not as a discrete, segregated activity, but as an integral component of individual and collective socioeconomic initiatives and efforts. Accordingly, one must include women's advances in politics, economics, and domestic life as additional avenues for breakthroughs in female education and learning.

Adopting a classical Marxist perspective, Eritrean leaders have viewed the economy as the decisive realm in which to secure the liberation of the Eritrean masses as a whole, and of Eritrean women in particular. Economic transformation is perceived as key to overcoming the oppressive class relations and impoverishment that have victimized the vast majority of both men and women. It is believed that the mobilization and integration of women into the labor force is essential for successful economic development of the nation. In the leadership's view, women's full participation in economic life as wage laborers helps to dissipate their traditionally inferior social status and subjugation. Accordingly, during the liberation struggle and since independence, a range of interventions to overcome obstacles and prohibitions to women's economic activity have been launched. The national Constitution[36] asserts that women have a right to work in all economic sectors and that the principle of "equal pay for equal work" must be gender-free. A decisive intervention establishes women's rights to own and work the land in the countryside, and for nomadic women to own herds.[37] As a modern economic sector has been revived and expanded during the liberation struggle and since independence, women have gained entry into a range of wage labor fields that under colonialism had been the preserve of men. Females work in rural poultry and vegetable cooperatives and state farms, in quarries and mines, in factories, and as part of maintenance and repair units. They have assumed frontline and administrative positions in the human service agencies proliferated first by the Front, and then later by the government. They have converted unpaid household activities into retail operations by selling foodstuffs, baskets, pottery, and processed hides. Women entrepreneurs, a recent phenomenon, have developed small-scale businesses, primarily in the service and retail sectors, owning and running restaurants, bars, groceries, and clothing stores.[38]

The Eritrean leadership also asserts that substantial interventions to open up the arena of politics to women are necessary if gender oppression is to be addressed and if women are to be mobilized for nation-building. While leaders regard economic rights as the fundamental lever for changing women's status, they have viewed political empowerment for women as key to energizing and guaranteeing the emancipatory process.

Beginning in 1974, women's political mobilization and integration became a major priority of the EPLF. It strove to eliminate the substantial obstacles to women's participation in political activity. During a succession of nationalist efforts prior to the EPLF, women had been relegated to highly circumscribed, marginal activity. The EPLF broke with this legacy. The Front, which prior to this point had been exclusively male, formally welcomed and recruited women to join its ranks as cadre, a step which concretely legitimized women's capabilities to play political roles.[39] In addition, the EPLF proclaimed women's right to vote and to run for office. Local organizers actively criticized men's resistance to this process. Under the EPLF's tutelage, women became a presence and had an active voice in the newly organized village and urban assemblies that were established in liberated regions.[40] One indicator of the political empowerment of women is that, at the point of independence in 1993, they represented 30 percent of the Front's membership.[41] However, despite its sustained push for inclusion of women in the political arena, the current government (and the EPLF) have never acknowledged a need for females to assume positions within the core national or regional leadership. There were no women in the EPLF's Central Committee and currently only a few women are in high government positions. None are viewed as key players in major policy decisionmaking.[42]

Women's political activism has, nonetheless, given them a major opportunity to exercise new skills. Previously confined to family life, women developed their capabilities as they increasingly spoke in public and participated in shaping group opinions and decisions in the transformed political arena. With their views about public matters now making a difference, women had new incentives to learn about and analyze regional and national issues. These activities were instrumental in breaking women's internalized view of themselves, upheld by men, that they were "naturally" weak, shy, indecisive, and deferential. The taboo on women being forceful and taking initiatives in public was weakened, and men began to face criticism for chastening and disciplining such women as "hard-headed" and "unruly."

A major EPLF initiative was to welcome women into the liberation Army as active combatants.[43] Thus, women gained entry into the independence struggle's highest status and most revered role, which once again broke decisively with male prerogatives, stereotypes, and self-stigmatization. Women had won access to the decisive fulcrum of the national liberation effort.[44]

In the mid-1970s, the EPLF established a women's organization, the National Union of Eritrean Women (NUEW).[45] The Front chose women cadre to head NUEW and to frame its mission, which was to engage Eritrean women activists at the grassroots levels; to form consciousness-raising groups so that women could break with internalized stigma and become active supporters of the Front's strategy to open up educational, political, and economic arenas to women; and to confront male domination legitimized by traditional and religious attitudes. The NUEW has continued since independence, and its branches have become ardent supporters of government initiatives that specifically abolished male privilege and of policy initiatives that support areas seen as central to the support and development of women, such as education, health care, and child care. Overcoming the initial resistance to unorthodox, militant female cadres, NUEW members entered the cloistered sanctums of women's *wushati* (or women's room)[46] and became highly adept at incrementally organizing cautiously conservative women. The NUEW has vigorously recruited women supporters for the Front and post-independence government that Eritrean male leadership could not have recruited. Nevertheless, while the NUEW has had an independent sphere of activity and significant Front and government support, those in its top ranks have always been selected by the national (male) leadership, which has also defined its overall mission and mode of operation.

During the liberation struggle and since independence, Eritrean leaders have crafted policies and programs that affect the realm of family life. These interventions into the family represent an additional route by which consciousness has been shaped and obstacles reduced that bear directly upon female's ability to gain access to education and opportunities for new learning and skills. Legislation has been enacted that abolishes customary common laws that enshrined male control over women in the domestic realm. Laws were passed that gave women rights equal to men's to choose a marriage partner, pursue divorce, and own family property. At the same time, they have encoded the preeminence of secular law over practices emanating from Coptic Christian and/or Muslim religious tenets that had legitimized women's submissiveness and absolute male authority in family matters.[47] These laws have had an enormous impact on Eritrean women's self-esteem and stature as full participants in family matters, and have also strengthened their sense of themselves as social beings and members of the larger society who are motivated to pursue schooling and educational goals, as well as economic and political interests.

The government has recognized that women are, by custom, singularly and disproportionately responsible for domestic labor and child care, and that these burdens impede their ability to pursue education, learn job-market skills, or fully enter into wage labor. Efforts have been made to lessen women's household work by establishing childcare centers, communal laundries, and flour mills. Attempts have been made to educate men so that they accept rather than block women from pursuing these alternatives to tending to children's needs or domestic chores. At the same time, the Eritrean leaders have claimed that a large-scale development of institutional infrastructure to lessen women's burdens in family life is contingent upon significant economic modernization. This is an example of a classical Marxist orientation that views economic advancement of the masses as the key catalyst for overcoming women's oppression and male dominance. Accordingly, the Eritrean leadership has abstained from pursuing initiatives to directly intervene in male privilege and sexism within the family. There are no educational campaigns to pressure, enlighten, or teach skills to men so that they can perform more household tasks, care effectively for children, or gain new appreciation for daughters. No programs have been created to challenge a culture that frees men to pursue public leisure activities and entertainment with each other, while women tend to their homes separately. Further, the government has been highly cautious in the area of sexual practices that oppress women. It has only tentatively and sporadically questioned customs, such as female seclusion, polygamy, and female circumcision. It seems probable that relatively unchallenged male sexism within family life emboldens fathers and husbands to undercut government-sanctioned drives to expand female access to educational opportunity.

Women's Perceptions and Experiences

Eritrean political leaders' goals and policies for advancing female opportunities in education need to be measured against the concrete aspirations and experiences of Eritrean women. This article seeks to establish a sense of grassroots perceptions and perspectives. A group of Eritrean women were interviewed about their encounters with education during the national liberation struggle and after independence.[48]

These women were drawn from a diverse range of ages, places of birth, ethnic groups, primary languages, religious affiliations, and educational levels (if any).[49] These women saw themselves as participating in the liberation struggle, and were aware of the post-independence government's goal of national reconstruction and development. They shared this perspective with the vast majority of contemporary Eritrean women and men. They represent both cadre and mass participants, the level and status of their activity varies, and there are significant differences in the degree to which they feel connected to (or distanced from) Eritrean leaders and nationally organized political efforts.

These women express the view that the decisive mid-1970s leadership decision to integrate women fully into national liberation and development was essential to insure the success of these efforts. They do not believe that the leadership's commitment to women's emancipation was inevitable, and they give male national leaders credit for this decisive break with the legacy of male supremacy. Genet, a single fifty-year-old civil servant with the Public Works Department in Asmara, says:

> Women's oppression is deep-seated and multifarious. . . . [Eritrean leaders] have embraced "the women's question". . . [which] has given women the opportunity to participate and to fight against their specific oppression. This is an important concession. . . . The [leaders] did not have to do that . . . it is a daring act.[50]

These women define education broadly. When they discuss education, they include both nonformal and formal learning, focus on both knowledge acquisition and skill building, place great emphasis on consciousness-raising activities, and highlight the positive psychological and developmental effects of education as much as its practical benefits. They often depict the revolutionary process itself as a nonformal setting that promoted the intellectual growth of its female participants. These women view education as a core arena in which reforms have had a significant impact on Eritrean women's gains toward emancipation. They generally regard the effects of opportunities for women in education as more substantial and fundamental than changes in the economy — the public realm viewed as the decisive lever for gender equality by Eritrean leaders. Keddes, a college-educated woman from a middle-class family, characterizes education as "pivotal" in enabling women to pursue new rights and access to female participation in politics and economic life:

> For women, education is a critical measure to deepen their awareness about and to develop the means of change in their personal lives. Also, through the acquisition of training and skills women can successfully move into public life that was previously inaccessible to them. I would also say that education is pivotal in transforming the entire society into an egalitarian social system and a productive economic entity.

Many women perceive education as necessary in order for women to recognize and understand the nature of their oppression and to overcome self-stigmatization and, thereby, to embrace and participate in emancipatory efforts. As Asma, a thirty-four-year-old Muslim woman from a peasant family, describes:

> Education [is] the major element in the creation of a new Eritrean woman. Education helps [women] to understand the need for that change, thus empowering us to become major protagonists in our own name.

Yelsu, a thirty-year-old Coptic Christian woman from one of the Highland regions, couples the depiction of education as the key to women's social liberation with the guarantee it provides that children — the future of the nation — will pursue educational advancement:

> Education of women is the sure way to promote the social position of women . . . but it [also] equips them to impart their knowledge and training to the chil-

> dren they bear and raise within the household. So the next generation would grow up with new attitudes and values.

Time and again, these women reflect on how their participation and achievements in education were unimaginable until the reforms advanced by the Eritrean leadership. They note the scarcity of learning opportunities available to girls, the economic pressures that prevented their participation in schools, and the traditional beliefs and attitudes against women's intellectual development. Leila, an ex-combatant from a nomadic peasant family, notes that in her village "it was unthinkable for a girl to be sent to school" or attain rudimentary literacy. Women from towns and cities indicate that there, too, girls who pursued schooling were extremely rare.

Women place great value on the institutionalization of a curriculum open to both genders in all its dimensions. They depict the constraints that had been previously placed on female students. Senayit, a thirty-eight-year-old front-line medic, states:

> Before, there was a differential between females' and males' educational goals. Girls who remained in school were urged to take home economics and home-making courses. . . . I had wanted to study the sciences. I dreamed of being a doctor. . . . There was no way I could do this in the [traditional] school system.

A reformed pedagogical approach that focused on lessons drawn from everyday life and concrete experience, rather than on rote textbook learning, greatly benefited female students, who had been steeped in the detailed narratives and ruminations of an oral culture. Some women indicate that schools' inclusion of collective manual labor as part of the educational experience and equal regard for both intellectual and physical activities also benefited females, who even more so than males had been traditionally restricted to and associated with manual tasks.

Many women characterize education (and revolutionary activity in general) as a "great awakener" that has catalyzed enormous growth in both understandings of self and of a larger social landscape. Twenty-six-year-old Mamet, a former member of the Eritrean Liberation Army, says:

> There is no yardstick to measure the revolution's influence over my life. Now I have better understanding about myself and others. . . . Before I came here, my interest in life was geared exclusively towards family affairs. I did not know anything about my country and the world beyond.[51]

Zewdi, a thirty-six-year-old Catholic single woman from a working-class background, says:

> I have undergone immense changes since I joined EPLF [and] because of . . . my academic achievement. . . . Today I can understand about my surroundings and about the world. My horizon has broadened.[52]

Emancipatory reforms for females in education are linked with interventions to achieve gender equality in the economy and politics. Senayit observes that the introduction of a gender-equal curriculum could not benefit females if the job market had remained rigidly segregated by gender: "[Gender-based curricula] reflected the sex-segregated labor force where women received lowly jobs and were easily dispensed with. Girls were [routed] into vocations such as secretaries and seamstresses." Sarah, a forty-five-year-old college graduate who holds a professional position at the Ministry of Culture, notes: "Because of the limitation of women's role [in the economy], women did not have the incentive to continue their education."

The Eritrean government regards economic modernization as the key factor in enabling females to fully access education. National leaders believe that once the nation has the financial capability to develop and distribute education resources and families have greater economic well-being, girls will be able to take fuller advantage of new educational rights and opportunities. In contrast to this official view, the women interviewed generally regard male dominance and sexist attitudes within the family as the major impediments to females' accessing and utilizing the reformed educational arena. Time and again, they delineate how traditional family beliefs and practices block female participation in schools and learning. Although they recognize this as a manifestation of patriarchy — the rule of the father — they note that mothers have helped reinforce the tenet that education is unnecessary and undesirable for girls.[53] Leila, a forty-year-old married Muslim woman, relates:[54]

> My father had some education but my mother did not go school. My parents felt that a girl should learn from her mother how to be a good housekeeper, mother and wife, and the man will take care of the activities outside the home. In fact I was told the Prophet Mohammed has said that women should concern themselves only with family activities. So, it was unthinkable for a girl to be sent to school.

Twenty-two-year-old Rishan states:[55]

> When I was a little girl, villagers had a tremendous curiosity and enthusiasm for education. The elders used to accept contributions from farmers and request that the Italian administration establish schools, but it was to send boys not girls . . . [by saying] contemptuously that "a female will always remain a female so why waste time educating her." Women have never been seen as having the ability to cultivate their minds.

Mamet agrees: she says that even in the urban areas, parents always feel conflicted about sending their daughters to school. Interviewees stress that families' opposition to female education is rooted in their view that the priority for daughters is to help mothers with domestic chores and to be trained and socialized to become obedient and dutiful wives. Families have viewed education as a source by which girls can become defiant and morally corrupt. Yelsu explains:

> With better education girls may refuse to marry the men who already have paid the dowry; scholastic ambitions might tempt girls not to give their full attention to their "proper role" as wives and mothers; higher education may instigate giving up one's culture and the traditional status accorded childbearing; and, moral danger arising from imported values and new ways of life. . . . [My parents felt] they were being very liberal by allowing their daughters to go to school in the first place. However, as the girl gets older, they worry she may be interested in boys and before it is too late they consent to the first eligible suitor who appears. In my own case, they insisted that my education had improved my chances for a superior husband and that they could not understand why I rejected him. They kept saying, "but he is from a good family, educated and well-off." They felt that I could not get a better suitor than him.

Given the weight that respondents place on the patriarchal family's traditional resistance to females' access to education, they are extremely heartened by the reforms in education that include pedagogical approaches that challenge male students' sexist sense of superiority, and that allow boys opportunities to work and study alongside girls.

Women's Perspectives on Other Realms for Learning

When the women interviewed discuss national policies to achieve gender equality in realms other than education — the economy, politics, and family life — they note and value the increased power and material benefits that females won through these reforms. At the same time, they stress that the emancipating policies in these realms also provided women with additional educational opportunities to develop knowledge, consciousness, and skills. Keddes readily links women's new economic rights to own property, till the soil, sell products, and be wage laborers to changing relations with their husbands: "She can be an independent person rather than an appendage to a man." She couples female economic emancipation with the broader endeavor of women gaining a "foothold [into and] . . . learn[ing] the skills of public life." She then asserts that to achieve all this, "a women needs to have . . . education. Schooling would enable a woman to know what is possible and to acquire training and skills." Many respondents often note the intellectual growth that occurs as women encounter new work opportunities. As Yelsu states: "Access to employment enabled women to gain not only personal earnings and economic security, but it also broadened their horizons towards new experiences and ideas that were previously inaccessible to them when they were isolated in their homes." These women stress that intensive education and consciousness-raising have been key in making men more accepting of female economic equality and in motivating women to pursue new economic opportunities. As Sarah says:

> Some conservative rural villages have accepted the notion of women's right to own land. But this happened after conducting a long and arduous political edu-

> cation and discussion with the entire village community and not the least with women themselves.

Leila describes vividly how things have changed for women:

> [When I was young,] it was forbidden for women to plough the land and engage in all kinds of activities like selling grains or vegetables . . . [our] society does not find it acceptable for women to do these things. [It] is considered an insult to her husband. . . . Even if she is an able-bodied women and her husband is sick or she becomes widowed, she has to hire a field hand to do this specific job. This rule is something that no woman would dare break for she will be an outcast. . . . Now [women] are doing all these new things. We [women] are opening our eyes to a new way of life. Even our husbands are open to these new ideas. I only hope it remains like this when the war is over. . . . I like it better this way.

To these interviewees, women's full and equal participation in politics is a critical milestone in the movement toward gender equality. They often speak of their newly gained political understandings and activity as eventually producing a consciousness about their own oppression as women and the need to overcome it. Zewdi notes that, when joining the Front and commencing political activism,

> all I wanted is [to] stand on equal grounds with the enemy and avenge the misery and devastation it has brought to our people. I learned that there were other dimensions to struggling for national liberation, that we need to eradicate other types of oppression in our midst. There is prejudice, poverty, and illiteracy and there is also gender oppression. [Eventually] I ma[de] the connection between my political and my personal oppression. . . . Now, I consider it a bonus to exercise my rights, not only as an Eritrean but also as a woman.

Women embrace their admittance to the army because it not only allows them to exercise their patriotic fervor and desire for national liberation, but also because it is a decisive "testing ground" to demonstrate that their skills and tenacity are equal to men's. As Sarah explains, "in the course of the liberation struggle, no women fighters have deserted . . . whereas there were many men who deserted."

These women often see political activism as yielding more than political gains. To them, it also empowers women and creates a consciousness that females are able to forge their own destinies. Yelsu says that "the emancipation of women is not something that will be handed to us. We should earn it, through our own struggle." These women recognize that women's political participation results in enhanced power, but they also value political work because it also gives females opportunities to learn and to acquire new skills. Genet explains:

> [As a top political organizer assigned to a rural village,] I find my work challenging and gratifying because I relate with different types of people and their

> issues. . . . [I] have a chance to upgrade [my] skills. . . . There are new issues and challenges that one runs into all the time. I am always learning.

The NUEW is perceived as guarantor of women's political space and its organizers are viewed as uniquely capable of opening other women's eyes to the nature and need to overcome female oppression. As Mamet relates:

> We can go to inner sanctum of women's *wushati* and talk to them. It's even better to have a meeting . . . there, because they become very animated and direct. . . . And joining an all-female organization does not violate their sense of propriety. . . . Through the local [NUEW] chapter, women can participate [fully] in public life.

The interviewees place great value on interventions to foster gender equality within family. As Genet notes, "women's oppression has thrived . . . in the privacy and quiet corners of people's homes."[56] Respondents credit the new egalitarian laws about marriage, family property ownership, and divorce with giving women privileges and autonomy that were once the exclusive preserve of their men folk. At the same time, they stress that new, more emancipated family dynamics help women to speak up for themselves and to expand their abilities. Women now share with men decisions about family budgets. They have greater voice in planning children's (male, as well as female) futures. They speak of a whole range of familial discussions and decisionmaking that their spouses now engage in with them "where there is respect for each other's views." Women who are widowed and divorced describe how egalitarian family laws enabled them to exercise new capabilities and rights to raise their children effectively.

Increased Criticism from Below and Indications of Demoralization: Shifts during the Early Post-Independence Years

Fourteen years after the initial interviews, which were conducted during the liberation struggle in 1983 and four years into independence, the commentary of women respondents indicated much continuity in their attitudes and perspectives. All spoke with energy about the successfully waged liberation war, the welcome end of combat traumas and losses, and the myriad tasks and changes occurring since independence. Many have positions integral to national reconstruction, and some are associated with the government or with nonprofit organizations that receive state funding. All speak with pride about their individual participation in Eritrea's struggle for and achievements under independence. Most remark, without regret, that they have participated in experiences and activities that could not have been anticipated, given their gender and, for many, economic background. Many possess an intimate knowledge of regions of the country, ethnic groups, and second (and third) languages that were not connected to their own birthplaces, identities, and upbringings — a form of cosmopolitanism that was rare amongst most Eritreans twenty-five years ago and unimaginable for its constricted and cloistered females.

Nevertheless, the interviewees are generally far more critical of and pessimistic in 1997 about the Eritrean leadership's efforts toward gender equality and women's emancipation than they were in 1983 in the midst of the liberation struggle. There are more indications of bitterness, charges of bad faith, and evidence of alienation and demoralization. Ironically, many look back on the liberation war as "a better time" for women's rights and empowerment — "when we were living most heartily." Even so, these harsher appraisals do not just focus on the years since independence, but also on the decades of the liberation struggle itself. The respondents' critical commentary focuses on general aspects of Eritrean women's condition and does not concentrate in particular on female access to and pursuit of education. However, their insights are suggestive of how and why the drive to create gender equality in the educational realm may be losing momentum.

A large number of respondents characterize women as experiencing a range of difficulties and encountering frustrations and disappointments. They believe there is a resurgence of male reactions against women's gains during the liberation struggle and that Eritrean leaders either minimize this phenomenon or do not regard challenging it as a major priority. Eritrean women believe that the government's predominant focus is on economic modernization and that it has displayed a tendency to regard women's emancipation as a side issue or distraction. Many of these critics believe that leaders point too readily to disappointments in current international financial aid or the low levels of national resources as a rationale for why there is waning momentum for women's advancement. They assert that their leaders have long overvalued large-scale economic development as a contingency for gains in gender equality. These women have a revisionist view (often amending their own earlier appraisals) that during the liberation struggle there were gaps in the Front's pursuit of women's emancipation and that, with independence, for a variety of reasons, these deficiencies have intensified.

A large number of women are critical about what they regard as the government's relative abandonment of women activists — particularly those who were combatants in the liberation army. In the view of those women interviewed, the condition of the vast majority of female cadre is not an "insiders" issue. They regard the status of former women fighters and society's regard for them as a reasonable indicator of how the masses of Eritrean women — and the struggle for gender equality — are faring in post-independence Eritrea. Female members of the liberation army were largely rural peasants and working class (in contrast to the small number of female cadre who served in administrative noncombat positions, who were more educated and came from families with better economic circumstances).[57] While these respondents feel that all Front activists — both men and women — have not received as much care as they deserve, they feel this tendency has been harshest on females in general, and military personnel in particular.

They note that women fighters often had little or no education prior to joining the struggle, and that while many attained literacy during the liberation years, their further education was stymied by the imperatives of war. Many developed new skills during the struggle, but they were inadequately developed and are not well matched to the peacetime economy. Further, unlike upper-level female noncombatant administrators, the women fighters have few networks among men, which are critical to advancing in post-independent Eritrean society. To its credit, Eritrea has undertaken a massive demobilization of its army, recognizing that modernization is the work of civilians and that a permanent mobilization can undercut economic and political development. However, a significantly greater percentage of women than men have been demobilized[58] and this has accelerated the difficulties of former female members of the liberation army. As Sarah relates:

> The [demobilized] women have few marketable skills . . . they live a miserable and impoverished life. They come and tell me that "you were right, we should have looked out for ourselves and acquired some education and useful skill. All we thought about was contributing to the revolutionary effort. Perhaps we were duped." Now, you see them in terrible shape, poorly clothed, unhappy, with *madia*[59] on their faces, walking the streets of Asmara.

Some respondents believe that women cadre faced covert and unsanctioned disaffirmation during the liberation years. They do not view this as having been imposed by male Eritrean leaders, but as a manifestation of chauvinist attitudes among Front members that were not effectively challenged either by the leadership or by women themselves. Noting that no women combatants ever achieved the three highest officer ranks in the army, Keddes said that the effect was to keep women locked in the ranks or lower leadership roles that, ironically, required more physically demanding activity:

> It meant women combatants had years of carrying heavy weapons and supplies, climbing difficult terrain. They sustained multiple injuries and eventually their performance stagnated or declined because age catches up on you. Even though there have been many skilled female combatants, they never rose beyond the rank of *hailee*60 — we hit a "glass ceiling." We were told that the promotion required a higher level of training and educational background. Of course many of the females were peasants, who became literate after they joined and did not get beyond sixth-grade level of education. Due to their upbringing, they were viewed as having tremendous ability to withstand the physical hardship of guerrilla fighting. So the men said women were put where their labor is needed most. However, this was an excuse, since these factors do not limit peasant or working-class men from acquiring high status.

During the liberation struggle, many women activists had much exposure to a collective life, which despite its gaps in gender equality allowed women to work and live side by side with men, to perform tasks formerly reserved for males, and, in many instances, to have their effectiveness judged without bias. As they often say, "the revolution was a great equalizer." In this context, they abandoned the subservient and diffident stance that women had traditionally assumed. In today's civil society and economy, these women are often penalized for their "emancipated ways." Discussing demobilized women, Rishan notes that they often

> cannot get a job, because they are discriminated against. Even when they seek jobs like waitressing or store clerk position, employers say "we want women who have pleasant smiles and look appealing." [More traditional] women break their gaze and smile, and can put up with occasionally verbal abuse from male bosses and coworkers. Whereas these women know their rights and expect fair treatment. So they are shunned.

Many parents of women activists have begun to castigate them for going on a wayward path and abandoning cherished traditions during the years of struggle. A number have one or two children or are childless, which is condemned as a symptom of failure. Many women note that there is currently a notable "conservative backlash" in civil society against "liberated females." For example, in towns and cities, there has been a resurgence of elaborate weddings, and women are returning to traditionally feminine dress and finery. Symbols of women's delicacy and submissiveness have regained renewed acceptability as well.

Women respondents also characterize a current resurgence of men's supremacist attitudes. They assert that Eritrean leaders have reduced their commitment to organized mass education and consciousness-raising around gender issues and that this emboldens men to behave chauvinistically. They believe that this trend is marked among many men who were active during the liberation struggle. For example, they note that the divorce rate among Front members is over 35 percent.[61] While some of these divorces can be viewed as an indicator of modernity, respondents believe that they are predominantly initiated by men, who pursue younger women as partners and largely abandon responsibility for the children from their first marriages. These women believe that one aspect of the "women's liberation" is that men have embraced open forms of irresponsibility that used to be condemnable. As Keddes explains, "now that men have no monopoly over family property, they believe it is alright to leave a woman outright and then, only through the goodness of their hearts, would they assist former wives in raising their children."

Analysis and Conclusion

The twenty-three year collective effort in Eritrea to address longstanding female oppression in general, and to eliminate women's exclusion from education in particular, has had substantial successes. Statistical data demonstrates that women have achieved significant access into the contemporary educational system that has developed during the past two decades. For example, in 1992–1993, 45 percent of primary school students and 28.5 percent of high school graduates were female. In addition, there were 3,085 women teachers representing 37 percent of elementary, 17 percent of middle, and 10 percent of high school faculties.[62] The magnitude of this achievement is appreciated when it is contrasted with Eritrea's traditional and colonial epochs, when women's involvement in education was viewed as largely unnecessary and undesirable. Nevertheless, while women now participate as students, teachers, and, to a lesser extent, policymakers, they are still in the minority. Further, after initial breakthroughs and successes, there is evidence of a leveling off of effort and success, as indicated, for example, by persistently high dropout rates for females and the government's inattention to the factors that promote that trend.[63]

National leaders have adopted comprehensive and creative policies to promote gender equity in education, which suggests the authenticity of their effort. During and after the liberation struggle, government officials have defined broadly the components of education, focusing not only on formal schooling and youth, but also on nonformal educational efforts, adult education, and on-the-job training as core elements of the new educational system. This has been advantageous for women, who have needed many and flexible opportunities for learning to overcome the diverse obstacles that had marginalized them historically. Nonformal educational programs have insured that, as women gain entry to education, it is not just a small, privileged minority who have become involved and that major deficits, such as pervasive female nonliteracy, are addressed. Adult education programs are available to the many middle-aged and elderly females who shouldered much responsibility for liberating the nation and stabilizing its independence. Adult education has also helped win parents' acceptance of the merits of schooling and their daughters' rights to become students. The official emphasis on consciousness-raising as a core component of education has been vital in motivating females to pursue educational opportunities and in lessening male opposition to gender equality in this realm. Educational policymakers' attention to skill development, and not simply to the acquisition of knowledge, has helped women grasp the relevance of education in enriched, concrete terms, in contrast to previous generations, who were led to view women's schooling as, at most, a transitory stepping stone to a more desirable husband.

The interviewees in this study testify to the efficacy and accomplishments of the contemporary effort to emancipate Eritrean women from the constraints that kept them from getting an education. They describe the radical departure of current educational policies from the legacy of female exclusion from schooling, delineate the manner in which institutional supports have facilitated their pursuit of formal and nonformal learning, and marvel at their significant individual advances in knowledge and skill. These women place great value on educational reforms undertaken in the context of a broad, far-reaching national campaign to overcome their oppression. They believe that their participation in new educational programs has often been catalyzed and strengthened by their involvement in the realms of politics, the economy, and domestic life. They are a living testimony to contemporary gains in educating women. From adolescents to grandmothers, from peasants residing in remote regions to inhabitants of the capital city, from those who have recently attained basic literacy to those who have attended college — Eritrean women collectively demonstrate an impressive level of intellectual curiosity, analytic adeptness, and confidence in the value of their own perceptions and opinions. They address a range of issues — national economic policies, power dynamics in local political organizations, the intricacies of male chauvinistic practices, the transmission of internalized stigma from mother to daughter, the effects of sexual mores — that were literally unimaginable as topics for women two decades ago.

I found evidence in my analysis of government documents, national newspapers, meetings with public officials, and 1997 interviews with Eritrean women that there is currently a loss of momentum and, perhaps, a reversal in the movement to fully integrate women into public life, including education. The majority of women are concerned and somewhat skeptical about the government's ability to sustain a commitment to advance women's rights and status. They note that leaders are increasingly preoccupied with economic development. They see evidence that high-level officials believe that to pursue vigorously "the women's question" distracts from the collective unity and sacrifice required for modernization. Women suspect that leaders are ceding a need for them to return to more traditional roles in order to stabilize a massive reconstruction effort. For example, respondents believe the government is complacent in not implementing the kind of infrastructural supports — such as daycare centers and laundry and cooking establishments — that are particularly vital to facilitate women's participation in educational, political, and economic activity. Women activists consistently place far greater emphasis than do government leaders on the need to aggressively confront male sexism and privilege within the family and the cultural beliefs that legitimize female subordination. The current official focus on economic development is viewed as intensifying the government's relative disengagement from the cultural struggle around women's emancipation. In addition, the rapid decline in mass consciousness-raising activities is viewed by women as a major setback in efforts to enhance women's self-esteem and to reverse male chauvinism. The interviewees believe that the government's posture has the effect — even if not intended — of lending support to a conservative backlash within society against gender equality and "the new emancipated woman." The social organization and culture forged within the Front during the liberation struggle allowed female and male members to live and work together in a way that was far more egalitarian than gender relations in the larger society.

Respondents poignantly characterize women cadre as increasingly ostracized in public and private life, and view the government's inattentive support of former Front members, particularly females, as contributing to their isolation and demoralization.

Official speeches and policy documents demonstrate the government's narrowing focus on economic modernization and a dearth of new ideas and programs to push forward on women's liberation. A female official, selected by the government, who monitors programs directed to women, conveys current official complacency when she asserts that governmental structural interventions to ensure gender equality have been "largely achieved and now it is women's turn and responsibility to move forward on their own."[64]

In my own view, there are significant indications that government policymakers are turning away from an active campaign to eliminate women's oppression. I believe that longstanding weaknesses and fault lines in the Eritrean leadership's pursuit of gender equality have contributed to this shift. First, despite significant advances in the public arena, women were never able to break into the highest rankings of national political leadership, and this was never established as an emancipatory goal. Further, the NUEW has never been a fully autonomous organization. Those in senior positions of NUEW have always been selected by the top male leaders of the government (and formerly the Front), who also have defined its overall mission and sphere of operation. NUEW has never departed from or critiqued the agenda and priorities of the national leadership. The assertion that NUEW funding comes solely from nongovernmental organizations (NGOs) seems more a government strategy to inspire NGO support than evidence that the women's organization has a truly independent financial base. Despite an impressive record of substantial creativity in mobilizing women at the grassroots level, the NUEW has never established itself as an independent player that can pressure policymakers to attend to women's interests. The EPLF's initial embrace of women's emancipation was tied to a strategy to fully enlist marginalized groups into the liberation war. Eritrean leaders' commitment to gender equality has never been fully extricated from this pragmatic instrumentalism, and has thereby been vulnerable, especially once a major component of that commitment — the war effort — was no longer a factor.[65] While Eritrean activists have lessened their theoretical reliance on classical Marxism,[66] this orientation is still influential in the nation's political dialogue, and it systematically demotes women's oppression by making it a condition dependent on more basic social inequities.[67]

Many of the women interviewed discuss how they embraced the national revolutionary leadership, admired its success in forging independence, and were exhilarated by its sponsorship of women's emancipation. They speak of their devotion, their willingness "to hold nothing back and make every sacrifice" to the revolutionary cause. They often note that — given the legacy of women's subordination — females have "a duty" to be extraordinary in their performance and "to pass every test," as Zewdi put it. These themes, which are persistent, suggest that, in some sense, women switched their dutiful allegiance from the father — the domestic patriarch — to the liberating nation and its male leaders. It is understandable that strands of subservience remain in how women have positioned themselves in relation to the contemporary struggle to create a modern Eritrea. In my own view, women's vigorous criticism of the national leadership and its policies signals a major step forward in female assertiveness and independence. While the critical attitudes of these women activists are generated by setbacks to the struggle for gender equality, they represent a maturation of their capabilities and confidence in shaping public life.

Finally, Eritrea's current context and situation — nationally and internationally — promotes obstacles and challenges to a vigorous pursuit of women's rights and equality. The people of the nation have undergone a harrowing and traumatic struggle to achieve peace and independence. There is an understandable yearning for calm, amicability, and freedom from conflict. In this atmosphere, many — including former female activists — are zealously seeking the normalization of everyday life. This can result in a decline in the collective will and interest to pursue arduous battles against forms of female subjugation that have been entrenched for centuries. Even when they suffered from massive exploitation themselves, Eritrean men vigilantly guarded and preserved their dominance over women. Imperial powers chose not to tamper with or challenge these male prerogatives. It has been indeed "a daring act" and enormously courageous that contemporary Eritrean male leaders and women activists made women's rights and equality a major component of their vision and program for liberation and social revolution. In these early years of independence, Eritrea faces the monumental task of national reconstruction within an international political arena and world economy that largely marginalizes Africa and exempts itself from financial support to Third World societies.[68] This creates more pressures to blunt a sustained mobilization against women's oppression within Eritrea — a social struggle that will inevitably generate domestically pronounced tensions and opposition. It will take many more "daring acts" by both national leaders and Eritrean women to push forward the struggle for gender equality.

Notes

1. *"Eritrea: New Society Is Being Born," Eritrea Information, 4,* No. 9 (1982), 12.
2. I have opted to use the term "emancipation," which is defined as a release from oppressive constraints. It is also the opposite of oppression, which is the imposition of unjust restraint on the freedom of individuals and groups. From these definitions it follows that there are conceptual connections between oppression and emancipation. The diverse Western feminist literature on women's liberation does not explicitly define the term, focusing instead on the question of *why* and *how* women are oppressed. However, feminists implicitly outline the concept of women's emancipation

by suggesting different strategies to achieve women's liberation. For the purpose of this article, I conceived the term "emancipation" as a process of setting women free from restraint. Emancipation is not viewed as some finally achievable state or situation, but rather as the process of eliminating forms of oppression as they continue to arise. Thus, the domain of women and human liberation is constantly redefined and extended. Eritrean women's emancipation is therefore viewed from a perspective that presupposes a dynamic rather than a static view of society. Because of this, education is viewed as a critical element in changing Eritrean women's self-concept, autonomy, and options to participate in a democratic society. For further discussion, see Asgedet Stefanos, "African Women and Revolutionary Change: A Freirian and Feminist Perspective," in *Mentoring the Mentor: A Critical Dialogue with Paulo Freire,* ed. Paulo Freire, James Fraser, Donaldo Macedo, Tanya McKinnon, and William Stokes (New York: Peter Lang, 1997); Andrew Parker, Mary Russo, Doris Sommer, and Patricia Yaeger, eds., *Nationalisms and Sexualities* (London: Routledge, 1992); Seth Kreisberg, *Transforming Power: Domination, Empowerment, and Education* (Albany: State University of New York Press, 1992); Carmen Luke and Jennifer Gore, eds., *Feminisms and Critical Pedagogy* (London: Routledge, 1992); Albert Memmi, *The Colonizer and the Colonized* (Boston: Beacon Press, 1967).

3. See Rosemarie Buikema and Anneke Smelik, *Women's Studies and Culture* (London: Zed Books, 1993); Ann Diller, Barbara Houston, Kathryn Morgan and Maryama Ayim, *The Gender Question in Education: Theory, Pedagogy and Politics* (Boulder, CO: Westview Press, 1996).
4. For a discussion on the EPLF's and the Eritrean government's education goals, see Ministry of Labor and Human Welfare Report, *Initial Report on the Implementation of the Convention on the Rights of The Child,* (Asmara, Eritrea: Government of the State of Eritrea, 1997), pp. 60–62. In addition, as works in critical pedagogy have pointed out, education can be an important site of ongoing contestation and control. Likewise, resistance theorists indicate colonial struggles are also a rejection of domination and an assertion of self-determination. So, both revolution and education are interdependent in asserting the possibility of human agency, or the belief in the individual's ability to make a difference, to bring about an egalitarian society. See Paulo Freire, *Pedagogy of the Oppressed* (New York: Continuum, 1970); Michael W. Apple, *Ideology and Curriculum* (New York: Routledge, 1990); Henry A. Giroux, *Theory and Resistance in Education* (South Hadley, MA: Bergin & Garvey, 1983); Paulo Freire and Donaldo Macedo, *Literacy: Reading the Word and the World* (Westport, CT: Bergin & Garvey, 1987); Paul Willis, *Learning to Labour* (New York: Columbia University Press, 1977).
5. The strategy of Eritrean education is to attack the structural constraints to women's access to education. See Asgedet Stefanos, *An Encounter with Revolutionary Change: A Portrait of Eritrean Women,* Diss., Harvard Graduate School of Education, 1988, p. 295; Sheila Parvyn Wamahiu, ed., *Girls' Education in Eritrea,* (Asmara, Eritrea: Ministry of Education and UNICEF, 1996), p. 6.
6. See Jane Gaskell and John Willinsky, eds., *Gender In/forms Curriculum: From Enrichment to Transformation* (New York: Teachers College Press, 1995); Miriam David, *The State, The Family and Education* (London: Routledge & Kegan Paul, 1980).
7. For detailed discussion on women's access to formal education during Italian and British colonial rule, see Stefanos, *An Encounter with Revolutionary Change,* pp. 203–206.
8. Stefanos, *An Encounter with Revolutionary Change,* p. 205.
9. Here, the term "traditional" is used to differentiate between socioeconomic structures that predated colonization and those that took shape during colonialism. Economic development theorists use the term traditional to suggest "backward" in contrast to "modern." They characterize traditionalists as "rural, unproductive, consumptive, uneducated, irrational, uncompetitive, unmotivated, acquisitive . . ." Modern is defined

as "urban, productive, autonomous, motivated, literate, rational, punctual, efficient . . ." See David McClelland, *The Achieving Society* (New York: Irvington, 1976, rpt.); Alex Inkeles and David H. Smith, *On Being Modern* (Cambridge, MA: Harvard University, 1974); Daniel Lerner, *The Passing of Traditional Society: Modernizing the Middle East* (New York: Free Press, 1958).

10. There was also a minority of Protestant and Catholic highlanders in traditional Eritrea. Stefanos, *An Encounter With Revolutionary Change,* p. 204.
11. There are nine distinct national/linguistic groups within Eritrea — Tigre, Kebessa (Tigrinya), Belen, Denkel, Sahho, Barya and Beza (Kunama), Ben Amir, and Beja. For a detailed account of the history of Eritrea and its sociocultural groups, see Stefanos, *An Encounter with Revolutionary Change,* pp. 70–186.
12. A people and socioeconomic system that do not fit into these broad categories are the Kunamas. They were both agriculturalists and pastoralists. They did not adhere to a monotheistic religion. Their society followed a matrilineal descent line. Social relations were relatively nonhierarchical.
13. Stefanos, *An Encounter with Revolutionary Change,* pp. 188–197.
14. These expectations were gleaned from my interviews with Eritrean women in 1983. See "Women's Perception and Experiences of Their Personal Status Within the Family," Stefanos, *An Encounter with Revolutionary Change,* pp. 348–353.
15. Women carry singular responsibility for household management. Asma, an interviewee from a peasant background, stated: "I rarely saw my mother sitting down doing nothing. She always worked. The work within the home is solely hers. She prepared the daily family meal, raised her children, and took care of the sick and the old in the family. My father did not perform any duties within the home even when it is not farming season, because tradition did not permit him to do so. [However,] my mother was also expected to 'lend a hand' during planting and harvesting season," Stefanos, *An Encounter with Revolutionary Change,* p. 346.
16. Studies of pastoral societies are comparatively sparse and a focus on women even more rare. In order to have a fuller picture of Eritrean women, the differing structures and experiences of semi-nomadic women should be studied in their own right. Stefanos, *An Encounter with Revolutionary Change,* p. 193.
17. By the 1940s, one-fifth of the Eritrean population was urbanized. See Jordan Gebre-Medhin, *Peasant and Nationalism in Eritrea* (Trenton, NJ: Red Sea Press, 1989), p. 61.
18. Italy, like all other European colonial regimes in Africa, had Victorian sensibilities about women's position within its own society and so was less interested in women in the colonies. For an analysis of colonialists' view of African women, see Fanon's classic analysis of Algerian women's position during French colonial period: Frantz Fanon, *A Dying Colonialism* (New York: Grove Press, 1965).
19. Italians had a separatist and functional view of education for Eritreans, which led them to a policy that government education can only go as far as the fourth-grade level. Kennedy Nicholas Trevaskis, *Eritrea: A Colony in Transition* (London: Oxford University Press, 1952), p. 33.
20. The various Catholic and Protestant missionaries were fiercely competitive among each other, which was aggravated by the fact that in the Highlands, where their activities were based, Eritreans were conservative Coptic Christians who viewed conversion as ludicrous. Promises of schooling and health services were used as major inducements to enter the mission orbit and become a convert. Stefanos, *An Encounter with Revolutionary Change,* p. 203.
21. Trevaskis, *Eritrea: A Colony in Transition,* p. 33.
22. In contrast to a rigid policy of noncontinuation of schooling beyond fourth-grade level, mission schools allowed some Eritreans to pursue their education further. Trevaskis, *Eritrea: A Colony in Transition,* p. 34.

23. Children who were fathered by Italians were conferred Italian citizenship and were permitted to enjoy the full benefit of Italian education in segregated parochial schools. Stefanos, *An Encounter with Revolutionary Change,* p. 204.
24. Trevaskis quotes from an official confidential memo to Italian headmasters by Signor Festa, Director of Education in Eritrea, in 1938: "By the end of fourth year, the Eritrean student should be able to speak our language moderately well; he should know the four arithmetical operations within normal limits; he should be a convinced propagandist of the principles of hygiene; and of history he should know only the names of those who have made Italy great." Trevaskis, *Eritrea: A Colony in Transition,* p. 33.
25. See Asgedet Stefanos, *Women and Education in Guinea-Bissau: An Analysis of Theory and Practice,* Qualifying Paper, Harvard Graduate School of Education, 1981, p. 19. Also, see Amilcar Cabral, *A Return to the Source* (New York: African Information Service and PAIGC, 1973); Donna Landry and Gerald Maclean, *The Spivak Reader* (New York: Routledge, 1996); Homi K. Bhabha, *Nation and Narration* (London: Routledge, 1990); Stephanie Urdang, *Fighting Two Colonialisms: Women in Guinea-Bissau* (New York: Monthly Review Press, 1979).
26. Family life worsened during British and subsequently under Ethiopian regimes: "The colonialists' neglect of the rural areas has caused the disintegration of Eritrean families. Starting from the Italian period, male members migrated to cities in search of work. Years went by before their families saw them and many did not return. Sometimes men decided to move on rather than come back penniless. As the situation worsened, both men and women increasingly began to go further and further away from their homes, to the other African countries, the Gulf states, Europe and the United States." Stefanos, *An Encounter with Revolutionary Change,* p. 371.
27. It was not desirable for Eritrean women to become maids in Italian homes.
28. Traditionally, some occupations were viewed as not "proper." For example, there was a deep-seated prejudice against musicians, singers, leather-workers, jewelry-makers, and blacksmiths. These groups were shunned and intermarried among themselves. Stefanos, *An Encounter with Revolutionary Change,* p. 198.
29. As has been discussed, the barriers for girls to access education had been sturdy and long-standing. Prior to the liberation struggle, nonliteracy among Eritrean women was over 90 percent. Seyoum A. Haregot, *The First Year: Fourth Quarter Report, May–July, 1996* (United Nations Office for Project Services, Second-Phase—Support for Public Sector Management Programme, Project ERI/94/006), p. 33.
30. "Relationship Between Society and School," *Eritrea Information, 5,* No. 3, (1983), p. 7.
31. "The Revolution School Achievement and Problems," *Eritrea Information,* p. 11.
32. Stefanos, *An Encounter with Revolutionary Change,* p. 298.
33. For example, there were themes of "mother's brigade," "mother's day," or "working-mothers" and the portrayal of women in official iconography "with a gun in one hand and a baby in the other" that were promoted as manifestations of interest in women's issues. However, there was no similar representation of men hailed as images of "fathers work-brigade" or "fathers with a child in one hand and a gun in the other." For a detailed discussion on this, see Stefanos, *An Encounter with Revolutionary Change,* p. 427.
34. "The Revolution School Achievement and Problems," *Eritrea Information,* p. 10.
35. Even though "basic education" (seven years of schooling) has been promoted as a requirement regardless of gender, the government has ceded that it has not created the educational capacity to make compulsory schooling a viable alternative. See Ministry of Labor and Human Welfare Report, *Initial Report on the Implementation of the Convention on the Rights of the Child,* pp. 64–73; Wamahiu, *Girls' Education in Eritrea,* p. 6; Department of Research, *Eritrea: Basic Education Statistics and Essential Indicators 1995/96* (Asmara, Eritrea: Ministry of Education, 1996).

36. See *Draft Constitution of Eritrea* (Asmara, Eritrea: Constitutional Commission of Eritrea, July 1996), p. 19.
37. Traditionally, property and livestock ownership had been an unassailable male prerogative. As the EPLF applied the principle of "land to the tiller" in liberated areas, it distributed land directly to refugees and landless peasants, a vast majority of whom were women. In post-independent Eritrea, the Land Reform Proclamation has provided equal access to female land ownership. See "National Democratic Program" in Stefanos, *An Encounter with Revolutionary Change,* pp. 446–447; *Draft Constitution of Eritrea,* p. 20.
38. The majority of women who are self-employed are found in the service and retail sectors, 38 percent and 39 percent, respectively, while only 18 percent are in manufacturing and less than 1 percent are in commercial farming. Haregot, *The First Year: Fourth Quarter Report,* p. 37.
39. The push for this shift came concurrently from below. Increasingly, in the cities and towns, females — particularly high school and college students — were becoming visible in organized nationalist clandestine activities. For a detailed discussion on women's political participation, see Stefanos, *An Encounter with Revolutionary Change,* pp. 279–285.
40. The Front's campaign for breaking with male political domination was clearly connected to its own needs for active supporters to wage the battle for national liberation under its leadership. The EPLF saw women, along with marginalized ethnic groups, landless peasants, and youth, as naturally more sympathetic to its egalitarian agenda and drive against traditional beliefs that upheld the status quo, than the men who had a grip on local and family privilege and power. For more information about the EPLF's view of gender equality, see Stefanos, *An Encounter with Revolutionary Change,* pp. 274–279.
41. The Minister of Education, His Excellency Osman Saleh, in his Opening Address to the Workshop on Girls' Education, in September 1996, Wamahiu, *Girls' Education in Eritrea,* p. 6.
42. In the executive branch, there are two women out of fourteen ministers — one is a Minister of Tourism and the other is a Minister of Justice; there are four women directors — of Postal and Communication, Central Personnel Administration, Social Affairs, and National Union of Eritrean Women. There are no women as provincial governors. While women comprise 31.3 percent of all government employees, they outnumber men in clerical and custodial services. Haregot, *The First Year: Fourth Quarter Report,* p. 37.
43. Women represented 20 percent of active combatants in 1983 and 30 percent in 1993. The inclusion of well-trained women into the army helped lessen the impact of the vastly larger number of troops under Ethiopian command. International journalists regularly highlighted the numbers and performance of female EPLF fighters as a unique feature in Eritrea's independence struggle. They observed that the Front's iconic imagery of a woman with a gun in hand was not solely a symbol of new female assertiveness and freedoms, but rather a familiar happenstance in areas under Front control. Stefanos, *An Encounter with Revolutionary Change,* pp. 274–279.
44. In interviews, women combatants said that they fought to the death, partly because of what they knew about the atrocities that Ethiopian soldiers inflicted on female POWs. They felt that the sexism of the enemy soldiers made them more determined as fighters.
45. All rural and urban residents were organized into one of "five mass organizations according to social class or groups — women, youth, peasants, workers, and professionals." Stefanos, *An Encounter with Revolutionary Change,* p. 271.

46. Among settled agriculturalists, *wushati* is a small room within the hut that is reserved for women only. Male members older than five are by tradition prohibited from entering this room.
47. See Stefanos, *An Encounter with Revolutionary Change,* pp. 292–293.
48. In 1983, I interviewed twenty-four women in eleven towns and villages in the northeastern and northwestern regions of Eritrea. I returned to Eritrea in January 1997 to do follow-up interviews, and was able to locate eighteen women from my original study and to broaden my sample to eight additional women, some of whom held key positions in the new post-independence government.
49. The interview sample represented an age range of sixteen to sixty-five; single, married, divorced and widowed; Tigre, Kebessa, Denkel, Sahho, Kunama, and Belen nationalities; Coptics, Muslims, Catholics, Protestants, and various African religious orientations; nonliterate to college-level education; political activists and non-activists; peasants, factory workers, medical doctors, and students.
50. During the national liberation struggle, Genet worked as a coordinator of refugee women in the village of Arrarib. She received her elementary education at a Catholic missionary school and had an arranged marriage at the age of fifteen. She subsequently resumed her schooling and got a certificate in business administration.
51. After military demobilization, Mamet invested the $4,000 [in U.S. dollars] compensation from the government in a cotton plantation project. Since the project was not well conceived, she along with many others lost her lifelong investment. She is presently unemployed. Her marriage failed, and she and her two small children are presently living with ex-combatant friends.
52. Zewdi works as a store clerk, after completing her high school level education.
53. As some respondents indicated, occasionally there were mothers and often brothers who were ardent supporters of their schooling.
54. Leila is of Sahho nationality. She and her husband own a gift store in Massawa.
55. Rishan, an ex-combatant, is presently working as a parking lot attendant in the capital city. Her parents are farmers and Coptic Christians from Kebessa. She was in fifth grade when she joined the liberation front.
56. Many respondents described vividly the low status of females within their families when they were children. Asma states, "In the family, a women is not considered an equal human being to a man. She is there to serve him. A father chooses her husband. . . . She is prohibited from leaving the house." Keddes adds, "In our home, our oldest brother assumed the second command to our father. . . . My mother deferred to him. Even my younger brothers had better rights than me. . . . Men do not want women to be independent. Even when they are oppressed themselves, men feel that women are their domain . . ." Sarah, who is from a middle-class urban family, says, "My mother kept careful watch over me. When parents find a girl playing with her brothers, she will be told to go inside the house and sit there or do something useful. If a girl protests, the explanation given by all mothers to their daughters is, 'boys can play and be rambunctious, but a girl must be quiet and stay in the house, and keep busy. Besides, a girl should not expect to be treated equally with boys.'"
57. In post-independence Eritrea, this same group of women currently occupy the mid-level administrative and moderately prestigious white-collar jobs. See Stefanos, "Appendix E: Biographical Charts," in *An Encounter with Revolutionary Change, pp. 466–467.*
58. Women representation in the military has been reduced from 30 percent to 10 percent. "Of those who were demobilized, only 14 percent had skills that can be translated into employment or income-generating activities." Haregot, *The First Year: Fourth Quarter Report,* p. 39.

59. Facial skin discoloration caused by stress.
60. The military hierarchy starts with being in charge of a *gujelle,* a unit of ten people; then *ganta* (composed of three *gujelles*); *hailee* (three *gantas*); *bottolini* (three *hailees*); *brigade* (three *bottolonis*), and finally *Kefle-Serawit* (three *brigades*). Sarah states "that up to the *hailee* level, the work is physically demanding — one has to be physically fit for a guerrilla warfare, carrying heavy weapons and supplies, walking and climbing difficult terrain. In addition, one has to endure multiple injuries. But, once you become a *bottolini* leader, what is demanded is leadership ability based on your experience and training for strategic plans and supervising ancillary divisions such as medical, economic, and other units."
61. Interview with the director of *BANA* — Eritrean Women War Veteran Association.
62. Haregot, *The First Year: Fourth Quarter Report,* pp. 4–50.
63. In 1997, Mamet provided two relevant examples of government disinterest — the decline in mass consciousness-raising programs to deal with parental attitudes toward female education and the dearth of interventions to lighten domestic labor, which gets relegated to females and promotes removing girls from schools.
64. This same remark was offered by the three women officials who held top positions within the post-revolutionary government.
65. Asgedet Stefanos, *An Encounter with Revolutionary Change,* William Monroe Trotter Institute Research Report No. 33 (Boston: University of Massachusetts, 1996), pp. 72–74.
66. Like most Third World revolutions, Eritrea's approach to women's issues was influenced by an instrumental reading of two well-known texts: Frederick Engels, *The Origin of the Family, Private Property and the State,* ed. Eleanor Burke Leacock (New York: International Publishers, 1972), and V. I. Lenin, *The Emancipation of Women* (New York: International Publishers, 1966). In this approach, moving women into the public sector was viewed as key to solving women's problems. The privileging of the role of production over women's familial relations has been functional to the struggle for national liberation during armed conflict and the drive for economic development after liberation. The appeal for women to fulfill the general needs of the society legitimizes the reproduction of sexual divisions of labor both in the work force and in the home.
67. According to Senayit, recent official theoretical acceptance of a mixed economy "with heavy emphasis on privatization is not advantageous to women, who will have difficulty gaining a foothold in the free-for-all of individual entrepreneurship — where men's longstanding dominance in business will have unchecked reign."
68. Although the Eritrean government does not have any debt to service, its ability to raise funds has been severely hindered by its devastated economy and the overall poverty of its people. Eritrea is one of the poorest countries in the world, with a GDP per capita below U.S. $120–$150, less than half the U.S. $300 average for sub-Saharan African countries. Ministry of Labor and Human Welfare Report, *Initial Report on the Implementation of the Convention on the Rights of the Child,* p. 5.

Nicaragua 1980:
The Battle of the ABCs

FERNANDO CARDENAL, S.J.
VALERIE MILLER

It is September 1980. Nicaragua is green from winter rains. The countryside that just two weeks ago was bustling with more than 50,000 young volunteer literacy teachers is quieter now. The National Literacy Crusade is over. The peasant-shirt, blue-jean uniforms of the young *brigadistas* ("student-volunteers") can no longer be seen in the far-away hills and valleys. Their footsteps no longer mark the mountain paths between San Rafael and Yall, but their voices and spirit remain, transformed and replaced by those of their students. Local people from Waslale and Wiwill now conduct the community study groups begun by the volunteers. From cotton fields to the jungle valleys, reading and writing continues.

In the cities, the buses overflow, crowded again with teenage faces. Endless registration lines of students surround the high schools and universities. The country begins another school year, which on the surface looks like any other. Yet, Nicaragua will never be the same again. The National Literacy Crusade has broken the patterns of the past and has laid the foundations for the future. In five months, more than 400,000 Nicaraguans learned to master basic reading and writing skills, and tens of thousands of young people and their families learned about rural poverty and peasant culture.

Nicaragua recently celebrated an educational victory that a little over a year ago would have seemed impossible. On August 23, 1980, the nation applauded the success of students and teachers of the National Literacy Crusade. We saluted their achievements, and we also saluted thousands of people who could not stand with us, those who had given their lives in battle to free this land. The National Literacy Crusade was a living tribute to their sacrifice, commitment, and hope. Their dedication and faith in the future made the campaign possible. Their memories live on in each one of us. This article is dedicated to them.

Nicaragua's struggle for self-determination had been going on for many years, but finally exploded on a massive scale in 1978. After decades of foreign domination, inequity, and military repression, the mounting rebellion could

Harvard Educational Review Vol. 51 No. 1 February 1981, 1–39

no longer be contained. As the battle intensified, young people went to the mountains and joined the liberation forces. Directed and organized by the Sandinista National Liberation Front (FSLN), they fought with an unshakable belief in victory and an uncommon courage against extraordinary odds. Civilians, organized into community-defense committees, added to their force. City people dug up the neighborhood streets to form barricades against tanks and troops. When the tear gas became too thick, housewives set out on their porches specially prepared tubs of bicarbonate of soda water for the young fighters to neutralize the burning chemicals. Women's groups organized clandestine hospitals in their homes. First- and second-graders served as couriers carrying important messages across battle lines. Businessmen led strikes and raised funds for arms. Market women hid ammunition at the bottom of baskets brimming with vegetables and carried out their missions walking confidently between rows of armored cars. Families carved out bomb shelters in their patios, using shovels and spoons. They created homemade hand bombs out of firecrackers and collected rocks to throw against Somoza's machine guns.

Despite this extraordinary display of courage and faith, the war was long and costly. Some 40,000 people were killed, 100,000 wounded, and 40,000 children orphaned. Somoza escaped with all the reserves in the Central Bank except $3.5 million, leaving an international debt of $1.6 billion. Yet, less than one year after victory, the nation was transformed from a violent war zone into one enormous school. The spirit and commitment of hundreds of thousands of Nicaraguans forged in combat became the moving force behind a massive literacy program. Young men and women who had taken up arms and gone to the hills now took up pencils and primers and returned to the mountains.

Where machine guns and bombs had filled the air such a short time ago, the sounds of ABCs and singing could be heard. Along the same paths where young fighters had rushed to battle, young literacy teachers set up blackboards and guided unsteady hands in writing their first words. In cornfields ravaged by war, beside the simple graves of fallen patriots, the literacy volunteers worked the land side-by-side with their adopted peasant families. In bomb-damaged factories, workers taught fellow workers the ABCs. The violence and destruction of yesterday had been replaced by the quiet pride of learning. A new nation was being born. One battle had been won and another begun. In these pages we will describe that second battle by explaining the origins of the campaign and its relationship to development. We will also examine some of the major problems that the Literacy Crusade confronted and the strategies developed to overcome them.

Origins of the Battle

On March 24, 1980, the entire country became engaged in a nationwide learning campaign. Student volunteers went to the countryside to teach literacy and learn the ways of peasant living, while urban workers and housewives taught and learned from people in the cities. The program was designed to help Nicaraguans acquire the skills, understanding, and empathy necessary for participation in a society undergoing rapid transformation.

The spirit that inspired the campaign had its origins in the early part of he century. The 1980 Literacy Crusade grew out of the liberation struggle begun by General Augusto César Sandino. The tensions that led to the struggle were related primarily to efforts to establish an interoceanic canal in Nicaragua. In 1909 Liberal President José Santos Zelays refused to grant canal rights to the United States. As a result, the State Department gave its support to the Conservative opposition which, when it took power, agreed to a permanent U.S. military presence and U.S. control of the economy through management of national bank, railway, and customs operations. In the 1920s the tension between the two parties escalated into open fighting. The buildup of the Liberal army in 1927 posed a serious threat to the Conservative regime. Fearing a loss of power and stability, the United States bolstered the marine presence. By a combination of political promise and military threat, the United States ambassador persuaded both parties to halt the fighting. General elections were agreed to and a National Guard was created to maintain the "peace." U.S. Marine commanders were put in charge of its training and organization, and Anastasio Somoza García was among its chosen officers.

However, General Sandino refused to accept the United States-negotiated accords. For seven years, Sandino and his peasant army battled against foreign intervention. Unable to defeat the increasingly popular general, the marines finally were forced to withdraw in 1933. With their departure, Sandino signed a peace treaty with the government, dismantled his army, and retired to organize peasant cooperatives in the north. The United States installed Anastasio Somoza as the head of the National Guard. In 1934 Somoza had Sandino assassinated, his cooperatives destroyed, and their members and families exterminated.

Throughout Sandino's struggle he had always wanted to assure his people's social and economic development. He set up cooperatives for agricultural production and, when possible, urged his troops to learn to read and write. He was especially proud of their educational achievements:

> I can assure you that the number of our illiterate officers can now be counted on fewer than the fingers of one hand. Unfortunately, due to a shortage of people who can teach, progress among the soldiers has been almost negligible.
>
> When General Pedro Altamirano first joined us he did not know how to read or write but . . . during the fighting and only because I insisted on it, Altamirano learned, stumbling and mumbling as he went along. Despite his age, he has made great strides since then, and now, as amazing as it may seem, he actually knows how to type — even if it is only with one finger.[1]

In the early 1960s, the FSLN took up Sandino's challenge. The struggle for both literacy and liberation was once again alive.

Development and Literacy: Yesterday

Under Somoza, Nicaragua was run as a family plantation. Development had been narrowly focused on modernizing the economy's agricultural export sector for the benefit of a small privileged minority. The promotion of universal literacy or adult education was irrelevant and potentially threatening. Under this economic system, national development programs were essentially used to enrich Somoza's personal fortune and to buttress the regime's power structure by providing his partners with lucrative business opportunities involving massive graft and corruption. While isolated sectors of the population benefited from the programs, the root causes of economic disparity and political injustice were never addressed. Ultimately, development projects led to the expansion of the government's corrupt patronage system and to the further impoverishment and repression of the majority.

Illiteracy was both a condition and a product of this system. In 1979 a special census revealed that more than 50 percent of the population was illiterate, a figure which soared above 85 percent in some rural areas.[2] This problem was never seriously addressed during the dictatorship because the promotion of universal literacy was neither politically advisable for the maintenance of the system nor economically necessary for its functioning. The development model of export agriculture depended upon a large pool of unskilled workers, and therefore it neither required nor encouraged an educated labor force. Politically, it was unwise for Somoza to undertake a genuine nationwide literacy program. Basic education would have provided the poor and disenfranchised with the potential tools to analyze and question the unequal power relationships and economic conditions under which they had lived. An illustration from the crusade underlines this point. A peasant is speaking during the dialogue section of the lesson:

> Somoza never taught us to read — it really was ungrateful of him, wasn't it. He knew that if he taught the peasants to read we would claim our rights. Ay! But back then, people couldn't even breathe. You see, I believe that a government is like the parent of a family. The parent demands the best of his children and the children demand the best of the parent, but a governor, like a parent, who does not give culture and upbringing to the child, well that means he doesn't love his child, or his people. Don't you agree?[3]

Under Somoza, literacy teaching was used as a cover for counter insurgency operations in the north. The "Plan Waslala," according to the Ministry of Education's own report in 1978, appointed more than 100 literacy teachers to act as spies and identify peasants sympathetic to the FSLN. Many people singled out by this operation later disappeared. Waslala itself was the site of an infamous concentration camp where hundreds of peasants had been savagely tortured and killed.

Development and Literacy: Today

With the recent triumph of the Sandinista Revolution, the meaning of development and education changed radically. The ideas of Julius Nyerere, President of Tanzania, seem especially appropriate for understanding the change. In his writings, Nyerere stresses that development means freedom and liberation. Development means people. But, as he emphasizes, people cannot be developed, human beings can only develop themselves. In the new Nicaragua, we also believe that development means freedom, a freedom that is based on liberation and popular participation. Such a process rests on the redistribution of the nation's power and wealth and on the thoughtful, creative involvement of people in community organization. Development in Nicaragua today requires that all aspects of society be examined and recreated to respond to the needs and aspirations of the majority. It involves a profound transformation of the social system and the creation of structures which promote permanent opportunities for learning and enhance equitable forms of economic and political participation.

We believe that in order to create a new nation we must begin with an education that liberates people. Only through knowing their past and their present, only through understanding and analyzing their reality can people choose their future. Education, therefore, must encourage people to take charge of their lives, to learn to become informed and effective decision makers, and to understand their roles as responsible citizens possessing rights and obligations. A liberating education nurtures empathy, a commitment to community, and a sense of self-worth and dignity. It involves people acquiring the knowledge, skills, and attitudes necessary for their new community responsibilities. Education for liberation means people working together to gain an understanding of and control over society's economic, political, and social forces in order to guarantee their full participation in the creation of the new nation. Literacy and permanent programs of adult learning are fundamental to these goals. We believe they are essential to the building of a democratic society in which people can participate consciously and critically in national decision making. The struggle to achieve these aims is long, and we are just beginning.

Soon after the triumph, the Government of National Reconstruction (GNR) and the FSLN proposed their first development plan. Education and literacy were among its top priorities. The program emphasized economic reactivation and national reconstruction and was founded on four major points. First, it established a socioeconomic policy based on a commitment to full employment, improved social services, universal literacy, land reform, self-sufficiency in basic food stuffs, increased production for the common good, and a mixed economy. Second, it encouraged popular participation through a network of citizens' and workers' associations, a representative legislative body, the Council of State, and a variety of public forums for open debate and dialogue between government and citizens. Third, the program called for the birth and affirmation of the "New Nicaraguan," revolutionary men and women, characterized by sacrifice, humility, discipline, creativity, love, generosity, hard work, and a critical consciousness. Finally, to accumulate the necessary capital for domestic investment and to pay the nation's staggering debt, it emphasized austerity. Salary differentials were drastically reduced, wages controlled, and luxury imports curtailed.

In their development plan, conducting a nationwide literacy campaign was one of the first priorities of the young government. In August 1979, just fifteen days after victory, Nicaragua's Literacy Crusade was born. The first goal of the campaign was to eliminate illiteracy. Specifically, this meant reducing the illiteracy rate to between 10 to 15 percent, establishing a nationwide system of adult education, and expanding primary school coverage through the country. Other important goals were to encourage an integration and

understanding among Nicaraguans of different classes and backgrounds; to increase political awareness and a critical analysis of underdevelopment; to nurture attitudes and skills related to creativity, production, cooperation, discipline, and analytical thinking; to forge a sense of national consensus and of social responsibility; to strengthen channels of economic and political participation; to acquaint people with national development programs; to record oral histories and recover popular forms of culture; and to conduct research in health and agriculture for future development programming.

Specifically, the Crusade was intended to help people acquire basic skills in reading, writing, math, and analytical thinking, and to develop an elementary knowledge of history and civics. Learning materials were chosen to acquaint people with the history of the Revolution, the national development plan, and the emerging political and economic structures. As a whole, the campaign was designed to sensitize the entire country to the problems and rights of the poor and to prepare citizens for their responsibilities in meeting the challenge of national development. The Crusade had one other important function: it gave the young people who had fought and suffered the traumas of the war a channel for their energy and enthusiasm. Their participation as volunteer teachers helped them make the transition between the violence of war and the challenge of transformation.

In its design and implementation, the campaign was eminently political and profoundly spiritual. First, it was aimed at giving the nation's poor and disenfranchised the skills and knowledge they needed to become active participants in the political process. In doing so, it consolidated a powerful new political force and challenged the power of large economic interests. Second, it was spiritual. The act of learning to read and write served to restore and nurture spiritual values which had for so long been suppressed. Dignity and self-worth took on new meaning as people began to gain confidence in themselves and their future. Literacy was considered much more than a basic human right. The FSLN called literacy "an apprenticeship in life because in the process the literate person learns his intrinsic value as a person, as a maker of history, as an actor of an important social role, as an individual with rights to demand and duties to fulfill."[4]

The means to carry out such an ambitious educational challenge emerged from both the philosophical principles and the practical experience of the Revolution. The actual strategies of battle provided a model for educational action. One of the fundamental tenets of the GRN and the FSLN was citizen participation: just as in war, victory rested on active community involvement. Triumph over illiteracy meant citizens learning from citizens, neighbors helping neighbors, an entire nation organized to educate itself. The specific strategy depended upon the network of citizens and labor associations that originally had been organized clandestinely for the war. The actual operation of the literacy struggle followed the same general lines as the liberation struggle — from isolated skirmishes and harassment of the enemy in the pilot project stage, to a national insurrection during the main implementation phase, on to the final offensive of accelerated study, and ultimately to the consolidation of the Revolution through the follow-up program.

The metaphors and terminology of the campaign were purposefully military — "The National Literacy Crusade: Heroes and Martyrs for the Liberation of Nicaragua," "the war on ignorance," "the cultural insurrection," and "the second war of liberation." The literacy warriors, or brigadistas, of the Popular Literacy Army were divided into brigades, columns, and squadrons and were located along six battlefronts identical to those of the war.[5] They joined forces with the Peasant and Workers' Militias and the Urban Literacy Guerillas. Each battle unit chose the name of a fallen combatant as a means of honoring his or her memory.

In no way was the use of military terminology designed to glorify war or violence. Anyone who lived through the horror perpetuated by Somoza's guard was acutely aware that the pain and trauma of violence and repression were not worthy of glorification. On the contrary, the choice of military metaphors was designed to help young volunteers integrate the memories of the past, transforming terms related to the war into positive associations with teaching and sharing. Military terminology also helped the brigadistas see the Crusade as a vital part of the nation's continuing liberation struggle and to understand that, as such, it demanded the seriousness, dedication and discipline of a military offensive. In essence, we wanted to make clear that peace-time battles demanded the same selfless, disciplined commitment as did the war effort; in fact, they demanded more.

The use of military terms and the naming of fallen heroes had a deeply spiritual significance. The Crusade owed its very existence to the Revolution and to the sacrifice of thousands of men and women who fought and died for liberation. By calling forth their names and memories, the young volunteers kept alive the courage and example of their fallen compatriots. A spiritual bond joined the living with the dead. It inspired greater levels of commitment and compassion and it spurred people on in moments of difficulty. Over 40,000 Nicaraguans died in the struggle's violence. The Crusade and its symbols were a living testimony to their sacrifice, dedication, and faith in the future.

The Challenge and the Problems

The challenge confronting the crusade staff would have discouraged most educational planners. At times we were overwhelmed. The lessons of the war, however, provided us with a special source of strength and inspiration. During the insurrection we had learned to take unimaginable risks. We learned about organizing, and about trusting in people's extraordinary capacity for daring, creativity, and perseverance. We were confident that we could translate that spirit into the Literacy Crusade. But, initially, we weren't quite sure how to prepare, organize, and mobilize the large numbers of people necessary for the battle or how to finance it. The problems appeared formidable.

Somoza had left the country destitute. We could not count on public financing. We estimated that we would need to raise approximately $20 million to support the effort. Since the war had affected much of the nation's transportation system, and years of government corruption had impeded the development of a rural infrastructure, new methods had to be devised to maintain communication with the isolated regions of the country, to transport the tens of thousands of brigadistas to the countryside, and to distribute massive amounts of equipment and teaching materials.

The long months of battle had destroyed industry so that supplying even the basic material necessities of the Crusade required herculean efforts. Machinery had to be imported, factories reorganized, cottage industries developed, and materials ordered from foreign markets to provide the necessary uniforms, lanterns, mosquito nets, boots, raincoats, malaria pills, water purification tablets, and study materials. Agricultural production had been interrupted, and scarcity in rural communities was commonplace. Basic foodstuffs first needed to be imported and then distributed to supply the brigadistas.

Because decades of repression had prevented the development of community groups and labor associations, the campaign had to depend on organizations that were still in their infancy for the crucial tasks of mobilizing and supporting the Crusade's volunteer personnel. Long years of neglect had deprived the poor of adequate health care and resulted in high levels of parasitic and skin infections, malaria, and malnutrition. Conditions in rural areas were especially severe. Medical supplies and basic health information would have to be provided to the brigadistas. To mount a campaign of such magnitude, a network of offices needed to be established. Since the number of trained and experienced administrators was limited, the Crusade would have to become a learning laboratory for educational managers.

Once launched, the Crusade confronted another series of problems. The rainy season began in May and continued throughout the duration of the campaign. As a result, many volunteers were isolated, and transportation and communication throughout the country were seriously impaired. Somoza sympathizers and former guardsmen created grave problems and tried to spread fear among the brigadistas and their families in an attempt to paralyze the Crusade. In certain regions, literacy teachers and personnel were threatened and harassed; nine were assassinated.

In the face of such complex difficulties, our inexperience weighed heavily on us. Out of the initial staff of seven, only two had worked in literacy programs, and none had ever been involved in a project of such magnitude. Our strategy for overcoming the team's lack of experience evolved over time. Basically it included study, long hours, hard work, collective problem solving, and hiring experts in adult education.

We spent the first month studying — reading about the experiences of other countries, discussing the small church-sponsored literacy projects that had been attempted in Nicaragua, talking with experts, writing position papers, and outlining a possible primer. We also had to spend time searching for desks and chairs. The Ministry offices had been left empty, and there were times when the team had to take turns using desks and either share chairs or sit on the floor.

To complete our national team, we hired selected experts in education from Argentina, Colombia, Costa Rica, Mexico, Honduras, Puerto Rico, and the United States. During the campaign they were joined by four Cuban specialists who had participated in the 1961 Cuban literacy campaign. As one of their first assignments, they were given a truck to pick up student desks from the university so that they would have a place to sit.

We also requested further technical assistance from a variety of organizations and institutions — UNESCO, the Organization of American States, the World Council of Churches, CELADEC (a Latin American Ecumenical group working in popular peasant education), CREFAL (Regional Center on Adult Education and Functional Literacy for Latin America), and Cuba's Ministry of Education. Cuban teachers who worked in Nicaragua's primary schools participated in the Crusade after classes. Spain, Costa Rica, and the Dominican Republic sent delegations of teachers to participate in the campaign. During the course of the program, additional international experts joined, including people from Canada, Chile, El Salvador, Peru, Spain, and Uruguay. More advisors also came from Colombia, Mexico, and the United States.[6]

At the end of September the core team of seven visited Cuba for a week. We interviewed the former director of the 1961 Cuban Literacy Campaign and spent four valuable days delving into the archives of their Literacy Museum. During October 1979 we organized an intensive one-week planning seminar with a team of experts from Mexico, Colombia, and the United States. After a careful clarification and analysis of the Crusade's proposed plan, we developed some general operational guidelines and began to define program structures and tasks.

As the work intensified, the core team met daily to identify and study specific problems as they emerged, and to seek effective responses. The staff labored fourteen to fifteen hours a day, seven days a week. This combination of commitment, intensive study, group problem solving, and the elaboration of easy-to-follow operational procedures enabled us to overcome many of our initial shortcomings. Before any program could be launched, however, we had to face the legacy of debt, destruction, and corruption left by the dictatorship. Serious problems of financing, health, food, transportation, and communication demanded immediate solutions.

Financing the Crusade

The crusade had to be financed from sources outside the government. We called in two specialists from the Ministry of Planning. After providing them with program details such as the Crusade's proposed scope, duration, and personnel and material needs, they developed a tentative budget calling for approximately $20 million (200 million *cordobas*).

We immediately set up a finance office. Requests for assistance were mailed to governments, institutions, and solidarity groups around the world. Official delegations were sent to the United States and to Europe. In Nicaragua, the Crusade established a program of Patriotic Literacy Bonds and encouraged community fund-raising efforts. Employees from all sectors, public and private, tithed one day's salary each month to the campaign. Marketwomen from Managua and peasants from distant mountain villages came to the national office in order to make their contributions personally. For example, three representatives of the Revolutionary Sports Committee of Chontales, two peasants and one young student, contributed 1,000 cordobas collected from community raffles. Enthusiastic high school students filled the city streets carrying tin cans. Following some of the same tactics used in the insurrection, they set up road blocks — to collect "pennies for pencils" — and called on radio stations to read official declarations of war against ignorance and to make appeals for financial help. Dances, song fests, concerts, and poetry readings all added to the fund-raising effort.

Including cash and materials, some 120 million cordobas were raised. Since the program had been carefully streamlined by cutting out all excess expenses, these funds covered the costs. Catholic and Protestant organizations were the first to contribute. The countries most generous in their donations were the Federal Republic of Germany, Switzerland, Sweden, Holland, and England, although people contributed from all over the world. In this way, they too formed part of the Crusade and shared in its achievements.

Health Problems

For decades, life in the countryside had meant poor health and early death. Malnutrition, malaria, measles, gastroenteritis, and mountain leprosy — a widespread skin infection that causes large scabs and scars — were common and sometimes deadly. To protect the brigadistas, inoculations were given, as well as basic health training which included malaria diagnosis and control. Each teaching squadron was provided with a first-aid kit with supplies sufficient for the duration of the Crusade.

Health problems, however, were more extensive and complicated than anticipated. Many older people attending literacy classes suffered from poor eyesight and therefore had difficulty reading. While eyeglasses had been ordered, their delivery was delayed, causing some people to withdraw, at least temporarily, from the campaign. Other program participants suffered from debilitating illnesses, making attendance sporadic. Volunteers suffered similar ailments. In some cases, disease prevented people from enrolling in the Crusade.

The first-aid supplies which had been carefully calculated to last five months usually ran out within two weeks. When confronted with the extent of illness and disease in the countryside, the brigadistas placed their first-aid kits at the service of the community. Medicine was immediately shared with their adopted peasant families. As a result, new supplies had to be ordered and special medical brigades formed. After a brief intensive training program, some 700 university medical students were placed throughout the country to serve as mobile health teams. Besides providing basic medical attention to volunteers, they also prepared them to give community classes in elementary health education. In addition, the brigades gathered vital information on national disease patterns and health conditions to be used in future health programming.

Food was also a problem. Without the timely organization of an emergency distribution system, food shortages would also have affected the brigadistas' health. Through the Institute of Basic Grain Distribution (ENABAS) volunteers were provided with double rations of basic foodstuffs both to feed themselves and to assist their host families. Weekend visits by parents and care packages from home helped improve the community diet.

Transportation and Communication

Nicaragua's poor transportation system hampered many aspects of the Crusade. Mobilization operations, supply distribution, and communication were all affected. For the March mobilization, brigadistas were dispersed gradually, their departures staggered over a four-day period. To accomplish the massive operation, the Crusade worked in coordination with the Ministry of Transportation and the Farmworkers' Association. They located, employed, and coordinated every available means of transportation — buses, boats, ferries, trains, dump trucks, jeeps, ox carts, horses, mules, donkeys, canoes, rafts, and, finally, feet. Some volunteers had to walk for two or three days to reach their assigned communities. During the campaign, helicopters were used for emergency medical rescues. Vehicles from every ministry and government institution were pressed into service for the distribution of supplies. Food, boots, uniforms, notebooks, pencils, pens, primers, medicine, lanterns, hammocks, and mosquito nets had to be delivered to all 144 municipalities. As winter approached, an emergency plan was instituted to accelerate the distribution process in order to provide sufficient supplies to those areas which would be isolated by the rains.

At the conclusion of the Crusade, the poor networks of roads and almost total lack of bridges exacerbated the problems of demobilization. By August, the winter rains had made many roads and rivers impassable. The lovely streams that the brigadistas had crossed on foot in the dry season had become swollen torrents, and the dirt roads had turned into muddy swamps. What had been a two- or three-day walk in March became a five- or six-day journey.

A carefully orchestrated eight-day demobilization program was put into action. At each point along the way, community organizations provided accommodations and hospitality for the footsore brigadistas. From the farthest sites, the young volunteers walked to area transportation points. From municipal centers, they were transported to department capitals, and then finally to Managua for the August 23rd celebration. Although there were many blistered feet, everyone arrived home safely.

Communication, while always a problem, was greatly improved through a network of forty-eight shortwave radios. Department offices and selected remote municipalities were given radio equipment and their personnel provided with training. A rotating team of volunteers staffed the central office twenty-four hours a day from March 10 to August 22. Besides maintaining communication in technical and administrative matters, the network served as a lifeline in case of medical emergencies.

Establishment of Records

Since government statistics were outdated and notoriously inaccurate, one of the first campaign tasks was conducting a census to establish actual levels of literacy and to ascertain the availability of volunteer teachers. With expert assistance, the census was planned and executed. Teams of volunteer census takers were trained and sent out into the field, and the results tabulated by citizens and labor organizations. Since this was our first experience in mass mobilization, the effort was not without its problems. Because the volunteer response in Managua was much greater than anticipated, not enough public vehicles had been secured for the operation. It was Sunday and all offices were closed. Not wanting to dismiss needed recruits, the Crusade's administrative coordinator borrowed money from his mother to rent private transport. No one was turned away. In all, the volunteers surveyed 1,434,738 people. Since the census tabulation would have absorbed all the nation's computer capacity for two weeks, a group of 2,500 volunteers received special training, and the tabulations were completed in ten days. The results indicated that 722,431 Nicaraguans were illiterate.

In addition, the census gave us a more complete picture of the country's illiteracy levels and their geographic distribution. As the Crusade progressed, however, it became clear that people's notions of illiteracy varied. Some who classified themselves as totally illiterate could recognize the alphabet and read simple words, but could not write. Exact skills were not known until brigadistas gave program applicants a qualifying test. This brief exam was the first in a series of three given during the campaign. The initial test was designed to determine the actual skill level of each participant, beginning with a simple exercise — drawing a straight line. This step was included so that those unable to continue beyond the first question would have some sense of accomplishment and understand that they too possessed the potential to master the alphabet. The next level of skill tested was the ability to write one's name, followed by reading and writing exercises — single words first, then short sentences. The test concluded with a comprehension exercise. People who completed all sections successfully were considered literate, and those who could read and write a few words were classified as semiliterates. Illiterates included people who could not read or write more than their own name.

An intermediate test was given to assess learner progress and diagnose individual study needs. The ability to read and write different syllabic families was determined so that specialized review could be oriented toward practicing those that had not yet been fully mastered. The final exam was administered by the literacy volunteer under the guidance of a technical advisor. It consisted of five parts which tested reading, writing, and comprehension skills. To be considered literate, participants had to write their name, read aloud a short text, answer three questions based on the reading, write a sentence dictated to them, and write a short composition. They were expected to be able to read with comprehension, pronouncing words as a whole and not as a series of isolated syllables. They were to write legibly, leaving appropriate spaces between words, and to spell phonetically. With such skills, participants were prepared within their vocabulary range to read newspapers, application forms, technical information pamphlets, and books.

Records kept on each student included such general information as name, age, sex, date of enrollment, residence, occupation, and past school attendance. A monthly progress chart indicated the lessons and exercises completed in both the primer and math workbook, as well as the total number of sessions attended. Test results for each of the three exams were recorded, as were observations about individual learning difficulties, health problems, and areas of personal interest for future study.

These reports reveal the history and progress of the Crusade. They also indicate the poor conditions under which the majority of Nicaraguans have lived and the tragic human costs of underdevelopment. According to the 1979 census, Nicaragua had an overall illiteracy rate of 50 percent, 30 percent in urban areas and 75 percent in the countryside. Children between ten and fourteen years of age accounted for 21 percent of the illiterate population. In the course of the campaign we discovered other dimensions of the illiteracy problem. As much as we did not want to accept the fact, some people simply did not have the capacity to master reading and writing skills in the campaign. Reports from volunteers and technical advisers indicated widespread learning difficulties and cases of disability. Poor health was the principal cause. Extensive malnutrition handicaps many Nicaraguans, impairing sight and hearing, limiting memory, and often causing early senility. Health statistics indicate that 25 percent of all newborns fall into the high-risk category. Many do not reach five years of age, and those who do suffer serious mental and physical disorders. About 9 percent of the population had severe learning disabilities that prevented them from studying.

Despite debilitating health problems and extreme hardships, 406,056 Nicaraguans learned basic reading and writing skills — an achievement that testifies to the creative power and determination of students and teachers alike. But initial statistics revealed that Nicaragua still had an illiteracy rate of 13 percent to overcome (6 percent urban and 21 percent rural). We believe, however, that by 1981 the rate will decrease as a result of the Crusade's follow-up program and the campaigns in English, Miskito, and Sumo.

Structural Organization: From Mountaintops to Managua

The success of the Crusade's administrative and support structure depended primarily on the participation of the citizen and labor associations. Though we did not know the kind of structure that would facilitate their involvement or exactly how to organize it, we learned much from the process. Since the campaign was an intensive, short-run nationwide project, it required setting up a massive organizational network that could effectively reach from isolated mountaintops down to the neighborhoods of Managua. With that in mind, we tried to develop a system that would be flexible and responsive at the local level and yet maintain a clear central direction and control. A single national coordinating structure took on the general management functions. Operational responsibilities were decentralized through a regional institutional network. In the field, the teachers' organization, ANDEN, and the Sandinista Young People's Association carried out organizational and implementation functions. Citizen groups, labor federations, and public institutions participated and supported the work at all levels. Two national congresses were held which brought together participants and staff to discuss program needs, problems, and solutions. Conferences began at the community level, proceeded to the municipal, on to the departmental, and finally to the national. In all, over 100,000 people participated.

To coordinate the campaign structures, the Crusade functioned in consultation with a National Literacy Commission. Presided over by the Minister of Education, Carlos Tunnerman, the National Literacy Commission, composed of delegates from twenty-five public and private institutions, workers' associations, and citizens' groups, assisted with resource mobilization and coordination. Parallel commissions were established on both the departmental and municipal levels with representatives from the same institutions and organiza-

tions as the national structure. Subcommissions were formed at the comarca and neighborhood levels.

The Literacy Crusade was organized as part of the Ministry of Education and therefore could draw upon any of the Ministry's technical or administrative support services. The campaign itself, however, was coordinated and managed by a single executive structure, the National Coordinating Board, headed by a National Coordinator and consisting of six divisions: Technical/Pedagogical; Production and Design; Technical/Organizational; Public Relations; Financial Promotion; and Administrative. A special subdivision was also established to design and implement the bilingual program.[7]

This administrative and organizational network was complemented by the actual operational structure in the field. The field network was directed by a variety of organizations and coordinated by the Crusade. For the rural work, the Sandinista Young People's Association was responsible for the organization, enthusiasm, and discipline of the teaching brigades. Made up of high school and college students, this group, known as the Popular Literacy Army (EPA), formed the bulk of the rural education corps. The Farmworkers Association (ATC) organized a small but effective teaching unit called the Peasants Literacy Militia (MAC) which worked alongside the EPA.

The Nicaraguan Educators Association (ANDEN) was in charge of the teachers who served as the technical support staff for the brigades and militia. Each squadron of about thirty volunteers was assisted by three professional teachers. ANDEN was also responsible for two of the Crusade's auxiliary activities, the Retaguardia, a summer daycare program for primary school children, and the Quincho Barrilete project, a literacy and basic education program for child street vendors. Cultural brigades for some 450 students were organized by the University and the Ministry of Culture to collect oral histories, promote popular culture, and conduct different types of research studies. In the cities, the volunteers were organized into two main forces: the Urban Literacy Guerillas, coordinated directly by the Crusade and made up of housewives, working students, professionals, and private citizens; and the Workers' Literacy Militia (MOA), coordinated by the Sandinista Worker Federation and composed of factory workers, office personnel, market vendors, and government employees.

Pedagogy in Practice: Revolution and Education

In designing the materials and methodologies for the Crusade, the liberation struggle served as inspiration and teacher. Its lessons were many, some pedagogical and some philosophical. Educational experiences carried out over the long years of fighting and community organizing had demonstrated the validity of a variety of teaching approaches and learning principles. Small study groups had met throughout the struggle to analyze, plan, and carry out war-related tasks; clandestine literacy efforts had been conducted as well. Learning in this context had been based on action and reflection. Lessons had a direct, urgent, and immediate application to reality. These experiences had combined such methods and techniques as experiential learning, dialogue, group discussions, and collective problem solving. They also revealed the tremendous creativity and capacity for learning that existed within people regardless of their educational background.

These experiences were enriched by the ideas and practice of Paulo Freire and others. At the beginning of the campaign, Freire had challenged us to create the best learning program we could. He stressed the importance of providing opportunities for learners to practice their creativity and added that within a liberating revolutionary process people would learn to read and write even with mediocre materials. The revolutionary context and methodology were more important than any isolated study program or particular teaching techniques. Literacy, he said, could only "have a genuine meaning in a country which is going through a revolutionary process."[8] With his challenge in mind, we faced two technical questions: how to design literacy materials for use by volunteer teachers and how to translate young people's enthusiasm and commitment into a minimum set of pedagogical skills.

The Crusade's education team attempted to address these questions first by studying Nicaragua's experiences in clandestine literacy teaching and then by analyzing other countries' programs in light of local needs. Cuba's literacy campaign was examined closely, as was that of Peru and those of the African nations of São Tomé and Guinea-Bissau, both of which had been greatly inspired by Freire. His thinking along with many other lines of Latin American thought and experience influenced the campaign, but the most important elements of the program emerged from the reality and needs of Nicaragua and the creativity of the Crusade's national education team. In all, five intense months were spent in developing and pilot-testing materials and methods. The resultant education program was a product of their collective effort. It was founded on dialogue and on a standardized national literacy primer.

We believed, as did Freire, that dialogue is critical to a liberating education and that, combined with a phonetics approach to teaching literacy, it surpasses any other method. Since we were engaged in carrying out a national literacy campaign in the context of profound social transformation, we focused on themes that were concerns of the society at large rather than on narrow issues of interest only to individual communities. Because it offered participants the power of the word and of history, the dialogue was highly political. By expressing their own opinions about their lives, their culture, their past and future, people would begin to develop and strengthen their creativity and analytical abilities as well as to see themselves as makers of culture and history. As Carlos Carrión, the FSLN representative to the Crusade, expressed it:

> The literacy methodology is intrinsically political. How? It's not just that we speak of Sandino or of Carlos Fonseca, or of the Frente Sandinista. The most political, the most revolutionary aspect of this literacy approach is the fact that we are providing scientific knowledge and analytical skills to our brothers and sisters in the fields and factories who do not know how to read or write — the skills to reason, think, compare, discern and the ability to form their own human and political criteria, their own critical framework.[9]

To help volunteers promote the process of dialogue we provided them with concrete, step-by-step guidelines. The five-step process contained a series of suggested questions designed to help participants develop both analytical skills and a profound sense of social responsibility. The questions proceeded from simple to difficult and encouraged the students to describe the contents of a photograph; analyze the situation portrayed; relate the particular situation to the life of the learner, to the community, and to the problems facing them; solve problems around issues identified by the group; and engage participants in transforming reality, committing themselves to solving the problem, and becoming active in the national programs of social change. During the course of the Crusade, however, we came to realize the obvious — that dialogue occurred both during the literacy teaching process itself as well as in the daily living experience, and that the latter was perhaps the richer and more profound exchange. We discovered that photographs needed to be chosen with great care to stimulate a critical discussion. The team had been limited not only by a certain inexperience but also by a lack of photographs from which to choose. After experimenting with line drawings, they discovered that photographs, despite the limited selection, were far more effective in stimulating dynamic discussion.

After twenty minutes or so of dialogue, the direct study of reading and writing skills began — first with a sentence, then a word, and finally a syllabic family. We expanded Freire's single-word approach by using a short phrase or sentence based on the photograph's theme as the starting point for literacy practice. The team felt that a sentence provided a smoother transition from complex discussion to the concrete study of syllables. Because sentences encompassed a whole thought, they were considered more appropriate for adult learning as well as more flexible in generating the study of syllabic families. After reading the sentence, a key word from each phrase was chosen and divided into syllables, from which one family of syllables was selected and studied. For example, in the second lesson the name Fonseca was divided, Fon-*se*-ca, initiating a study of the syllabic family, sa, se, si, so, and su. Writing exercises were introduced and recognition exercises were used to help the participants identify the syllables as phonetic units. As learners mastered the individual syllables, they went on to use them to build new words, thus practicing their creativity and skills in manipulating the written language.

The specific teaching materials we used consisted of the elementary literacy primer, *Dawn of the People,* a teacher's manual, the *Teachers' Guide for Literacy Volunteers,* and an arithmetic workbook, *Math and Economic Reconstruction: One Single Operation.* During the Crusade, teaching games stressing learner creativity, such as a type of syllabic Scrabble, were developed and distributed. In addition, during the entire year of 1980, the national match factory produced all matches in special boxes decorated with the alphabet to be used as letter building blocks.

The primer was divided into twenty-three lessons, each accompanied by photographs and practice exercises, and was organized into three major areas: the history and development of the Revolution; the socioeconomic programs of the Government of National Reconstruction; and civil defense and community participation. Some of the specific lesson themes were "Sandino, guiding force of the Revolution"; "Work is the right and duty of every citizen"; "Spend little, save resources, and produce a lot — that is Revolution"; "The FSLN led the people to Liberation"; "With organization, work, and discipline we will be able to build the nation of Sandino."

The teacher's manual provided step-by-step instructions on the use of the literacy methodology and also contained detailed back-up readings for each of the twenty-three themes. It gave the brigadistas the necessary social, politi-

Ejercicio C

1.- Leamos la oración :

La Reforma Agraria recupera la producción de la tierra para el pueblo.

2.- Leamos la palabra :

tierra

3.- Separemos la palabra en sílabas :

tie rra

4.- Leamos las sílabas :

rra rro rre rru rra

5.- Leamos y escribamos las sílabas :

rra rro rre rru rri

rre rri rro rru

6.- Formemos y escribamos palabras combinando las sílabas conocidas:

cal, and economic information to generate a knowledgeable discussion and dialogue. Since the Crusade was considered a reciprocal learning process, the handbook also outlined a systematic set of study activities for the volunteers. The basis of their learning was their own living and teaching experience. As such, they were responsible for conducting a careful research study of their communities and keeping a field diary of their activities.

A Pedagogy of Shared Responsibility

To prepare the immense teacher corps to use the program's materials and methods, a national training program of short, intensive workshops was conducted. The first training materials explained to the brigadistas their revolutionary educational role as literacy promoters:

> You will be a catalyst of the teaching-learning process. Your literacy students will be people who think, create, and express their ideas. Together, you will form a team of mutual learning and human development. . . . The literacy process is an act of creation in which people offer each other their thoughts, words, and deeds. It is a cultural action of transformation and growth.[10]

Training, therefore, required that all participants take on new educational roles in what we called a pedagogy of shared responsibility. The traditional model of the active, all-wise professor and passive, ignorant pupil was specifically rejected and replaced by one in which the traditional teacher became a type of learning coordinator. The role of the workshop director was one of facilitator, a role that involved motivating, inspiring, challenging, and working with the participants who were encouraged to become active problem solvers. Participants were the foundation and wellspring of the process. Their responsibilities were to explore, research, and create. Small-group study, team teaching, and problem solving affirmed this new relationship. Under the coordination of two facilitators, workshop members were given a variety of educational tasks to accomplish. During the training, they reflected upon the group process and their progress, integrating both theory and practice.

Our primary purpose in training was to have people master the materials and methods while developing skills necessary to solve social problems creatively and sensitively. Methods were chosen to enhance the initiative and imagination with which people acquire and apply knowledge. The specific techniques used were simulations, role playing, group discussions, debates, murals, poetry, drawing, songs, and some artistic forms of expression from Nicaraguan folklore. Each workshop began with an introductory presentation exercise to acquaint participants with each other and to establish a congenial, dynamic learning environment. The participants were initially divided into working teams of about six people each, which formed the principal base of learning for the entire workshop. The small group chose the name of a fallen combatant for their symbol and wrote up his or her biography, hanging it on the wall for others to read. In their teams, participants then discussed the meaning of the Crusade and why they had decided to become volunteers, listing their responses on large sheets of paper and tacking them on the wall for presentation to the group. To conclude the first exercise, they were asked to create some two-line, rhyme-slogans which summarized their discussion. This technique had its roots in Nicaraguan traditional culture, where couplets are a popular literary expression, and in the war. During the long years of struggle, short chants which synthesized and captured the spirit of popular demands and aspirations had been used to animate demonstrations and harass the National Guard.

During the workshop, the rhymes took on a life of their own. Groups used their spare time trying to create new and more imaginative ones. They would practice them together in a corner and in a moment of relative silence between activities shout out their creation with great pride and enthusiasm. They then prepared a carefully written copy of their work so others could join them in shouting their couplet. The effort generated a spirit of lively rivalry and boosted energies when long hours of work became heavy and fatiguing. It also served as a positive means to gauge involvement and comprehension levels. If for example a group didn't understand an exercise or a reading, invariably a humorous couplet indicating their confusion and frustration would surface. At the end of the workshop the walls told the story of training. They were covered by summaries of group discussion and popular poetry.

To implement the training program, a decentralized four-stage model was designed. The program's success depended on its multiplier effect: beginning with seven national trainers, it was expected that in less than four months almost 100,000 people would be prepared. From December to March, workshops were held across the country. The driving force behind the training was the "group of eighty." Forty university students and forty teachers were specially selected for an intensive two-week preparation program and a one-month field experience. From their ranks, forty were chosen to train approximately 600 students and teachers in the next phase. During late February these 600 people prepared more than 12,000 people, most of whom were teachers. They, in turn, conducted the eight-day intensive workshops for thousands of literacy volunteers. Once the Crusade began, permanent training workshops were given for those people who still wished to enter the program. A radio show broadcast twice daily, together with special Saturday seminars conducted by squadron technical advisors, provided a continuing in-service training for the volunteers.

The Continuing Challenge

We are presently involved in designing and establishing a permanent system of adult education. In October 1980 three new Crusades began — in English, Miskito, and Sumo — for Nicaraguans who do not speak Spanish as their native language; and in 1981 we are hoping to launch a Health Crusade along the same lines as the literacy campaign. So much needs to be done. The hundreds of thousands of Nicaraguans who mastered basic reading and writing skills have just begun their studies. Their skills are still fragile.

The Literacy Crusade is only a first step in a long process of education and social creation. For the moment, we are in a transition that began in the final month of the Crusade — a time for people to practice and strengthen their literacy and math skills. The transition program arose from a natural phenomenon occurring in the literacy groups. As the most advanced students finished the primer, they began to concentrate on helping fellow students in mastering skills. When the campaign terminated, outstanding literacy graduates or educated members of the community were chosen to continue the work of the learning group. After being given some basic training by the Crusade's teaching supervisors, the new educational coordinators were provided with a carefully designed teacher's guide and a set of follow-up reading materials that stressed collective study and action as the fundamental basis for community learning. These community learning groups are supported by the network of mass citizen and labor organizations. The work of the coordinators is bolstered by specially selected traveling "promoters" who serve as liaisons to the regional adult education offices and provide the community groups with encouragement, orientation, and extra learning materials when available. Rounding out the transition program is a radio show for the study groups, broadcast twice daily on all national channels.

The challenge for the future is awesome. Expectations are great, problems complex, and resources scarce. In the face of new tasks, the example and lessons of the campaign provide the inspiration and hope for tomorrow. As one young literacy volunteer expressed in August, "The Crusade is like the source of a river of popular knowledge which will flow onward forever."

Life as a Brigadista

Before we conclude, there is one more aspect of the Crusade that needs to be presented — the experience of being a brigadista. Life as a volunteer in the countryside was hard work. Tasks filled the day. Mornings were spent laboring alongside peasant *compañeros;* late afternoons and evenings were dedicated to leading study sessions in homes, patios, or front yards. The experience can best be described by those who were there. We have gathered some quotes which convey how the brigadistas lived and worked and how the campaign touched their lives. No one can explain it better.

> Dear All,
>
> I arrived here on this mountain top yesterday on the back of a mule. . . . We left Saturday from Managua at 3 A.M. in a caravan of 70 buses and dump trucks, about 1,500 university students in all, complete with a gasoline truck and an

army escort to protect us during the 20 hour journey. We spent most of the time singing, shouting cheers, and waving. It was incredible, really! Even though it was nighttime in every village and town along the way, people left their homes to wave at us. Of course, they knew we were members of EPA. Women would offer us oranges and bananas and shout up at us, "Take care! See you when you return. We love you!" They would throw us kisses too. One old man, he must have been at least 70, ran beside the bus smiling up at us shouting EPA, EPA, EPA. I didn't know whether I was crying from the dust, the cold, or the wind, or the emotion I felt at seeing what a revolution can really mean. . . .

Many Hugs, Gabriella

* * *

I am really impressed how some of these kids came prepared and equipped. One of the boys looks like he is ready to fight the crocodile that always shows up in the jungle movies wanting to eat Tarzan. Another one has all the trappings of a walking Boy Scout Store. It's a sure sign of how ignorant most of us are about how people live in the countryside.

The hardest part for the volunteers is the loneliness and isolation, finding themselves suddenly living among strangers with whom, at least up till now, they have little in common. The feeling is one of anguish and insecurity. Thank God because of their political spirit and Christian faith, none of my brigadistas have deserted. Everyday they seem to adjust and find themselves enjoying life here more.

I can understand the horror of some of the parents from the capital when they come to visit their children and find them living in peasant "homes." What I don't understand is why they are so horrified that their kids will have to spend 5 months in these conditions and not that 70 percent of the Nicaraguan people have to suffer this misery their entire lives.

Educational Advisor
Los Santos

* * *

To my literacy teacher and compañero: Guillermo Briones Cisñero

My friends, Nicaragua is free.
The oppression of Somoza is defeated
For with the rumbling of bullets,
    Anastasio and son ran far away.
And now with the shouting of ABCs,
    Ignorance flees and joins them in Paraguay.
These verses I do recite
    in honor of Guillermo, my friend and compañero
Because I respect him like no other
    and love him like an older brother.

Anselmo Hurtado Lopez

* * *

Dear Mom and Dad,

I am fine. I arrived safe and sound but please send me 20 cans of grape juice. The well is filled with mud and the river is far away. . . .

Love, your son

* * *

Dear Folks,

I'm learning a lot. I now know how to milk a cow and plant vegetables. The other day I was with Don Demesio roping a steer but I'm so stupid that I frightened the thing and we had to work twice as hard to catch it again. . . . The rains are constant. The soles of my boots came unglued and I had to sew them with a needle they use to make sacks with.

Love, David

* * *

It's difficult sometimes. Tomasita is smart and wants to study but her baby cries a lot and she can't put him down. I visit her three times a day just on the chance she'll be free but . . . she's only on lesson 4. . . . Camilo doesn't seem to assimilate his sounds very well. Of course he does need glasses. He's 67. . . . Socorro and Joaquina are way ahead on lesson 14 but Julio left to pick coffee and Catalina's in bed with malaria. . . . Vicente has improved incredibly since he fell off his mule. He was really a lazy bum before. But now, with his broken arm, he's quite serious and dedicated, even though he's had to learn to write all over again with his left hand.

Guadalupe from the Brigade Enoc Ortez
in a report to her teaching supervisor

* * *

Eight ex-national guardsmen crossed the border from Honduras yesterday and murdered the literacy teacher Georgino Andrade.

Newsbroadcast, Managua
May 19, 1980

* * *

The struggle is long and sometimes cruel. What's needed above all, my dear friend, is love and commitment. Remember, "the freedom of a people is not won with flowers." We are young and we are called upon to build the new, to create what our heroes and martyrs would have wanted. Put yourself in the place of Georgino Andrade. You wouldn't like it, if out of fear, the cause you gave your life for wasn't continued.

Letter to boyfriend Brigadista
from girlfriend Brigadista

* * *

The Literacy Crusade taught us two things. One, what our own children are capable of doing and of becoming. Two, what our country is like and how gentle and how poor our people are in the countryside.

Mother of three literacy volunteers

* * *

We take our malaria medicine twice a week and we're supposed to use our water purifying tablets. . . . The sicknesses among the children are many. Eight children in the next valley died last month of measles, three from the same family. It's unbelievable the inhuman conditions these people live under. I feel indignation and rage at not being a doctor.

Brigadista
Atlantic Coast

* * *

The Crusade has been carried out by the kids of Nicaragua, the wonderful kids who under the leadership of the *Frente* fought the tyrant — intelligent kids, sacrificing, determined — idealists and realists all at the same time. For me the principal lesson of the campaign is that now Nicaragua knows that it can count on this treasure for its future. Not all the best children died in the war. With the living, we can carry out the other necessary wars to be fought, the war against social injustice, the war against poor health, the war against disease.

The Crusade is over. The People of Nicaragua and the commitment of the *Frente* made it possible. Thanks to their efforts Nicaragua will be totally different in the future. It will be a better nation, a nation that all Nicaraguans deserve. If that's not a triumph, excuse me, but then what the hell do you call a triumph?

Priest,
Squadron Teaching Supervisor

Reflections

Thinking back over the last year, the most important lesson we learned will probably be the most difficult for educational planners to apply. In the final analysis, the success of the campaign depended not on scientifically tested educational theories, or complex planning systems, or even sophisticated curriculum design. The ultimate success of the Literacy Crusade depended on a commitment of the spirit — a commitment of a people and a government born of a liberation struggle. Only that kind of creative force could generate and maintain the levels of sacrifice and dedication required to accomplish such a task.

For when all is said and done, the crusade is not a story of complicated techniques or complex cost-benefit analysis. It is a story of people and the extraordinary potential for liberation and creation that exists within nations.

It is about thousands of problems, big and small. But most of all it is a story about the creative intelligence of people and the courageous sacrifice of thousands of Nicaraguans who gave their lives so that intelligence and creativity could flourish. It is a beginning.

Its promise can probably best be described by the words of a peasant speaking to the mother of his young literacy teacher: "Do you know I am not ignorant any more. I know how to read now. Not perfectly, you understand, but I know how. And do you know, your son isn't ignorant any more either. Now he knows how we live, what we eat, how we work and he knows the life of the mountains. Your son, ma'am, has learned to read from our book."

Notes

1. Quoted in José Román, *Maldito Pais* (Managua: El Pez y La Serpiente, 1979), p. 135.
2. Ministry of Educatión, *La Educación En El Primar Año De La Revolución Popular Sandinista* (Managua: Author, 1980), p. 162.
3. Auxiliadora Rivas and Asunción Suazo, conversation in literacy class, Masaya, Nicaragua, May 4, 1980.
4. Unpublished Report on Literacy Crusade by FSLN (Sardinista National Liberation Front), December 1979.
5. Brigades were made up of all those brigadistas in one municipality; columns were made up of four squadrons where possible and each squadron contained thirty brigadistas and one to three education advisors.
6. In all, the Crusade's National Office employed the services of the following international experts: 2 Argentinians, 1 Canadian, 1 Chilean, 5 Colombians, 1 Costa Rican, 4 Cubans, 2 Salvadorians, 1 Honduran, 2 Mexicans, 1 Peruvian, 1 Puerto Rican, 4 Spaniards.
7. The Technical/Pedagogical Division had four sections — Curriculum, Research, Training, and Library/Museum — and was designed to provide the educational expertise for the program. The Technical/Organizational Division essentially served as a support-control structure for the literacy promoters and as a liaison to the different sponsoring organizations. It had four sections: Statistics and Census; the Popular Literacy Army (EPA) and the Urban Literacy Guerillas (GUAS); the Mass Citizen and Labor Organizations; and the Internal Technical Secretariat. The Administrative Division was separated into two departments: Logistical Support, which was made up of Supplies, Health, Food Distribution, Transportation, Communication and Maintenance, and Plant Maintenance; and the Department of Administration, which contained Control, Accounting, Personnel, and Budget. The departments and municipalities were each structured along lines similar to the national — Technical/Pedagogical, Statistics and Census, Logistical Support, and Publicity.
8. Paulo Freire in conversion with Fernando Cardenal, Nicaragua, Oct.–Nov. 1979.
9. Carlos Carrión, speech before First Congress of the National Literacy Crusade, June 17, 1980.
10. Cruzada Nacional de Alfabetización, *Cuaderno de Orientacions* (Managua: Ministry of Education, 1979), p. 1.

The photographs in this article were taken during the Literacy Campaign and were provided by the authors.

About the Contributors

Thea Renda Abu El-Haj is an assistant professor in the Department of Educational Theory, Policy, and Administration at the Graduate School of Education at Rutgers University in New Jersey. Her research focuses on transnational immigration and citizenship education, concepts of educational justice manifest in policy and practice, and critical analyses of race, gender, class, and disability in schooling. Her publications include *Elusive Justice: Wrestling with Difference and Educational Equity in Everyday Practice* (2006), and "Race, Politics, and Arab American Youth: Shifting Frameworks for Conceptualizing Educational Equity," in *Educational Policy* (2006).

Charles J. Beirne, S.J., is a Jesuit priest and visiting professor at the Graduate School of Education at Fordham University in New York City. He was the principal at Colegio San Ignacio in San Juan, and Regis High School in New York City. He also served as associate dean of the Business School at Georgetown, and as academic vice president at Santa Clara University, the Universidad Centroamericana in San Salvador, and the Universidad Rafael Landivar in Guatemala. From 2000 to 2007, he was president of Le Moyne College in Syracuse, New York. He is also a consultant in higher education to the Jesuit of Africa. His books include *The Problem of Americanization in the Catholic Schools of Puerto Rico* (1975) and *Jesuit Education and Social Change in El Salvador* (1996).

Hanna Buczynska-Garewicz is currently professor emerita of philosophy at College of the Holy Cross and has also served in that capacity at the Polish Academy of Science and Humanities in Warsaw. She has lectured extensively in the United States and abroad on semiotics and is an active member of the Polish Semiotic Society. Among her numerous philosophical publications are "Sign and Evidence," in *Semiosis* (1977), "Sign and Dialogue," in *American Journal of Semiotics* (1983), and "Sign and Cogito," in *The Sign and its Systems* (1984).

Fernando Cardenal, S.J., served as the national coordinator of the Nicaraguan Literacy Crusade and the minister of education for the Sandinista government. He is the current director of the Fé y Alegría ("Faith and Happiness") school system in Nicaragua. He is a Jesuit priest and liberation theologian.

Jocelyn Anne Glazier is an assistant professor of teaching and learning in the School of Education at the University of North Carolina at Chapel Hill. Her research and teaching interests include teacher education, critical pedagogy, and social justice. Glazier's research has been published in numerous journals, including *Teachers College Record, Journal of Adolescent and Adult Literacy,* and *Teaching Education.*

Jonathan David Jansen is honorary professor of education at the University of the Witwatersrand in Johannesburg, South Africa. Jansen's research is broadly concerned with educational change and, more recently, educational leadership in postconflict societies. He currently serves as vice president of the South African Academy of Science. His books include *Knowledge in the Blood: Confronting Race and the Apartheid Past* (2009) and, with Saloshna Vandeyar, *Diversity High: Class, Color, Character and Culture in a South African High School* (2008).

Susan M. Kardos is an independent researcher and a research affiliate of the Project on the Next Generation of Teachers at the Harvard Graduate School of Education. Her work focuses on school organization, improvement, and leadership; new teacher induction and support; education policy; and Jewish education. She is coauthor of *Finders and Keepers: Helping New Teachers Survive and Thrive in Our Schools* (with Susan Moore Johnson and The Project on the Next Generation of Teachers, 2004) and "Research-Based Evidence and State Policy: Bridging the Gulf," in *The Role of Research in Education Improvement* (with Robert B. Schwartz, 2009). Kardos has also created a documentary film on the reclamation and recreation of Jewish memory in post-Holocaust, post-Soviet Ukraine.

Christopher Kruegler directed the Program on Nonviolent Sanctions in Conflict and Defense at Harvard University from 1985 to 1991. After a series of other roles in higher education and research administration at Harvard and elsewhere, he took up practice as a human resources consultant, and is now an Assistant Dean for Human Resources in the Faculty of Arts and Sciences at Harvard.

John E. Mack, M.D. (October 4, 1929–September 27, 2004) was a professor of psychiatry and chairperson of the Executive Committee for the department of psychiatry at the Harvard University School of Medicine. Among his many professional interests were the application of psychological insights to biographical study and to social and political problems in the nuclear age, and research on spiritual or transformational human experiences.

Khalil Mahshi is a program officer at UNESCO's International Institute for Educational Planning (IIEP) in Paris, where he manages education development projects and is involved in research on education in emergencies and reconstruction. At IIEP he also helps to train educational planners from education ministries. Before joining IIEP, he was director general of international and public relations at the Palestinian Ministry of Education and Higher Educationfor six years, where he worked on the design and implementation of development projects. He also coordinated the production of the first five-year national education development plan.

Valerie Miller is the senior adviser and cofounder of Just Associates, a global network of activists, educators and scholars focused on women's empowerment, leadership, and movement-building. She is coauthor of *A New Weave of Power, People and Politics* (2007), an advocacy and organizing guide, and *Critical Webs of Power and Change* (2005), an evaluation sourcebook. She has served as Oxfam America's policy director, an adviser to UNICEF and Alas de Mariposa, an instructor of online courses, and a collaborating researcher with the Institute of Development Studies.

Mokubung O. Nkomo is a professor in the Faculty of Education at the University of Pretoria in South Africa. He is the author of numerous articles in academic journals; author of *Student Culture and Activism in South African Black Universities* (1984); editor of *Pedagogy of Domination* (1990); coeditor of *Reflections on School Integration* (2004); coeditor of *Within the Realm of Possibility* (2006); and coeditor of *Diversity and Social Cohesion in Education: Transnational Reflections* (forthcoming).

Patricia Parkman has conducted numerous workshops on nonviolence; her professional focus is on the study of the history and potential of nonviolent action in Latin America. Her publications include *Nonviolent Insurrection in El Salvador: The Fall of Maximiliano Hernández Martínez* (1988) and *Insurrectionary Civic Strikes in Latin America 1931–1961* (1990).

Asgedet Stefanos is a professor of critical pedagogy, African studies, and women's studies at the University of Massachusetts Boston's College of Public and Community Service. Her teaching, scholarship, and service focus on gender and education in African societies. Professor Stefanos has written about efforts to incorporate women into the formal and nonformal educational systems in Guinea Bissau, and has written several articles and a forthcoming book based on extensive field research on women's educational experiences in Eritrea.

David Tyack is the Vida Jacks Professor of Education and Professor of History Emeritus, at Stanford University. His publications include *The One Best System* (1974), *Seeking Common Ground* (2003), and (coauthor with Larry Cuban) *Tinkering Toward Utopia: A Century of Public School Reform* (1995).

About the Editors

Elizabeth E. Blair is a doctoral candidate at the Harvard Graduate School of Education and a cochair of the *Harvard Educational Review.* Her current research examines how late adolescents conceptualize intimacy in relationships. She is also a researcher for an NSF-funded study on teaching, learning, and gender dynamics in undergraduate engineering programs, serves as a thesis adviser for the Harvard College Department of Women and Gender Studies, and is the senior resident tutor for Adams House at Harvard College. She previously taught violence-prevention courses in middle and high schools and coordinated a university/public school service-learning partnership.

Rebecca B. Miller is a doctoral candidate at the Harvard Graduate School of Education and the manuscripts editor of the *Harvard Educational Review.* Her research bridges the fields of education and science and technology studies to examine the educational efforts of academic scientists, particularly through undergraduate courses designed for nonscience specialists. Her most recent work focuses on the social and political purposes of general science education in the United States during the early cold-war period. Before enrolling at Harvard, she conducted research in biochemistry and biophysics, worked as a freelance science writer, and directed the development of online science and medicine courses at Columbia University.

Mara Casey Tieken is a doctoral candidate at the Harvard Graduate School of Education and a cochair of the *Harvard Educational Review.* Her research focuses on the role that the public school plays in rural southern communities. As a research assistant for the Massachusetts Charter School Dissemination and Replication Project, she recently coauthored a book that explores the practices of five high-performing urban charter schools. She has also participated in research projects studying education organizing and adolescent moral development. Trained as a public school teacher, she previously taught third grade and adult education in rural Tennessee.